ENGLISH GRAMMAR
Principles and Facts

Jeffrey P. Kaplan
Department of Linguistics
San Diego State University

PRENTICE HALL   Englewood Cliffs, New Jersey 07632

Library of Congress Cataloging-in-Publication Data

Kaplan, Jeffrey P.
    English grammar.

    Bibliography: p.
    Includes index.
    1. English language--Grammar--1950-   . 2. English
language--Grammar, Generative. I. Title.
PE1106.K37 1989   428.2   88-23175
ISBN 0-13-280967-2

Editorial/production supervision: Martha Masterson
    and Arthur Maisel
Cover design: Ben Santora
Manufacturing buyer: Ray Keating

© 1989 by Prentice-Hall, Inc.
A Division of Simon & Schuster
Englewood Cliffs, New Jersey 07632

Printed in the United States of America
l0 9 8 7 6 5 4 3 2

ISBN 0-13-280967-2

Prentice-Hall International (UK) Limited, *London*
Prentice-Hall of Australia Pty. Limited, *Sydney*
Prentice-Hall Canada Inc., *Toronto*
Prentice-Hall Hispanoamericana, S.A., *Mexico*
Prentice-Hall of India Private Limited, *New Delhi*
Prentice-Hall of Japan, Inc., *Tokyo*
Simon & Schuster Asia Pte. Ltd., *Singapore*
Editora Prentice-Hall do Brasil, Ltda., *Rio de Janeiro*

CONTENTS

A NOTE TO STUDENTS

The purpose of this book is to help you understand grammar, English grammar in particular.

Grammar, as it has usually been taught in schools, has struck many people as dry and boring. One reason for this may be the fact that grammar in our culture has long been regarded by many, including some grammar teachers, as a set of rigid prescriptions focussing on error correction. A different conception of grammar forms the basis of this book: grammar thought of as a marvelously intricate set of principles and rules governing what is and what is not "in" a language, according to judgments of native speakers of that language.

The widespread attitude that grammar is entirely a matter of correctness or incorrectness is undoubtedly connected to the common feeling that one's own speech is full of grammatical errors. The feeling (held by most speakers of English) that one's language is bad, somehow or other, almost inevitably makes thinking about grammar painful. To redress this hurt is one goal of this book.

The mid and late fifties saw the advent of a revolution in linguistic scholarship: transformational grammar. Since that time, transformational grammar, as broadly conceived, has produced an explosion of interest in English grammar and a corresponding exponential growth in the number of linguists studying it, resulting in deep study of the subject in unprecedented ways. A great deal (relatively speaking) is known about the subject. The aims of this book are: First, to present to you some important facts of English grammar, some of which have been known for a long time, some of which are products of the transformational revolution; and second, at the same time to introduce you to a linguistic, i.e., scientific, way of thinking about grammar. A third aim, overtly addressed primarily in the first chapter, is to challenge the attitude that variation in language—as among, for example, different "accents" or dialects—is a matter of correctness or incorrectness, and in the process, to encourage you to respond to language variation with delight.

The object of the book throughout is to involve you in the facts of English, with as little linguistic theory as possible, but with guidance and training toward "thinking like a linguist" about grammar. Thus, coverage of the facts will be broad, and selectively deep, emphasizing argumentation and motivation for grammatical analyses—always from the facts; arguments based on the structure of some particular version of grammatical theory will be excluded.

To understand this book, you need no previous knowledge, except the perfect unconscious knowledge of English grammar that every adult native speaker of English automatically possesses.

A NOTE TO INSTRUCTORS

This book is designed for undergraduate (and beginning graduate) classes in English grammar or in linguistics focussing on English.

It presupposes no previous experience with linguistics.

Chapter One, somewhat polemical, lays a descriptivist foundation, arguing against prescriptivism on the basis of facts about variation and change. The rest of the book proceeds straightforwardly, without polemics, through phonetics, phonology, morphology, word classes, simple phrase structure, grammatical relations, complex sentences, relative clauses and participles, and anaphora. The minimal syntactic theory introduced relies on phrase structure. The idea of different levels of structure is stressed in phonology and morphophonemics, and in the discussions of noncanonical simple sentences and complex sentences. While the framework is transformational more often than not, transformations are used only implicitly. The main reason for this is to avoid bogging down in the theory-driven details of derivations and transformational formalizations. Another reason is to accord with the replacement by most modern theories of the bulk of transformational machinery by other devices. Also to avoid theory-driven issues, traces are only hinted at, and never discussed as such.

Much more prominent than theory is methodology—i.e., argumentation and syntactic reasoning—because an important goal of the book is guiding readers to think of grammatical analyses as empirically motivated.

There is more in this book than can be properly covered in a one semester course. The core of the book is Chapters Four, Five, Six, and Seven, that is, the material on word classes and subclasses, on phrase structure, and on grammatical relations. But a big piece of Chapter Six, that dealing with the internal structure of NPs, with some detailed work on $\overline{N}$s, could easily be omitted, especially in lower-level classes. Instructors may or may not opt to include phonology, morphology, and morphophonemics (Chapters Two and Three), and will doubtless vary in whether, or how much, to deal with complex sentences and anaphora (Chapters Eight–Ten). Chapter One stands by itself, and, except for a small amount of introductory information about semantics and notation (and except for its introductory tone), could be read last as well as first.

ACKNOWLEDGMENTS

Thanks go to my wife, Peri L. Good, for her ideas, love, support, patience, and faith; to my colleague and friend Charlotte Webb for her phonological wisdom and good common-sense ideas about Chapter One and the phonology and morphology chapters; to my colleague and friend Mary Ellen Ryder for her insightful comments on the morphology chapter; and to my colleague and friend Gregory Ward, for his extensive, deep, knowledgeable, and wise assistance with every chapter, as to both content and form.

Errors and limitations are of course my own.

Chapter One

SOME WAYS OF THINKING ABOUT GRAMMAR

PRESCRIPTIVE VS. DESCRIPTIVE GRAMMAR

Prescriptive Grammar

Most familiarly, 'grammar' means the rules governing how a language is supposed to be used. In this sense, 'grammar' is prescriptive. Mostly, prescriptive grammatical rules are phrased as prohibitions. Some prohibitions have to do with *sentence structure:*

1. DO NOT "split an infinitive," as in *to reluctantly leave*
2. DO NOT end a sentence with a preposition, as in *Who did she go with*

Some have to do with uses of particular *types of words:*

3. DO NOT use a plural pronoun with a singular antecedent, as in *If anyone comes in late they should go quietly to the rear*
4. DO NOT use double modals, as in *I might could help you*

Some have to do with how you are supposed to use *individual words:*

5. DO NOT use *impact* as a verb, as in *This program is intended to impact the trade imbalance*
6. DO NOT use *hopefully* as a sentence adverb, as in *Hopefully this book will be fascinating*

In prescriptive grammar, authorities about the language—dictionary writers, editors, critics, writers and other literary folk, and English teachers—lay down the law about how the language is supposed to be used.

Prescriptivists often take the position that they are defending virtue, value, and honor against ignorant or lazy corruption. Observe the tone of the following comments by drama critic John Simon in his *Paradigms Lost: Reflections on Literacy and Its Decline* (New York: Clarkson N. Potter, Inc., 1980):

7. a. I was reading an article . . . where, disbelieving, I found: "Each of Mr. Fugard's plays . . . are themselves acts of contrition and ennoblement." The subject, *each*, is clearly singular, yet [the article's author] and the copy editor were content to let it multiply miraculously—an excellent thing in loaves and fishes, but sinful in syntax. What are we coming to when our big newspapers and their writers see no difference between singular and plural? (p. 24)
   b. Nearly every change in language does, in fact, begin with some form of illiteracy, but an illiteracy that is seldom, if ever, inventive. . . . Bad usage is . . . the dirty work of private, individual batrachians . . .
      Nevertheless, ignorant, obfuscatory, unnecessary change, producing linguistic leveling and flatness, could be stopped in its tracks by concerted effort. (p. 39)
   c. The fact that some people are too thickheaded to grasp, for example, that "anyone" is singular, as the "one" in it plainly denotes . . . (p. 40)

As you can see, Simon's ire is directed against both what he regards as bad usage as a result of thickheadedness and what he regards as unnecessary change.

Interestingly, there has long been concern about language change, on the assumption that change often means change for the worse. In the late 1700's there were public complaints about the use of *existence* for *life, novel* for *new, capture* for *take,* and *inimical* for *hostile,* and a century later, *The Spectator,* a British journal of culture, criticized the use of *demise* for *death* and *phenomenal* for *extraordinary*.[1] A 1960 article in *The Atlantic Monthly*[2] fulminated against errors of "diction," objecting to the following, among others:

8. a. Ask whoever you see.
   b. He works faster than me.
   c. I can't imagine it being him.
   d. Nobody was killed, were they?
   e. These kind of men are dangerous.
   f. That's her at the door now.
   g. The data is now in.

EXERCISE 1. For each sentence in the list above, what do you think would be the corresponding "correct" form? Which of these "correct" forms would you use in casual speech? Which ones would you use in formal writing?

---

1. Daniels, Harvey A. "Old Scolds Never Die," article in *Chicago Tribune,* Nov. 21, 1976.
2. Follett, Wilson. "Grammar is Obsolete," *The Atlantic Monthly,* February 1960, p. 73–76.

In our discussion to follow, we shall see that there is no evidence that linguistic change can be identified with linguistic decline. To the contrary, a language, through being used, adapts to meet the changing needs of its speakers. Language change has always been with us; consequently it is reasonable to conclude that such change is natural.

Descriptive Grammar

In the modern science of linguistics, grammar is "descriptive" rather than prescriptive. The aim of descriptive grammar is to describe the grammatical system of a language, that is, what speakers of the language unconsciously know, which enables them to speak and understand the language. For instance, it is part of the grammatical knowledge of all speakers of English that while sentences 9a, b, and c (below) are grammatical, 10a, b, and c are not:

9. a. The Celtics are likely to win.
  b. This is the pen that I had lost.
  c. America is between the Atlantic and the Pacific.
10. a. *The Celtics are probable to win.
  b. *This is the pen that I didn't know where I had put.
  c. *The Atlantic is what America is between the Pacific and.

An asterisk preceding a sequence of words means that the sequence is **ungrammatical**. What ungrammatical means will become clear as we proceed; for the time being, interpret it as meaning simply "incorrect."

You may wonder why the sequences of (10) are of concern at all. In no way do they represent problems in English usage; no speaker of a "substandard" dialect uses them; and no foreigner learning English would erroneously produce them. Much more relevant, you might imagine, would be presumably ungrammatical sequences like these:

11. a. Ann and Sally don't know nothin'.
  b. He ain't here.
  c. She be here.
  d. I go to the movies a lot anymore.

However, the first three of these are fully grammatical in certain dialects of English, and the fourth exemplifies a point of grammar that is used without adverse reaction by many English speakers, even if not by a group identifiable as speaking a dialect. That is why no asterisk precedes them.

What does it mean to say something is "grammatical in certain dialects of English"? And what is the significance of saying that a given grammar point is "used without adverse reaction"? These questions will be addressed later in this chapter.

Sentences 10a, b, and c (above) are important because the ways they are ungrammatical shed light on the rules governing grammaticality.

Throughout this book, we will examine scores of ungrammatical word sequences with the idea of using them to understand what makes grammatical sentences grammatical.

In descriptive grammar, the interest is not in what should be, but in what is: the language that people use all the time, the whole range of different varieties they use in their normal everyday lives, including the varieties they use in their most casual or intimate moments, as well as the varieties they use in their formal, careful speech and writing. In the practice of descriptive grammar no judgment is made about what is right or wrong; speakers of the language are held to be the highest authorities. Literally, "what they say goes." "Correct grammar," i.e., grammaticality, is exemplified in ANY sentences and discourses felt by a native speaker to be the normal way to talk.

EXERCISE 2.

A. Consider the task of getting someone to loan you a book. How would you ask to borrow a book from the following people?
1. Your roommate
2. Your father
3. Your professor
4. Another professor, whom you don't know
5. Your little brother or sister
6. Your grandmother
7. Your mother-in-law
8. Someone in your neighborhood whom you always had trouble with when you were a child

B. Write a couple of brief (one- or two-paragraph) descriptions of an event you have participated in. Address one to your best friend and one to a relative you are not particularly close to. Then make a list of all the differences between the two versions.

"Anything goes."—BUT.

If you are wondering whether descriptive linguists believe that, linguistically speaking, anything goes, the answer is YES—in their role as linguists, that is. Naturally, as native speakers of a language, say, English, they have the same kind of reaction any educated person might have toward imprecision in language use, or bureaucratic gobbledygook, or manipulatively deceptive language use. Linguists get just as offended as the next person by misleading uses like *incursion* for *invasion* and *disinformation* for *lie,* and are bothered just like anyone else by unnecessarily complex discourse like this World War II blackout directive submitted to President Roosevelt:

12.	Such preparations shall be made as will completely obscure all Federal buildings and non-Federal buildings occupied by the Federal Government during an air raid for any period of time from visibility by reason of internal or external illumination. Such obscuration may be obtained either by blackout construction or by termination of the illumination. This will, of course, require that in building areas in which construction must continue during the blackout, construction must be provided that internal illumination may continue. Other areas, whether or not occupied by personnel, may be obscured by terminating the illumination. (Associated Press dispatch, 11 March 1942, quoted in Bolinger 1975, p. 258)[3]

But what bothers linguists about such examples is their manipulativeness or their obscurity, not the linguistic structures or words used.

Descriptive linguists, as ordinary people (i.e., not in their linguists' role), often have private pet peeves about language change. For instance, one descriptive linguist I know—let's call him "G"—regrets the weakening of the distinction between *imply* and *infer,* and feels that someone who says something like the following is grammatically "wrong":

13.	That article inferred that Washington was a Marxist.

If you are wondering what's wrong with it, you've lost the distinction, which is (or was) that *infer* can have only a human subject which stands for the person who derives a notion from something, whereas *imply* (taking a wider range of subjects than *infer*) goes in the other direction. That is, whatever does the implying gives the notion to someone else—the one who infers it. So, for G (and for most, probably all, prescriptivists) sentence (a) below is "right" and sentences (b) and (c) are "wrong":

14.	a.	Smith implied to Wesson that the FBI was on her trail.
	b.	*Smith inferred to Wesson that the FBI was on her trail.
	c.	*That article inferred that the moon was green cheese.

On the other hand, G rather likes the weakening of the rule that states that *anymore* can be used only in negative contexts—

15.	I don't eat chocolate anymore.

---

3. The newspaper dispatch containing this text pointed out that President Roosevelt amended the text to the following:
Tell them that in buildings where they have to keep the work going, to put something across the window. In buildings where they can afford to let the work stop for a while, turn out the lights. (Associated Press dispatch, 11 March 1942, quoted in Bolinger [1975], p. 258)

—and himself now says such things as

16. I go to late movies a lot anymore.

No doubt many readers will find this barbarous. Others will be surprised that anyone would object.

There is an interesting difference between these two cases. The first, the one that G objects to (personally, not as a descriptive linguist), involves a threat to a useful meaning distinction. The second, the one G himself uses, is merely an extension of a word use to a new grammatical environment, a change in grammatical patterning without a meaning change. Originally the use of *anymore* was restricted to occurrence in agreement with a preceding negative:

17. a. Sandy sleeps late.
　　　b. *Sandy sleeps late anymore.
　　　c. Sandy doesn't sleep late.
　　　d. Sandy does*n't* sleep late *anymore.*

Its new use, as in *Sandy sleeps late anymore,* is an extension to an affirmative, rather than negative, environment. Its grammatical restrictiveness with respect to negation is gone (for speakers like G). But there is no loss of a meaning distinction.

EXERCISE 3. Which of the following changes represent a loss of a meaning distinction? Which ones represent a strictly grammatical change with no loss of a meaning distinction?

1. The loss of the *who/whom* distinction
2. The use of *disinterested* as a synonym for *uninterested*
3. Allowing *they* to refer back to a singular word like *anyone,* as in *if anyone arrives late, they should go to the back*
4. Saying *Alice is not as tall as Marya* instead of *Alice is not so tall as Marya*
5. Saying *I was literally climbing the walls* when you mean that you were distraught, but not that you were physically ascending walls
6. Using *most* for *almost,* as in *Most everybody likes pancakes*
7. Saying *between you and I*

Language history teaches us that it is common for useful distinctions to remain in the language, despite being threatened. In the same 1960 *Atlantic Monthly* article mentioned before, we see the same objection to the weakening of the *imply/infer* distinction as G's today:

18.   . . . smoke *implies* fire, but when you smell smoke you *infer* fire. It is a clear loss . . . when we ignore the differentiation. . . . *Infer* is being so chronically abused by many who should know better that lexicography no longer quite sees what to do with it, but a decent writer sees, and he is quite aware that the widespread confusion makes the English vocabulary not richer, but poorer. (Wilson Follett, "Grammar is Obsolete," *The Atlantic Monthly*, December 1960, p. 76)

But the distinction is still with us, albeit in danger. One can be reasonably confident that 25 years from now linguistic curmudgeons will be complaining about the ongoing weakening of the *imply/infer* distinction, just as G does today and Wilson Follett did 25 years ago in *The Atlantic Monthly*. The linguist Geoffrey Nunberg points out that "the battles over grammar, like other battles for souls, are won at the individual level."[4] As individuals continue to hear about the *imply/infer* distinction, it is entirely possible that enough of them will be persuaded of its usefulness to preserve it. There is a smaller chance of this happening with the *anymore* rule.[5]

However, it is by no means the case that all useful distinctions are preserved, or that speakers always act rationally in deciding in what directions a language will change. Consider *ain't*. Once a perfectly respectable contraction of *am not*, with some pronunciation change (as with *will not* ⇒ *won't*), it became stigmatized a few hundred years ago, resulting in an unfortunate gap in the conjugation of *be*. After sentences like *He's late.*, we can form tag questions like *isn't he?*, but after sentences like *I'm late.*, there is no "right" form to use. To fill the gap, we produce *aren't I*, which, if you think about it, is as grammatically illogical as any usage criticized by prescriptivists. So the tendency to preserve useful distinctions is just that, a tendency, and sometimes linguistic changes are, as prescriptivists claim, for the worse. However, no great harm has resulted from the stigmatization of *ain't* or the existence and use of grammatically "illogical" forms like *aren't I*.

Similarly, no great harm will come to our language, or to communication in English, if the *infer/imply* distinction disappears. The loss of a distinction between a pair of words does not destroy the capacity of human beings to recognize and use the meaning difference formerly encoded in the two words. Speakers will simply invent different ways to encode it.

It has been speculated, but never proven, that the grammatical structure of a language channels the way its speakers think and view the world. But if grammar does affect thought in this way, it does so only in a sug-

---

4. Nunberg, Geoffrey. "The Decline of Grammar," *The Atlantic Monthly*, Dec. 1983, p. 44.
5. The linguist William Labov quotes the following conversation between himself and a person providing him with linguistic data:
W. L.: Around here, can you say, "We go to the movies anymore"?
Salesgirl: No, we say "show" or "flick." (1972, p. 309)

gestive or predisposing way, not as an ironclad straitjacket on mental processes. Speakers of languages without grammatical tense have no trouble distinguishing earlier from later, and speakers of languages without a grammatical distinction between first-hand reports and second-hand reports (e.g., English) have no trouble distinguishing between the degrees of trust to be placed in the reports. For this reason, it probably makes sense not to worry about changes in a language lowering the general intellectual level of its speakers.

Despite their inevitable personal biases in language, *in their role as scientists,* descriptive linguists observe, record, and try understand these linguistic innovations, without deciding from personal taste, or even from expert knowledge, that the innovations are *wrong.* They are neither wrong nor right; rather, they are just a fact of linguistic life.

The connection between language change and supposedly incorrect grammar is strong, as we will see below. Our next topic is language variation, to be followed by a consideration of language change. At this point, you should be clear about the distinction between "prescriptive" grammar and "descriptive" grammar. Descriptive grammar is the framework of modern linguistics, and of this book.

VARIATION IN ENGLISH

Let's begin with an exercise.

EXERCISE 4. For each of the expressions below, put a check mark in the proper column or columns. If you have heard the expression before, check *Have heard.* If the expression is something you say, check *Say.* If you think it is typical of some particular group of English speakers that you are not a member of, for example, some group whose members you believe usually speak "substandard" English, or speakers who live in some particular geographical area, check *Other group.* (Do not check this category if you believe nobody would say the expression.) If you believe the expression is "incorrect grammar," check *Incorrect.* (Rely both on your intuitions about what is English, and on what you have learned in school.) (NOTE: For many of the expressions listed, you will want to write more than one check mark.)

Expression	Have Heard	Say	Other Group	Incorrect
1. This shirt needs ironed.	____	____	____	____
2. They might should go.	____	____	____	____
3. You like her, and so don't I.	____	____	____	____
4. She always be late!	____	____	____	____
5. Don't nobody know that.	____	____	____	____

	Expression	Have Heard	Say	Other Group	Incorrect
6.	That is John book.	___	___	___	___
7.	There's a new house abuilding over there.	___	___	___	___
8.	My brother a fireman.	___	___	___	___
9.	There goes the man that I told you about him yesterday.	___	___	___	___
10.	I haven't got any.	___	___	___	___
11.	We've some money for you.	___	___	___	___
12.	I asked him if he could come out and play.	___	___	___	___
13.	I asked him could he come out and play.	___	___	___	___
14.	I know where he.	___	___	___	___
15.	It's a fly in my soup!	___	___	___	___

If you compare your responses to this exercise with those of others, you will probably find a good deal of variation. This is to be expected, and may give you some idea of the range of people's judgments about what is correct. Also, you probably have several check marks in Column 4, "incorrect." However, only sentence 14 is ungrammatical in all varieties of English. All the rest are quite normal sentences for a sizable number of native speakers of English.

For a descriptivist, the basis for judging the grammaticality of an utterance is the feelings of the speaker of the utterance. The most common indication of these feelings is what is normally said. For example, if I (a native Pennsylvanian) have a conversation with a person from the Southeast, say, Georgia, I may hear something like the following—

19. I might could do that.

—which I would not say (it is ungrammatical according to the rules of my dialect) but which is perfectly fine in my interlocutor's dialect. That is, in certain areas of the United States no one blinks an eye or raises an eyebrow at such a sentence; it feels perfectly natural to speakers of the dialect in which it is grammatical. No one who uttered such a sentence naturally would, on hearing a recording of it, say, "Oh, no, that doesn't sound right."—except, possibly, as a result of prescriptivist training in schools. Because of the effect of some aspects of schooling, a speaker of such a sentence might say, "This is bad grammar, and should not be used, but is used by everybody around here." (Or one may hear ". . . but I say it all the time.") Descriptive grammarians would not take this kind of reaction as evidence that the sentence in question was ungrammatical for the person who uttered it. On the contrary, it would be a fairly strong indication of grammaticality.

The Dimensions of Variation

A language can vary within itself along at least four dimensions: time, space, social group, and style. Variation in time means language change. Variation in space means geographical dialect differences. Variation according to social group means differences in language form or language use depending on what social group the speaker belongs to. Social groups can be defined in this regard in any number of ways: by socio-economic class, by gender, by race, by occupation, by age, by political party, and in numerous other ways. Variation according to style means the different ways a person, for example, you, speaks (or writes) depending on the immediate situation and purpose in speaking (or writing).

Sets of co-occurring linguistic features in a place or typical of a group are usually accorded the label **dialect**. The distinction between a dialect and a language is fuzzy, and, in popular parlance, sometimes depends on nonlinguistic—e.g., political—facts. For instance, even though the people on both sides of the Spanish-Portuguese border speak essentially the same way, what they speak is called Spanish on one side and Portuguese on the other. To an outsider, the language of China is Chinese, despite there being at least five major regional versions of Chinese, which are not mutually intelligible.[6] This political aspect to the language-dialect distinction led one linguist to say, "A language is a dialect with an army and a navy." Of course, a more useful characterization of the distinction is in terms of mutual intelligibility: dialects are mutually intelligible, languages aren't.[7]

Variation in language can be discovered on several "levels" of language: the level of pronunciation, the level of grammar, and the level of vocabulary, among others.

Variation in time will be discussed later. Here are some examples of variation along the other dimensions:

Variation in space (geographical dialects)

By pronunciation

In New York City, eastern New England (for example, the Boston area), and certain areas of the South (Richmond, VA, Charleston, SC, and

---

6. The Chinese dialects are united not only by their speakers' common nationality, but also by their writing system. The Chinese writing system, in which characters stand for meanings, rather than sounds, is the same in all Chinese dialects. To help their interlocutors understand, people from different areas of China sometimes draw characters in the air as they converse with each other.

7. Even this is not completely reliable, since intelligibility admits of degrees.

New Orleans, LA, for example), an *r* that occurs at the end of a word, or before a consonant, can be dropped. Hence the parody of a Boston accent pronouncing *I parked my car in Harvard Yard* as "*I pahked my cah in Hahvahd Yahd.*" Elsewhere in the country this *r*-dropping does not occur.

By grammar

Around Pittsburgh, it is common to omit *to be* between the verb *need* and a passive participle, that is:

20.   a.   This shirt needs to be ironed.
            ⇓
          b.   This shirt needs ironed.

Elsewhere this grammatical pattern does not occur.

By vocabulary

In Boston, what is called *soda* in most parts of the country is called *tonic*. In California, many call it *coke*—that is, *coke* is not only a brand name, but also a common noun denoting any number of types and brands of soft drink. In the Philadelphia area, a *hoagie* is a submarine sandwich (also called, in other areas, a *sub*, a *torpedo*, a *poor boy*, and a *grinder*). In parts of the South, a *spider* is a frying pan. What Easterners call *lightning bugs* are *fireflies* elsewhere. It is easy to come up with hundreds of additional examples.

Variation by social group

Any social groups you pick will have some language differences. We will draw our examples here from two of the most influential ones: gender and race. In our examples drawn from the racial dimension, we will go into some detail, because the differences between the variety of English spoken by many members of a minority group—Black Americans—and standard English are generally not understood as representing equally valid systems, which, from a scientific point of view, they do. Rather, they are usually conceived of in terms of a distinction between correct and incorrect speech. For numerous educational and social reasons it is important to understand them properly.

Black English developed out of the special situation in which slaves and their descendants found themselves, in the 17th, 18th, and 19th centuries, and has endured partly because of the wide social distances that have separated blacks and whites in the U.S. since emancipation. Slave traders made a practice of separating kidnapped Africans from the same linguistic areas and grouping captives from linguistically disparate areas, so that communication difficulties would make revolt less likely. In the New World, slaves were of course socially separate from their masters, and received no overt English instruction, learning English "naturalistically," primarily from fellow slaves. The linguistic situation was rich with diversity, offering a variety of African sources as well as a range of English dialects—those of overseers as well as masters. In this situation, linguistic change and development was rapid, with considerable amalgamation and adaptation of elements from various African languages, as well as from English. (In fact, some of the main features of Black English today are ambiguous in their roots: we can't tell whether they have an African or English origin, the features being found both in English dialects and in West African languages.) The social separations between whites and blacks that have scarred American history up to the present have accentuated the differences between standard English and Black English. In light of this, it may be surprising that Black English is as similar to standard English as it is.

It is important to point out here that the term "Black English" is something of a misnomer, for two reasons. One, the term suggests that all black people, and only black people, speak Black English. In fact, many black people speak standard English, and many white people speak a variety of southern English that is very similar to Black English. Two, the term suggests that Black English is monolithic, whereas it is actually a gradient ranging from speech forms like those of standard English to those characteristic of the in-group speech of black inner-city youths. In most cultures around the world, non-standard speech forms show this kind of variation, and Black English is no exception. In short, the rules of Black English we discuss next are *variable* rather than *categorical*.

However, outside the South, Black English is spoken natively essentially only by black people. The term is therefore useful because of this association between language and race. More importantly, because Black English patterns that diverge the most from standard English have come to indicate (erroneously, of course) to many people a lack of intelligence, it is important to understand the structure underlying these non-standard patterns—so that the erroneous inference from non-standard speech to a lack of intelligence can be corrected. So, in order to study it conveniently, we will make the simplifying assumption that Black English is a homogeneous structure, even though the reality is the opposite.

With this in mind, let's look now at a few salient features of modern Black English. (Note: The somewhat intricate descriptions that follow will not only give you information about Black English, but will also give you your first taste [in this book, at any rate] of descriptive linguistic analysis.)

A pronunciation rule of Black English

One pronunciation rule of Black English deals with word-final consonant clusters. Words like *mist, clasp,* and *desk* are often pronounced *miss, class,* and *dess* by black speakers. The reason is that, in Black English, certain types of word-final consonants can be omitted in pronunciation. This omission is not due to laziness or incompetence in speaking. Rather, it is rule-governed. The rule—i.e., the circumstances under which this omission can occur—is complex. First, the consonant that can be dropped must be a "stop." A "stop" is a speech-sound which is made by completely closing off, or *stopping* (however briefly), the airflow from the lungs. The stops of English are [p], [t], [k], [b], [d], and "hard" [g]. If a stop is the second sound in a pair of word-final consonants, it can be dropped if both sounds are *voiced* or both are *voiceless.* The sounds [s], [t], [k], and [p] are all voiceless, in contrast with their respective "voiced" counterparts, [z], [d], [g], and [b], which are made with the vocal cords vibrating. Words like *mist, clasp,* and *desk* can therefore be pronounced *miss, class,* and *dess,* because they end with a pair of voiceless consonants ([st], [sp], and [sk]). Words with a pair of voiced final sounds—*grabbed, bend,* and *breathed* (don't worry about the spelling; focus on the sounds: [bd], [nd], and the [voiced "th"d]), for example—can also lose their final sound, resulting in *grab, ben, breathe.* The rule, in short, is:

21. Rule: A word-final "stop" can be deleted when it occurs after a consonant with the same voicing value (voiced or voiceless).

To figure out whether or not a word is subject to this rule, you need to determine whether or not it ends with the right kind of consonant cluster: a consonant followed by a stop, with both sounds having the same voicing. You can tell whether a sound is voiced by placing your finger on your "Adam's apple" and trying to sense a vibration during the pronunciation of the sound.

EXERCISE 5. Which of the following words are subject to Rule (21)? (Be sure to focus on pronunciation, not spelling.) For each word subject to this rule, state how application of the rule would cause it to be pronounced.

slept	warned
gained	brags
washed	blabbed
belt	added

Sometimes the operation of this rule can leave a past tense verb with the same form as its present tense: *grab,* past tense: *grab;* present tense: *breathe,* past tense: *breathe;* present tense: *dress,* past tense: *dress.* An understandable inference in reaction to this is that many Black English speakers don't know past tenses. But they do; Rule (21) is just a *pronunciation* rule. Past tenses made irregularly (*broke, took, ate, came, went, swam, thought, bit,* etc.) are produced by Black English speakers just as they are by standard English speakers. Moreover, regular past tense forms are understood even when they are not produced. The situation is in a way like speakers from [r]-dropping areas who delete their word-final and pre-consonantal [r]'s (e.g., in *car* and *yard*). Just because they don't pronounce these [r]'s doesn't mean they don't recognize the ("abstract") presence of an [r] in these words.

Another common reaction is that, even if the irregular verbs mark the past tense, information is lost in the regular past tense verbs. However, those who have this reaction fail to remember that several English verbs form their past tense with a "zero" suffix—*put, cut, hit, beat,* for example—and this is true in all dialects. No one feels that information is lost in a sentence like *They put the books on the shelf,* because, of course, almost all the time the intended time reference is made clear by the surrounding context. It should be noted that the pronunciation rule under discussion here (Rule 21) also exists in standard English, although its operation is more restricted. In a phrase like *cold beer,* the pair of voiced sounds at the end of *cold,* [-ld], can lose the [d], resulting in *col' beer,* for all speakers of English. A final consonant can be dropped even when what is lost is meaningful, as in *I miss' my bus* for *I missed my bus.* But for speakers of standard English, in *cold eggs,* the [d] does not drop, nor does the [d] in *I missed eleven buses.* In standard English, the rule applies, but not when a word beginning with a vowel follows.

Three grammatical rules of Black English

Be-less sentences. One of the stereotypes about Black English is that it lacks the verb *be.* Black English sentences like the following—

22. a. Tim over there.
    b. She late.
    c. My father a fireman.

—are stock material for jokes and put-downs. Black people are sometimes sensitive about them, to the point of denying that they exist. But they do exist, and it is important to understand their structure. The most striking thing about their structure is how similar they are to common standard

English sentences. The superficial differences mask an underlying similarity.

Briefly, the Black English *be*-dropping rule says the following:

23.   Black English *Be*-Deletion Rule:
Present tense forms of *be* (*is, are,* and *am*) can be omitted only where they can be contracted into the forms *s, 're,* and *'m.*

For instance, *he's here, they're standing,* and *I'm swimming* can become *he here, they standing,* and *I swimming,* respectively. However, *is* in *I know where he is* cannot be contracted. If you try to contract it, you get **I know where he's,* which is ungrammatical. Just as it cannot be contracted, in both standard English and Black English, it cannot be deleted in Black English; if you delete it, you get **I know where he,* which could not possibly occur in Black English—i.e., it is ungrammatical.

To understand the conditions on contraction and deletion of forms of *be,* consider the following. Certain expressions normally occur after a verb—for instance, location expressions, as in *She is <u>in the corner</u>* or *Greg was <u>over there</u>.* When such an expression is the focus of a question, though, it is "moved" from its basic post-verbal slot: Rather than *Do you know he is <u>where?</u>,* we have *Do you know where he is?* This "movement" is reflected even in so-called indirect questions, which aren't really questions at all: *I know where he is.* Diagrammatically:

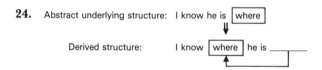

24.   Abstract underlying structure: I know he is [where]

Derived structure: I know [where] he is _____

In both standard English and Black English, forms of *be* can be contracted only under the following conditions:

25.   English Contraction Rule (All Dialects):
Present-tense forms of *be* (*is, are, am*) can be contracted only where no word or phrase has been "moved" from the position right after the *be* word.

Thus, no contraction is possible in *I know where he is,* because the word *where* was "moved" from its position directly after *is.* Consequently, no English speaker—black or white—would ever say **I know where he's* or **I know where he.* Of some interest is the fact that the contraction rule is exactly the same in Black English and in standard English. This means that the Black English deletion rule can be seen as just an extension of a "reduction" process (contraction) that applies in both standard English and Black English. So another way to put the rule is:

26. Black English Contraction Rule (Simple Version):
Black English can delete only where standard English can contract.

So Black English sentences lacking *be* are not nearly so different in grammatical structure from their standard English counterparts as they seem.

EXERCISE 6. For each of the following sentences, state: (a) whether or not a contracted form is possible for it; (b) its contracted form, if it has one; (c) the corresponding Black English sentence resulting from *be*-deletion.

1. We are ready to help you.
2. Ready we are to help you.
3. The concert is on the 26th.
4. I know when the concert is.
5. The concert is in the stadium on the 26th.
6. Max told me where the concert is on the 26th.
7. Max told me that the concert is on the 26th.

Invariant *be* sentences. The Black English *be*-less construction is quite different, in form and also in meaning, from the construction represented in the following:

27.   a.   Shauna be late.
    b.   He be working.
    c.   I be in bed.

This construction, known as "invariant *be*," due to the fact that *be* does not change into *am, is,* and *are,* is not contractible (and hence not deletable), and has a meaning different from the contractible-deletable forms, and different from anything so compactly sayable in standard English. It means "typically," "habitually," "repeatedly." So *Shauna be late* means that Shauna is usually late, not that she is late now.

EXERCISE 7. Translate the following Black English sentences into standard English.

1. My brother a fireman.
2. My brother be working.

3. My brother working.

4. Yesterday when my brother work he bought this ticket.

Now explain, for each sentence above, exactly how it is different from its standard English counterpart. Use the terminology and framework for description used in our discussion above.

Multiple negation. Sentences with multiple negation, like this one—

28. I don't know nothing about none of those.

—are supposedly illogical because the negative cancel each other out, as minuses do in math. Indeed, in some constructions, they do, for example: *I do NOT know NOTHING about stereochemistry—I know at least a little bit!* However, in Black English, multiple negation can occur also as a form of grammatical "agreement." The way the agreement works is simple. Whenever an indefinite word (*some, something, someone, a, an,* etc.) follows a negative (*not*), it changes its form to agree with it:

29. Indefinite Agreement Rule:
An indefinite word that follows a negative in a sentence must agree with the negative.

This rule actually is observed in all dialects of English, not just Black English. To see this, consider the affirmative version of sentence (28): *I know something about some of those.* In standard English, if we negate this, simply by adding *not,* we must also change the form of the indefinite words to *any.* In Black English, the required change is to *no* or *none.* Diagrammatically:

30. Underlying structure:
I know something about some of those.
⇓
Derived structure after the insertion of *not:*
I don't know something about some of those.
⇓
Further derived structure, after adjustment of *some:*
a. in standard English—
I don't know anything about any of those.
b. in Black English—
I don't know nothing about none of those.

The rules in the two dialects are identical except for requiring a different form of negative agreement: *no* or *none* vs. *any.*

There are numerous other areas of Black English grammar that deserve discussion, but this should suffice to show you that Black English is complexly structured (at times in ways suprisingly parallel to standard English), and that Black English speech is not a failed effort to speak "correctly." It is not a mere collection of mistakes; like all languages and dialects, it is rule-governed.

Vocabulary differences by social group

Here let us leave race and turn briefly to gender as a correlate of language differences. Are there any words that men use but women don't, and are there any words that women use but men don't? In a word, yes; a commonly offered example is taboo words (curse words, "four-letter words"), allegedly used less by women than men. But many women say that in groups made up of women only, taboo words are common. Possibly, in mixed groups, women do not use taboo words as much as men do.

Other examples of words used more by women than by men are certain adjectives. There are some English adjectives that men are simply not culturally permitted to use:[8] *adorable, darling, sweet* (as applied to actually non-sweet objects like cars, houses, and pictures), and perhaps *cute* (as applied to most objects, but not women). Color terms are another example. There are many color terms that most American men do not know and whose referents they cannot identify: e.g., *puce, vermillion, mauve,* and *chartreuse.* And there are others that are understood but rarely used by men: e.g., *peach, lemon, sand, ivory, rose, emerald, navy,* and *eggshell.*

EXERCISE 8. Gather some physical samples of different colors, for instance swatches of fabric. Some of the samples should be "cardinal" colors, such as a strong fire-engine red and bright lemon yellow; others should be "borderline" colors, such as mauve, magenta, and yellow-green. Present the colors to subjects, one sample at a time, and ask the subject simply to name the color. See if you can correlate the responses with gender and with other characteristics of subjects, such as age, socio-economic status, etc.

Variation in individual style

In pronunciation

Almost everybody "drops the *g*" at the end of an *-ing* suffix in casual speech, while retaining it in careful speech. Similarly, most people destress

---

8. Except in certain subcultures, e.g., gay.

the vowels in words like *and, the,* and *of,* compared with their pronunciation in isolation. *And* has a vowel like that in *man* in isolation, but the vowel is suppressed in casual speech, so that the word is pronounced either [n] or with a destressed vowel our spelling system has no standard spelling for. *The* has a vowel like either "ee" or "uh" in isolation, but a destressed vowel in casual speech.

Cases of social variation are frequently stylistic as well. The *r*-dropping rule of New Yorkers is a good example, for in addition to being geographically defined, it is a social marker as well. In New York, members of lower socio-economic classes tend to omit *r*'s more than members of higher classes. But almost all New Yorkers drop *r* more in casual speech than in formal, careful speech. This was demonstrated in the mid-1960s in some revolutionary sociolinguistic studies by William Labov (see Labov 1972). Labov conducted sociolinguistic interviews with New Yorkers from a wide range of social classes, pioneering ingenious ways of getting his subjects to produce a range of speech styles, from the most casual, with the speaker paying the least attention to form, to the most formal and careful. Across both social class and individual style, the percentage of *r*-retention and *r*-dropping varied according to degree of formality.

In grammar

Certain grammatical constructions seem to be largely restricted to very formal speech, or to writing. Here are three examples, all constructions which will be discussed later in this book.

31. absolute constructions:
His wire cage now ready, Luis grabbed the pigeon and put it in.
32. nonrestrictive relative clauses (those with commas):
My brother, *who is a circus acrobat,* is coming to visit this week.

In less formal speech we are likely to hear *My brother—he's a circus acrobat—he's coming to visit this week* or *My brother's a circus acrobat and he's coming to visit this week.*

33. *do so:* If you can persuade him to go, please do so.

In less formal speech we are likely to hear . . . *do it* or just *do.*

In vocabulary

Similarly, certain pairs of synonyms are specialized for more formal or less formal contexts: *utilize* vs. *use; inquire* vs. *ask; illumination* v. *light; personnel* vs. *people* or *workers* or *employees; beverage* vs. *drink.*

EXERCISE 9. Construct a large 3 × 3 grid, with the top labeled, from left to right, GEOGRAPHICAL, SOCIAL, and STYLISTIC, and the left axis labeled, from top to bottom, PRONUNCIATION, GRAMMAR, and VOCABULARY. In each cell put two additional examples of the nine kinds of language variation we have discussed. Your chart should look like this:

	Geographical	Social	Stylistic
Pronunciation			
Grammar			
Vocabulary			

THE EFFECTS OF PRESCRIPTIVISM

Different attitudes toward different types of variation

Interestingly, people have different sorts of attitudes toward the different kinds of variation. The attitude many people have toward vocabulary variation is one of amusement. It tickles their interest that speakers from Philadelphia call a submarine sandwich a *hoagie,* that a skunk is a *polecat* in much of the South, and that a water fountain for many midwesterners is a *bubbler.*

Pronunciation variation gets a mixed response. Often, in conversation, it is not noticed at all. Some pronunciation differences are regarded as quaint—for instance, *r*-deletion, to speakers from *r*-pronouncing areas (most Americans from outside eastern New England find Boston accents rather charming). Others are greeted with surprise: Eastern speakers who become aware that Western speakers do not distinguish the vowels of *cot* and *caught* are surprised, but not particularly amused—but neither do they find this loss of a distinction "wrong" or "right."

Sometimes, though, pronunciation different from one's own is thought to be either "right" or "wrong." Most Westerners believe it is "right" to use, as they do, the same first-syllable vowel in *Mary, merry,* and *marry*; that is, they find their own pronunciation "right." Both New Yorkers and non-New Yorkers find the stereotyped Brooklyn *boid* ("bird") and *t'oity-t'oid* ("thirty-third") "wrong." In fact, pronunciation is the main input into tests of "linguistic insecurity." These tests work in the following manner. A person is presented with a list of English words which are known to have alternative pronunciations—e.g., *vase, nuclear, escalator, aunt,* and—in New York—words with preconsonantal or final *r,* or word-initial *th*—and asked two questions: "How do you pronounce this word?" and "What is the correct way to pronounce it?." The percentage of cases in which different answers are given to the two questions is the person's "index of linguistic insecurity.[9]"

Grammatical variation elicits attitudes that are much more negative, and more rigid; there is hardly any tolerance for grammatical differences at all. The reason is presumably that since communication takes place via complex phrases and sentences, not just sounds or isolated words, the rules governing the structure of phrases and sentences are unconsciously regarded as sacred. This attitude is manifested in the common misconception that correct grammar is co-extensive with "making sense." But it is possible to make perfectly good sense, i.e., be meaningful, without being grammatical, and it is possible to be grammatical without making any sense at all. An example of the former is **Joe arrived before Muffy will leave,* which violates a sequence-of-tense rule—a grammatical rule—but is, in terms of meaning (rather than structure), perfectly fine. An example of the latter is *My brother is an only child,* which makes sense only on a metaphorical reading; otherwise it is contradictory (not making any sense), although it is fully grammatical.

More importantly, it is possible to make sense by means of different grammatical forms from those sanctioned by the grammatical powers-that-be. William Labov's seminal paper "The Logic of Non-standard English" (1969) showed that valid argumentation is not dependent on what grammatical rules govern one's sentences, or on what dialect they are from. Labov contrasted two tape-recorded discourses, one produced by a young black street gang leader in Harlem, speaking Black English, and one produced by a middle-aged middle-class black New Yorker, speaking standard English. The former discourse was succinct, interesting, and logically impeccable; the latter was wordy and uninteresting, and had logical gaps.

Certain aspects of minority dialects have been claimed to represent illogical thinking. Two examples discussed above are multiple negation and the absence of some *be*'s in Black English. All you have to see to understand

9. Labov (1972), p. 117–118.

that these are not illogical is evidence from other languages which have not been accused of illogic. Many languages express the meaning of *He doesn't have anything* with the word for 'nothing' where standard English has *anything;* e.g., Spanish *No tiene nada* translates into English literally as "Not he-has nothing," i.e., "he doesn't have nothing." But no one ever claims Spanish is illogical. Similarly, many languages lack verbs translatable into English as present tense *be;* Russian is an example. In Russian, to say "John is a man" you say *Ivan chelovek,* literally "John man." (Russian also lacks articles.) So *be* is not needed in Russian to communicate the idea that X is Y. Yet no one has claimed Russian is illogical, nor should one. A Black English sentence of that form, without *be,* is just as logical. No communicative or logical loss is brought about by the absence of *be.*

How Prescriptivism Can Hurt

Little social harm comes from the anecdotal and scattered objections of prescriptivists to innovations like *to impact,* "positive" *anymore,* and the like, or from complaints about changes like the loss of the *infer/imply* distinction. These cases are not markers of particular social groups which are discriminated against. Harm may come, however, from attacks on linguistic systems which are standard for certain social groups. When black six-year-olds pronounce *mist* or *missed* as *miss,* or *jumped* as *jump,* they are simply following a rule of their dialect (in these words the two word-final sounds are [-pt]; by Rule 21, the [t] is dropped), and it is unnecessarily critical to tell them that they are "wrong."

Imagine a first-grade class. Reading aloud, a black child encounters the sentence *Spot jumped over the fence.* The child says: "Spot jump over the fence." The teacher, meaning well, and believing that the child has made a reading error, corrects her: "No, Sheila, Spot *jumped.*" The child may not know what she is being corrected for, because for her, many occurrences of the form *-ed* are, in effect, silent letters, much like the *-b* on the end of *bomb,* and when she hears the teacher's *jumped,* she disregards the final [-t] sound much the same way adults often unconsciously disregard pronunciation differences in dialects different from their own. Though she pronounces *jumped* as *jump,* the child may be reading correctly—deriving information from the written page—but *pronouncing* it in a way different from what the teacher is used to accepting as correct. This is not a reading problem, if by "reading" we mean deriving meaning from writing.

Black English is different from standard English in a number of ways, not just in the few ways we have discussed in this chapter. It is entirely possible that the amount of criticism children receive for their natural, home-acquired language—criticism both overt and subtle, in terms of well-intentioned corrections—is enough to have a negative effect on the children's attitude toward school and learning.

A More Rational Approach

The reality is that standard English (the ill-defined version of English that prescriptivists would have us aspire to) is in no way intrinsically superior to Black English or any other dialect of English; it is just the dialect of the powerful. (Standard dialects always are: standard French, the French of the Academy, is Parisian, the dialect of the capital; standard British English is that of upper-class London; standard Russian is Muscovite; etc.) Many complex historical forces, which we will not go into here, have operated together to determine whose speech would be the American standard, but there is nothing intrinsically more logical, beautiful, efficient, or systematic about it as compared to any nonstandard dialect, or any other standard English dialect (e.g., British), for that matter.

Consequently, the most rational attitude toward language variation may be to delight in it![10] If you can't, or don't want to, catch the linguistic bug of fascination with linguistic form, it makes sense to at least take an attitude of relaxed unconcern and detachment regarding language variation. Remember that it's just historical accident, not intrinsic linguistic superiority, that selects standard dialects, and that nonstandard dialects are just as rule-governed as standard ones are.

An entirely different issue is how to educate speakers of nonstandard dialects. Our society is not free of linguistic prejudice, to put it mildly, and linguistic prejudice is often compounded with racial and other sorts of prejudice. To deal with the realities of the world, then, in particular those of the marketplace, it ought to be communicated to users of *be*-less sentences and other nonstandard English forms that different varieties of English are judged by the society to be appropriate to different situations or contexts. It is *useful* to be able to produce standard English in certain circumstances (e.g., job interviews and formal written papers) and just as useful, and appropriate, to use nonstandard (notice: not *sub*-standard) English in others (having a beer with a friend). In each situation, a speaker who produces the inappropriate variety—standard or nonstandard—may be subject to criticism.

LANGUAGE CHANGES

The evidence of language change is easy to find: if you examine some works of English literature from a few hundred years ago, and contrast

---

10. This is the attitude most linguists take. It is common for linguists to make themselves obnoxious at parties by asking strangers to repeat themselves when they have produced some fascinating novel pronunciation, word, or sentence structure. Non-linguists often feel self-conscious or irritated in the face of such single-minded attention to the form, rather than the content of what they're saying. Sometimes they mistakenly feel criticized. This, of course, is an understandable effect of the pervasive influence of prescriptivism.

them with some works from today, you will discover a large number of changes.

Vocabulary and Meaning Change

Changes are easy to find in the vocabulary of a language and in word meaning. Hundreds of years ago the English word for 'uncle' was *eme.* There used to be an English word *poppet,* which meant 'doll.' In old English *flesh* meant 'edible flesh,' i.e., 'meat,' in addition to what it means today, and *meat* meant *any* food (as in the still-alive expressions *meat and drink* and *nutmeat,* frozen phrases which preserve the old meaning). The ancestor word for *hound* meant 'dog' generally, not just one breed, and *dog* meant a particular breed.

Grammatical Change

It is also easy to find examples of grammatical change. English used to have a set of noun endings which signaled what role the noun had in its sentence: whether it functioned as subject, direct object, indirect object, or possessive. (These concepts will be discussed in Chapter Seven.) For example, the word meaning 'stone' had the following forms in Old English:

34. *stan* (subject and direct object form: as in *The stone fell and I threw the stone*)
   stanes (possessive form: as in *The stone's weight*)
   stane (indirect object form: as in *give the stone a whitewash*)

English also used to make negative sentences differently from the way it does now. In the 15th and 16th centuries, sentences were negated simply by attaching *not* to the end of the sentence: *I see you not;* or by inserting *not* after the verb: *This man is not of God, because he keepeth not the sabbath day (New Testament,* John 9.16).

It is possible to see the evidence of grammatical change in the variety of English today, e.g., in the variations discussed above. The seeds of change are in this variation. Usually the change is marked by the competition between a couple of variants, one of which is viewed as correct, the other as incorrect. We discussed one case of this earlier, "positive *anymore,*" as in *I go to movies a lot anymore,* which most English speakers believe to be "wrong," yet many use. Certainly this "positive *anymore*" was incorrect (in the sense that it was simply not English—it was not something that anyone would ever say), but has become correct for many speakers—again, "correct" in the sense that they use the expression without thinking about it, and don't feel that there's anything wrong with it when it is used. Another case, perhaps easier for some to accept, is the weakening of the *who-whom* distinction. *Whom* used to be required whenever the word functioned as direct object—as in *You kissed whom?* or *Whom did you kiss?*, or as object of a preposition, as in *With whom did you dance?* or *Whom did you dance with?*. This rule has been weakened, so that today a "moved" *who(m)*, as in *Whom did you kiss* _____ or *Whom did you dance with* _____[11] is required only in formal contexts. In fact, in casual situations, if someone uses *whom* in the ways shown in the examples just given, the speaker will probably be subject to criticism!

Pronunciation Change

Changes in pronunciation are also easy to find. These are interesting because they provide an explanation for some of the bizarre facts about English spelling, the strange silent letters and other features of spelling which distance it from a simple "one letter = one sound" system.

The most significant set of sound changes in English was the Great Vowel Shift, which took place between about 1400 and about 1600. This set of changes is interesting because it is responsible for some of the quirks of English spelling and the widespread systematic differences between the English spelling system and that of continental European languages.

In the Great Vowel Shift, the vowel in words like *bite, wise,* and *by,* which had been pronounced like "ee" as in our current pronunciation of *see,* became a diphthong. (A diphthong is a double vowel sound in which the first part makes a smooth transition into the second. Examples are the vowel sounds of *I, now,* and *toy.*) The diphthong which developed was the one in which the first part is the vowel of the first syllable of *father* and the second part is the "ee" sound. That is, around 1400 *bite* was pronounced as *beet* is today, but by about 1600 it was being pronounced "ah-ee" (or "uh-ee") as it is today. Most European languages use the written vowel "i" to stand for an "ee" sound. English used to, but the Great Vowel Shift moved the pronunciation of English words spelled with an "i" away from this European standard.

In a similar change, the vowel in words like *house* and *loud,* which had been pronounced the way the vowel of *Sue* is today, also became a diphthong—one in which the first part was the vowel of the first syllable of *father* and the second part the "u" vowel. (The reason that *house* and *loud* are spelled with *ou* is that English had borrowed from French the spelling "ou" for the vowel sound of *Sue.*)

The Great Vowel Shift was "great" because it affected all the vowels of English. Here are the rest of the changes:

---

11. The "_____" stands for where *who(m)* was "moved" from.

35.   THE GREAT VOWEL SHIFT

	Pre-1400 Vowel Pronunciation	Post-1600 Vowel Pronunciation
beet, freeze, see:	like that of modern *fate*	"ee"
beat, please, sea:	like that of modern *bet*	like that of modern *say* (A later change produced the modern "ee" sound.)
goose, fool:	like that of modern *home*	"oo" as in modern *Sue*
broken, rose:	like that of a modern New Yorker's pronunciation of *law*	as in modern *hope*
hate, graze, name:	like that of the first vowel in modern *father*	like modern *bet* (and later as a result of another change, with its current vowel)

THE SIGNIFICANCE OF VARIATION AND CHANGE

Arguments against prescriptivism can be derived from our discussion of variation and change. From the historical side, it is simply the case that a language changes, as part of its nature, in particular as part of its embedding in culture (which itself changes). There is no evidence that any particular historical stage of a language was, or is, any better than any other. A language's changing does not change its speakers' ability to communicate meanings. Consequently, there is no scientific basis for opposing language change.

From the side of variation, varied systems—e.g., geographical or social dialects—are equally capable of the expression of thoughts and feelings (they're equally capable of the expression of logical arguments, for instance) and equally highly structured. Since they are equally capable, one variety or another does not deserve stigma, at least from an objective, scientific perspective. And from the recognition of the complexity of structure in nonstandard dialects comes another reason for appreciating their validity: if they are complexly structured, their features cannot be regarded as erroneous attempts to approximate the standard. Consequently, from an objective point of view, all varieties are equally legitimate, rather than some (or one) being good and some bad, some right and some wrong.

OTHER SENSES FOR 'GRAMMAR'

Besides the descriptive/prescriptive opposition we have been discussing, there are other meanings for the term "grammar."

A Global Sense For 'Grammar'

Within framework of descriptive grammar, sometimes the term 'grammar' is used to stand for ALL the knowledge that a native speaker has about his or her language. Naturally, this includes facts about the structure of words and sentences. It also includes pronunciation rules (e.g., the fact that the regular English past tense ending shows up as the sounds [-t], [-d], or "[-id]" (as in *walked, played,* and *batted,* respectively); and the fact that every word-initial [p], [t], and [k] in English is made with a distinct puff of breath after it, called "aspiration"). Phonological facts like these are the topic of Chapters Two and Three. 'Grammar' in this grand sense also includes facts about meaning of words (such as the fact that the meaning 'mammal' is included in the meaning of *horse,* but not vice-versa) and the meaning of sentences (such as the fact that in *Ellen is sorry that Ruth has left Harry* it is assumed—"presupposed"—that Ruth has indeed left Harry, but this is not presupposed in *Ellen suspects that Ruth has left Harry*). It includes, too, facts about the organization of whole discourses, such as the fact that normally a person would not start a discourse with something like *What my sister did at her wedding was spill the rice;* that is, normally one would not burst into a room and produce this sentence as one's initial utterance. In other words, 'grammar' in this wide sense includes everything a native speaker knows about his/her language which enables him or her to speak and understand it.

This knowledge is not conscious, of course. English speakers can no more list on a piece of paper the rules of English grammar than they can explicitly describe the "rules" for bicycle riding—i.e., the "rules" we follow which govern balance and steering. The technical term for this sense of 'grammar' is **competence**. It is distinguished from **performance**, which is what speakers do (competence being what they know). Performance includes mistakes; competence doesn't. Thus, if you, by mistake, say *flop tight* instead of *top flight,* this is not an example of your competence—your knowledge—but simply a mistake, a failure of performance. (However, it is a fact of your competence in English that you would never, even by mistake, say **tlop fight* or **fop tlight,* because English pronunciation rules—part of competence—don't permit word-initial [tl-] combinations, whereas the possibility of a mistake like *flop tight* is included in every native speaker's competence in English.)

One manifestation of competence is the ability native speakers of a language have to judge instantly whether a particular combination of elements (words, sounds) is "grammatical" or "ungrammatical" in the language. "Grammatical" and "ungrammatical" are here taken widely, as meaning "possible or impossible in the language." Not just sequences of words, but also sequences of sounds, can be ungrammatical, e.g., **[tlop]*.

Note that "impossible in the language" is different from "not in the language." There are plenty of sound sequences which are not in the language in the sense of being words: [flin], [snawk], [snep], [barg]. But these are possible words, and could be coined—e.g., by creative advertising agencies, as names for new products—and are quite different from *[tlop], *[srip], *[fsap], *[ngombe], and the like, which at this stage of English could not be English words. No advertising agency, no matter how creative, would come up with them. So the notion "possible/impossible in the language" equivalent to the notion "grammatical/ungrammatical," deeply involves things which have not yet been produced as English, yet which are English, and even "in" English. The same is true, in an even more obvious way, on the level of sentences. Most of the sentences that are produced in speech or writing, when people use English, are produced for the very first time. Another way to put this is that speakers (and writers) say (and write) new things nearly all the time. As we experience the world, we have new things to say about it.

An interesting consequence of this view of grammaticality is that knowing a language means knowing some "rules" (the technical linguistic term), or processes of construction, which can produce an infinite number of new combinations of language elements. It is *not* the case that knowing a language means simply having memorized a list of possible combinations. (Since the possible combinations are infinite, there are too many.) The nature of these "rules" is part of the subject matter of the field of linguistics: their nature, how they interact, how they change, how they are actually represented in people's minds. In this book we won't be concerned about such topics, fascinating as they are. We will be concerned instead with the facts of the structure of English words and sentences, the effects of these rules.

A Narrow Sense For 'Grammar': Morphology and Syntax

The term 'grammar' is often used to refer to a particular body of information about a language: that having to do only with the structure of words and of sentences.

Morphology

Morphology is the study of words, including:

Inflection

Inflection refers to the way English makes related forms of words of the same "part of speech," such as plurals and possessives of nouns and past tenses of verbs. What is meant by "of the same part of speech" is that, for example, from the noun *cat* we can form the plural noun *cats,* which is the same part of speech (it's a noun) as the original *cat.* Similarly, the verb *brag* can be made into the verb *bragged* by attaching the past tense *-ed* to its end.

Derivation

Derivation refers to the rules governing how added prefixes or suffixes can create new words typically of a different "part of speech." For example, in English, so-called "manner" adverbs are formed from adjectives by suffixing *-ly* to them, as with *rapid* (adjective) + *-ly* = *rapidly* (manner adverb). Another example is how certain verbs can be made into nouns by having *-ment* added to their end *excite:* (verb) + *-ment* = *excitement* (noun).

Syntax

By **syntax** (the technical term for sentence structure) is meant, for example:

Grouping

In grouping the words of a sentence, they fall into chunks, or phrases. A sentence is not made up just of a sequence of words; some words that are next to each other go together more closely than others. For instance, in the sentence

36. Max's very impressive solo showed off his expertise.

the adjacent words *Max's* and *very* do not go together nearly as tightly as do *very* and *impressive;* and the words *showed off* go together much more closely than do *off his.* That is, if we "box" together words that go together into "phrases," we don't get something like (a) below, but rather something like (b):

37. (a) Wrong:

(b) Right:

When all the phrases of a sentence have been established, the sentence can be seen to have a hierarchical structure, with smaller phrases nesting inside larger ones. For instance, in this sentence, the phrase *very impressive* nests inside the larger phrase *very impressive solo,* which itself is a part of the even larger phrase *Max's very impressive solo.* When we bracket the parts of the sentence that go together, we get the following:

38.

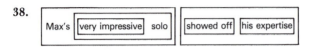

Functions

The function of certain chunks of words in sentences, as, for example, "subject" or "direct object" or "predicate." What these terms mean will be addressed in Chapter Seven. Briefly, words or phrases functioning as **subject** in English generally make the verb agree with them:

39.   Joe like-<u>s</u> Mary; Joe and Bob like-Ø[12] Mary.
         ⇑   ⇑
       subject   subject

Words or phrases functioning as **direct object** occur, typically, directly after the verb and are movable by a process called passivization:[13] *Shakespeare wrote <u>histories and comedies; Histories and comedies</u> were written by Shakespeare.*

Predicates make statements about things (the "things" generally being represented by words or phrases functioning as subject). The part that functions as predicate of *Shakespeare wrote histories and comedies* is *wrote histories and comedies.*

After we deal with pronunciation (phonology), in Chapter Two, our exclusive focus will be grammar in this narrow sense. In fact, after Chapter Three (which deals with morphology), our focus will be even narrower; the rest of the book will deal with syntax.

EXERCISE 10. Four senses of the term 'grammar' have been discussed: prescriptive, descriptive, global (overall linguistic competence), and narrow (morphology and syntax). For each of the following facts or rules of English, identify it as prescriptive or descriptive and as global or narrow.

1.   The rule that in a formal written paper you should not use contractions.

---

12. The "Ø" stands for an unpronounced suffix.
13. "Passivization" turns an "active" sentence, like *Shakespeare wrote histories and comedies* into a "passive" one, like *Histories and comedies were written by Shakespeare.* (The verb changes to "past, or passive, participle" form; the preposition *by* is inserted; a form of *be,* such as *were,* is inserted; and the phrase functioning as "direct object" gets shifted from its original post-verbal position to sentence-initial position and now functions as "derived" subject.)

2. The fact that English has some irregular past tenses, like *bought, ate,* and *went.*

3. The (presumable) fact that in *George chopped down the tree,* the sequence *chopped down* is a phrase, but *down the* is not.

4. The rule that present tense third person singular verbs in English have to agree with their subjects (e.g., *snores* has to have an [-s] enging in *Sarah snores*).

5. The rule that you can't begin a word in English with the [ng] sound.

6. The rule that *less* is used with mass nouns, like *money,* and *fewer* is used with count nouns, like *nickels.*

7. The fact that in English adjectives do not have to agree with the nouns they modify in gender or number (in contrast to many languages, like French, Spanish, and German).

8. The rule that in English normally adjectives precede the nouns they modify.

9. The prohibition against using *ain't.*

10. The fact that the English words *bull, ram, man, stag, stallion,* and *drake* all contain a feature of meaning not found in *woman, book, ewe,* and *patriot.*

WRITING

One obvious side of language we have neglected so far is writing. The reason we have neglected it is that it is really a derivative part of language. There are many languages which have no writing system, and one can have a perfect (though unconscious) knowledge of a language without being able to write it at all. Earlier, in the context of our discussion of Black English pronunciation, we mentioned that in some dialects of English an [r] could be either pronounced or not pronounced, depending on a pronunciation rule. Notice that we did not say "the letter *r*" can be either pronounced or not; an abstract [r], which either shows up in actual pronunciation or doesn't, may be present even in the language system of a nonliterate speaker! Bostonians—even preliterate ones, like young children— who drop the "r" in *fourteen* pronounce it in *four o'clock,* showing that *four* has an abstract [r] that is phonetically realized (i.e., pronounced) between vowels, but omitted before a consonant. You can know the system of your language perfectly without being able to read or write the language. Our focus of interest is therefore always on the unconsciously known language system of speakers, not on the written language. Writing is just a way to represent a language, and the structure of the language exists independently of the "channel" (e.g., speech, writing, telegraphy) it is sent out over. However, speech is the natural channel for language; all naturally evolved human languages use the channel of speech, and only some speech communities have developed writing systems. The channels different from speech that have developed in some communities (for instance, the community of the deaf, in which sign language is used) have developed in response to special needs.

There is, however, one way in which writing is more than just a representation of a language most naturally represented in speech. Some grammatical constructions are largely restricted to writing, only very rarely occurring in speech. A few of these were discussed above.

SOME BASIC NOTIONS OF SEMANTICS

Although a rich tradition in semantics exists independent of grammar, and much grammatical analysis is done with as little reference to meaning as possible, there are nevertheless pervasive connections between semantics and grammar, and no understanding of grammar is possible without familiarity with some rudimentary semantic notions.

We will not attempt here to say what meaning is. We will, however, survey some important concepts that bear on that large question. One idea is that meaning is **reference**: the use by a speaker of a word or phrase to refer to, or uniquely pick out, a particular object (thing, idea, quality, event, process, etc.) in the world (the real one or imaginary ones). The technical term for this object is **referent**. According to this notion, the meaning of *car* in *I want the car* is the four-wheel motor vehicle—the thing itself—that I am talking about and that my hearer knows about. The reference of *Mick Jagger* is that musician, the person himself.

Although reference is clearly an important part of meaning, it can't be all there is to it, since there are pairs of words and phrases that have the same reference—that refer to the same thing—that clearly have different meanings. One (famous) example is *the morning star* and *the evening star*. Both REFER to the planet Venus, but both MEAN different things, as is clear from the fact that *The morning star is the evening star* communicates a piece of information, unlike *The morning star is the morning star*. It's easy to find additional examples. One is *the instructor of this class* and whatever the instructor's name happens to be—let's say *Ms. Schmoo*. Despite having the same referent, these expressions intuitively "mean" different things. Notice that someone might say *I am looking for the instructor of this class* and, on another occasion, *I am looking for Ms. Schmoo*. If the speaker doesn't know that Ms. Schmoo is the instructor of this class, the two sentences would not mean the same, despite having two expressions with the same reference (the same person) in identical frames (*I am looking for . . .*). So meaning, whatever it is, must be more than just reference.

Related to the notion of reference is **denotation**. The denotation of a word is the set of its possible referents.

(Obviously, reference and denotation are applicable to the meanings of nouns, although they are insufficient by themselves to characterize these meanings. We won't go into this here, but reference and denotation are also applicable to the meanings of other kinds of words, albeit in complicated ways. Just as with noun meanings, meanings of other types of words cannot be fully characterized in terms of reference.)

The concepts of reference and denotation have to do with word-meaning. Other concepts important to word-meaning are **synonymy, homonymy** and **antonymy**. Synonyms are words with the same meaning, like *stop* and *cease*. Homonyms are words with the same pronunciation but different meanings, e.g., *sun* and *son,* and the two words *bank* (the edge of a river and the financial institution). Antonyms are opposites. There are different kinds of antonyms: "binary" ones, like *dead* and *alive*, which exhaust all possibilities, "graded" ones, like *hot* and *cold,* which are at opposite ends of a continuous scale, and "converses" like *buy* and *sell,* which denote the same event from different sides, with mirrored word order: *Joe bought the car from Fred—Fred sold the car to Joe.*

We have not, of course, defined the concept "meaning of a word." All we have done is mention a few concepts that are relevant to the problem of devising a satisfactory definition and that are important to understanding meaning.

Notions important to sentence meaning—just as hard to define as word-meaning—include the following.

Entailment (also called **logical consequence**) is the relation between a pair of sentences (strictly, a pair of **propositions**, which we will discuss below) when the second necessarily follows from the first. Another way to put it is to say that in any possible "world"—i.e., in any logically possible circumstance, conceivable or not—whenever the first sentence is true the second is also. Examples:

40. a. Karen killed Brian.
    b. Brian died.

    c. Lee kissed Kim passionately.
    d. Lee touched Kim.

The relevant verb here is **entail**; we would say sentence (40a) entails sentence (40b), and (40c) entails (40d).

Another basic concept is **paraphrase**, which can be defined as mutual entailment, or, less precisely, as "meaning the same thing." Examples of paraphrase pairs:

41. a. Reggie kicked the ball.
    b. The ball was kicked by Reggie.

    c. David sent a poem to Peri.
    d. David sent Peri a poem.

You can see that under whatever conditions it is true that Reggie kicked the ball, it must also be true that the ball was kicked by Reggie, and vice versa. Hence (41a) and (41b) mutually entail each other. The same holds for (41c) and (41d).

Paraphrase, of course, isn't restricted to sentence pairs; there exist paraphrase "sets" made up of numerous related sentences.

EXERCISE 11. List as many paraphrases as you can for the sentence *Mary bought a blue dress for Susie.* Exclude from your list paraphrases making use of synonyms.

Another significant notion is **anomaly**, which is the property of not making sense because of contradictory combinations of meanings. The sentence *Curious green ideas sleep furiously* is anomalous. This sentence was used by the linguist Noam Chomsky in his book *Syntactic Structures* (The Hague: Mouton, 1957) to argue that grammaticality and "making sense" are distinct properties of sentences.

Another significant concept is **proposition**. A proposition is the meaning of a sentence, that which can be true or false. A proposition is independent of language—that is, the same proposition can be expressed in English, Swahili, French, or Japanese. Different paraphrases in one language can express the same proposition, too.

NOTATIONAL CONVENTIONS

Since this book is written in English, and its topic is English, we need ways to distinguish our uses of English from our mentions of it, our examples. Logicians generally have solved this problem by using single quotes: Socrates was a man, but 'Socrates' was his name. We'll do the same sort of thing, but we'll need more than one way to represent our examples, because English, like any language, exists on a number of levels. There's the level of raw speech sound, for instance. For this, we'll use phonetic transcription, to be described in Chapter Two. Phonetic transcription will always be placed in square brackets: [pʰali wãnts ə kʰrækɾ] "Polly wants a cracker." For the level of organized sound, the phonemic level, at which only language-specific sound distinctions are marked, we'll use slanted lines: /pali wants ə krækɾ/.

When our focus is not sound or sound structure, examples of language data will be given in two ways: within a paragraph, in which case it will be italicized, and as set-off numbered examples, in which case it will be presented in normal typography.

Ungrammatical examples will be marked with a preceding asterisk (*), and questionable examples with a preceding question mark, as is traditional in linguistics.

ADDITIONAL EXERCISE

1. Write a short paper comparing and contrasting the concept of grammaticality discussed in this chapter and the concept of grammatical correctness you are familiar with from school.

2. Write a short paper about your personal experiences with prescriptive grammar. Try to identify some grammatical patterns of your speech which you were taught were wrong. How did you feel about what you were taught? (It is common to simply believe that what you were taught was right.) How do you feel now about language variation? Do you agree or disagree with the point of view expressed in the chapter?

REFERENCES

BOLINGER, DWIGHT. 1975. *Aspects of Language,* 2nd ed. New York: Harcourt, Brace, Jovanovich.

CHOMSKY, NOAM. 1957. *Syntactic Structures.* The Hague: Mouton.

DANIELS, HARVEY. 1976. "Old Scolds Never Die." *Chicago Tribune,* Nov. 21.

FOLLETT, WILSON. 1960. "Grammar is Obsolete." *The Atlantic Monthly,* February, 1960, pp. 73–76.

LABOV, WILLIAM. 1969. "The Logic of Nonstandard English." In James E. Alatis, ed., *Report of the Twentieth Annual Round Table Meeting on Linguistics and Language Studies,* Washington: Georgetown University Press, pp. 1–43.

_____ 1972. *Sociolinguistic Patterns.* Philadelphia: University of Pennsylvania Press.

NUNBERG, GEOFFREY. 1983. "The Decline of Grammar," in *The Atlantic Monthly,* Dec. 1983, p. 31–46.

Chapter Two

THE STRUCTURE
OF ENGLISH SOUND

THE FRUSTRATIONS OF ENGLISH SPELLING

Most of us have struggled from time to time with the inconsistencies and peculiarities of English spelling. I remember being amazed, at the age of seven, that *egg* was not spelled *a-i-g*, which in my dialect more closely reflected its pronunciation. Much later, I remember explaining to my six-year-old son why *tree* was spelled with an initial *t* instead of a *ch*, which also seemed a closer approximation to the pronunciation. My explanation—my first effort at communicating the mysteries of phonology—was that the word really was pronounced with a [t] sound, but when we say it fast it comes out similar to [ch] before the next sound, the [r]. I can also remember, in second grade, learning incorrectly the "*i* before *e* rule": "*i* before *e* except after *c,* or when sounded like *a* as in *neighbor* and *weigh.*" My version went "*i* before *e* except after *c* or when sounded like *a* in a neighboring way." It was one of those things you took on faith, no matter how little sense it made. I remember trying bravely to convince myself that the "sh" sound, as in *shell,* was ACTUALLY the [s] sound followed by the [h] sound, and pronouncing them together rapidly resulted in the "sh" sound. You can see that I was naively optimistic, taking seriously the idea that LETTERS stood for SOUNDS.

This is not to say that there is no correspondence between letters and sounds. On the contrary, we shall see that despite a far from perfect letter-to-sound correlation, English spelling nonetheless is reasonably systematic.

Let's begin our look at English sounds and sound structure with a catalog of ways that English spelling fails to match neatly with English pronunciation. Imagine a perfect spelling system, one in which there is a consistent correlation between letter and sound (the way the International Phonetic Alphabet is, as we'll see). Let's list ways that English fails to match this standard. (A notational warning: Throughout this chapter, we will use italicized letters (*a*, *b*, *k*) to stand for spellings, and square-bracketed symbols ([a], [b], [k]) to stand for sounds.)

First, *a given letter, or spelling, may have two or more pronunciations.* Symbolically:

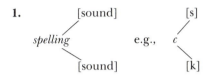

Examples abound: *c* in *ice* and *cake; s* at the beginning and the end of *sees* (it's pronounced [s] at the beginning but [z] at the end); *g* in *get* and *huge; x* in *axe* and *xylophone; th* in *thin* and *this; qu* in *loquacious* and *torque.* Vowels deviate from the ideal more than consonants. Take *u* and *a* as examples: *u* is pronounced differently in *put, cut, Sue,* and *suite,* and *a* is pronounced differently in *father, mat, mate,* and *can.*

Second, *two or more letters or spellings may represent the same sound.* Symbolically:

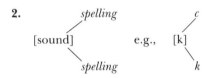

Again, examples are easy to find: the [k]-sounds in *cake* (the first one is represented by *c*, the second by *k*); the [ǰ], or "soft *g*" sounds in *judge,* spelled by *j* and *g;* the [f] sound, which can be represented by the letter *f* or by the letter combination *ph* (this two-letter symbol is another kind of deviation from an ideal alphabet, as we shall see directly below). Again, vowels deviate from the ideal even more than consonants. In most dialects of American English the [a] sound of the *a* in *father* can also be spelled with an *o*, as in *shop*, and in western American dialects, with *au* or *augh* as in *taut* and *taught*. The unstressed vowel represented by the underlined letters in *idea, a box of beans*, and *She saw the car the thief stole* has at least three different spellings, *a, o,* and *e.*

Third, *a single sound may be represented by a SEQUENCE of letters.* A perfect writing system ought to have exactly one symbol for one sound, in sequence as well as in the ways discussed above. The English spellings *sh, ch, ph* (representing [f]), and *th* illustrate the problem.

Fourth, the converse of the two-successive-letters-for-one-sound case, *a single letter may stand for two successive sounds.* One example of this in English is the letter *x*, which most of the time stands for the sounds [ks], as in *axe*. The vowel *i* as in *five* is another: it stands for a sequence of sounds we might better spell *"ah-ee."*

Fifth, *letters may be silent*, e.g., the *k* in *knife*, the *p* in *psychic*, and the *b* in *dumb*. These letters have no effect, unlike the final *-e* in words like *mate*, *cope*, and *hide*, which, while silent itself, cues the pronunciation of the preceding vowel.[1]

EXERCISE 1. Five categories of deviations from the phonetic ideal have been discussed. They are:

a. A given letter or spelling may have two or more pronunciations.

b. Two or more letters or spellings may represent the same sound.

c. A single sound may be represented by a sequence of letters.

d. A single letter may stand for two successive sounds.

e. Letters may be silent.

Identify which deviation category, a–e, or none of them, is exemplified by each of the following:

1. the *e* at the end of *line*.

2. the way *n* is pronounced in *thank* and *than*.

3. the pronunciation of the underlined letters in the following words: *leaf, see, machine, Caesar*.

4. the way *c* is pronounced in *medicine* and *medical*, *electricity* and *electrical*, and *reciprocate* and *reciprocity*.

5. the different pronunciations of *th* in *this* and *think*.

The Reasons for "Unphonetic" Spelling

Why is English spelling so filled with these inconsistencies? In short, for two main reasons: (1) language change and (2) the conservative nature of spelling.

The type of language change that has affected spelling is, of course, pronunciation change. All the changes, for example, of the Great Vowel Shift (1400–1600) have left their mark on our spelling. Before the Great Vowel Shift, the vowel in *bite* and *wise* was pronounced "ee"; the vowel in *beet, freeze,* and *see* was pronounced rather like the *ay* in *say;* the vowel in *beat, please,* and *sea* was pronounced "eh" (that is, as currently in *bet*); the

---

1. Silent letters which have no effect are also different from the *g* in *sign* and the final *b* of *bomb;* the *g* and *b* connect *sign* and *bomb* to their relatives *signal* and *bombard*.

vowel in *foul* and *house* was pronounced "u" (that is, as currently in *moo*); the vowel in *fool* and *goose* was pronounced "oh"; the vowel in *rose* and *no* was pronounced like a New Yorker's *caught;* and the vowel of *hate* and *name* was pronounced "ah."

Relics of pre-Great Vowel Shift patterns can be seen in certain pairs of related words, one of which retains something closer to the pre-Shift pronunciation: *please - pleasant, crime - criminal, sane - sanity.*

In many ways the pre-Shift spelling more consistently reflected pronunciation. The same symbol, *i*, was used for the vowels in *machine* and *bite*, and this made sense, since in these words the letter *i* was pronounced identically. The same goes for the *a* vowels in *name* and *father*, the *ea* vowels in *please* and *pleasant,* and the *a* vowels in *sane* and *sanity.* Moreover, words with different vowel spellings like *ea* and *ee* in *heat* and *see* were pronounced differently; today, the spelling masks the sameness of pronunciation.

Some characteristics of pre-Shift spelling derived from French borrowings, not only of words, but of general rules of spelling. For instance, the word *foul* was borrowed from French, with the spelling *ou* to represent the sound [u], that is, the sound of the vowel of *moo* and *shoe* today. But also, in general, the spelling *ou* was borrowed from French to represent the [u] sound even in words not borrowed from French—e.g., Germanic *house* (Old English *hus,* pronounced [hus] "hoos" before the Great Vowel Shift). The borrowing of spellings for non-borrowed words could only occur in a largely illiterate society, in which a small class of educated persons could easily make decisions about spellings. This of course was the case in medieval England. Some aspects of modern spelling are the result of these decisions.

So the pronunciation of English changed, in a direction away from spelling. Why didn't the spelling keep pace? In other words, why was English spelling so conservative? And why is spelling in general so conservative? By the same token, why can't English spelling reform now? This is the topic of the next section.

Why Not Spelling Reform?

One obstacle to spelling reform is the inertia caused by the permanence of writing. Unlike speech, which is gone the moment it is uttered, writing endures. Books and papers can last for centuries. So spelling tends to remain the same because what is printed or written tends to remain in physical existence. Wholesale spelling reform would require rewriting the entire corpus of English writing from the past several hundred years (not just literature, but also newspapers, journals, textbooks, government records, etc.). If this were not done, persons who learned to read in the new system would have a very difficult time reading anything written in English before the spelling change.

Another obstacle in the way of spelling reform comes from the association speakers of English make between standard spelling and literacy, or "being educated." Reformed spellings might suggest, to many people, lack of education, or even stupidity. How do you feel about "Meny sikologists definitly beleev that dreams have grate hiden significense"? Does it strike you as the product of an uneducated person? Recall the use of "eye dialect" in literature to suggest rusticness and lack of education, even when the pronunciation of the eye dialect spelling is identical to that of the standard spelling, for instance, cases like "yore" and "yew" for "your" and "you."

Nonetheless, spelling reform has at times been attempted. The British playwright George Bernard Shaw (d. 1950) was one who strongly favored spelling reform. (Shaw is responsible for the parody of English spelling in which *fish* is spelled *ghoti: gh* as in *tough, o* as in *women, ti* as in *station.*) In fact, Shaw set aside a large sum of money in his will to be used to advance the cause of spelling reform.

Earlier, in the 1830s, in the United States, the editors of Webster's dictionary actually achieved some reform, abolishing British *u*'s in *hono(u)r, colo(u)r,* and the like. In this century, the *Chicago Tribune* tried to "simplify" the spelling of many words, including the following:

3.   Examples of the *Chicago Tribune*'s simplified spellings:
ameba, altho, burocracy, definitly, dialog, drouth, frater (for *freighter*) genuinly, hocky, midrif, prolog, skilful, tho, thoro, thru

The *Tribune* began using spellings like these in 1934. The effort was controversial, and the paper's commitment to spelling reform waxed and waned more than once. Public opinion never strongly favored spelling reform, and the *Tribune*'s efforts at reform received significant negative reaction. In 1974 the effort was given up, with the retention of a few relics (e.g., *tho* and *thru*).

Another reason that English spelling has not been reformed to any significant degree is the vast extent of dialect variation in English. If reform were instituted, which dialect would be chosen as the basis for spelling? Throughout the English speaking world, and even within the U.S., there are many different regional pronunciations. To some extent there is a national standard, as heard, for example, in the speech of television network newscasters. But respected as this speech is, it has not had the effect of homogenizing regional dialects into, or even in the direction of, the national standard.[2] If anything, regional dialects are even more distinct than before the advent of television. The regional varieties of American

---

2. According to William Labov, "people do not borrow much from broadcast media or from other remote sources, but rather from those who are at the most one or two removes from them in age or social distance" (1972, p. 180 FN).

English don't quite carry the prestige of newscaster speech, but may be regarded locally as entirely acceptable for all kinds of speech interactions. In Boston, no stigma is attached to [r]-dropping, and in Knoxville and Atlanta no stigma is attached to the replacement of diphthongs like those in *oil* and *sky* by "monophthongs," giving rise to pronunciations like "all" and "skah," respectively. And there is an unconscious national ambivalence about which pronunciation of words like *caught* is correct, the eastern one or the western one. (Western readers can approximate the eastern pronunciation by pronouncing *caught* with an initial consonant and vowel like those of *core*, and replacing the final [r] with a [t]; and Eastern readers can match the Western pronunciation by pronouncing *caught* like *cot*.) In light of facts like these, if we were to reform English spelling to make it more accurately reflect pronunciation, whose pronunciation would it reflect— that of residents of Atlanta, Boston, Seattle, London, Melbourne, New Delhi,[3] or somewhere else?

PHONETICS

During the age of European exploration (c. 1400–1900) amateur linguists lacked a consistent way to represent the sounds of the languages spoken in Africa, Asia, the Americas, and the Pacific region. Each of the various European spelling systems (e.g., English, French, Dutch, Portuguese) had its own spelling problems (akin to those identified above for English). Linguistic field work on non-European languages was greatly facilitated by the development of the International Phonetic Alphabet (IPA) in 1889, which developed out of the (mainly historical) linguistic scholarship of the 19th century.

The IPA (and the slightly different phonetic alphabet we will use, which will be presented below) is a set of symbols for speech-sound, each of which has an agreed-upon phonetic interpretation. This interpretation is **articulatory**; that is, the "meaning" of each symbol is how the sound represented by the symbol is produced.

Since the interpretation of the phonetic alphabet is articulatory, to understand it you need to know something about articulation. This is one reason to look at articulatory phonetics. Another, equally important, is that articulatory phonetics provides a basis for understanding phonological rules, which describe how combinations of linguistic elements are pronounced. Phonological rules will be discussed later in this chapter.

---

3. In several former British colonies, a sufficiently large population of native or second-language English speakers has developed so that actual standard regional dialects of English can now be said to exist.

Articulatory Phonetics

The way we create speech sounds is by exhaling air from our lungs and modifying the shape of the moving column of air by altering the shape and position of our **articulators**—the lips, tongue, teeth, and different areas of the roof and back of the mouth. Blowing across the mouths of bottles with different amounts of water in them can give you an idea of how modifying the shape and size of a column of air can change sound.

One important dimension by which sounds can be classified is the location of the main constriction placed in the way of the column of air being exhaled. We will discuss this in detail below, but for now notice the difference between how a [k] is made and how a [p] is made. The difference is the location of the closure. The closure for a [k] is made near the back of the mouth, and for a [p] in the front. Not all sounds involve a complete closure; in [s], [z], and [r], for example, there is only an approximation of two articulators to each other.

One difference between **vowels** and **consonants** is the degree of closure; vowels are made with essentially no closure—the column of air is relatively unobstructed as it moves out—while consonants are made with at least some closure. To see this, contrast the first vowel sound in *father* (whose phonetic symbol is [a]) with [f], [s], and [z], holding each sound for several seconds (that is, say [aaa..aaa..fff..fff], etc.).

A second dimension by which sounds differ is whether the vocal cords are vibrating or not during sound production. You make your vocal cords vibrate by holding the cords close together, in a state of tension, so that air exhaled between them causes them to vibrate. You can arrange your vocal cords in two other states. One is tightly closed, so no air can exit. This is the position they are in when you lift a very heavy object—closing off the chest cavity with a quantity of air inside lends rigidity to your torso, adding strength for lifting. It is also the vocal cord position immediately before coughing. The other position is wide open, so air exits unobstructed, as in natural breathing, and in the utterance of [h]. Sounds with vocal cord vibration are **voiced** and sounds without it are **voiceless**. Contrast [s] and [z], again holding the sounds for several seconds. (As you try this, be sure not to whisper; say the sounds loudly!) Try it with two fingers placed against your **larynx** ("Adams apple"). You should be able to feel a pronounced vibration when you say [zzzzzzz].

All English vowels are voiced,[4] but English consonants are divided into voiceless and voiced ones.

---

4. Not so in all languages. Japanese has voiceless vowels. However, they are restricted to occurrence between voiceless consonants. Since [s] and [k] are voiceless, the [u] in *sukiyaki* is voiceless, resulting in a pronunciation which may sound like [skiyaki] to English speakers.

EXERCISE 2. Use the finger-on-the-throat test (holding the pronunciation of the sounds for several seconds) to determine whether the following sounds are voiced or voiceless:

1. [v] as in *loving*
2. the first sound in *think*
3. [m] as in *ember*
4. [f] as in *off*
5. the middle consonant in *measure*
6. the middle consonant in *mother*
7. the middle consonant in *witches*
8. the initial consonant in *jump*
9. [l] as in *yellow*

It is sometimes a little difficult to tell impressionistically whether [p], [t], [k], [b], [d], and "hard *g*" are voiced or voiceless. Use the finger-on-the-throat test with the following words to see if you can tell: *pass, tussle, kiss, bash, dish,* and *gush.* If you can't tell for sure, you'll have to just memorize that [p], [t], and [k] are voiceless, and that [b], [d], and [g] are voiced.

The voiceless sounds of English, then, are:

[p t k f s h]; the initial sounds of *think, chew,* and *shoe;* and the middle consonant in a casual pronunciation of *cotton, Latin,* and *kitten.* (We will go over the phonetic symbols for these, and other, sounds below.)

And the voiced sounds are:

All vowels; [b d v z r l m n w y]; "hard *g*"; the middle consonant of *measure;* the final sound of *fudge;* the initial sound of *this;* and the final sound of *sing.*

Most voiceless sounds have a "voiced counterpart," one made in exactly the same way (that is, as we shall see directly below, produced at the same place of articulation and with the same manner of articulation). For instance, the voiceless [p] has a voiced counterpart [b], [f] has [v], etc. Say the following pairs of words aloud, paying special attention to the pronunciation of the underlined letters:

4. pill - bill tan - Dan kill - gill fan - van thigh - thy Sue - zoo mesher - measure chunk - junk

The only voiceless sounds without voiced counterparts are [h] and the middle consonant of *cotton, kitten,* etc. The phonetic symbol for this consonant is [ʔ]. It is easy to see how these sounds could not possibly have voiced counterparts, once you understand how you produce them: you make an [h] by opening the vocal cords widely, so air rushes between them without obstruction. Since your vocal cords are so far apart, they couldn't possibly be close enough to be caused to vibrate by the passage of air between them; and you make a [ʔ] by quickly and completely closing the vocal cords and then releasing them. Say *uh-oh;* the "catch" in the middle is a [ʔ]. Since the very "tools" you need to produce voicing are busy doing something else, a voiced [ʔ] would be impossible.

Point of articulation

Point of articulation is the location of the main obstruction to the outward airflow.

As we discuss point of articulation, we will also introduce the phonetic symbols used for each sound. There is a consistent and strict correlation between sound and symbol—the rule is, very strictly, ONE SYMBOL = ONE SOUND—so that anyone who knows the phonetic alphabet can read aloud anything written in it, from any language whatsoever. (Obviously, the idea is that the phonetic alphabet should be free from all the problems of the spelling system of English or any other language.) Earlier in this chapter the International Phonetic Alphabet (IPA) was mentioned. In the early years of the 20th century American linguists developed a phonetic alphabet slightly different from the IPA; this phonetic alphabet is the one we will adopt.

Since the point of articulation parameters are different for vowels and consonants, we will discuss them separately.

Point of articulation for consonants

There are eight points of articulation for consonants in English. Points of articulation are labeled anatomically, by the two parts of the mouth that come together to close off or constrict the airflow. These are called **articulators.** From the front of the vocal tract to the back, here are the points of articulation, together with the sounds produced at each one:

Bilabial: The articulators are the two lips. Sounds: [p b m w].

Labiodental: The articulators are the lower lip and the upper teeth. Sounds: [f v].

Interdental: The articulators are the tongue tip and the teeth. The tongue tip protrudes slightly between the teeth. This point of articulation is rare among the languages of the world. Sounds: the "*th*" sounds of *think* and *then,* with the following phonetic symbols: [θ] for the "th" sound of *thin, ether,* and *moth,* and [ð] for the "th" sound of *this, either,* and *thy.*

Note the difference between [θ] and [ð]. [θ] is voiceless, and [ð] is voiced. Convince yourself of this, using the finger-on-the-throat test, with *ether* and *either*, in each case speaking the word aloud and prolonging for several seconds the "th" part ("E..th-th-th..er. Ei..th-th-th..er.").

Alveolar: The articulators are the tongue tip and the "alveolar ridge, the ridge behind the upper front teeth. Sounds: [t d s z l n].

Alveopalatal: The articulators are the tongue tip and the area from the alveolar ridge back to the palate, the central area of the roof of the mouth. Sounds: those represented by the underlined letters in *shoe, measure, church, fudge*. The phonetic symbols for these sounds are as follows:

[š]: the "sh" sound of *shoe*
[ž]: the "zh" sound of *measure* and *azure*
[č]: the "ch" sound of *church*
[ǰ]: the "j" or "soft *g*" sound of *fudge*[5]

Palatal: The articulators are the blade of the tongue and the palate, the central area of the roof of the mouth. Sounds: [y r].

Velar: The articulators are the back of the tongue and the velum, the "soft palate" near the back of the mouth. Sounds: [k g] and the final sound of *sing*, phonetic symbol [ŋ].

Glottal: The articulators are the two vocal cords. Sounds: [ʔ h].

The following diagram displays these points of articulation.

5.   **POINTS OF ARTICULATION OF ENGLISH CONSONANTS:**

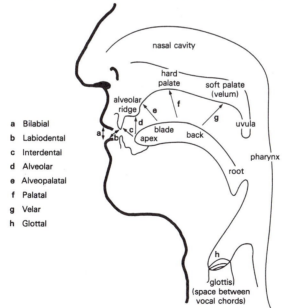

a Bilabial
b Labiodental
c Interdental
d Alveolar
e Alveopalatal
f Palatal
g Velar
h Glottal

5. The International Phonetic Alphabet (IPA) uses different symbols for these sounds: [ʃ] for [š], [ʒ] for [ž], [tʃ] for [č], and [dʒ] for [ǰ].

Point of articulation of vowels

Contrast the vowel sounds in *key, coo,* and *hot* to get a feel of the range of point of articulation in vowels. If you pronounce *key* with a very high, tight vowel sound, you'll feel your tongue blade almost touching your alveolar ridge or palate. Pronouncing *coo* with a very high, tight vowel, you'll feel near tongue contact in the back of your oral cavity, with your velum. Saying *hot,* you'll feel nothing close to tongue contact during the vowel production, and in fact your mouth will be fairly wide open.

The phonetic symbol for the vowel in *key* is [i]; for the vowel in *coo* is [u]; and for the vowel in *hot* is [a].

Both [i] and [u] are considered **high** vowels, because the tongue is in a high position, almost touching the roof of the mouth, while [a] is a **low** vowel, because the tongue is low (since the mouth is open).

The difference between [i] and [u] is along a **front - back** dimension, [i] being a **front** vowel and [u] being a **back** one. [a] is also a back vowel.

The other front vowels (in addition to [i]) are those in *hit, late, let,* and *hat.* The vowel of *hit* is considered high, those of *late* and *let* are considered **mid**, and that of *hat* is low. The other back vowels (in addition to [u] and [a]) are those in *book, boat,* and *lawn* (pronounced with a New York accent).

There are two **central** vowels: the unstressed vowel of the first syllable of *about* and the stressed vowel of *nut* and the first syllable of *mother.* On the height dimension these are considered mid.

Here are all of the phonetic symbols for English vowels, listed by their point of articulation:

FRONT:

High:

[i]: the second vowel of *machine;* the vowel of *see, sea,* and *me.*
[ɪ]: The vowel of *bit, did,* and *lip.*

Mid:

[e]: The second vowel of Spanish *hablé;* the vowel of French *et.* In English this vowel occurs in a diphthong (discussed below) as in *play, mate,* and *hey.* The diphthong symbol is [ey] (sometimes written [ei]).
[ɛ]: The vowel of *bet, dregs,* and *neck.*

Low:

[æ]: The vowel of *lap, mat,* and *Jack.* (In some dialects, notably that of the central midwest, centering around Chicago, the vowel in these words is closer to [ɛ]. Readers who speak such a dialect should think of eastern or western speakers' versions of *Jack* or *lap* to get a fix on [æ].)

CENTRAL:

Mid:

Stressed:

[ʌ]: The vowel of *hut, mud,* the first syllable of *mother.* This vowel is always stressed ("accented").

Unstressed:

[ə]: The unstressed vowel of the first syllable of *above* and the last syllable of *sofa.* This vowel, called "schwa," is always unstressed. It often occurs in rapid, casual speech, as the vowel of small words like *the* and *of,* as in a casual pronunciation of the following sentence:

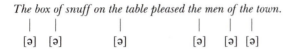

The box of snuff on the table pleased the men of the town.
  | | | | | |
 [ə] [ə]   [ə]   [ə] [ə] [ə]

It is easy to confuse [ə] and [ʌ]. A good mnemonic for distinguishing them is the word *above.* The phonetic transcription of *above* is [əbʌv]. The first vowel is unstressed, so it is [ə]. The second vowel is stressed, so it is [ʌ].

(There is actually no phonetic difference between [ə] and [ʌ]; they are the same sound, the former always being unstressed and the latter always being stressed. By rights, then, there should be just one phonetic symbol for this single sound. But a conventional practice has developed of distinguishing the stressed and unstressed versions of this sound by means of these two symbols.)

BACK:

High:

[u]: The vowel of *shoe, Sue,* and *zoo.*
[ʊ]: The vowel of *put, should,* and *book.*

Mid:

[o]: The vowel of *boat, so,* and *Moe.* In American English this is usually diphthongized to [ou] or [ow].
[ɔ]: The vowel of middle Atlantic speakers' pronunciation of *caught, law, dog, fought,* etc. The vowel has disappeared in the speech of many Americans, particularly those from the West, except before [r] in words like *for* and *core.* It is present in British English. If you pronounce *caught* like *cot,* you may be able to produce [ɔ] by mimicking the speech of the movie or TV actors from New York (they often play New Yorkers).

Low:

[a]: In the speech of most Americans, the vowel of *hot* and of the first syllable of *father.*

The chart below displays the height and location along the front-back dimension for all the American English vowels.

6.   American English Vowels

	FRONT	CENTRAL	BACK
HIGH	[i]		[u]
	[ɪ]		[ʊ]
MID	[ey]	[ə] [ʌ]	[o]
	[ɛ]		[ɔ]
LOW	[æ]	[a]	

In this chart, the low vowels are closer together on the front-back dimension than the high vowels are. This is because there is less distance between the sites of closest approximation of tongue to palate in [æ] and [a] than is the case with [i] and [u].

Manner of articulation

Manner of articulation is the kind of obstruction created by the articulators.

Manner of articulation in consonants

Stops momentarily halt the outward airflow by means of a total closure: [p t k b d g ʔ].

Fricatives create a friction or hissing noise. The airflow continues, but is obstructed enough for friction to occur: [f v θ ð s z š ž h].

Affricates are combinations of stop plus fricative: [č ǰ]. You can see that these sounds are combinations of a stop followed by a fricative by saying some words slowly: *watch* and *church* for [č], *badge* and *judge* for [ǰ]. If you hold the final sound in each for a few seconds, you can feel the [t] closure as the first part of [č] and the [d] closure as the first part of [ǰ]. Thus perhaps *watch* ought to be transcribed phonetically [watš] rather than the customary [wač], and *judge* ought to be transcribed [ǰʌdž] rather than the customary [ǰʌǰ]. However, phonological patterns argue against this: for example, English does not generally permit words to begin with a stop followed by a fricative. English could not contain words like *tsip, pshelly, kfab, gzip,* and the like. But words can begin with [č] and [ǰ]. The phonological pattern thus suggests that English speakers tend to unconsciously think of [č] and [ǰ] as single sounds rather than as sequences. Hence in our phonetic transcriptions we will use [č] and [ǰ].

Nasals are sounds in which the air being exhaled passes out through the nasal passage rather than the mouth: [m n ŋ]

Liquids are two sounds that are acoustically, rather than articulatorily, very similar: [r l]

Glides (semivowels), sounds which are between vowels and consonants: [w y]. If you say these quickly, they are consonants; if you say them slowly, they are the vowels [u] and [i]. These consonants can appear at the periphery of syllables, as in [wɛst, yɛs, haw, tɔy] (*west, yes, how, toy*), and the vowels appear as syllabic cores, as in [rum, sit] (*room, seat*).

This chart summarizes the classification of English consonants.

7.

ENGLISH CONSONANTS:

	stop	fricative	affricate	nasal	liquid	glide
bilabial	p b			m		w
labiodental		f v				
interdental		θ ð				
alveolar	t d	s z		n	l	
alveopalatal		š ž	č ǰ			
palatal					r	y
velar	k g			ŋ		
glottal	ʔ	h				

In this chart, wherever you see a pair of sounds—e.g., [p b]—the first one is voiceless, the second one voiced.

Chart (7) summarizes ENGLISH consonants. There are numerous other consonants in other languages. For instance, German and Spanish contain velar fricatives. German has a voiceless velar fricative (phonetic symbol [x]) at the end of names like *Bach* and words like *noch* ("still, yet") (this sound exists also in Scottish English: *loch*), and Spanish has both a voiceless and a voiced velar fricative (phonetic symbol [ɣ]). The voiceless one appears, for example, in *jota* ("letter 'j'"), and the voiced one in, for example, *lago* ("lake"). Some West African languages have bilabial fricatives as well as stops (phonetic symbols: [ɸ] for a voiceless bilabial fricative, which is rather like the sound you make blowing out a candle, [β] for a voiced bilabial fricative). Hebrew and Japanese both have a voiceless alveolar affricate [ts].

Manner of articulation in vowels

The vowels [u], [ʊ], [o], and [ɔ] are not only "back," they are **round** as well, meaning that their production is accompanied by lip rounding. English has no front round vowels, but many languages do, including French and German (French *rue* "street" and German *müde* "tired" have high front round vowels, which you can produce by configuring your lips and tongue as if to whistle, and then saying [i]).[6]

The sounds in the pairs [i] - [ɪ], [e] - [ɛ], [u] - [ʊ], and [o] - [ɔ] are distinguished from each other by a **tense-lax** opposition. In each pair just listed, the first vowel listed is tense, or produced with relatively greater musuclar tension, the second lax, or produced with relatively less muscular tension.

EXERCISE 3. Translate the following phonetically transcribed English words into English spelling.

[ošənz]
[lʌki]
[θru]
[tɛləvižən]
[sips]
[čæt]
[beyðz]
[məšinz]
[lʊkt]
[ɔfən]
[mæθ]
[nɪpi]
[bʌd]
[bɪŋgo]

EXERCISE 4. Transcribe the LAST sound of each of the following words with the correct phonetic symbol.

drives
following
baked
scissors
catch
language

---

6. French and German also have mid front round vowels: French *oeuf* "egg," German *Goethe* (the name).

Mac
moth
mash
idea
pass
brainy
she
wires

Exercise 5. Phonetically transcribe the following words.

eats
know
knee
mast
bet
lick
look
shoes
cot
putted
opened
wax
seems
robbed
songs
wreathe
caught
helped
ears
fastened
oceans
acknowledge

Additional vowels: diphthongs

The vowel sounds of *cow, boy,* and *sky* are called "diphthongs." The word "diphthong" comes from the Ancient Greek word *diphthongos,* meaning "two sounds" ("di" (= two) + "phthongos" (= voice or sound)). The diphthong in *cow* starts out with an [a] sound and then makes a transition to an [u] sound. So the phonetic symbol for this sound is [au], and the transcription for *cow* is [kau].[7] But a common transcription for *cow* is [kaw], since a [w] is, articulatorily, a rapid produced [u] (conversely, a reasonable transcription for *week* might be [uik], if the [u], the initial sound, is uttered slowly).

The diphthong in *boy* starts out with an [ɔ] and ends with an [i]. So the transcription for *boy* is [bɔi]. Usually [y] is used instead of [i], hence: [bɔy]. The [w] of the [aw] diphthong and the [y] of the [ɔy] diphthong are "glides," that is, transition sounds. That's why they're used in transcriptions of diphthongs, which are inherently transitional.

The diphthong in *sky*, as you might predict, is [ai]. It may also be— and more commonly is—written [ay].

EXERCISE 6. Transcribe the following words phonetically:

joyful
mine
clown
I
annoys
around
laundry
malign
itchy
beauty
ground
dry
stayed

Additional consonants: syllabic ones

Usually a syllable has a familiar vowel at its core. However, at times [r], [n], [l], and rarely a few others, like [s] in *psst!* and [š] in *shh!*[8] are found. Words like *bird, shirt,* and *lurk,* in most American dialects, have "syllabic r,"

---

7. Actually, in most American dialects, the first part of this diphthong is a sound about midway between [a] and [æ]. There is no commonly accepted symbol for this sound. However, it is common practice to use [a] for the first part of this diphthong.

8. Words like *psst* and *shh* are unusual in two respects: first, as indicated here, they are unusual in terms of syllable structure, and second, they have no grammatical function at all—they bear no grammatical connection to other words in a sentence.

symbolized [ɹ], at their core. The phonetic transcription of *bird,* in the speech of most Americans, is [bɹ̩d]. This syllabic [ɹ] is phonetically a blending of the vowel [ə] with [r]. Similarly, *satin* can have a syllabic [n̩], and *bottle* can have a syllabic [l̩]. No [ə] blends with syllabic [n̩] or [l̩], though; they're just syllabic consonants. Words like *satin* and *bottle* have alternative pronunciations, one with a [ə] before a nonsyllabic consonant, and one without a [ə] but with a syllabic consonant: [sætɪn] and [sæʔn̩], [batəl] and [batl̩].

Sometimes the difference between a syllabic consonant and a nonsyllabic consonant preceded by [ə] is subtle—and sometimes arbitrary in impressionistic transcription. Sometimes syllabic [ɹ] is transcribed as [r] with a preceding [ə]: [bərd] rather than [bɹ̩d] for *bird.* But for most American dialects the syllabic [ɹ] transcription is closer to articulatory reality.

Exercise 7.

A. Translate the following into normal English spelling:
[wɹ̩dz] [šʌtl̩] [kaʔn̩] [kʌmfɹt] [wɹ̩ði] [sɪʔn̩]

B. Phonetically transcribe the following:
mirthful heard heart burdens satin metal

Phonetic transcription is intended to reflect as closely as possible the phonetic (articulatory) reality of speech as produced on some occasion by some speaker. So the phonetic transcriptions of words can vary according to the dialect of the speaker, and even according to the style a given speaker uses at different times, in different situations. The name *Carol* might be pronounced [kærəl] by an American from the northeast, [kʸɛrəl] (the raised [y] indicates a very slight "y" sound) by a Californian, and [kæəl] by an [r]-deleting Southerner. In careful speech, you might, for *satin,* say [sætɪn], while in everyday casual speech you would probably say [sæʔn̩].

PHONOLOGICAL RULES: SOUND ADJUSTMENTS TO ENVIRONMENT

The location of a sound relative to other sounds, or in a particular position in a word (like the beginning or the end), often results in a change in the sound. For example, every English [p], [t], or [k] produced in the utterance of the following words is accompanied by a little puff of breath, called "aspiration": *pill, pass, tin, tassel, kiss, care.* You can experience the aspiration by holding your palm or a light sheet of paper very close to your mouth as you say these words in a normal tone. You will feel a puff of breath on your palm, and the puff will move the paper. However, the instances of [p], [t] and [k] in words like *spill, option, sting, settler, scare,* and *success* are never pronounced with aspiration. Try the palm or paper test to see. On the basis of this data, a first approximation of the phonological rule governing aspiration might be:

8. Rule: [p], [t], and [k] become aspirated when they occur word-initially.

This rule is exceptionless—which you can prove to yourself by collecting several dozen words starting with [p], [t], and [k], and trying the hand-before-mouth or paper-blowing test—but below the level of conscious awareness. All native speakers of English obey it, all the time, but few are aware of it.[9]

All scientific statements, including linguistic rules like Rule (8), are better when formulated as generalizations. We can make Rule (8) more general by noticing what [p], [t], and [k] have in common that sets them apart from all other sounds: the fact that they are voiceless stops (and they are the only voiceless stops). So let us reformulate Rule (8) as follows:

9. Rule: Voiceless stops become aspirated when they occur word-initially.

Is it really just stops that are voiceless that get aspirated? Try voiced stops ([b], [d], and [g]) to see. Pronounce *bill, dill,* and *gill.* Is there aspiration? Try saying them with the hand-in-front-of-mouth test and the paper-blowing test. You should be able to confirm rule that word-initial voiced stops are not aspirated.

The correct phonetic transcription for initial voiceless stops contains a symbol for the aspiration. The standard symbol is a small raised "h":

10. *pill:* [pʰɪl]   *tea:* [tʰi]   *cash:* [kʰæš]

Unaspirated voiceless stops are transcribed without such a symbol:

11. *spill:* [spɪl]   *steed:* [stid]   *scat:* [skæt]

Rule (9) is a phonological rule specifically of English, not of language universally. Spanish initial voiceless stops are not aspirated. Spanish *pero* ('but') is transcribed [pero].[10] This consistent difference between English and Spanish is partly responsible for native English speakers often sounding "funny" when learning Spanish, because they unconsciously transfer the English aspiration rule to the new language.

Another phonological rule of English that operates below the level of

---

9. Perhaps only those who have had an introductory linguistics course or have read this or some other introductory linguistics book.
10. Actually, the [r] should be different, to distinguish the alveolar-apical (using the tip of the tongue) Spanish [r] from the palatal-dorsal (using blade rather than tip of the tongue) English [r].

conscious awareness shows up in the difference between the vowels in the words in Columns A and B below:

12. **COLUMN A**　　**COLUMN B**

COLUMN A	COLUMN B
leak	league
wrote	rode
suit	sued
crap	crab
wreath	wreathe
luff	love
batch	badge

Try to see what the difference is between the Column A vowels and the Column B vowels. Say the words aloud in a normal way. You should be able to notice a slight but consistent greater duration or length in the Column B vowels as compared with the Column A vowels. The Column B vowels are truly longer (unlike so-called "long" vowels like the *o* of *cope* as compared with the *o* of *cop*, as described in school grammar books).

Now try to figure out the phonological rule. What other phonetic characteristic is vowel length (or shortness) correlated with?

On the basis of the data given in (12), the rule might be

13.　Rule: Vowels become lengthened when they occur before a voiced sound.

Of course, we could state the rule in the "opposite direction." Rule (14) describes the same fact as does Rule (13).

14.　Rule: Vowels become shortened when they occur before a voiceless sound.

Which way should we state the rule? Does it matter? It depends. If the only data the rules are expected to cover is that given in (12), both the formulations are equally right, and there is no basis for choosing between them. But if we have additional data, say, that given in (15), it does make a difference which formulation we choose.

15.　tea, toe, slaw, bow, say, ma

Are the vowels in these words long or short? Compare *tea* with *teak, toe* with *tote, ma* with *mop:* clearly the vowels in the words given in (15) are long. This requires a change in our rule, to account for long vowels not only before voiced sounds, but also before nothing, i.e., at the end of a word. We could revise Rule (13) to read as follows:

16.　Rule: Vowels become lengthened before a voiced sound and at word-end.

How about Rule (14)? How would it be revised? The answer is not at all. Our data in (15) does not change the observation that vowels get shortened before voiceless sounds.

The choice between Rule (14) and Rule (16) depends on what is taken as "basic"—what the rule is assumed to apply to. If short vowels are taken as basic, then Rule (16) will be chosen. If long vowels are taken as basic, then Rule (14) will be chosen. Notice, now, that one of these two approaches is simpler than the other. Rule (16) mentions two separate environments in which something happens to vowels. Rule (14) mentions only one. Therefore Rule (14) is simpler, and—all other things being equal—to be preferred.

This can be regarded in a slightly different way. The Rule (16) approach assumes that short vowels are the normal case, and that they get changed into longer ones in two special cases: when they occur before voiced sounds and when they occur at the end of a word. The Rule (14) approach assumes that long vowels are the normal case, and that they get changed into shorter ones in one special case: when they occur before voiceless sounds.

Looking at the fact that there are two separate environments in which long vowels appear, but only one environment in which short vowels appear, it makes sense to conclude that long vowels are "basic," since they occur in a wider range of environments—in a sense, "more commonly." Short vowels seem to be the "exception," the special case for which a rule is required. Therefore Rule (14) is to be preferred.

The phonetic transcription of long and short vowels has to be distinguished. There is no standard symbol for vowel shortness. Two standard notations for vowel length include simply doubling a vowel symbol, so that the transcription for *league* is [liig] (while that for *leak* is [lik]), and placing a colon (":") after a long vowel ([li:g] for *league*).

In light of our analysis of long vowels as basic, perhaps we should revise our vowel chart for English (6), replacing all the short vowel symbols with long vowel symbols. Because there are some additional complications,[11] we won't bother with this, but that doesn't affect the basic correctness of the analysis.

A third unconscious, and automatic, phonetic adjustment to environment that occurs in English is the nasalization of vowels when they occur before nasal consonants. Contrast the pronunciations of *bead* and *bean*, paying attention to the vowels. (When you say the words aloud, hold the

---

11. E.g., that long vowels are found only in stressed syllables; our analysis so far is limited to that environment. Also, it is typographically inconvenient to write double vowels or vowels with colons in every case.

vowels unnaturally long.) You should be able to hear (or feel) the nasal quality of the vowel in *bean*. All vowels that occur before nasal consonants get nasalized in this way:

17. Rule: Vowels occurring before nasal consonants become nasalized.

The phonetic symbol for a nasalized vowel is a tilde ("˜") above the vowel. So the correct phonetic transcription for *bean* is [bĩ:n] (or [bĩĩn]). (Notice that the vowel is marked as being long, since the following sound, [n], is voiced).

Abstract and Surface Phonological Representations

We have discussed sound adjustments to environment in terms of rules applying to sounds and changing the sounds in some way. Voiceless stops "become" aspirated word-initially, vowels "become" short before voiceless sounds, and vowels "become" nasalized before nasal consonants. This metaphor of "becoming" can be reflected in the form of our descriptive statements (rules): basic forms undergo certain changes and turn into "derived" forms. The basic forms are called "abstract" or "underlying," and the derived forms are called "surface" or "phonetic." A special notation is sometimes used for the two types of forms, slanted lines surrounding underlying forms, square brackets surrounding surface forms. Like this:

18.   /pɪl/   [pʰɪl]
      Abstract/Underlying → Surface/Phonetic

The arrow represents the effect of Rule (9), "Voiceless stops become aspirated word-initially." /pɪl/ is the underlying form of the word *pill* and [pʰɪl] is the surface form—the pronounced, phonetic form. Underlying forms lack any indication of aspects of pronunciation which are due to general phonological rules (in this case, the aspiration rule). Think of underlying forms, then, as items from which the effects of all phonological rules have been factored out.

The underlying form /pɪl/ is assumed to be the basic form in which we store the word *pill* in our mental dictionary. The characteristics of the pronunciation of *pill* are therefore due to two different things: (1) its underlying form, which states, in part, that the first sound in *pill* is a voiceless bilabial stop, and (2) general phonological rules, one of which accounts for the fact that the initial sound is aspirated. In other words, we don't know that the initial [p] in *pill* is aspirated as a particular fact about that word; we know it as a general fact about initial voiceless stops in English.

EXERCISE 8. For each of the following words, give its underlying form and its phonetic (surface) form. Assume that vowels are underlyingly long.

	bean	badge	writes	con	prime	pond	post
Underlying:	/___/	/___/	/___/	/___/	/___/	/___/	/___/
Phonetic:	[___]	[___]	[___]	[___]	[___]	[___]	[___]

Optional Phonological Rules

The rules discussed above—aspiration, vowel lengthening, and vowel nasalization—are "obligatory" rules, meaning that they must apply whenever they can. (As we have seen, in English *all* word-initial occurrences of voiceless stops are aspirated, *all* occurrences of vowels before voiceless sounds are short, and *all* occurrences of vowels before nasal sounds are nasalized.) There are other phonological rules which are optional, that is, they sometimes apply, sometimes not, depending on a variety of factors.

One such rule is the optional change, in casual speech, of alveolar stops to match the place of articulation of following stops, as in the following words and phrases. (Vowel length is not marked in this data set.)

19.

	Careful Speech:	Casual Speech:
get Paul	[gɛt pʰɔl]	[gɛp pʰɔl][12]
football	[fʊtbɔl]	[fʊpbɔl]
pat Carl	[pʰæt kʰarl]	[pʰæk kʰarl][12]
that girl	[ðæt gr̩l]	[ðæk gr̩l]
red pony	[rɛd pʰõni]	[rɛb pʰõni]
had bluefish	[hæd blufɪš]	[hæb blufɪš][12]
had ketchup	[hæd kʰɛčəp]	[hæg kʰɛčəp]
good God	[gʊd gad]	[gʊg gad][12]

In the casual version of *get Paul*, the alveolar [t] changes to a bilabial [p] to resemble the bilabial [p] of *Paul*. In the casual version of *football*, [t] likewise becomes [p] to match the bilabial [b] that follows it. Notice that the adjustment is only in place of articulation, not in voicing; [t] does not become [b]. In *pat Carl* and *that girl* the [t] changes to a velar [k] to match the alveolar [k] of Carl and [g] of girl. Similar changes happen to [d] in *red pony, had bluefish, had ketchup,* and *good God.*

---

12. This transcription is slightly misleading. Actually, there is no evidence for double, i.e., long, consonants in English, as the two [p]s in [gɛp pʰɔl], the two [k]s in [pʰæk kʰa:rl], the two [b]s in [hæb blufɪš], and the two [g]s in [gʊg ga:d] suggest. The two identical consonants simplify to one.

The technical term for such sound adjustments is **assimilation**, which can be defined as the process of a sound's changing to resemble more closely a neighboring sound. In the example discussed above, alveolar stops **assimilate in place of articulation** to a following stop. Often languages have **total assimilation**, which is what happens when a sound changes to match exactly a neighboring sound. We will discuss an example of this in English in Chapter Three.

Two other optional sound changes that correlate with formality level are the change, under certain conditions, of [t] to [ʔ], and under other conditions, of [t] to [D], a "flapped" alveolar stop made by rapidly touching the tongue tip against the alveolar ridge and then instantly releasing it— sort of between a [t] and a [d]. The sound [D] occurs in the underlined position in *butter*. Try to figure out what the conditions are for each change, using the following data. In the data below, the first column represents painfully formal pronunciation or pronunciation aimed at carefully following spelling, the second everyday casual speech. An acute accent mark (′) means that the vowel preceding it is stressed.

20.

	Careful Speech or Spelling Pronunciation:	Casual Speech:
button	[bʌ′tə̄n]	[bʌ′ʔn̩]
baton	[bətʰā′:n]	[bətʰā′:n]
butter	[bʌ′tr̩]	[bʌ′Dr̩]
battle	[bæ′təl]	[bæ′Dl̩]
kitten	[kʰɪ′tə̄n]	[kʰɪ′ʔn̩]
mountain	[mãw′:ntə̄n]	[mãw′:nʔn̩]
sitting	[sɪ′tɪŋ]	[sɪ′ʔn̩]
stapler	[stey′plr̩]	[stey′plr̩]
Plato	[pʰley′to]	[pʰley′Do]
tea	[tʰi:]	[tʰi:]

You can see from the casual pronunciation of *button, kitten, mountain,* and *sitting* that the change [t] → [ʔ] occurs in casual speech after a stressed syllable and before an unstressed syllable of the form [n̩]. From the other words in this table you can see that in other environments this change does not take place. From *baton* (which is the same in careful and casual speech), you can see that [t] does not become [ʔ] before a stressed syllable. From *stapler* and *tea* (also the same in careful and casual speech) you can see that the change does not occur unless [t] follows a stressed syllable. From *butter* and *battle* you can see that in order for the change to take place, [n̩], not just any syllabic consonant, must be the following unstressed syllable. The rule, then, is:

21. Rule: [t] → [ʔ], optionally, in casual speech, between a stressed syllable and an unstressed [n̩] syllable.

And from *butter, battle,* and *Plato* you can see that the change [t] → [D] occurs in casual speech after a stressed syllable and before an unstressed syllable of other types from [ṇ]—in this data, syllables containing [ɾ], [ḷ], and [o]. The rule for this change is:

22. Rule: [t] → [D], optionally, in casual speech, between a stressed syllable and an unstressed syllable of any type except [ṇ].

"Optional" does not mean the same as "in casual speech," although optional changes appear much more in casual speech than in careful speech. One option that is not dependent on formality level is the choice between released and unreleased word-final stops. You can choose to end a word whose final sound is any of [p t k b d g] with either a little explosion of air, or without one, i.e., with your outward airflow still stopped. For instance, you can end a word like *lip* with your lips either open (released) or closed (unreleased).

Phonemes and allophones

Until now we have simply described aspects of the English sound system, without regard to how we figure out what the system is. It can be instructive, however, to imagine being a foreign linguist who knows nothing about English and must discover its sound patterns from the beginning.

We have observed that certain sounds have optional or obligatory variants in certain environments. Voiceless stops, for example, have to be aspirated whenever they occur word-initially. Putting yourself in the role of a foreign—let's say, Martian—linguist, you wouldn't know, at first, that [p] and [pʰ], or [t] and [tʰ], were related to each other. You would have to notice first that there are two kinds of voiceless stops in this strange language, English, aspirated ones and unaspirated ones. Suppose that you had a fair bit of experience analyzing other Terran languages, and had just finished an exhaustive study of Igbo (a Nigerian language). In Igbo, aspirated and unaspirated stops are NOT related to each other; they contrast with each other. [apʰe] and [ape][13] are different words. [apʰe] means 'sharpening,' and [ape] means 'pressing.' Of course, as you can see from these examples, the reason [p] and [pʰ] contrast in Igbo is that they can occur in exactly the same environment: between [a] and [e]. The difference

---

13. Actually, since Igbo is a tone language, in which the pitch at which a vowel is pronounced can distinguish meaning, the correct transcriptions are [àpʰé] and [ápè]. (The tone sequence on the two syllables of the first word is "low" - "high"; the tone sequence in the second word is "high" - "low."). This doesn't invalidate the point being made, though. Although the tone differences prevent the cited pair from being minimally distinguished by [pʰ] and [p], in fact they are contrastive in Igbo, as are other voiceless aspirated and unaspirated stops, for which minimal pairs can be found. The Igbo data is from Ladefoged (1968).

between Igbo and English in this regard, then, is that in Igbo aspirated and unaspirated stops do not occur in separate environments, but in the same environment, whereas in English the two types of stops never occur in the same environment. As a Martian linguist, you would have to discover this. Knowing how Igbo works, you might assume as a working hypothesis that English, too, contrasted [p] and [pʰ], and you would search your data lists (gathered in the traditional way in linguistic field work from native English speakers bilingual in Martian and English) for English word pairs like the Igbo [apʰe] - [ape]. Such a pair is called a "minimal pair." Of course, you wouldn't find any. What you would find, instead, is the rule we have already discussed (Rule 9), that is, an environmental specialization for aspirated and unaspirated voiceless stops: one type occurring always in one kind of environment, the other never occurring in that environment. Such a situation is called **complementary distribution**. (The **distribution** of a linguistic element—here, a sound—is the union of all the possible environments in which it can occur.)

Whenever two sounds are phonetically similar (like [p] and [pʰ], both sounds being voiceless and bilabial and stops) and are in complementary distribution, they "count as" the SAME sound, for speakers of the language in question. This is true despite the actual physical sound difference. Since the two sounds never occur in the same environment, speakers don't notice the difference between the sounds; the difference doesn't stand out. On the other hand, when two only slightly different sounds—like [p] and [pʰ]—occur in exactly the same environment, as they do in Igbo, the difference stands out. The reason it stands out is that the difference is what distinguishes one word from another. The phonetic difference, small as it is, expresses a meaning difference.

The psychological significance of this is that for speakers of a language in which a pair of phonetically similar sounds are in complementary distribution, the sounds are regarded as being the same, even though they are actually phonetically (that is, physically) different. On the other hand, the same pair of phonetically similar sounds in a language in which they are not in complementary distribution, but in contrast, count psychologically—for speakers of that language—as completely different sounds.

Sounds which are phonetically different but which "count as" the same are called **allophones**. A set of such sounds which contrasts with other sets is called a **phoneme**.

In Igbo, [p] and [pʰ] represent different phonemes. In English, the same sounds are allophones of one phoneme.

	Igbo		English	
Phonemes	/p/	/pʰ/	/p/	
	|	|	╱ ╲	
Allophones	[p]	[pʰ]	[p]	[pʰ]

The English phoneme /p/ is actually the set {[p], [pʰ]}. Some phonemes have only one allophone, like Igbo /p/ and /pʰ/. English /h/ is another. Its only allophone is [h].

You can see from this last statement that the notation introduced earlier for underlying vs. surface levels of representation of words applies to phonemes and allophones too. Phonemes are written between slanted lines, and allophones, being actual sounds, are written in square brackets.[14] Besides being sets of allophones, phonemes are mentally real sound units. Allophones are their different manifestations in actual speech when they occur in different environments. You can see how phonemes are mentally real by noticing that spelling systems are more or less true to phonemes, not allophones. (Spelling systems represent speakers' ideas about what the sound structure of words is.) English has one *p* letter for the /p/ phoneme, not two, one for the aspirated allophone [pʰ] and one for the unaspirated allophone [p]. Similarly, English uses one letter, *t*, for [t], [tʰ], [D], and [ʔ], all allophones of the /t/ phoneme. (Recall the discussion about Data Set 20.) And in the same way, English doesn't use separate spelling symbols for nasal and nonnasal vowels, since these are not phonemically distinct.

EXERCISE 9. Most speakers of American English have two allophones for the /l/ phoneme, one which shows up, for example, in words like *leap,* and one which shows up in words like *all.* Separate phonetic symbols are used, of course: [l] for the /l/ in *leap* and [ł] for the /l/ in *all.*

A. On the basis of the data given below, what determines which kind of /l/ appears in a word?

[l]	[ł]
leap	hill
lake	Paul
lip	oil
legs	full

B. Suppose there is a dialect[15] of English in which the following transcriptions are basically accurate (here we will ignore vowel length and nasalization, for simplicity):

---

14. Actually, there is a difference between the meaning of the square brackets in phonetic transcription and the meaning of square brackets around allophones. Phonetic transcription, strictly speaking, is a record of the pronunciation of one speaker on a particular occasion. Allophones are systematic, part of a language's structure, and therefore independent of time and place and speaker. Both are "tokens" of phonemes, but at different levels. The sounds recorded in a phonetic transcription are tokens of allophones as well as of phonemes.

15. Not necessarily, but possibly, a real one.

leak	[lik]	*hill*	[hɪɫ]	*all*	[ɔɫ]
long	[ɫɔŋ]	*Luke*	[ɫuk]	*late*	[leyt]
locate	[ɫokeyt]	*lend*	[lɛnd]	*last*	[læst]
luck	[ɫʌk]	*peel*	[pʰiɫ]	*lick*	[lɪk]
pale	[pʰeyɫ]	*shell*	[šɛɫ]	*shall*	[šæɫ]

The allophones [l] and [ɫ] are in complementary distribution in this dialect. On the basis of this data, state the distribution. (State in what environments, distinct from each other, [l] and [ɫ] occur.)

Taking off from the data discussed in Exercise 9, let us consider a different English dialect,[16] one in which the following transcriptions are basically accurate (as in Exercise 9, for simplicity we'll ignore vowel nasalization and length).

23.

all	[ɔɫ]	*oil*	[ɔyɫ]	*leak*	[lik]
luck	[ɫʌk]	*luck*	[lʌk]	*Luke*	[luk]
Luke	[ɫuk]	*lake*	[leyk]	*log*	[lag]
log	[ɫag]	*keel*	[kʰiɫ]	*lane*	[leyn]

The double occurrences of *luck, Luke,* and *log* are not misprints. They reflect alternative ways to pronounce these words in this dialect. Are [l] and [ɫ] in complementary distribution in this dialect? Obviously not; the environments in which they occur overlap. Here is a harder question: in this dialect, are [l] and [ɫ] allophones of one phoneme, or are they contrasting phonemes? The answer is that they are allophones of one phoneme, even though they are not in complementary distribution. Even though they occur in the same environments, [l] and [ɫ] do not represent different phonemes, because the choice between one and the other does not result in a meaning difference. The key idea characterizing allophones of one phoneme is LACK OF CONTRAST, not complementary distribution. Complementary distribution is one way, not the only way, sounds can be noncontrastive. In the dialect exemplified in (23), [l] and [ɫ] are non-contrastive because they are in "free variation" before mid and back vowels. We briefly discussed a case of free variation earlier, although we didn't label it as such: the option of released vs. unreleased stops (p. 60).

Notation for Phonological Rules

We have already seen that our notation marks the underlying level of phonological structure with slanted lines, as in /k/ for a phoneme, /kæ:n/ for the underlying form of a word. The physically real phonetic level is

---

16. Again, not necessarily, but possibly, a real one.

marked by square brackets: [kʰ], [kʰæ̃:n]. It is customary to use a small arrow, "→," for "becomes," in phonological rules, then, "V → [+nasal] before a nasal." ("V" stands for "any vowel.")

Notice that there are two parts to every phonological rule: the part that tells what happens (e.g., "Voiceless stops become aspirated . . ."), and the part that tells under what circumstances—really, in what environments—it happens (e.g., ". . . word-initially"). A piece of formal notation has been developed for this. Here is a formal rendition of the aspiration rule just quoted:

24. $\begin{bmatrix} -\text{voice} \\ +\text{stop} \end{bmatrix} \rightarrow [+\text{aspirated}] \, / \, \#\underline{\hspace{1cm}}$

The part of the rule on the left side of the slanty line should be easy to understand. It says anything which is "[-voice]," i.e., voiceless, and which is "[+stop]," i.e., a stop, becomes aspirated. What is new to you is the slanted line and the number sign "#" and the blank space after it.

The slanted line is shorthand for "in the following environment." The number sign, #, stands for "word boundary." Imagine that every word has one of these before it and one after it. This is because it is common for word boundaries—beginnings and ends of words—to be relevant environments in phonological rules. The blank space (_____) stands for where the sound occurs that the rule deals with.

Our rule means "Voiceless stops become aspirated in the environment 'at word beginning'." So the blank space is found after the word boundary sign.

EXERCISE 10. Translate the following phonological rules into normal English. "V" stands for "any vowel" and "C" stands for "any consonant."

1. V → [+nasal] / _____ [+nasal]

2. /o/ → [ɔ] / _____ [+nasal]

3. $\begin{bmatrix} +\text{stop} \\ +\text{voice} \end{bmatrix} \rightarrow [+\text{fricative}] \, / \, V\underline{\hspace{0.5cm}}V$

4. $\begin{bmatrix} +\text{stop} \\ +\text{alveolar} \end{bmatrix} \rightarrow [+\text{bilabial}] \, / \, \underline{\hspace{0.6cm}}[+\text{bilabial}]$

5. /r/ → Ø $\Big/ \begin{matrix} \underline{\hspace{0.5cm}}\# \\ \underline{\hspace{0.5cm}}C \end{matrix}$

EXERCISE 11. Translate the following hypothetical phonological rules into formal statements.

1. Vowels lose their voicing between voiceless consonants.
2. Nasals are syllabic word-initially before stops.
3. /l/ is deleted word-finally and before consonants.
4. The second of a pair of voiced consonants at word-end is deleted.

SUPRASEGMENTALS

Our discussion so far has dealt with individual sounds—[m], [k], [æ], etc.—and how they are represented both mentally (on the phonemic or underlying level) and physically (on the phonetic level). But there are two other important aspects of sound structure that co-exist with the individual (or "segmental") sounds, sitting on top of them, as it were: the "suprasegmentals," **intonation** and **stress**.[17]

Stress

Stressed syllables are produced with greater energy, in particular with a greater quantity of air expelled from the lungs, than with unstressed syllables. The capitalized syllables in the following words are stressed:

25. PHOtograph, phoTOGraphy, photoGRAphic, CONduct, conDUCT, antidisestablishmenTARianism

As you can see, in English there is no constraint governing which syllable of a word—first, second, last, etc.—can be stressed. Some languages do have such a constraint; in Swahili a phonological rule always stresses the next-to-last syllable in a word:

26. a. kuPIka   'to cook'
    b. aliyoPIka   '. . . which he/she cooked'
    c. alianDIka   'he wrote'
    d. aliniandiKIa   'he wrote to me'

---

17. Another suprasegmental is **rate** of speaking, which varies across speakers and within the speech patterns of an individual, both as a function of style and to communicate need for haste or its opposite (*Take your time*, said slowly).

Some languages, for example French, stress all syllables in a word about equally.

Hearers' perceptions of stress depend on three distinct aspects of speech sound, **pitch**, **length**, and **loudness**. **Pitch**, the acoustic frequencies of the sound of a syllable, is the most important. The higher the pitch, the greater the perceived stress. Length and loudness are secondary determinants of perceived stress.

English stress has several functions: to signal emphasis, with an implied contrast, as in *Bill AND Judy went;* to signal explicit contrast, as in *Donna called Hank a Californian, and then HE insulted HER;* and to indicate the part of speech of a word, as in the following:

27. | Nouns | Verbs |
|-------|-------|
| CONduct | conDUCT |
| PERmit | perMIT |
| INsult | inSULT |
| a STRIKEout | to STRIKE OUT (*or* strike OUT) |

Intonation

Intonation is the rise and fall of pitch (frequency) in a sentence.

The importance of intonation is clear from the different ways a sentence can be uttered, each way corresponding to a different interpretation. Consider *They visited Max in New York.* With steady down-trending intonation,

28.

They visited Max in New York

The sentence has a neutral assertion interpretation. With a pitch uptrend, and sudden upshooting intonation at the end,

29.

They visited Max in New York

The speaker is inquiring; this is normal yes-no question intonation. With (usually) a flatter initial contour, it is found in Yes-No questions with the standard word-order for that sort of question:

30.

Did they visit Max?

With a flat contour followed by an upshoot which doesn't go as high as it does in a yes-no question, optionally followed by a small drop,

31.

(a)   They visited Max in New York

(b)   They visited Max in New York

you are making a list, on which the visit to Max is one entry (preceded and followed, perhaps, by *They saw Sheila in Albany* and *They stopped off at Sammy's in Jersey City*).

Wh-questions like *Who did you see?* or *What happened?* have a downtrending intonation contour, just like neutral assertions.

32.

Who did you see?

Tonic syllable

These intonation contours are inaccurate in one respect: there is usually a single stressed syllable that is more prominent than any other in the stretch covered by the intonation contour. (A short sentence has one intonation contour, while a longer one may have two or more.) In *Who did you see?* this **tonic syllable** would most likely be *see:*

33.

Who did you see?

(It could be other syllables, though, resulting in different interpretations: *who, did,* or *you.*) Often, the tonic syllable marks new information as opposed to information already known by the hearer. In a conversation about why Max isn't present, if you, but no one else, knows why, you could say *Max has gone fishing,* with stress on the first syllable of *fishing* (in a word with more than one syllable, if the word bears tonic stress, that stress falls on the syllable which gets word-stress in isolation: *FISHing,* not *fishING).:*

34.

Max has gone fishing

But in a conversation about fishing, in which you offer the new information that Max likes to fish, you might say *Max has gone fishing* with the following intonation contour:

35.

Max has gone fishing

EXERCISE 12.

A. Draw the intonation contours, including an indication of tonic stress, that would be likely to characterize the utterance of the following sentences:
1. "Where is my brown alligator wallet?" (said impatiently)
2. "What were you doing last night?" (said angrily by parent to teenager)
3. "He may be small, but he's fast."
4. "If anybody comes in late, they should go quietly to the back."
5. "I'll show him a thing or two!"

B. An intonation contour used in lists was given. At what part of a list would the following intonation contour occur?

They visited Max in New York

SUMMARY AND CONCLUSION

In this chapter we have accomplished five things. We have seen how English spelling is inadequate as a consistent representation of sounds. We have discussed the version of the phonetic alphabet in common use by American linguists. We have examined the ways in which English sounds are produced, and, at the same time, described and classified speech sounds in terms of their mechanism of production. We have looked at phonological rules, and the relation between underlying phonological form and surface phonetic form, with some examples from English. Finally, we have taken a brief look at stress and intonation.

In the latter part of the next chapter, we will look again at phonological rules and underlying forms, in order to account for the varying phonetic forms certain meaningful elements of English can take—for example, the pronunciation of the past tense form sometimes as [d] (*grabbed*), sometimes as [t] (*talked*), and sometimes as [əd] (*batted*).

ADDITIONAL EXERCISE

Spanish has some sounds that are not present in English. Two of these are:

a *voiced bilabial fricative,* [β], made by placing the lips closer together almost as if for a [b], but not touching, and vibrating the vocal cords;

a *voiced velar fricative,* [ɣ], made by approximating the back of the tongue to the soft palate (velum), the same place of articulation as a [k] or [g], but not touching it, and vibrating the vocal cords.

IN ADDITION, the Spanish voice stop [d] is made *dentally,* rather than alveolarly, as in English. That is, a Spanish-speaker makes a [d] by placing the tip of the tongue against the inner surface of the upper front teeth, rather than against the alveolar ridge (as in English).

1. With these facts in mind, consider the following PHONETIC data from Spanish.

[aðios]	'goodbye'	[kaða]	'each'
[desear]	'to desire'	[dose]	'twelve'
[duðar]	'to doubt'	[dar]	'to give'
[olviðar]	'to forget'	[naða]	'nothing'
[mundo]	'world'	[toðo]	'all'

Are [d] and [ð] allophones of one phoneme, or members of different phonemes? Provide evidence.

2. Now consider the following additional phonetic data from Spanish, which contains the sounds [b] and [β] (again, [β] is a voiced bilabial fricative).

[bien]	'well'	[akaβar]	'to end, finish'
[blaŋko]	'white'	[aβoɣaðo]	'lawyer'
[ambiente]	'atmosphere'	[beβer]	'to drink'
[ariβa]	'above'	[arbol]	'tree'

Are [b] and [β] allophones of one phoneme, or members of different phonemes? Provide evidence.

3. Now consider a final set of phonetic data from Spanish, this time focusing on the two sounds [g] and [ɣ] (which is, as mentioned, a voiced velar fricative).

[paɣar]	'to pay'	[gramatika]	'grammar'
[aβoɣaðo]	'lawyer'	[galeria]	'gallery'
[aɣo]	'I make, do'	[gustar]	'to like, please'
[iŋgles]	'English'	[diɣa]	'say'

Are [g] and [ɣ] allophones of one phoneme, or members of different phonemes? Provide evidence.

4. Now rethink your answers to questions 1, 2, and 3, and unite the findings about [d] and [ð], [b] and [β], and [g] and [ɣ] into a SINGLE generalization governing all three pairs of sounds, rather than three separate statements. (Hints: i) What do [b], [d], and [g] have in common? ii) What do [β], [ð], and [ɣ] have in common?)

REFERENCES

LABOV, WILLIAM. 1972. *Sociolinguistic Patterns*. University of Pennsylvania. ("On the Mechanism of Linguistic Change").

LADEFOGED, PETER. 1968. *A Phonetic Study of West African Languages*. Cambridge University Press.

Chapter Three

THE STRUCTURE OF ENGLISH WORDS

Consider the word *antidisestablishmentarianism,* supposedly the longest non-technical word in English. Even if you don't know its meaning, you can make a partial guess: it must be a philosophy or world-view (*-ism*) involving opposition to something (*anti-*); and what it opposes must be "disestablish-ing"—i.e., those who subscribe to it must favor the maintenance of the status quo in some area. (Actually, the word names a 19th century British movement which favored retention of the Anglican Church as the official church of England.)

You are able to make guesses about the meaning of this words be-cause you know its component parts: *anti-, dis-, establish, -ment, -ary, -an,* and *-ism.* Such components of words are called **morphemes**. The meanings of complex words are directly related to the meanings of their component morphemes.

Basically a morpheme is a minimal stretch of language which has a meaning. (We will amend this definition significantly later in this chapter.)

The idea of a morpheme being "minimal" is important. *Disestablish* is not a morpheme; it is a stretch containing two minimal elements which carry meaning (morphemes), *dis-* and *establish.*

A morpheme can be a single syllable (*dis-*), or several syllables long (*establish, Connecticut*). It can even be less than a syllable, like the morpheme *-s* (for 'plural') at the end of *dogs* and *cats.*

EXERCISE 1. Divide the following words into morphemes.

grandmother	playfully	desks	Oklahoma
algebraic	activity	always	unhappily

It's not quite so easy working on unfamiliar languages, but the process of identifying morphemes is the same. Minimal elements are isolated by comparing words that are partly similar in both form and meaning. Here is an example from Swahili:

1. tumefika   'we have arrived'
    amefika   'he/she has arrived'
    nimefika   'I have arrived'

From these three words, we can isolate the morphemes *tu-*, *a-*, and *ni-*, meaning 'we', 'he/she,' and 'I,' respectively. Continuing the example:

2. tutafika   'we will arrive'
    tulifika   'we arrived'
    nitafika   'I will arrive'

Adding this data to that in (1), we can isolate the morphemes *-ta-*, *-li-*, and *-me-*, meaning 'future,' 'past,' and 'perfect,' respectively, and *-fika*, meaning 'arrive.'

EXERCISE 2.

A. Based on what you have just learned about Swahili, if *jua* means 'know,' how would you expect to say 'I will know'? How about 'we have known'?

B. Here is some data, given phonetically, from Turkish. Identify all morphemes and their meanings.

[baš]	'head'	[dostlar]	'friends'
[bašlar]	'heads'	[yaš]	'age'
[bašlarda]	'in (the) heads'	[kol]	'arm'
[kušlar]	'birds'	[pullar]	'stamps'

After you have identified all morphemes and their meanings, predict the Turkish words for the following meanings:

'friend': _____   'in the stamp': _____
'in the arm': _____   'arms': _____

TYPES OF MORPHEMES

Bound and Free Morphemes

The underlined morphemes in the following words are **bound**:

3. boys   played   unhappy   studying

This means that they occur only attached to other morphemes, never **free** as words by themselves. Free morphemes can occur alone as words:

4.   boy   play   happy   study

Roots, Stems, and Affixes

Besides being free morphemes, the items listed in (4) are **roots**, that is, basic single-morpheme forms to which **affixes** (the general term for prefixes and suffixes) can be attached. In English most roots are free morphemes, but not all. For instance, the words *chronology, chronic,* and *chronograph* all contain the root *chron-* (meaning, basically, 'time'), which is not free, but bound, because it never occurs alone as a word. Similarly *renovate* and *novice* contain a bound root *nov-* (meaning, basically, 'new'). (The bound-free distinction once led an undergraduate linguistics club to sell T-shirts inscribed with the slogan "Free the bound morpheme!")

Stems are also forms to which affixes can be attached. Stems differ from roots in that they may be made up of more than one morpheme. All roots are stems, but many stems are not roots (but contain them). Stems are sometimes created by the juxtaposition of two roots in a compound. Both *baby* and *sit* are roots (and stems), but *babysit* is a stem (but not a root)—because *-er* can be attached to it.

Stems can also be formed by adding meaningless elements to certain roots. The *-n-* in *binary* and *trinity* is one such stem-forming element, attached to the roots *bi-* ('two') and *tri-* ('three'). Another is the *-o-* in *chronograph* and *chronology*. Another is the *-a-* that shows up before *-tion* in words like *computation, conversation,* and *formation*. We know that this *-a-* is a separate element, not part of either the root or the suffix *-tion*, because the roots *compute, converse,* and *form* exist without it, and because *-tion* often occurs without it—for example, in *retention, absorption,* and *prediction*.

Are these stem-forming elements morphemes? No, if by "morpheme" we mean "minimal element with a meaning," because stem-formers have no meaning or grammatical function. They are present only for phonological reasons, the specifics of which we won't go into here: *-n-*, for example, to break up the vowel-vowel sequence that would occur in *bi-* + *-ary* in *binary*, *-a-* and *-o-* similarly to break up uncomfortable consonant-consonant combinations, for example in *form* + *-tion* or *chron-* + *-logy*. (There was a time when linguists generally believed that all the phonemes of a word must be assigned to some morpheme, so there couldn't be non-morphemic parts of words. This view of morphology is not held today.)

In the examples we have looked at so far, a word containing more than one morpheme is made up of a root, possibly a stem-forming element, and possibly prefixes and suffixes. Each morpheme is a continuous, uninterrupted stretch, and the morphemes chain together like railroad cars, occasionally linked by non-morphemic stem-forming elements. This is the usual case. However, there are a couple of more complex cases:

Discontinuous morphemes occur in two separate parts. English has three cases which can be analyzed this way: the **perfect**, the **passive**, and the **progressive** constructions. The perfect construction, as in *You have eaten my soup*, is made up of *have* and a verb with a "past participle" ending (in this case, *-en*). The form that conveys the "perfect" meaning (existence of an event or situation in the past which has some special relevance to the present) is two separate speech-stretches: *have* and the suffix *-en*. As a result, it is possible to analyze the perfect construction as being made up of two morphemes, not three, in the following way:

5.

Two other English constructions which can be analyzed this way are the **passive**, the *be Verb-en (by...)* construction (e.g., *The cake may be taken by Max*) and the **progressive**, the *be Verb-ing* construction (e.g., *She will be eating my soup*). The discontinuous morphemes here are *be..-en* and *be..-ing*.

One other complication in morphological structure is the existence of **infixes**. An infix is a bound morpheme occurring right inside another morpheme, unlike the other affix types, prefixes and suffixes, which are bound morphemes attached to stems to the left and right, respectively. English has no infixes, but they are not uncommon in the languages of the world. Bontoc (spoken in the Philippines) has infixes, as can be seen in the following words:

6. [fikas]   'strong'   [fumikas]   'he is becoming strong'
        [kilad]   'red'   [kumilad]   'he is becoming red'

In Bontoc, [fikas] and [kilad] are single morphemes. So is [um]. [um] is an infix which occurs after the initial consonant of a root.

English has some morphological phenomena which at first glance look like infixation, but are better described otherwise. Plurals like *geese* for *goose* and *feet* for *foot* do not contain infix morphemes, despite appearances, because [gs] and [ft] are not morphemes. Rather, what English has in words like these is the result of a replacement process, a kind of morphological irregularity. This kind of irregularity will be taken up in a later section of this chapter.

"Lexical" and "Grammatical" Morphemes

Lexical morphemes express meanings that can be relatively easily defined by using dictionary terms or by pointing out examples of things, events, or properties the morphemes can be used to refer to: *tree, burp, above, red, pseudo-, anti-, ism, honest.*

Grammatical morphemes have one (or both) of two characteristics. First, they express very common meanings, meanings which speakers of the language unconsciously consider important enough to be expressed very often. Verb tense morphemes are an example. English requires essentially every sentence to have a tense:

7. a.   Max cried   b.   Phyllis will leave
            ↑   ↑
         past tense   future tense

    c.   To be or not to be, that is the question
                                          ↑
                                    present tense

Another example is morphemes expressing noun **number** (singular vs. plural); most nouns can be made plural, and most nouns, when used, are either singular or plural. Tense morphemes and the plural morpheme are thus grammatical.

The idea of common expression of meanings can be generalized to include, as grammatical, morphemes which are obligatory in certain contexts and express no meaning: for example, the tense-carrier morpheme *do,* which is used in interrogative and negative sentences when no helping verb ("auxiliary") is present (e.g., *Do they drink? They don't drink*). This "dummy" *do* is discussed in Chapter Six in connection with negation and yes-no questions.

The other characteristic that grammatical morphemes may exhibit is the expression of relations within a sentence (instead of denoting things, properties, or events in the world). The verb suffix *-s* for third-person-singular-present-tense, for example, besides indicating tense, marks "agreement" between subject and verb (with a present tense verb, a singular third-person subject calls for a verb ending in *-s*):

8. a.   That dark-haired man clearly resembles Humphrey Bogart.
            ↑   ↑
         singular subject   singular verb form with 3rd-
                                     person singular *-s* ending

    b.   Those guys clearly resemble the Four Horsemen.
            ↑   ↑
         plural subject   plural verb form
                              with no ending

Another example is the use of the *-'s* ("possessive") suffix on a noun to indicate that the noun is the logical subject of a nominalized[1] verb: *Rob's*

---

1. Meaning simply a verb that has been turned into a noun, here, by the addition of *-ing.*

driving. (*Rob* is the "logical subject" of *driving,* because the meaning of *Rob's driving* includes the idea: "Rob drives," in which *Rob* is the subject.)

The definition of "grammatical morpheme" is disjunctive: any morpheme is "grammatical" if it fits either (or both) of our two characteristics: (a) it expresses a very common meaning or is specifically required in some context; or (b) it expresses a relation within a sentence rather than denoting things (activities, properties, etc.) in the world.

Some of the most commonly used grammatical morphemes in English are bound: for example, the three *-s* morphemes (plural, possessive, and third-person-singular present tense on verbs—e.g., *he sleeps*), past tense *-ed, -ing,* comparative *-er,* superlative *-est,* and past participle *-en* (as in *taken*). Others are free—that is, independent—words. A few examples of free grammatical morphemes are *the,* passive *by* (as in *he was seen by the queen*), *as,* the infinitive marker *to* (as in *We like to eat ice cream*), *that* (as in *We think that he will win*), and, as mentioned, "dummy" *do* (*Who do you like?*). Free grammatical morphemes are also called **function words.**

Some of the free grammatical morphemes have homonyms which are lexical, for example locative *by* as in *she is by the door,* directional *to* as in *go to your room,* and main verb *do* as in *do your homework.*

The distinction between "grammatical" and "lexical" morphemes is distantly related to the distinction between the "grammar" and the "lexicon," i.e., between what is regular in a language (grammar) and what is idiosyncratic (lexicon). Here we are using "grammar" in the narrow sense of "syntax + morphology." Your **grammar,** in this sense, contains GENERAL information about words, morphemes, and sentences—for instance, the fact that nouns can be made plural, that verbs are tensed, and that passive sentences (e.g., *The cake may be taken by Max*) contain subject and direct object noun phrases in the reverse of the basic order (*Max may take the cake*). Your **lexicon** is your mental dictionary, your very large mental list of the morphemes of English. In your lexicon, the information you store for each morpheme includes its meaning, its particular grammatical characteristics (e.g., its part of speech—noun, verb, or whatever), and what sequence of phonemes it is composed of. Your lexicon thus contains IDIOSYNCRATIC information about each morpheme or word—for instance, the fact that the irregular plural of *man* is *men,* that *put* begins with a voiceless bilabial stop (instead of, say, with a voiced one), and that the meaning of *desk* includes the notion "furniture."

EXERCISE 3. Determine whether the following morphemes are grammatical or lexical. Give your reasoning. There is not necessarily a clear answer in all cases; if not, discuss.

1. The words *fish, book, light, sky,* and *turn.*
2. The suffix *-like* as in *childlike.*

3. The suffix -*ed* on the verb in *We walked for six hours.*
4. The suffix -*ize* in *prioritize, randomize,* and *socialize.*
5. The adverb-forming suffix -*ly* as in *slowly, quickly, eagerly.*
6. The word *of* meaning 'possessive,' as in *the property of the Duponts.*
7. The word *of* in these examples: *this unit of meaning, that piece of cake, a blade of grass.*

Inflection and Derivation

Another useful morphological distinction is between two kinds of bound morphemes: **inflectional** and **derivational**. Roughly speaking, a derivational morpheme creates—"derives"—a new word when attached, while an inflectional morpheme creates a new form of the old word. For example, the derivational suffix -*ly* changes *eager* into another word, *eagerly*. But the inflectional suffix -*s* (plural) just makes a word plural, rather than creating a new word; *tables* is generally felt to be a form of the word *table*, not a completely separate word.

There are only eight inflectional affixes (all suffixes) in English:

9. **ENGLISH INFLECTIONAL SUFFIXES:**

plural (-*s* and its irregular variants, e.g., as in *men*)
-*'s* (possessive)
-*s* (verb suffix for third person singular present tense)
-*ing* (verb suffix meaning "in process': *is reading*)
-*er* (comparative: *smarter*)
-*est* (superlative suffix: *smartest*)
"perfect" suffix on verbs (-*en*, as in *he has taken the cake*, and variants, e.g., -Ø, as in *has put*)
past tense (-*ed* and irregular variants, as in *bought* and *ate*)

All other affixes are derivational.

Domain size difference between inflectional and derivational morphemes

We said above that a derivational morpheme creates a new word, while an inflectional morpheme creates a new form of a word. Here is a sharper difference: Notice that the inflectional suffix -*s* meaning 'third person singular present tense' occurs with all verbs (*swims, sleeps, brags*, etc.). Similary, the inflectional suffix meaning 'past tense' (-*ed* and its irregular variants) occurs with all verbs, the inflectional affix meaning 'plural' occurs with almost all nouns, and the inflectional affix for adjective comparison

(*-er* and its variant *more*) occurs with most adjectives (*sicker, more ill*).[2] But consider the derivational morpheme *-ment*, which, when added to verbs, creates nouns, as in the following:

10. a.   *govern* (verb) + *-ment* = government (noun)
     b.   *discern* (verb) + *-ment* = discernment (noun)

The form *-ment* occurs with relatively few verbs (*govern, discern, abut, judge, achieve, amuse,* etc.), and is impossible with most:

11. a.   *order* (verb) + *-ment* = *orderment
     b.   *direct* (verb) + *-ment* = *directment
     c.   *negotiate* (verb) + *-ment* = *negotiatement

This difference between inflectional and derivational affixes is quite general: inflectional affixes can occur with all, or most, members of the word class to which they get attached, while derivational affixes occur only with members of a relatively small proper subclass of the large class to which they get attached. Here are two examples showing the restrictedness of derivational morphemes: The derivational prefix *in-*, meaning 'not,' is added to adjectives, e.g., as in *inoperable, intolerant,* and *infrequent,* but is impossible with most adjectives (e.g., *inreadable, *inforgiveable, *infat, *insmall*). The derivational suffix *-ize*, which creates verbs from adjectives and nouns, e.g.,

12. a.   *legal* (adjective) + *-ize* = *legalize* (verb)
     b.   *regular* (adjective) + *-ize* = *regularize* (verb)
     c.   *rational* (adjective) + *-ize* = *rationalize* (verb)
     d.   *computer* (noun) + *-ize* = *computerize* (verb)

is impossible with most adjectives (*notationalize, *happyize, *sickize, *awfulize*) and most nouns (*deskize, *companyize*).

Since inflectional morphemes are relatively unrestricted (and correspondingly very common), they are considered grammatical, while most derivational morphemes are considered lexical. However, grammatical vs. lexical and inflectional vs. derivational are two different distinctions. The suffix *-ing* that forms a noun from a verb, as in the noun *swimming* (as in

2. But not all. There are numerous adjectives which cannot occur with comparatives or degree intensifiers like *very* and *quite: dental, chemical, corporate, criminal, dramatic, total, sheer, main,* and many more. But despite there being many of these adjectives which cannot occur with *-er* or *more*, it still makes sense to call *-er/more* inflectional, since these forms occur with a large subclass of adjectives. Interestingly, adjectives which cannot occur with *-er/more* also share the property of not being able to occur "predicatively," i.e., after verbs like *be*. Most adjectives can occur "attributively," before nouns (*red house*), and predicatively, after verbs (*house is red*). But adjectives of the *dental, chemical,* etc., class, can only occur before nouns: *dental assistant,* never *this assistant is dental*. Adjectives of this sort are discussed in Levi 1973.

Swimming is good for you) from the verb *swim*, is grammatical, because of its meaning. But it is derivational, because it makes a noun from a verb, thereby making a new word. So while all inflectional morphemes are grammatical, derivational morphemes can be either grammatical or lexical. (However, the vast majority are lexical.)

EXERCISE 4. We have identified two differences between inflectional and derivational morphemes: inflectional morphemes don't create new words, while derivational morphemes do, and inflectional morphemes are relatively unrestricted in occurrence, while derivational morphemes tend to be restricted. What additional difference between inflectional and derivational affixes in English is shown by the following data?

a. babysitters, *babiessitter
b. nation, nationality, nationalities, *nationsality
c. red, redden, reddening, *reddingen

Productivity

Closely related to the concept of domain size is the concept of **productivity**. Some morphemes are **productive**, meaning that they can be used to create new words. Others are unproductive, appearing only in already existing forms. All inflectional morphemes are productive, and many, but not all, derivational ones are. The adjective-forming derivational prefix *pre-* is productive; it can be attached to just about any noun which can be interpreted as having a definite time referent (*pre-1957, pre-Sputnik, pre-New Deal, pre-Kennedy, pre-Vietnam War, pre-marriage, pre-tornado*). The adjective-forming suffix *-ose*, as in *verbose* and *bellicose,* seems unproductive, occurring only in *comatose, grandiose, lachrymose,* and a few others. The prefix *omni-* is relatively unproductive, existing only in *omniscient, omnivorous, omnipotent, omnipresent,* and a few others; hypothetical forms like *omnivident* 'all-seeing' and *omniferent*[3] 'all-bearing' seem unlikely. However, speakers who enjoy making new words based on Latin could coin new *omni-* words which might be accepted in certain restricted contexts. The Oxford English Dictionary lists several which have been coined, including *omnibenevolent, omnierudite, omnilegent* ('all-reading'), *omnilingual,* and even *omniferous* ('all-bearing'). These words surely are not familiar to most English speakers, nor do most English speakers invent new *omni-* words. Certainly *omni-* used to be more productive than it is now. Most likely one reason for its decline in productivity is the smaller number of Latin-literate

---

3. *Omni-* attaches only to Latin-origin roots.

members of the English-speaking community. The moral of this is that productivity is a gradient, rather then binary, and it is possible that very few morphemes, if any, are totally unproductive. Even *cran-*, which used to occur only in *cranberry*, can be found in words denoting mixtures of cranberry and other juices, and seems productive: knowing *cranberry* and *cran-apple*, I was not suprised to encounter *crangrape*, and *cranpear* seems a reasonable new form.

The test for productivity is whether or not the form can be used in new words, not how restricted the form is. The suffixes *-ist* and *-ism* can be attached only to morphemes which include in their meaning something interpretable as a policy or philosophy or world-view (*socialism, Zoroastrianism, revisionism*); it would be hard to have **of-ism, *ditch-ism, *button-ism*. But within that constraint, *-ism* and *-ist* are productive. As new philosophies are invented or recognized, so are new *-ism* words to name them (*Nazism, ageism, sexism, Reaganism*).

EXERCISE 5. How productive is the suffix *-able* which is attached to verbs to make adjectives (*wash* (verb) + *-able* = *washable*)? Is it attachable to all verbs? If not, can you define the subset of verbs to which it is attachable? Is it productive within that subset? Give examples.

Some Important Derivational Morphemes

Members of the major word classes (nouns, verbs, adjectives, and adverbs)[4] can include characteristic derivational affixes. Here are some:

13.   **DERIVATIONAL AFFIXES IN NOUNS:**

-age (appendage)	-ity (scarcity)
-al (arrival)	-let (kinglet)
-ance (acceptance)	-ling (princeling)
-ant (assistant)	-ment (government)
astro- (astrophysics)	neo- (neophyte)
-er (baby sitter)	-ness (closeness)
-ful (handful)	non- (nonentity)
-icle (particle)	-ocrat (aristocrat)
-ism (socialism)	-ship (stewardship)
-ist (socialist)	-tion (absorption)
-itis (sinusitis)	-ure (departure)

---

4. The rest (prepositions, pronouns, articles, etc.) are "minor," as we will see in Chapter Four.

14. **DERIVATIONAL AFFIXES IN VERBS:**

-ate (satiate)   -ize (regularize)
de- (deregulate)   re- (rewrite)
-en (harden)   un- (undo)
-ify (glorify)

15. **DERIVATIONAL AFFIXES IN ADJECTIVES:**

-able (readable)   -like (childlike)
-al (accidental)   -oid (humanoid)
anti- (anti-war)   omni- (omnivorous)
-ary (visionary)   -ory (regulatory)
-ent (confident)   -ous (porous)
-esque (Romanesque)   pan- (panoceanic)
-ful (peaceful)   pro- (pro-war)
-ic (linguistic)   semi- (semilogical)
in- (intolerant)   super- (superabundant)
-ish (boyish)   trans- (trans-Siberian)
-ive (active)   ultra- (ultrasensitive)
-less (powerless)

16. **DERIVATIONAL AFFIXES IN ADVERBS:**

-ly (beautifully)   -wise (timewise)

17. **DERIVATIONAL AFFIXES IN MEMBERS OF MORE THAN
ONE WORD CLASS:**

-an (American [noun and adjective])
-ly (friendly [adjective], eagerly [adverb])
post- (postscript [noun], postdate [verb])
pre- (preview [noun and verb])

THE HIERARCHICAL STRUCTURE OF WORDS

Consider *unlovable*. It is made up of three morphemes: *un-*, *love*, and *-able*. There are three possibilities for how they might be connected:

18.

un love able   un love able   un love able
(a)   (b)   (c)

Alternative (a) reflects the claim that neither *unlove* nor *loveable* are meaningful combinations. Alternative (b) reflects the claim that *unlove*, but not *loveable*, is a meaningful combination. Alternative (c) reflects the claim that *loveable*, but not *unlove*, is a meaningful combination. Diagrams like these can be regarded as indicating a (metaphorical) sequence of combining morphemes into a word. Alternative (a) represents simultaneous combination, (b) combination of *un-* and *love* before the attachment of *-able*, and (c) the combination of *love* and *-able* before the attachment of *un-*. Obviously alternative (c) makes the most sense. So (c) is the best representation of the internal structure of *unlovable*.

What would the hierarchical structure be for *universality*? Presumably the following:

19.

universe al   ity

This makes sense because *universal* is a meaningful combination of morphemes, while *ality* isn't.

EXERCISE 6. Draw diagrams of the sort just discussed to represent the hierarchical structure of the following words.

1. troublesomeness   **4.** adjustments

2. lovelier   **5.** monstrosities

3. unworkable   **6.** grandmothers

Categories Within Words

Let us return to the complex word *universality* for a moment. We know more about this word than just its hierarchical structure as indicated in (19). For example, we know that it is a noun. We also know that it contains *universal*, which is an adjective. But the adjective *universal* is itself made up of the noun *universe* plus an adjective-forming suffix *-al*. We can easily put this "part of speech" information into our hierarchical diagrams:

20.

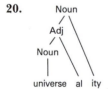

universe   al   ity

Before going on, we need to quickly go over some basic definitions of "parts of speech." Parts of speech are the topic of Chapter Four, where they will be carefully defined, but in order to follow the current discussion you need to be able to label words as nouns, verbs, adjectives, or adverbs. So here are some simplified definitions:

21. Approximate definitions of "parts of speech":

    Noun: A noun is a word that can follow *the:* the <u>boat</u>, the <u>universe</u>, the <u>rationality</u> of this decision.

    Verb: A verb is a word that can have a tense morpheme attached to it: <u>played</u>, <u>swims</u>.

    Adjective: An adjective is a word that can occur between *the* and a noun: the <u>awful</u> truth, the <u>yellow</u> train, the <u>criminal</u> lawyer.

    Adverb: An adverb is a word that ends in *-ly*: slowly, embarrassingly.

With parts of speech minimally defined in these ways, you can make some useful judgments about hierarchical structure. What is the hierarchical structure of *reappearance?* You might think there would be two possibilities:

22.

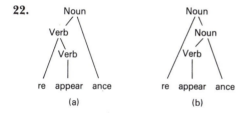

       (a)   (b)

But in fact structure (a) is right, (b) wrong. The reason is that the prefix *re-* attaches to verbs to form derived verbs:

23. **re-** + **verb** = **derived verb**

adjust	readjust
appear	reappear
write	rewrite
consider	reconsider
calibrate	recalibrate
align	realign

But *re-* doesn't attach to nouns:

24. **re-** + **noun** = ***noun**

table	*retable
grass	*regrass
alliance	*realliance
government	*regovernment

So *re-* is "first" attached to the verb *appear,* and only "then" is the suffix *-ance* attached to the verb *reappear.* This is why (22a) makes more sense than (22b).

EXERCISE 7. Draw hierarchical structure diagrams, with part-of-speech labels, for the following words:

1. undeniable   **4.** unpalatable
2. thickeners   **5.** revision
3. unforgivability   **6.** resubmission

WAYS OF FORMING NEW WORDS

As our language changes, new words are created through a variety of creative mechanisms. Besides derivation, important processes include compounding, the use of acronyms, extending brand names to the realm of common nouns, "blends," "zero-derivation," and extending the domain of derivational morphemes.

Compounding

Words like *baseball, handbook, toothpick, White House,* and *lawn mower* are compounds, which can be defined as words containing at least two roots. As you can see, compounds are sometimes spelled as single words, sometimes as word sequences.

EXERCISE 8. Draw hierarchical structure diagrams for the following words:

1. baseball   **2.** basketballs   **3.** wallpapered

The stress pattern generally reveals whether a pair of words is a compound or a pair of unattached words. In a compound noun, the first word is usually stressed, the second de-stressed. Contrast *I visited a white house in my neighborhood* and *In Washington I visited the White House.* In the first example, *white* and *house* receive equal, separate stress. In the second, *white* receives stress but *house* is de-stressed.

The meaning of a compound may be systematically related to the meanings of its components via a number of different rules. Consider *bartender,* whose meaning is "one who tends bar." Many compounds have the same pattern, which can be abbreviated as follows:

25. N V + -er = one who V's N, i.e., N   V
                                                  | |
                                               bar tend -er

Compounds which fit this pattern include *baby sitter, window washer, garbage collector,*[5] *man-eater, house painter.*
    A related meaning pattern is the following:

26. N V + -er = that which V's N

This pattern shows up, for example, in *lawn mower, trash compactor, air cleaner, word processor,* and *can opener.*
    Yet another meaning pattern is the following:

27. N_1 N_2 = N_2 to contain N_1

It shows up in *bookcase, birdcage, cigar box, ashtray,* and *trashcan.*

EXERCISE 9. The compound nouns listed here manifest meaning patterns different from those we have just examined. For each, figure out its meaning pattern. How many different meaning patterns are needed for the twelve compound nouns?

1. vacuum cleaner
2. polarizing filter
3. breakwater
4. pressure cooker
5. cleaning woman
6. killjoy
7. gas mower
8. windsurfer (the object, not the person)
9. cleaning solution
10. pickpocket
11. magnifying glass
12. know-it-all

On the other hand, many compounds have idiosyncratic meanings which are different from the sum of the meanings of their parts. *Girlfriend* means more than just a friend who is a girl, *sweetheart* relies on metaphor to relate its form and its meaning, *overlap* can denote only a state, never an

---

5. Don't worry about the spelling difference between *-er* and *-or* in this and other examples. They represent the same morpheme.

event (an overlap exists, rather than happens; liquids, for example, don't overlap, although they do lap over, the edges of containers), a *firing squad* is not just a squad that fires, but one that executes by firing, *sandpaper* has a narrower meaning than just 'paper with sand (on it),' and both *bag man* and *bag lady* mean more than 'man (woman) with a bag.'

Acronyms

Another word-formation process turns word-initial letter sequences into ordinary words: *laser* from *light amplification by stimulated emission of radiation*, *NATO* from *North Atlantic Treaty Organization*, *radar* from *radio detecting and ranging*, *NOW* from *National Organization of Women*.

Brand Names

This word-formation process turns brand names into common nouns: *kleenex, xerox, scotch tape, victrola*.

Blends

Still another word-formation process combines the first part of one word with the second part of another: *brunch* from *breakfast* and *lunch*, *smog* from *smoke* and *fog*, and *motel* from *motor* and *hotel*.

Morphological Reanalysis

Naive native speaker analysis of morphologically complex words is responsible for such new directions as the invention of the productive compounding root *-burger*, based on the original *hamburger*. *Hamburger* was originally short for *hamburger steak*, presumably because hamburgers originated in Hamburg, Germany. English speakers thought there was a morpheme boundary between *ham* and *burger*, possibly because *ham* is an independent morpheme denoting a kind of meat. This analysis made possible the derived *cheeseburger, beefburger, steakburger, pizzaburger, chiliburger*, etc. Another example of morphological reanalysis is some speakers' occasional shift of the morpheme boundary in *another*, resulting in phrases like *a whole nother*. An older example is how the word *pea* acquired its present form: in old English, the word was *pease*, in both singular and plural. The final [z] came to be interpreted as the plural, resulting in the new singular form *pea*.

Functional Shift (Zero-Derivation)

An important source of vocabulary development is the use of a word as a different part of speech from its original form. Numerous English words that can now be both nouns and verbs began life as verbs only: *walk, hunt, laugh, run,* and many more. Many others were originally only nouns:

sight, float, interface. Functional shift can also move a word from one sub-class of a part of speech to another, as when an auto salesman praises his product by calling it *a lot of car,* in which the **count** noun *car* is used as a **mass** noun. (Count nouns are those which get plurals and can be modified by "counting" words like *many* and cardinal numbers; mass nouns are those which don't get plurals or numbers and can be modified by "mass quantity" words like *much.* Examples of mass nouns are *salt, water, rice,* and *butter.*)

Extending the Domain of Derivational Morphemes

Another word-formation process, often criticized by prescriptivists, is making a derivational morpheme more productive than it was. One frequently criticized example of this is the extension of *-ize* to create forms like *prioritize* and *containerize.*

This kind of word-creation is found frequently in a child's first language acquisition. When my son was four, he began extending the adjective suffix *-ish* beyond words like *reddish* to all gradable adjectives, inventing words like *hungryish* and *coldish.*[6]

EXERCISE 10. Classify the following words in terms of their origin: compounding, acronym creation, making a brand name a common noun, blending, re-analyzing morpheme boundaries, functioned shift (zero-derivation), and extending the domain of a derivational morpheme:

1. yuppie   **2.** a steal   **3.** to badmouth
4. workaholic   **5.** walkman   **6.** modem
7. sellathon

Idioms

An important area of grammar that doesn't fit neatly into either morphology (word structure) or syntax (sentence structure, the topic of Chapters Six–Ten) is idioms, some of which are exemplified below:

28. a. to kick the bucket
    b. to throw in the towel
    c. hold your horses
    d. to put one's best foot forward
    e. to sell down the river
    f. to eat one's hat
    g. to put one's foot in one's mouth
    h. to throw one's weight around

6. He also used *-ish* as a free morpheme: JK: *Are you hungry?* PK: *Ish.*

An idiom is a complex expression whose meaning is not the sum of the meanings of its parts. As idioms, *to kick the bucket* means "to die," *to throw in the towel* means "to surrender," *hold your horses* means "wait, stop," and *to sell down the river* means "to abandon, betray." Of course, these all have literal, nonidiomatic meanings as well. As idioms, they are subject to special restrictions. In general, unlike ordinary phrases, idioms are subject to the syntactic restriction that they can't have their word order changed. You can't say **The bucket was kicked by my old tomcat* to mean "my old tomcat died," although if your old tomcat actually physically kicked a bucket, you could. Similarly, with idiomatic meanings, *the towel was thrown in, his hat was eaten,* and *his best foot was put forward* are impossible, although they are fine with nonidiomatic interpretations. *Hold your horses* is subject to a functional restriction as well: it can occur only as a command or request: *Hold your horses! I'd like you to hold your horses on that, if you could,* never as an assertion: **Max was holding his horses.* So idioms have two characteristic properties: their meaning is not a function of their subparts, and they do not behave syntactically like phrases, since they can't have their internal structure rearranged.

Although an idiom is a phrase, i.e., a sequence of words, it is in some ways like a single word: words can't have their component morphemes rearranged, and while word meanings are often a direct function of the meanings of their parts, they aren't always, as we saw in our discussion of compounds. Moreover, unlike phrases, idioms are finite in number, as are words. Of course we wouldn't want to push this parallel too far, since in other ways idioms act like phrases: they appear to have structures parallel to normal phrases, e.g., *eat one's hat* seems to be structured just like *eat one's spinach,* and intonationally idiomatic phrases have normal phrase contours.

EXERCISE 11. Examine several idioms (from the list above as well as from your own experience) with respect to the claim that some interpretations of idioms have a base in metaphor. Which idioms clearly have a metaphoric base? What metaphors are involved? Which idioms don't have a metaphoric base, as far as you can tell?

HOW LANGUAGES DIFFER MORPHOLOGICALLY

We have seen that some English words are made up of a single morpheme, like *swim* and *California.* Others are made up of two morphemes: *boys, baseball.* Others contain three morphemes: *unhappily, subclasses;* and others contain more, like *antidisestablishmentarianism.*

On the average, how morphologically complex is English? In other words, on average how many morphemes tend to be in a typical English word? A quick way to approximate an answer to this is to compute the average number of morphemes per word in a particular discourse, and the relative proportion of one-morpheme words, two-morpheme words, etc. The figure arrived at will vary according to genre and style, of course. Newspaper opinion columns and advertisements average around 1.35 morphemes per word, with well over 90 percent of the words containing one or two morphemes.[7]

Spanish is somewhat more complex, tending to pack more morphemes into most words. Newspaper opinion columns average around 1.5 morphemes per word.[8]

To give you some idea of how languages can vary in morphological complexity, here is some information on three languages which differ strikingly from English in morphological structure.

Swahili words tend to have more morphemes than English or Spanish. Each of the three Swahili expressions below is a single word:

29. a. atakupenda 'he/she will love you':
   [a   -ta -ku -penda]
   'he/she-will-you-love'
   b. unaitwa 'you are wanted':
   [u -na   -it   -wa]
   'you-present-want-passive'
   c. aliyemwona 'the one who saw her'
   [a   -li -ye -mw   -ona]
   'he/she-past-who-him/her-see'

A meaning expressed as a three-, four-, or even five-word sentence in English can be encoded as a single word in Swahili.

Greenlandic Eskimo is even more morphologically complex:

---

7. I applied this simple procedure to two paragraphs (169 words) in a newspaper opinion column, and found 112 one-morpheme words, 54 two-morpheme words, and 3 three-morpheme words, for an average of 1.35 morphemes per word. The same figure was derived from a 256-word travel advertisement in a magazine (183 one-morpheme words, 62 two-morpheme words, and a handful of longer words). Casual conversation tends to be morphologically simpler: in a tape recording of a casual conversation I found 406 one-morpheme words and 102 two-morpheme words, for an average of 1.2 morphemes per word. Textbook discourse tends to be morphologically more complex: in a 167-word paragraph in an introductory linguistics textbook I counted 89 1-morpheme words, 66 2-morpheme words, 11 3-morpheme words, and 1 4-morpheme word, for an average of 1.54 morphemes per word.

8. In two paragraphs (220 words) from a Spanish newspaper opinion column, I found 123 one-morpheme words, 85 two-morpheme words, 2 two-morpheme words, and 1 4-morpheme word, for an average of 1.5 morphemes per word.

30.   nanoq illumiisimavoq 'the bear has been in the house'
    [nano-q   illu -   mii -sima - voq]
    'bear-intrans.subj   house-in-   has-indic. 3 sg.'[9]

([q] stands for a voiceless uvular stop, a sound made in the very back of the mouth—like a [k] but made much farther back.) In this example, you can see that Eskimo has a verb form (a single word) that encodes the meaning "has been in the house."

At the other extreme is Chinese, in which all words are 1 morpheme long:

31.   'They heard us'
    [ta mʌn tin lʌ wo mʌn][10]
    'he plural hear past I plural'

A language like Chinese, with a consistent one morpheme per word, and in which elementary meaning concepts tend to get expressed by separate morphemes, is called **analytic** (or **isolating**). At the other extreme, a language like Greenlandic Eskimo, with polymorphemic words, is called **polysynthetic**. English sentences like *Jack and Jill will try to stay here now*, with nothing but one-morpheme words, can make English look analytic, and English is certainly more analytic than it was several hundred years ago, when, for example, it had endings on all nouns. (Recall our discussion of grammatical change in Chapter One.) We have seen, though, that many English words have complicated word-internal morphology, and a sentence like *Those plainclothesmen infrequently reassessed their unworkable courtroom procedures*, with nothing but polymorphemic words, can make English morphology look complex, although not nearly as complicated as that seen in Greenlandic Eskimo.

Morphological complexity is assessed not just on how many morphemes make up words, but also on how easy it is to see the morpheme boundaries. A language with predominantly polymorphemic words in which the morphemes have well-marked edges, like Swahili, is called **agglutinating**. If you look back at our Swahili example, (29), you'll easily be able to identify individual morphemes. Greenlandic Eskimo is not agglutinating, because it has too much smearing of morpheme boundaries and complex pronunciation changes when morphemes come together, a hint of which can be seen in the following:

32.   a.   [amiq] 'hide'   [ammit] 'hides'
        b.   [nuyaq] 'hair'   [nutsat] 'hairs'

---

9. Grammatical abbreviations: "Intrans. subj." means that this morpheme is used to mark subjects of intranstive verbs, verbs that don't take direct objects. "Indic. 3 sg." means that this morpheme indicates a third person singular subject, and at the same time "indicative" mood, the normal verb form for expressing assertions. See below, and Chapter Five.

10. Chinese is a tone language, but tone is not marked here.

c. [naalagaq] 'master'   [naalakkat] 'masters'
d. [igalaaq] 'window'   [igalassat] 'windows'[11]

Languages which do not pack so many morphemes into words as Greenlandic Eskimo, but which have some changes of pronunciation as morphemes adjoin each other, are called **fusional**. Another property of fusional languages is the bundling of several features of meaning into a single morpheme. In English this property can be seen in the meaning of the -*s* ending on verbs, as in *sleeps, rises,* etc., which means "present tense, third person, singular, indicative.[12]" One language usually called fusional is Spanish. In the following example, observe how a number of features of meaning are expressed by a single form, as the endings express not only tense (present) but also person and number information. Observe also how determining morpheme boundaries is no simple matter. Is the morpheme for 'speak' [abl]? Or is it [abla], with some pronunciation changes, e.g., a loss of an [a] before [o] or [e]?

33. a. [ablar]   'to speak'
     b. [ablo]   'I speak'
     c. [able]   'I spoke'
     d. [ablas]   'you (singular speak'
     e. [abla]   'he/she/it speaks'
     f. [ablan]   'they speak'

These parameters for morphological complexity are not parallel; analyticity vs. polysynthesis has to do strictly with number of morphemes per word, whereas agglutination vs. fusion has to do with how much blending occurs at morpheme boundaries.

Most languages cannot be labeled simply as one or another of these types. Rather, most show a mixture of properties having to do with morphological complexity. Nonetheless it is possible—roughly—to arrange languages along a scale of morphological complexity:

34. Scale of morphological complexity:

Most complex	$\rightarrow$	$\rightarrow$	$\rightarrow$	Least complex
Polysynthetic		Agglutinating	Fusional	Isolating
Eskimo		Swahili	Spanish	Chinese

English fits between Spanish and Chinese on this scale.

11. This data is from Robert Underhill's review of *Topics in West Greenlandic Phonology*, by J. Rischel, *Language* 53.4, 1977, pp. 944–948.
12. We'll define these features in Chapter Five. Probably the troublesome ones are "third person" and "indicative," which mean roughly "he/she/it/they" and "used for assertions," respectively. "Indicative" is a **mood**, and contrasts with **subjunctive**, which is used in certain expressions of wishing (e.g., *Long live the king;* note the absence of an ending on the verb *live*).

THE PRONUNCIATION OF MORPHEMES

At the beginning of this chapter a morpheme was defined as a minimal form with a meaning. But a morpheme can vary in pronunciation, much the way a phoneme can. Consequently we must return now to some of the notions developed in Chapter Two, including the idea of underlying form and the concept of phonological rules. Let's start with an exercise.

EXERCISE 12. Pronounce the following words, paying attention to how you say the past tense endings. What are the different ways past tense -*ed* can be pronounced?

spilled	blabbed	kissed	baked	played
added	decided	batted	wished	buzzed
watched	hugged	lived	crammed	grinned
hopped	scribbled	composed	judged	denied

The three ways past tense -*ed* are pronounced in English are [d], [t], and something between [ɪd] and [əd]. We'll use the latter notation, recognizing that it is inexact.

How do you know which of these three endings to use, when you pronounce an "-ed" past tense? Which ones would you use with the following nonsense verbs—*to snurp, to blorg, to grubbet?* Presumably, [t], [d], and [əd], respectively, producing [snɾpt], [blɔrgd], and [grʌbətəd]. The fact that you instantly know which ending to use with a "verb" you have never encountered before is strong evidence that you know, unconsciously, a rule which determines the phonetic form of the "-ed" past tense ending. To find out the nature of this rule, try this exercise:

EXERCISE 13. Phonetically transcribe the last sound before the "-ed" ending in each of the verbs in Exercise 12, and see if you can find a correlation between the kind of verb-stem-final sound and the pronunciation of the past tense morpheme.

Hopefully, you found that the pronunciation [əd] was found after alveolar stops (after [t] and [d], that is), [t] after voiceless sounds (except [t]), and [d] after voiced sounds (except [d]). This pattern makes for relative ease of pronunciation: first, [t], a voiceless sound, follows any voiceless sound (except another [t]), and [d], a voiced sound, follows any voiced sound (except another [d]). Recalling our discussion of assimilation in

Chapter Two, you should recognize this as an example of assimilation in voicing. Second, [əd] follows [t] or [d]. Because it is very hard to pronounce, as distinct sounds, a pair of adjacent alveolar stops, as in [ædd] or [bætd], we insert a [ə] between the end of the verb stem and the past tense ending. Not surprisingly, the general term for this phonological process is **insertion**. Both assimilation and insertion often operate in a language in order to facilitate pronunciation.

We have, then, three forms of the past tense morpheme: [t], [d], and [əd]. Each occurs in its own special environment, with no overlap (i.e., no linguistic environment in which more than one of these occurs). That is, these three forms occur in complementary distribution. Do you see the resemblance to phonemes and allophones? The technical term for a pronunciation of a morpheme reflects the parallel: an **allomorph** is a version of a morpheme, just as an allophone is a version of a phoneme. The English past tense morpheme has three regular allomorphs, [t], [d], and [əd], in complementary distribution. (It has irregular allomorphs too, which we will discuss later in this chapter.)

A Formal Description

Describing such a pattern of occurrence of allomorphs in terms of underlying forms and formal, explicit rules, as we did in Chapter Two in connection with phonemes and allophones, can bring out some heretofore hidden aspects of the pattern. To figure out formal rules, we first select— perhaps arbitrarily—one of the allomorphs as "basic," the one which will be the underlying one in our description. To this basic allomorph, together with the root it gets attached to, phonological rules will apply to derive the proper phonetic forms. Let's (arbitrarily) select [d] as the basic allomorph of the past tense morpheme. To posit an underlying form of a word that contains more than one morpheme, we simply combine the basic allomorphs. This means that we will say that—underlyingly—the word *kissed* has the form /kɪsd/; [kɪs] and [d] are added together to make the underlying form /kɪsd/. (Just as in Chapter Two, we will use slanty lines to indicate underlying forms.) To this abstract, underlying form, /kɪsd/, at least one phonological rule must apply to create the actual phonetic form of the word—the one that is actually uttered: [kɪst]. The rule that applies, of course, is one that turns [d] into [t] after a voiceless sound at the end of a word, i.e., devoices the underlying /d/ to assimilate it to the preceding voiceless sound:

35. /d/ → [-voice]/[-voice] _____ #

(Recall that the symbol # indicates word boundary.)

A word like *buzzed* will have an underlying form just like its phonetic form: /bʌzd/ for its underlying form, built by adding /d/ to [bʌz], and [bʌzd] for its phonetic form. Since underlying form and phonetic form are the same, no rule is needed.

Now how about a word like *added*? Starting with our basic allomorph, /d/, the underlying form of *added* would be /ædd/, formed by attaching /d/ to the stem [æd]. What phonological rule can you invent which will turn the underlying form /ædd/ into the phonetic form [ædəd]? How about this one:

36. $\emptyset \rightarrow \text{ə}/\text{d}\underline{\hspace{1cm}}\text{d}\#$

This rule says that "zero"—i.e., a little piece of nothing—turns into [ə] between a pair of [d]'s at the end of a word. In other words, the rule says to insert a [ə] between the word-final [d]'s, thereby turning /ædd/ into [ædəd]. The rule should be more general, though, to cover cases like *bat* (past tense *batted*) where [ə] is inserted between a [t] and a [d], so a better rule might be the following:

37. $\emptyset \rightarrow \text{ə} \Big/ \begin{bmatrix} +\text{alveolar} \\ +\text{stop} \end{bmatrix} \_\_ \text{d}\#$

This rule inserts a [ə] between an alveolar stop—i.e., a [t] or [d]—and a word-final [d].

Summarizing these ideas diagrammatically:

38. *kissed*:

Underlying form:	/kisd/
	↓ Devoicing rule, i.e.,
Phonetic form:	[kist] /d/ → [-voice]/[-voice]__#

buzzed:

Underlying form:	/bʌzd/ No rule applies
same as phonetic form:	[bʌzd]

added:

Underlying form:	/ædd/
	↓ [ə]-insertion rule, i.e.,
Phonetic form:	[ædəd] $\emptyset \rightarrow [\text{ə}]/\begin{bmatrix} +\text{alveolar} \\ +\text{stop} \end{bmatrix}\_\_\text{d}\#$

batted:

Underlying form:	/bætd/
	↓ [ə]-insertion rule
Phonetic form:	[bætəd]

EXERCISE 14.

A. Apply the analysis just discussed to the following past tense forms of verbs. For each word, show the underlying form and the result of any rule applications.

washed   dried   admitted   designed   decided

B. Try another analysis of the same past tense forms of verbs, based on selecting [əd] as the basic allomorph for the past tense morpheme. Figure out phonological rules and state in what order they must be applied. In each case, show the underlying form and the result of any rule applications. NOTE: Do not attempt to formalize your rules in the notation we have developed; just state them in ordinary English prose.

C. i. Now try a third analysis, based on selecting [t] as the basic allomorph for the past tense morpheme. Figure out and formalize phonological rules and state in what order they must be applied. In each case, show the underlying form and the result of any rule applications.

ii. How do words like *carrot* and *target* pose a serious problem for this analysis?

EXERCISE 15.

A. Identify the different pronunciations of the English plural morpheme, by transcribing the plural endings of the following nouns:

sizes	cars	rugs	habits	birds
cups	sacks	wishes	screens	myths
cliffs	edges	buses	porches	windows
seas	pens	paragraphs	debts	tendencies

B. Figure out and state specifically what determines which pronunciation of the plural shows up in a given word.

C. Using the same approach as discussed for the past tense morpheme (above), select one of the allomorphs of the plural morpheme as basic, and propose phonological rules to derive the phonetic forms of this morpheme as needed. Show how your analysis works for selected nouns, by positing underlying forms for plural nouns and showing the effect of your phonological rules.

D. Try two other analyses, each one based on a different basic allomorph for the plural morpheme. (Don't formalize your rules here in our notation; just use ordinary English prose.)

Other Regular Phonological Rules for Allomorphs

Say the following words aloud:

39. *hymn*   *hymnal*
       damn   *damnation*

You can see that the morphemes *hymn* and *damn* have two allomorphs, one occurring when no other morpheme is attached to it, and one occurring when some other morpheme is attached:

40. Allomorphs for the morpheme *hymn:*
      [hɪm] when nothing follows
      [hɪmn] when another morpheme is attached
Allomorphs for the morpheme *damn:*
      [dæm] when nothing follows
      [dæmn] when another morpheme is attached

Since [-əl] is a suffix which occurs elsewhere—as in *comical, regimental,* and *recital*—it makes sense to assume, as we have done above, that [-əl] is the suffix rather than some hypothetical [-nəl]. The underlying form for *hymn*[hɪm], then, is /hɪmn/, and that for *damn*[dæm] is /dæmn/. This small class of words (others: *autumn - autumnal, solemn - solemnity*) shows the effect of a phonological rule which deletes an [n] word-finally after an [m]:

41. [n] → Ø/m_____#

The rule is productive, in the sense that if you encounter a word spelled with a final *n* after an *m*, you know to treat it as silent. Here is a made-up word: *trimn*. How would you pronounce it? Most likely [trɪm].

Let's summarize this analysis:

42. Underlying form: *hymn*: /hɪmn/

Since this morpheme has no
other morphemes attached,
this phonological rule applies: n → Ø/m___#

producing this phonetic form: [hɪm]

If a suffix is attached to the underlying form, the phonological rule won't apply: e.g., if we begin with the underlying form /hɪmnəl/, for *hymnal*, the phonological rule cannot apply, since it calls for a word-final [n]. In /hɪmnəl/ the [n] is word-internal.

Harking back to our discussion in Chapter Two about the frustrations of English spelling, the words *hymn* and *damn*, despite their silent *n*, are not spelled so unhelpfully; the *n* marks their connection to related words.

EXERCISE 16. After examining the following words, propose underlying forms for them and a phonological rule to turn the underlying forms into the proper phonetic forms, where necessary. Base your analysis on the one just discussed.

(Note: Consider only the presence and absence of a phonetic [g]; pay no attention to the vowel alternation between [ay] and [ɪ].

malign	-	malignant
sign	-	signature, signal
resign	-	resignation

EXERCISE 17.

A. After examining the following words, propose underlying forms for them and a phonological rule to turn the underlying forms into the proper phonetic forms, where necessary.

iamb	-	iambic
bomb	-	bombard
crumb	-	crumble

B. Are the underlying forms for *thumb* and *tomb* like or unlike those for *iamb* and *bomb*? Why?

Assimilation of Nasals

Let's look now at some more widely-used phonological rules. How do you pronounce the prefix meaning 'not' in the following words?

43.   a.   impossible, imbalance, immaterial
      b.   i.   indecisive, intangible, innumerable, insincere
           ii.   inability, inedible, inoperable
         iii.   inhuman, infallible, invalidate
      c.   inglorious, inconceivable, inquietude
      d.   illegal, illicit
      e.   irreparable, irreverent

In (a), the pronunciation is [ɪm]; in (b) it is [ɪn]; in (c) it is [ɪn] in careful speech and [ɪŋ] in casual speech; in (d) it is [ɪl]; and in (e) it is [ɪr]. This data, then, reveals five allomorphs for this morpheme: [ɪm], [ɪn], [ɪŋ], [ɪl], and [ɪr]. Is the choice among them rule-governed? Sure. When the root to which this prefix gets attached starts with an [l], the allomorph is [ɪl]; when the root starts with an [r], the allomorph is [ɪr]; when the root starts with a bilabial sound—[p], [b], or [m]—the allomorph is the one that ends with the bilabial [m], [ɪm]; when the root starts with a velar sound—[g] or [k]— the allomorph is [ɪn] in careful speech, [ɪŋ] in casual speech; and otherwise, the allomorph is [ɪn].

To formalize this in terms of underlying forms and phonological rules, we first select a basic allomorph. The best one to pick is [ɪn], because it is found in the widest range of environments: not only before alveolar sounds—which is expected due to assimilation between the [n] and the following alveolar sound—but also before [f], [v], and vowels. (Observe this in the data.) When an [n] is followed by a labiodental sound or a vowel, clearly no assimilation has occurred; [n] and labiodentals, and [n] and vowels, are about as different as sounds can be. So [ɪn] must be the basic allomorph, the "unmarked" one, the usual one. It then changes—driven by assimilation—into [ɪm], [ɪŋ], [ɪr], and[ɪl] in the proper environments. Formally:

44.   **UNDERLYING FORMS:**

impossible:	/ɪnpasəbl̩/
imbalance:	/ɪnbæləns/
indecisive:	/ɪndisaysɪv/
inedible:	/ɪnɛdɪbl̩/
inhuman:	/ɪnhyumən/
infallible:	/ɪnfælɪbl̩/
inglorious:	/ɪnglɔriəs/
illegal:	/ɪnligl̩/
irreverent:	/ɪnrɛvərənt/

45.   **PHONOLOGICAL RULES:**

$/n/_{not}$ → [l]/_____[l]
$/n/_{not}$ → [r]/_____[r]
$/n/_{not}$ → [m]/_____[+bilabial]
$/n/_{not}$ → [ŋ]/_____[+velar] (OPTIONALLY)

The subscript indicates that the /n/ that is subject to these rules is the /n/ of the prefix meaning 'not.' Such an indication is necessary because not all /n/'s assimilate in the ways described in these rules, as can be seen in *sunlight, generally* ([jɛnrəli]), and *Sinbad* (in careful speech).

46. Phonetic forms:

impossible:	[ɪmpasɪbl̩]	
imbalance:	[ɪmbæləns]	
indecisive:	[ɪndisaysɪv]	(just like the underlying form)
inedible:	[ɪnɛdɪbl̩]	"
inhuman:	[ɪnhyumən]	"
infallible:	[ɪnfælɪbl̩]	"
inglorious:	[ɪŋglɔriəs]	
illegal:	[ɪligl̩] (the two [l]'s collapse to one)	
irreverent:	[ɪrɛvərənt] (the two [r]'s collapse to one)	

Recall our Chapter Two discussion of assimilation. Here, /n/ **assimilates totally** to a following liquid (that is, to an [l] or [r]), and **assimilates in place of articulation** to a following bilabial or (optionally) a following velar. Otherwise it remains [n].

Consider now briefly the prefix *un-*, which has a set of allomorphs very similar to that of *in-*. How is *un-* pronounced in the following words?

47. a.   unbreakable, unpacified
   b.   i.   undecided, untainted, unsafe, unnatural
        ii. unearth, unobjectionable
   c.   uncover, ungallant
   d.   unloved
   e.   unreturnable

If you collect data from casual speech, you'll find that for many speakers of English the allomorphs of *un-* are [ʌm], [ʌŋ], and [ʌn]—the first two occurring before bilabials and velars respectively, in casual speech, and the third occurring everywhere else (i.e., before all other sounds in both careful and casual speech, and before even velars and bilabials in careful speech).

From Productive Rules to Irregular Allomorphs

Let us return to the English past tense and plural patterns. The assimilation and deletion rules you discovered for the past tense and plural are productive. As productive rules, they are applied to new nouns and verbs entering the language (the plural of *kleenex* is [kʰlinɛksəz], with a plural form [-əz], due to the final [s] on /klinɛks/; the plural of *laser* is [lezɹz], with a voiced [z] following the voiced [ɹ]; the past tense of the verb *to lase,* formed from *laser,* is *lased* [lezd], with a past tense form [d], due to the voiced [z] preceding it). These productive phonological rules are also applied widely—too widely, in fact—by adults and children learning English as a second language, and by children learning English as their first language. Both children acquiring English as their first language and students of English as a second language make errors like *bringed,* and similarly children aged two or three produce plurals like *mans* [mænz] and *sheeps* [šips], and past tense verbs like *goed* [god] and *sleeped* [slipt]. The very fact of too-wide application—known in the child language acquisition literature as **overgeneralization**—proves the productiveness of these rules.[13]

But productive phonological rules alone are not enough to account for the range of allomorphs certain morphemes can have. For there are irregular plurals and past tenses, in nouns like *men, women,* and *children* and verbs like *came, went,* and *took.* And while most verbs have **past participle** forms (used with *have* as in *have taken*) which are identical to their past tense forms (e.g., from the verb *address* we can form *addressed,* which is both the past tense and past participle form), some past participles end with *-en*

---

13. Since children's overgeneralizing often follows a language acquisition stage in which verb forms are produced correctly, parents are sometimes puzzled. But children's overgeneralization of rules is a sign of linguistic progress, since it indicates learning a general rule, which is clearly progress as compared with knowing isolated forms, which is what is going on in the previous, "correct" stage.

(*take;* past participle *taken*) and some have a root-internal vowel change (*drink;* past participle *drunk*). What is to be made of this irregularity?

Besides the allomorphs accounted for by productive phonological rules, morphemes can have irregular allomorphs. Some of them are completely irregular; that is, if a morpheme is new to you, there is no way to predict what its allomorph will be when placed next to other morphemes. The word *children* provides two examples: the irregular allomorph *-en* [ən] of the plural morpheme, and the irregular allomorph of *child*, [čɪldr], that precedes the plural ending.[14]

Some irregular allomorphs are not totally irregular; that is, there is a pattern, although it is not phonological. For instance, for many English speakers, the irregular allomorph [Ø] of the plural morpheme shows up after nouns like *fox, bear, fish, deer, sheep,* and *moose.* (Saying that the allomorph is [Ø] means that the plurals of these nouns are *fox, bear,* etc.— identical in form to the singular.) These nouns have in common the fact that they denote animals that people either hunt or raise on farms. Such nouns often use the plural allomorph [Ø]. Not all such nouns do, of course; exceptions include *pig, chicken,* and *snake.*

EXERCISE 18. Plural nouns like *fish, sheep,* and *bear* have the same form as their corresponding singulars. In plural uses, how can you tell they are plural?

Let's look at some irregular allomorphs English verbs have. The English past tense morpheme can show up irregularly as follows:

48. Irregular past tense allomorphs in English:

[Ø]: in some monosyllabic verbs: *cut, hit, beat, put,* etc.
Vowel change in verb stem, i.e., a replacement:

[ey] → [u]:	in *take, mistake, shake, forsake*
[ey] → [ɔ]:	in some verbs ending in [r]: *wear, tear, bear, swear,* etc.
[i] → [o]:	in *steal, speak,* etc.
[i] → [ɛ]:	in *meet, read, bleed, lead,* etc.
[ɪ] → [æ]:	in *drink, begin, stink, sink,* etc.
[ɪ] → [ʌ]:	in *dig, cling, spin, sting, win,* etc.
[ay] → [o]:	in *ride, rise, write, stride,* etc.
[ay] → [aw]:	in *bind, find,* etc.
[ʌ] → [ey]:	in *come, become*
[o] → [u]:	in *blow, grow,* etc.

14. The reason for assuming that the plural ending is [-ən] rather than [-rən] is that the allomorph of the plural morpheme [-ən] appears after *ox* too, in the form *oxen* [aksən], and we therefore achieve some economy by assuming the same allomorph. If we assumed the plural form in *children* was *-ren*[rən], we would have one more plural allomorph, and just as many allomorphs of *child,* since we need two anyway, due to the vowel difference between *child* and *children*—[cayld] vs. [čɪldrən].

Vowel change in verb stem plus suffix:
[i] → [ɛ] plus suffixed [-t]: in *sleep, keep, feel,* etc.
Final consonant replacement:
[d] → [t]: in *bend, build, send,* etc.
Irregular verb classes with only one or two members:
be, give, eat, go, teach, light, buy, etc.

Replacement processes, such as the stem vowel changes listed above, are themselves the allomorphs. That is, one of the allomorphs of the English past tense morpheme is the replacement process [ey] → [ʊ].

Formally, these irregular allomorphs occur in specific lexical (not phonological) environments: [Ø] occurs after *cut, hit, beat, put,* etc.; the allomorph "[ey] → [ʊ]" occurs in the words *take, mistake,* etc.; and so on. Each environment has to be specified as a list of words.

Although a small bit of regularity can be seen here (e.g., the fact that [Ø] occurs mostly with monosyllabic verbs ending in [t], for the most part these irregular facts have to be learned—even if unconsciously—one by one, by both first and second language learners. As isolated facts not part of a general rule, these are lexical rather than grammatical facts.

EXERCISE 19. Which verb classes, from the list above, do the following verbs fit into in terms of how they form their past tense?

dive, shed, sweep, rend, weave, throw, know

EXERCISE 20. Using the following nouns—and any others you can think of—determine what classes of nouns exist in English with respect to irregular allomorphs of the plural morpheme:

man, woman, child, sheep, fish, deer, ox, alumnus, mouse, analysis, foot, tooth, trout, larva, alumna, hypothesis, stimulus

---

Another Kind of Irregularity

What is surprising about the plurals of *wife, knife, hoof, wolf, elf,* and *life?* Let's look at these words phonetically:

49.	Singular noun	Plural noun	Singular noun	Plural noun
	[wayf][15]	[wayvz]	[wʊlf]	[wʊlvz]
	[nayf]	[nayvz]	[ɛlf]	[ɛlvz]
	[hʊf]	[hʊvs]	[layf]	[layvz]

15. In some dialects of English, the vowel of some of the singular words listed here is [ʌy] rather than [ay]. In this dialect, [ʌy] occurs before voiceless sounds, [ay] elsewhere.

If we look just at the plural words, we'll see nothing exceptional here. The plural morpheme has the form [z], exactly what it should after a voiced sound, [v] (see Exercise 15). But if we look at both singulars and plurals, we see a strange alternation between [f] and [v] in the roots. How can we describe this?

One way is to say each root listed here has two allomorphs, e.g., for *wife* [wayf] and [wayv]. They occur in complementary distribution, but the distribution is not phonetic. Rather, it is grammatical: the allomorph which ends with [v] occurs before the plural morpheme, and the allomorph that ends with [f] occurs elsewhere. (Note that the allomorph containing [f] occurs before the -'s possessive: *wife's* [wayfs].) To describe this formally, let's assume that the basic allomorph of these roots is the one with [f], and that the basic allomorph of the plural morpheme is [z]. Since the relevant environment for the choice between [wayf] and [wayv] is the grammatical nature of the next element, the plural morpheme [z] has to be identified as plural: [z_{pl}]. That is:

50. Underlying form: /wayfz_{pl}/ (i.e., [wayf] + [z_{pl}])
     Rule: /wayf/ → [wayv]/__/z_{pl}/
     Produces: [wayvz]

Words like this are relics of an old English rule which voiced fricatives that occurred between voiced sounds. In Old English, there was no phonemic distinction was between [f] and [v], [s] and [z], and [θ] and [ð]; the voiced ones occurred between voiced sounds, the voiceless ones elsewhere. A number of words in Old English had no suffix in certain forms, but had suffixes in other forms. In some cases the addition of a suffix, e.g., for plural, had the effect of placing a voiceless fricative between a pair of voiced sounds, resulting in its becoming voiced. This is the source of the [f]-[v] alternation in the words discussed above; the subject-form plural of *wives* was [wivan], though the singular was [wif]. Even though the ending [-an] has disappeared, the voicing of the morpheme-final labiodental has been retained in words such as these. (It hasn't been retained though, in many other final-[f] words, as can be seen in the plurals of *cliff, cuff, safe, sheriff, chief,* and *grief.*)

SUMMARY AND CONCLUSION

In this chapter we have examined how we can describe the internal structure of words in terms of their ultimate meaningful building-blocks, morphemes. We have also looked at how the pronunciation of morphemes can change depending on environment. The model we have adopted for describing such changes makes crucial use of abstract underlying forms and rules for turning them into phonetic forms.

We shall have nothing more to say in this book about pronunciation.

Our next agenda item is pure grammar in the narrow sense: word classes or "parts of speech."

ADDITIONAL EXERCISES

1. Both *in-* and *un-* are derivational suffixes that can be prefixed to adjectives (*insincere, uncomfortable*). Which is more productive? Investigate this by collecting a few dozen examples of words containing each prefix. Are there any restrictions on historical origin of the words to which each prefix can be attached? Use a good dictionary to research this.

2. To get an idea of the degree of morphological complexity in English, and how it can vary for genre or discourse type, figure out the average number of morphemes per word in a variety of types of data, e.g., a newspaper sports column, classified advertisements, a children's book, a technical report.

3. Which of the following word sequences can be considered compounds? Why? *stock market, stock market analyst, cheesecake, chocolate cream pie, apple pie, convenience store, neighborhood store, wood shop, wood fence, paper route, paper route collection book, electrical engineer, mud hut, mud pie*

4. Speculate about the reasons for the following "errors" in morphology found in children's acquisition of English as a first language:
   1. Daddy, I need to be change-you'd!
   2. I want another napple!
   3. Look how she standups! (from Cazden 1968, quoted in Reich 1986)
   4. Child: What's this, Daddy?
      Father: That's a bruise.
      Child: Look, Daddy! Here's another bru! (Reich 1986)
   5. Child: Somebody's at the door.
      Mother: There's nobody at the door.
      Child: There's yesbody at the door. (Reich 1986)
   6. a. We goed to the store.
      b. Eric putted the marble in there.
      c. Those womans don't talk right.
      d. My foots hurt.

5. Consider the following data from a language called Egaugnal:[16]

Singular form:	Plural form:	English translation:
[onit]	[onide]	'finger'
[rek]	[reke]	'chair'
[stel]	[stele]	'road'
[tap]	[tabe]	'button'
[fliz]	[flize]	'mountain'
[elup]	[elupe]	'chain'
[surk]	[surge]	'sky'

Identify all Egaugnal morphemes, and their allomorphs, that are found in this

---

16. This data was provided me by Charlotte Webb.

data. For morphemes with more than one allomorph, hypothesize underlying forms and a phonological rule which can derive the proper phonetic forms.

REFERENCES

CAZDEN, C. B. 1968. "The Acquisition of Noun and Verb Inflections," *Child Development* 39, pp. 433–448.

LEVI, JUDITH N. 1973. "Where Do All Those Other Adjectives Come From," in *Papers from the Ninth Regional Meeting, Chicago Linguistic Society*, ed. by C. Corum, T. C. Smith-Start, and A. Weiser, Chicago: Chicago Linguistic Society, pp. 332–345.

REICH, PETER A. 1986. *Language Development*. Englewood Cliffs, NJ: Prentice-Hall.

UNDERHILL, ROBERT. 1977. Review of J. Rischel, *Topics in West Greenlandic Phonology* (Copenhagen: Akademisk Forlag, 1974), *Language* 53.4, December, pp. 944–948.

Chapter Four

"PARTS OF SPEECH"

In grade school you probably learned that a noun was a "person, place, or thing," a verb was an "action word," an adjective either a "quality" or a "word that modifies a noun," and an adverb a word that "modifies a verb, adjective, or another adverb." You also probably learned about pronouns ("words that stand in place of nouns"), prepositions, conjunctions ("words that join things together"), and possibly other kinds of words as well. These are the traditional "parts of speech."

The traditional term "part of speech" is puzzling; it's not clear why kinds of words—really, classes of words—should be "parts" of speech any more than, say, phonemes, allophones, morphemes, allomorphs, or even phrases or sentences. In fact, instead of "part of speech," linguists usually employ the terms "word class" or "grammatical category." The term "grammatical category" is a useful one, since it captures an important aspect of a "part of speech," namely, that all tokens of a particular part of speech share important grammatical characteristics that other parts of speech lack. The term "word class," however, is valuable in its simplicity, and is certainly an improvement over "part of speech."

In this chapter we will examine what it means for a word to be a noun, a verb, an adjective, an adverb—the "major" word classes—and similarly, what it means for a word to be a preposition, pronoun, article, or other "minor" category. (As we will see, the traditional definitions you learned in school are sometimes vague, overlapping, or contradictory, leading to possible confusion in attempting to apply them.)

MAJOR AND MINOR CLASSES

Word classes can be divided into two groups: **major** and **minor**. The major classes—nouns, verbs, adjectives, and adverbs—have a great many members (very roughly, a hundred thousand nouns, for example). In contrast, minor classes have few members. It's easy to list all the articles of English: *a, an,* and *the.* (That's all.) There are only four coordinate conjunctions: *and, or, but,* and *nor.* There are maybe 70 prepositions, and approximately a dozen subordinate conjunctions: *when, since, because, after, before, while, although, as, whenever, until, as, unless,* and *if.*[1] Major class words tend to have meanings which can be captured in easy dictionary-type definitions, or can be shown "ostensively"—by pointing to an example in the world (e.g., "Horse means *that* kind of animal," uttered while pointing to a horse). Such meanings are called "referential," since they involve, or allow, reference to actual things, actions, events, or properties.[2]

Minor class words tend not to have referential meanings. That is, their meanings are not easily specified by means of a neat definition; how would you define *the,* or *of?* They rarely can be ostensively defined; you would certainly have a hard time pointing out something in the world which was an example of *and.* Sometimes the "meaning"—if that is indeed the proper term—of a minor class word is its grammatical function. (Recall our discussion about "lexical" and "grammatical" morphemes in Chapter Three.) For instance, the "meaning" of *that* in *Everybody believes that the President deserves respect* is simply that a sentence follows it (*the President deserves respect* is a sentence, albeit an embedded one). Here the word *that* simply announces the grammatical category of the immediately following sequence of words, a purely grammatical function. Sometimes the "meaning" of a minor class word is **metalinguistic**, that is, its meaning makes reference to words, often those around it (as, in fact, with the *that* just discussed). Another example is the word *too,* as in *I love chocolate mousse, and you are fond of rich, sinful desserts too.* In this example the "meaning" of *too* is that there is some kind of significant identity of meaning between the two clauses joined by *and.* Minor class words are much more likely to convey metalinguistic meanings than major class words.

Another characteristic of major classes as opposed to minor ones is that major classes are receptive to new members. We can all think of new nouns, verbs, and adjectives (new adverbs are harder to come up with) that have entered English fairly recently, often originating in slang or casual contexts: *teflon, yuppie, nerd* (nouns); *scam, boot up, book* (verbs); *rad, gnarly, killer, tubular* (adjectives). As a result, major classes are sometimes called

1. The exact number isn't important. It's imprecise because of uncertainty about whether to count "complex" subordinate conjunctions like *as soon as* as subordinate conjunctions.
2. Even the "actual" things which reside in our imaginations, like unicorns.

open classes. On the other hand, minor classes are not receptive to new members; they're **closed**. (Try to think of the last slangy new article, conjunction, pronoun, or preposition you learned. It's unlikely you can think of one.)

The reason for this difference has to do with a difference in the kind of meanings major and minor class words have. As mentioned above, the "meaning" of a minor class word is sometimes its grammatical function, and is frequently metalinguistic, whereas the meaning of a major class word is typically its ability to refer to something, or some action, or event, or quality, in the (real or imagined) world. The things (and events, etc.) that we refer to with words can, and do, change with the tides of history. As a language changes to reflect changed culture, old words die and new words are introduced. But grammatical functions and metalinguistic comments are relatively immune to cultural shifts. As a result little change occurs among minor class words as compared to change among major class words.[3]

Since there are so many members of major classes, we need operational definitions, i.e., definitions which will enable us to identify members of each major class. With minor classes, which have few members, operational definitions are less important. With this in mind, let us proceed to examine the major classes.

MAJOR CLASSES

Nouns and Verbs

The only things many people remember from English grammar lessons are the traditional definitions of nouns and verbs: a noun was "a word that names a person, place, or thing," and a verb was "an action word" or "a word that names an action or state." In the vast majority of cases these definitions work fine. The vast majority of nouns do "name" (better: "can be used to refer to") persons, places, or things, and verbs do indeed indicate actions or states. For example: *Joe, Marilyn Monroe, neighbor,* and *mankind* all can be used to refer to people; *San Diego, Asia, Jerusalem,* and *Saskatchewan* all name places; and *tree, dog, stick, table,* and *acorn* all can be used to refer to things—and all are nouns. *Walked, ran, ate, snoozed, blabbed,* and *burped* are all action words, and are verbs. Looking at the issue from the side of meaning, concepts having to do with things—entities in the world with relative permanence, and with spatial boundaries—tend to be encoded linguistically as nouns, and concepts having to do with states or

---

3. But change among minor class words does occur, of course. Pronouns are minor class words which have changed rather dramatically in the last four hundred years (only 16 generations or so): *thee, thou, thy,* and *thine,* once entrenched, are no longer viable.

events—"entities" that are dynamic, changing, lacking in stability through time—tend to be encoded linguistically as verbs. But taking these tendencies as definitions leads to problems.

Problems with the Traditional Definitions of "Noun" and "Verb"

One problem with the traditional definition of noun and verb is that since it is meaning-based (a noun is defined as a word having a certain sort of meaning), it ought to be universal—valid in all languages, that is. But concepts that are encoded linguistically as nouns in one language may be encoded as verbs or adjectives in others. In English we normally say *I'm hungry,* using an adjective to describe how we feel, but in Spanish one says *tengo hambre*—literally, "I have hunger," using a noun, *hambre,* to describe the same feeling. English, of course, has the noun *hunger* as well as the adjective *hungry,* but do these words MEAN different things? (For instance, does *hunger* stand for a "thing" while *hungry* doesn't?) Or do they merely have different grammatical properties? What this means will be taken up below.

Consider next abstract nouns like *honesty, poverty, beauty,* and *truth.* Of course these don't indicate persons or places, but could they possibly stand for things? This is actually a philosophical question, not a grammatical one. A follower of Plato might believe that they do. Plato believed that "qualities" like truth and beauty which were observable in the everyday world as properties of people or things (or events, for that matter) were just poor shadows of eternal "Forms" which ordinary people could not perceive directly. Thus a Platonist might argue that words like *honesty* at least indirectly can refer to actual things (the Forms).

One might claim, more simply, and without any reference to Plato, that abstract nouns do indeed indicate "things," the things being the abstract qualities "truth," "beauty," etc. However, there is no evidence for the existence of these so-called things; it may make as much sense to say that abstract nouns are simply abbreviations, in noun form, for repeated instances of verb + adjective constructions (*is honest, is true, is beautiful,* etc.), and that they are used, as nouns, in sentence slots which require nouns rather than adjectives (e.g., _____ *is in the eye of the beholder*). That is, the abstract "qualities" may be fictions; the only reality may be the repeated instances of behavior or appearance: repeated instances of "being honest," "being beautiful," "being true," etc. Perhaps English speakers are deceived by the structure of their language into believing that since there are abstract nouns, there must be abstract objects or "things." That is, since prototypical nouns (*stick, tree,* etc.) denote things, a noun like *beauty* may lead an English speaker to believe that it denotes a thing too, despite the absence of any evidence of this "thing"'s existence.

No proof can be given that abstract nouns do or do not indicate things. If you believe that they do, abstract nouns present no problem to you for the idea that nouns indicate persons, places, or things. If you don't, you will need somehow to modify your definition of noun, so as to account for abstract nouns. If you modify it to include "qualities" ("qualities" not equalling "things"), you may intrude into the territory of adjectives, which are sometimes said to indicate qualities.

Whatever you make of this minor detour into philosophy, much more serious is the problem raised by words like *rodeo, party, storm, fight* and *arrival*. Let's consider all of these in cases where they are unquestionably nouns, as, for example, in the following sentences.

1. a. The *rodeo* was fun.
    b. At the *party* we danced till three in the morning.
    c. A big *storm* was brewing up in the mountains.
    d. Did you see the *fight* between Ali and Norton?
    e. Scarlett's *arrival* was tempestuous.

Any English teacher will tell you that the italicized words in (1) are nouns, but by our traditional definitions of noun and verb (noun = word which indicates person, place, or thing; verb = word which indicates action or state) they ought to be verbs. Why? Because they clearly are used to refer to events, happenings, actions. That is, *rodeo, party, storm, fight*, and *arrival* are without doubt "action words," not person, places, or things. If action words are verbs, these words should be verbs. But they're not. Why not?

Grammatical characterizations of "noun"

What makes *rodeo, party, storm,* and *fight* as in (1) nouns, not verbs? A commonly given answer is "the way they're used." This answer reflects an unconscious awareness that an important aspect of "nouniness" or "verbiness" is grammatical, and that it is possible to determine from grammatical characteristics what "part of speech" a particular word is.

What makes an English noun[4] a noun, from the grammatical, rather than semantic, point of view? A number of characteristics:

i) the possibility of occurrence after an article or similar word, as in (1 a), b), and d) above, or after an article and adjective, as in (1c). Nouns occur after articles (and adjectives): *the tree, a bird, an apple, the big palooka.* Verbs don't: **the dived, *a walks, *an entered, *the grinned.*

ii) the possibility of occurrence with the possessive *-'s;* only nouns can

---

4. A grammatical approach to defining word classes, clearly, will have to be language-specific, not universal.

occur with this form: *a tree's leaves, Jo's car, virtue's reward,* etc.; verbs can't: **walked's, *enter's, *burped's.*

iii) the possibility of occurrence with the plural *-s: tables, chairs, desks, virtues.* This plural element occurs with no other word class in English, although verbs can have a "zero" suffix indicating plural when a verb agrees with a plural noun:

2.   *The boy-s*   *like-∅ the picture.*
             ↑   ↑
         plural noun form   plural verb form

Contrast the following:

3.   *The boy*   *like-s the picture,*
             ↑   ↑
         singular noun form   singular verb form

where a singular noun requires a singular verb.

The kind of characteristic exhibited by nouns that we have just discussed is one of **co-occurrence**, that is, possibility of "occurrence-with." Nouns, and only nouns, can occur with the various items listed (and in the stated order, e.g., *after* articles, not before them). Co-occurrence properties of word classes can be regarded as test environments: any word which can fit into an environment established as characteristic for a word class can be taken to be a member of that word class.

Another kind of characteristic has to do with function. Only noun phrases can function as "subjects" of sentences, while verb phrases, adjective phrases, and other phrasal categories (which will be discussed in detail in Chapter Six) cannot. What subjects are will be discussed in Chapter Seven. For the moment we'll have to settle for examples. In the following sentences, the noun phrases functioning as subjects are underlined. In each one the main noun (sometimes called "head noun") has been capitalized.

4.   a.   All those scary man-eating MONSTERS left quietly.
          b.   Some of the STUDENTS who took the test said it was easy.
          c.   A big fat old MECHANIC chased us away.
          d.   Some lovely old TREES stood atop a lonely hill.
          e.   My new FRIEND sent a bunch of roses to Emily.

Another function that only noun phrases can fulfill is that of "direct object," also to be defined in Chapter Seven, but exemplified below, again, underlined with capitalized head nouns:

5.   a.   With the ten dollars, Mo bought some LOBSTERS for Jane.
          b.   Jo kicked the polka-dotted SOCCERBALL across the field.
          c.   Unfortunately we scratched the TABLE with that nice finish.

Direct objects generally represent the entity acted upon by the verb—the thing that the action happens to. Only noun phrases can function as direct objects.

Another function noun phrases can fulfill is "indirect object." An indirect object is, roughly speaking, a noun phrase that stands for the entity which receives the benefit of the action identified by the verb. Here are some examples, again underlined with their head nouns capitalized:

6. a. With the ten dollars, Mo bought some lobsters for <u>JANE</u>.
  b. We gave <u>my sixth grade TEACHER</u> a box of candy.
  c. Jo sent a <u>flowered box of matches</u> to <u>MO</u>.
  d. Smith baked <u>the INVENTOR of the frisbee</u> some nice cookies.

Again, only noun phrases can function as indirect objects.

To summarize: an English noun is a word for which any one (or more) of the following characteristics holds:

1. It can occur directly after an article (*the tree*).[5]
2. It can occur immediately before, or including, the possessive morpheme (*John's, John's*).
3. It can occur immediately before, or including, the plural morpheme (*trees, trees*).
4. It can be the head word of a phrase functioning as subject, direct object, or indirect object.

These grammatical properties may bear some relation to the semantic nature of prototypical nouns (those which denote things), since things can be identified uniquely (and therefore be used with the definite article *the*), things can possess, things can be counted (and hence pluralized), and things can receive action, or receive things (and hence function as direct object and indirect object). However, events can also be identified uniquely, be counted, and receive action (as when they are altered by some other event). Consequently this apparent semantic basis for the grammatically defining properties of nouns cannot be taken too seriously.

Grammatical characterizations of "verb"

What about verbs? We need a new definition, because the traditional semantic definition "action word" unhelpfully included *fight, rodeo, storm,*

---

5. This must be refined, since adjectives and adverbs can occur directly after articles, though always in expressions that modify nouns:
  i. The *red* ball (adjective)
  ii. A *rapidly* disappearing type of behavior (manner adverb)
  iii. The *very* beautiful dancer (intensifier adverb)
  We can modify our partial definition of noun by restricting the test environment to sentence-final position: only nouns can occur after an article at the end of a sentence.

party, and *arrival* as verbs when they were clearly used as nouns. To come up with a new definition, we need to ask: What is grammatically unique about verbs? Well, just as there are certain forms that occur only with English nouns, so also with English verbs. *-ed,* meaning "past tense," is one. Only verbs can occur with this morpheme: *walked, missed, blabbed, snored;* but nouns can't: **presidented, *doorknobbed, *lawned.*

Another form that occurs only with verbs is the present tense *-s* that appears on the end of a verb whose subject is a third person singular noun phrase. (The "persons" are: first person = the speaker, second person = the hearer, third person = some other person or thing.) Examples: *Joe snores, The president burps, The guy over there smells funny.*

Not only CAN verbs (and only verbs) co-occur with a tense ending; they TYPICALLY do. Every English verb, used as the main or only verb of a sentence, must have a tense. This reflects a common semantic characteristic of verbs, the fact that they are "time words," most of the time making some time reference. (A German word for 'verb' is *zeitwort,* meaning "time-word.")

Another form that occurs only after verbs is *-ing.* The underlined portions of the following words are all verbs: *sleeping, breathing, flying, reading.* However, the whole word containing *-ing* may or may not be a verb. When it follows *am, is, are, was, were,* or *be,* as in *Mo is sleeping,* it is a verb. (As you can see, we'll have to refine our definition to allow for verbs not only occuring before, but also containing, key morphemes like *-ed* and *-ing.*) When it occurs otherwise, for example sentence-initially as a subject, it is a noun, as in *Burping can be fun.* (Such a noun is called a **gerund,** or verbal noun. Gerunds will be discussed later in this chapter.) Nouns and members of other word classes cannot occur before *-ing: *desking, *ofing, *verying, *mying, *beautifuling.*

At this point something needs to be said about "cross classification," that is, the ability for many words to be either a noun or a verb, depending on how they are used. *Fight, storm,* and *party,* for example, can be nouns or verbs. When used with an article (*a fight, a storm, a party*) they're nouns; when used with a tense morpheme (*They fought fair and square, The angry professor stormed out of the class, We partied all night*) they're verbs.

EXERCISE 1. For each of the following words, decide whether it is a noun, a verb, or neither, and show why, using the grammatical definitions we have provided. If the word is cross-classified, i.e., can be both a noun and a verb, say so, and show it with evidence for membership in both classes.

Example: typewriter: Noun only. Occurs with plural: *typewriters,* possessive: *the typewriter's ribbon,* and after articles: *the typewriter.* Cannot be a verb: **He typewritered all afternoon.*

1. table	7. skin
2. create	8. partition
3. concise	9. destroy
4. enslave	10. person
5. attack	11. appear
6. visualize	12. visualization

Adjectives

Here is a short list of adjectives: *big, small, tall, interesting, lousy, smelly, beautiful, grand, red, clever, usual, fancy, wooden, brilliant, shiny, cloudy, former, good.*

Traditionally, adjectives are either "words which modify nouns" or words which indicate "qualities." The former is preferable, because it is possible to make some sense of "modify nouns," whereas it is unclear what "qualities" are. If qualities indeed exist, they may be referred to by nouns, not by adjectives (*beauty, weight, softness*).

Regarding adjectives as noun-modifying words is helpful also because the position immediately before a noun is one of the two main places where adjectives occur, as in *large car, pretty girl, expensive watch, lousy game, blind umpire.* This is the **attributive** position. (The other position, after a "linking" verb like *be, seem,* or *appear,* is the **predicate** position.)

What does it mean to say "adjectives modify nouns"? Generally, in a sequence of the form ADJECTIVE + NOUN, the meaning of the adjective is added to the meaning of the modified noun, so that, for example, *red car* communicates more than does *car* alone. Often, this added meaning enables the hearer (or reader) to pick out the unique thing, in the world, that the speaker is referring to (e.g., *No, dummy, the red car, not the blue one.*).

This modification, however, can occur in several different ways. Here are three examples. Consider *red car* as compared with *large car* and *good car.* There is a set of red things in the world (not just the real world, but the world of our minds as well, and including the past and the future), including cars, sunsets, books, hair, flowers, etc. There is also a set of cars (again, in the present, real world, as well as in various worlds of our imaginations and the worlds of the past and the future). The intersection of these two sets is the set of red cars, the set of objects that you can refer to by means of the phrase *red car.*

7.

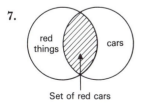

Set of red cars

Adjectives like *red* we can thus label "set-denoting" adjectives.

A more complicated case can be seen in *large car*. As we have seen, there exists a set of cars, i.e., a set of things which could conceivably be referred to by the word *car*. But, unlike the case with *red*, there is no well-defined set of large things. There are large mountains, trees, land masses, and the like, but there are also large bicycles, books, decks of cards, coins, human cells, molecules, and atomic nuclei. You can see that the meaning of an adjective like *large* contains an inherent notion of relativity. Not so an adjective like *red*. While something may be more red than something else, how red it is does not depend on what the thing is, whereas with *large* you do have to know what the object is, and, in fact, what the normal size range is for objects of that sort. If you come across an unfamiliar object, you can't appropriately label it large or small until you know how big typical objects of that sort are. Thus *large* is inherently comparative, and part of the meaning of the adjective *large* is its relativity to the noun it modifies.[6] Let's label adjectives like *large* "relative-to-noun" adjectives.

Now consider *good*. Just as with *large,* there is no set of good things; the interpretation of *good* is relative to the modified noun. Good cars are good in different ways from good food, good sex, good music, and good students. (To be sure, all these examples of *good* have something in common; that is what allows us to use the same word for all these cases.) But *good* has an extra degree of relativity. What is good music to my 17-year-old son is not necessarily good music to me. People have different tastes, and make different, and entirely appropriate, judgments of goodness. This relativity of judgment does not exist with *large;* generally speakers agree about the applicability of *large*. So, unlike *large,* the interpretation of *good* is relative not only to the modified noun, but also to the person whose judgment results in labeling something "good," the "user" of the word *good.* Let's call adjectives like *good* "relative to noun and user."

In summary, we have identified three semantically different types of adjectives (note that there are more): set-denoters like *red*, whose meaning includes potential reference to a set of red things, and whose meaning does not include an element of relativity to the modified noun or to the user; relative-to-modified-noun adjectives like *large;* and adjectives relative to both modified noun and user like *good*.

EXERCISE 2: For each of the following adjectives, say which of the three types discussed above it is an example of, and explain why.

blind, short, expensive, married, transparent, round, interesting, famous

---

6. There is another sense of *large*, one which relativizes size only to humans. This is the sense that appears in *Look, germs are little, and mountains are large, and that's that.*

Grammatical characteristics of adjectives

Although you probably have a fair idea of what adjectives are from their function of modifying nouns, it is also possible (and useful) to have at your fingertips some structural characteristics of adjectives. What morphemes co-occur with adjectives, and only adjectives? What sentence environments do adjectives, and only adjectives, occur in? (That is, before, or after, or between what types of words or phrases can only adjectives occur?)

Morphologically, the *-ly* ending indicating "manner" occurs for the most part after adjectives: *large - largely, beautiful - beautifully, quick - quickly, eager- eagerly, useful - usefully.* (There are a few nouns which can occur before *-ly:* e.g., *friend (friendly), bubble (bubbly), love (lovely),* but most of the pre- *ly* words are adjectives.) The *-ly* ending itself usually marks an adverb: with a few exceptions like *friendly, bubbly, lively, lovely, and deadly*—adjectives all—a word ending with *-ly* is an adverb, but the part before it is an adjective:

8.

Another morphological characteristic of many adjectives is that they can occur before the comparative and superlative suffixes *-er* and *-est*, or after *more* and *most* (which can be considered allomorphs of *-er* and *-est*): *larger, largest; more beautiful, most beautiful.* However, adverbs can also occur with *more* and *most*—e.g., *more slowly*—so this property cannot be taken as definitional. Moreover, there are numerous adjectives which cannot occur with comparative and superlative suffixes: *criminal, constitutional, legal, former, fake, agricultural, financial, economic,* etc. (Expressions like **This amendment is more constitutional than that one* are impossible.)

Syntactically (meaning "with respect to sentence structure," or, more generally, "having to do with sequences of words"), adjectives can occur between articles (such as *the* and *a*) and nouns: *the large car, a strange forest* (attributive position), and at the end of a sentence after a form of *be: The forest is strange.* (predicate position). Neither of these slots is fully definitional for adjectives, but both are useful indications that the word in question is likely to be an adjective. The slot *Article_____ Noun* is not hospitable to verbs, adverbs, and minor classes: **the reads boy, *a quickly horse, *the of table, *an it chair,* but, besides adjectives, it can accept nouns: *the stone wall, a coffee bean, the truck tire.* It is sometimes said about these constructions that the modifying nouns are "used as adjectives." Indeed they are, if that means "used to modify nouns." However, they are unlike typical adjectives in three ways:

i. They don't occur before *-er* or *-est* (**This tire is trucker than that one*), or after *more* or *most* (**This wall is more stone than that one; *That wall is the most stone of all*);

ii. Many do not occur in the "predicate" position (**This tire is truck*)—although some do (*This wall is stone*);

iii. They never occur before *-ly* (**The country wall stood there stonely*).

Moreover, the modifying nouns are nouns by our previous definition, in that they can (although not in the contexts exemplified in this paragraph) take possessives and plurals, and occur after articles.

Let's define adjectives with a combination of positive and negative attributes: for our purposes, an adjective will be any word which has one or more of the following positive attributes:

9.   i. it can occur between *Article* and *Noun*
     ii. it can occur in the slot *(Art) N is* _____.
     iii. it can occur before (or contains) *-er* and *-est*, or after *more* and *most*
     iv. it can occur before *-ly*

and in addition has all of the following negative attributes:

10.   i. it cannot occur with a plural
      ii. it cannot occur with a possessive
      iii. it cannot occur in the slot *(Art) N* _____ *Verb*.

EXERCISE 3. For each word below, show, using the positive and negative attributes listed above, that it either is or is not an adjective.

beautiful, handsome, stinky, house, tree, behind, disk, circular, world, legal, criminal, constitutional

---

Adverbs

Adverbs are hard to understand as a class, because they don't form a very neat class. In fact, for some purposes they are better described as not being a single class at all, but four unrelated classes. This will become clear as we proceed, beginning with the traditional definition of adverbs.

The traditional definition of adverbs

Your probably learned that an adverb was defined in something like the following terms: "a word that modifies a verb, an adjective, or another adverb." So adverbs include words like *cleverly, eagerly, quickly,* and *politely,* which modify verbs (e.g., *Jo politely answered the question,* in which the adverb *politely* modifies the verb *answered*); and words like *very, too, extremely,* and *slightly,* which modify adjectives or adverbs (e.g., *Jo is very tall,* in which the adverb *very* modifies the adjective *tall,* and *Jo reads extremely quickly,* in which the adverb *extremely* modifies the adverb *quickly*). This definition is not bad, except for two problems: (1) it does not include certain kinds of words which are usually called adverbs, and (2) it turns out that there are worlds of difference between basically verb-modifying adverbs on the one hand, and basically adjective- and adverb-modifying adverbs, on the other, so much so that "adverb," as a name of a grammatical category, doesn't have much meaning.

Grammatical characterization of adverbs

Before going into this, let us see what adverbs are like from a structural perspective. First, a simple morphological signal of adverb-hood is the presence of the *-ly* suffix. Almost all words ending in *-ly* are (traditionally) adverbs: *quickly, easily, obviously, certainly, reluctantly, heavily, brightly,* . . . You are therefore fairly safe in labelling such words as adverbs, but there are a few *-ly* words which are adjectives: *deadly, lively, lovely, friendly, bubbly,* and several more. (These are adjectives, by our definition (9) and (10): they fit the first three positive attributes, and they have all of negative attributes.)

Syntactically, most adverbs can occur after *more* and *most: More easily, most clearly, more reluctantly, most politely.* However, adjectives can also occur after these words (*more important, most beautiful*), so this alone won't suffice to identify adverbs.

Adverbs are fairly free as to where they can occur in a sentence. They can occur sentence-initially: *Certainly he will be elected, Reluctantly, she opened the door.* They can occur sentence-finally: *He jumped the fence easily, She spoke politely.* Since nouns can occur in these positions, these positions are not definitional for identifying adverbs. Adverbs can also occur in various sentence-internal positions, for example between a subject noun phrase and a verb (main or auxiliary), for instance:

11. a. He certainly sent Mary a card.
    b. He certainly should send Mary a card.

Another place hospitable to adverbs is between auxiliary verb and main verb:

12. He should certainly send Mary a card.

However, other auxiliaries can occur in these places, for instance:

13. a.   He may send Mary a card.
   b.   He should have sent Mary a card.
   c.   He should have sent Mary a card.

So, there is no fail-safe morphological characterization of adverbs—the ending *-ly* occurs on some adjectives, as well as many adverbs—and there is no syntactic environment which is hospitable only to adverbs. Consequently, we cannot define adverbs structurally, as we could for nouns, verbs, and adjectives.

Fortunately, this isn't as bad as it appears, because from a semantic, or functional, point of view, there are classes of adverb which are dramatically different from each other, so different that the whole class "adverb" is called into question.

Different kinds of adverbs

Let's begin with an exercise.

EXERCISE 4. Examples were given above of basically verb-modifying adverbs: *cleverly, eagerly, quickly, politely.* Examples were also given of basically adjective- or adverb-modifying adverbs: *very, too, extremely, slightly.* For each word in the following list, say which of these two types it is, and provide an example of its use in a sentence about Elmer Fudd, drawing an arrow to the word it modifies.

Example: *secretly:* Verb-modifying adverb.
    Elmer Fudd secretly planted some carrots where he thought Bugs couldn't find them.

mighty, sleepily, passionately, hungrily, awfully, somewhat, greedily, loudly, quite, terribly, rather

---

You probably came up with a pair of lists like this:

Verb-Modifying Adverbs:	**Adjective and Adverb Modifying Adverbs:**
sleepily, passionately, hungrily, awfully, greedily, loudly, terribly	mighty, awfully, somewhat, quite, terribly, rather

There are two adverbs which occur in both lists: *awfully* and *terribly*. You can say *I slept terribly* or *I slept awfully*, using them as verb-modifying adverbs; and you can say *That bed was terribly* (or: *awfully*) *uncomfortable*, using them as adjective-modifying adverbs. So these two adverbs are cross-classified; they're members of both the verb-modifying class and the adjective- or adverb-modifying class. The rest of the adverbs are not cross-classified. They are members of only one class each. The latter case is typical. Almost all adverbs are members of just one (sub-) class of adverbs.

What is important is that the two subclasses have nothing in common, except their *-ly* morphology (and that is by no means always there). Consequently, it makes sense to say there are two unrelated word-classes in the traditional "adverb" class:

14.

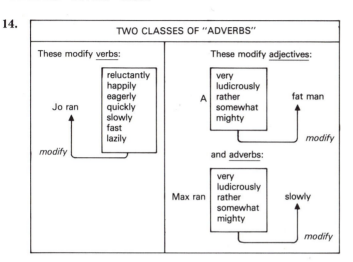

Because of their function and meaning, verb-modifying adverbs are usually called **manner adverbs**, because they can usually be paraphrased "in an X manner," where "X" is the adjective stem the adverb is derived from, as in the following:

15. Smith ran <u>easily</u>. = Smith ran <u>in an easy manner</u>.

Adjective and adverb-modifying adverbs are often called **intensifiers**, because many of them intensify the interpretation of the adjective or adverb they modify. Some, however, minimize it—

16. a. After spilling the spaghetti, I was <u>slightly</u> embarrassed.
    b. Yes, you were <u>a little</u> red.

Another term for this class of adverbs is **degree adverbs**.

Now into which class shall we place adverbs like *scientifically* and *logically*? They can modify verbs—

17. a. He thinks (*verb*) scientifically.
    b. He computes (*verb*) logically.

So they look like manner adverbs. And they have the typical manner-adverb paraphrases: *He thinks in a scientific manner, He computes in a logical manner.* But they can also modify adjectives, which is a problem, if we define manner adverbs as those that modify verbs:

18. a. That is scientifically impossible (*adjective*).
 b. Your claim is logically ridiculous (*adj*).

So they look like intensifiers as well.

We can get some insight into these words by noting that when they modify adjectives, as in (18), these adverbs don't have the typical manner adverb paraphrases of the form "in an X manner":

19. a. *That is impossible in a scientific manner.
 b. *Your claim is ridiculous in a logical manner.

Rather, they have paraphrases of the following sort:

20. a. That is impossible from the perspective of science.
 b. Your claim is ridiculous from the perspective of logic.

Intensifiers never have paraphrases of this sort:

21. a. *Mo is tall from the perspective of somewhat.
 b. *Jane was pretty from the perspective of very.

So words like *scientifically* and *logically* can't be intensifiers. What are they, then, when they modify adjectives? We can get a clue from the following data involving *economically:*

22. a. He shops economically, with money-saving coupons. =
 b. He shops in an economical manner, with money-saving coupons.
23. a. The President's budget is economically unsound ≠
 b. *The President's budget is unsound in an economical way.
 c. The President's budget is unsound from the perspective of economics.

Sentence (23a) is paraphrased not by (23b), but by (23c).

Observe that *economically* is derived from *economical* (= 'parsimonious') in (22a), but from *economic* (= 'having to do with economics') in (23a). The word *economically* is therefore actually a pair of homonyms: a manner adverb in (22a), with the appropriate paraphrase in (22b), and some other kind of word in (23a), which lacks the manner adverb paraphrase, as shown in (23b), but which has the kind of paraphrase observed for *scientifically* and *logically.* This suggests that when words like *scientifically* and *logically* modify adjectives, they are not manner adverbs. We have seen that they are not intensifiers either. They must be another kind of word.

Let's call them "denominal" adverbs, since they are derived ultimately from nouns (*science, logic, economics*). (*Nominal* is the adjectival form of *noun.*)

One further, and significant, complication having to do with manner adverbs shows up in connection with words like *mentally* and *physically*, as in *That instructor is mentally ill, not physically.* In such a sentence *mentally* and *physically* modify an adjective, *ill*, yet the sentence has a manner adverb-type paraphrase. *The instructor is ill in a mental manner (not in a physical one).* The simplest conclusion to draw from this is that manner adverbs can sometimes modify adjectives. But they can't modify all adjectives, only those that are part of predicates denoting processes or temporary states, like being ill. (Others include "being polite," as in *She was being obviously polite*, i.e., "polite in an obvious manner," and "being solicitous," as in *He was sarcastically solicitous*, i.e., "solicitous in a sarcastic way.") Predicates denoting enduring states like "being tall" won't allow manner adverbs. So—if manner adverbs can modify some adjectives—we need to define manner adverbs as words which have "in an X manner" paraphrases, NOT as "verb-modifying" words as we did above.

EXERCISE 5. Classify the underlined words below as manner adverbs, intensifiers, or denominal adverbs, and explain the basis for your choice.

1. That operation is medically unnecessary.
2. Senator Blowhard's amendment is constitutionally unsound.
3. We had a totally awesome time last night.
4. Eskimo verbs are morphologically complex.
5. President Nixon may have been criminally dishonest.
6. Some exam questions were impossibly difficult.

To complicate the "adverb" picture further, consider adverbs like *obviously, certainly, luckily,* and *unfortunately.* What do you think they modify, in sentences like the following?

24. a. Obviously you aren't interested in me, so goodbye.
    b. You certainly know how to show a person a good time.
    c. Well, I found out what you're really like, luckily.
    d. Unfortunately, some relationships end up this way.

The best answer is that they modify the whole sentence they are attached to, as the following paraphrases suggest.

25. a. That you aren't interested in me is obvious.
    b. That you know how to show a person a good time is certain.

    c. That I found out what you're really like is lucky.
    d. That some relationships end up this way is unfortunate.

The stretch from *that* to *me* in (a), and the analogous stretches in (b)–(d), contain sentences—*you aren't interested in me,* etc.—with a *that* attached. (As we observed earlier, the *that* in such sentences indicates that what immediately follows is an embedded sentence—a sentence within a larger sentence.) The relationship between the sentences of (24) and those of (25) supports the idea that *obviously, certainly, luckily,* and *unfortunately* modify sentences:

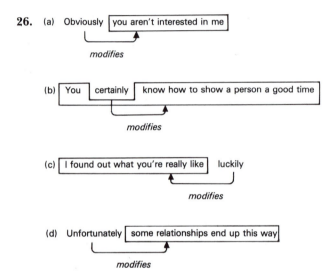

Adverbs like these are called, not surprisingly, **sentence adverbs**, since they modify sentences.

    Observe that there is nothing that sentence-adverbs have in common with manner adverbs, denominal adverbs, or intensifiers, in terms of what they modify. (About the only thing they do have in common is their *-ly* morphology, which, again, is not always present.) Moreover, there is hardly any overlap in subclass membership. There are a few adverbs which are cross-classified between the manner class and the sentence-adverb class. *Obviously* and *sadly* are two:

27. a. as manner adverbs:
      i. Drunk, and pleased to see the Playboy of the Month, Sandra leered obviously.
      = Drunk, and pleased to see the Playboy of the Month, Sandra leered in an obvious manner.
      ii. Tom smiled sadly. = Tom smiled in a sad manner.

b. as sentence adverbs:
   i. She obviously loves ice cream too much.
   = That she loves ice cream too much is obvious.
   ii. Sadly, ice cream is highly caloric.
   = That ice cream is highly caloric is sad.

But the majority of sentence adverbs can only be sentence adverbs, and the vast majority of manner adverbs (and intensifiers and denominal adverbs, of course) cannot be sentence adverbs. Trying to find *that . . . is 'adjective'* paraphrases, and not finding any, shows this. In the following example, the manner adverbs in Set A are given sentence-adverb-type paraphrases in Set B, the results being ungrammatical.

28. **Set A (manner adverbs):**   **Set B:**

   Mo smiled happily.   *That Mo smiled is happy.
   Al ran quickly.   *That Al ran is quick.
   Max reluctantly ducked.   *That Max ducked is reluctant.
   Lu ate hungrily.   *That Lu ate is hungry.

The same result happens when we try to find *that . . . is 'adjective'* paraphrases for denominal adverbs:

29. **Set A (Denominal adverbs):**   **Set B:**

   Eskimo is morphologically complex. *That Eskimo is complex is
                                       morphological.
   Your amendment is constitutionally *That your amendment is unsound
   unsound.   is constitutional.

A final comment on sentence adverbs is needed, in connection with the notorious word *hopefully*. *Hopefully* is a manner adverb when it occurs as in (a) below, but a sentence adverb when it occurs as in (b):

30. a. Marlene smiled hopefully at the hostess.
     b. Hopefully it won't rain on our parade tomorrow.

It is easy to see that (a) contains a manner adverb: the desired paraphrase exists, *Marlene smiled in a hopeful manner at the hostess*. But it is not easy to see that (b) contains a sentence adverb, since the desired paraphrase does not exist: **That it won't rain on our parade tomorrow is hopeful*. This fact may underlie prescriptive complaints about the use of *hopefully* as in (b) above, which is allegedly ungrammatical. (A prescriptivist would probably say that *hopefully* can't modify a sentence because *hopeful* can only modify noun phrases denoting sentient creatures, not things like sentences. People can be hopeful; facts or propositions can't.) The problem is that sentences like

(30b) are, from a descriptive point of view, clearly grammatical, in the sense discussed in Chapter One, because they are produced and understood, without a trace of negative reaction, by the vast majority of English speakers. As descriptivists, we must describe the language that is, not the one we or some language authority would prefer. The most reasonable interpretation of the lack of the usual type of paraphrase for *hopefully* sentences is that the language is changing so as to permit at least one sentence adverb to lack a paraphrase of the *that [Sentence] is Adj* type. Best to regard this as a quirk in the grammatical patterning of the word *hopefully* rather than an indication that sentences like (30b) are ungrammatical.

Now *hopefully* in (30b) clearly modifies the embedded sentence *it won't rain on our parade tomorrow;* hence it must be labeled a sentence adverb. A paraphrase suggesting that it is a sentence adverb is *One hopes that it won't rain on our parade tomorrow,* in which the embedded sentence functions as direct object of *hopes.* (A possibly more comfortable paraphrase is *It is hoped that. . . .*)

Time adverbs

We have not yet mentioned time adverbs like *yesterday, tomorrow, soon, now,* and *then,* and time adverbial phrases like *as soon as possible, next week,* and *the day before yesterday.* Clearly these are not intensifiers—they don't modify adjectives or adverbs. They are not manner adverbs; this follows from the fact that they cannot be paraphrased "in a such-and-such manner":

31. a. Max left yesterday ≠ *Max left in a yesterday manner
    b. Stephanie is leaving tomorrow ≠ *Stephanie is leaving in a tomorrow manner
    c. Jo is reading now ≠ *Jo is reading in a now manner

Nor, of course, are they denominal adverbs.

They are, rather, sentence adverbs. Each one modifies the sentence to which it is attached:

32.

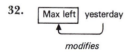

This can be seen from the fact that a paraphrase is possible in which a time adverb is turned into a predicate about the sentence, i.e., in which the sentence functions as subject and the time adverb functions as predicate:

33. a. Max left yesterday = Max's leaving was yesterday
    b. Stephanie is leaving tomorrow = Stephanie's leaving is/will be tomorrow
    c. Jo is reading now = Jo's reading is now

Some time adverbs are cross-classified as nouns, as can be seen from the fact that they can occur with a possessive -'s suffix and can function as subject and direct object.

34. a. Tomorrow's picnic should be fun.
   b. Yesterday was wonderful. (*Yesterday* functions as subject.)
   c. I'm just going to love next year. (*Next year* functions as direct object.)

Others, like *soon* and *now,* are just time adverbs.

To sum up: we have identified, primarily by means of paraphrase relations, four types of adverb: manner adverbs, denominal adverbs, sentence adverbs, and intensifiers. The first three have characteristic paraphrases, the fourth no characteristic paraphrase.

EXERCISE 6. For each word in the following list, identify it as a *Manner, Adverb, Intensifier, Denominal Adverb,* or *Sentence Adverb,* and provide evidence, in the form of paraphrases, for your decision. Some words in the list are cross-classified.

   1. strangely
   2. politically
   3. beautifully
   4. possessively
   5. literally
   6. undoubtedly
   7. today
   8. statistically
   9. demographically
   10. quite

We are now on the brink of winding up our examination of the major word classes. First, however, a comment about how our various (sub-) classes of adverbs fit with the major/minor, or open/closed, word class distinction.

Manner adverbs are an open class, since they can proliferate without limit. However, they proliferate only as forms derived from adjectives. In a way, then, the adjectives are the true open class, manner adverbs only derivatively so.

Denominal adverbs are open as well, but again only derivatively so, since they are based on nouns.

The same kind of openness holds for sentence adverbs derived from adjectives (*obvious* → *obviously, clear* → *clearly,* etc.). The class does not easily admit new members of other kinds, though *hopefully* is evidence that it is not completely inhospitable.

Intensifiers, however, basically a nonderived class, are essentially a closed class as well. We do not coin new words like *very, somewhat,* and *rather.* The intensifier class may admit new members, however, as derived manner adverbs take on intensifier uses, e.g., *extremely,* originally a manner adverb (= "in an extreme manner") but used as an intensifier in sentences like *She is extremely beautiful,* which is not very well paraphrased *She is beautiful in an extreme manner.*

This concludes our preliminary look at the major word classes. Next on the agenda is the minor classes.

EXERCISE 7. Identify the word class of every underlined word below.

1. I heartily accept the motto, "That government is best which governs least," and I should like to see it acted up to more rapidly and systematically . . . most governments are usually, and all governments are sometimes, inexpedient. (Henry David Thoreau, *Essay on Civil Disobedience*)

2. There is no Rule in Heaven that language has to be logical, orderly, and coherent any more than there is some Law of Nature that requires football players to stay within the lines. . . . Your language can be illogical, disorderly, and even incomprehensible—in fact, sometimes it *should* be so—but you won't be writing discursive prose. (Richard Mitchell, *Less Than Words Can Say* (Boston: Little, Brown, 1979, p. 43)

3. You are about to try the most technologically advanced shaving edge you can buy. Wilkinson Sword, with a world-wide reputation for innovation, brings you still another advance in razor blade technology, the first third-generation stainless steel blade. (quoted in Edwin Newman, *Strictly Speaking* (New York: Bobbs Merrill, 1974, p. 133))

MINOR CLASSES

Minor classes, so called because of their few members and their typically grammatical rather than referential meaning, include articles, demonstratives (e.g., *this*), quantifiers (e.g., *all, some,* and *many*), conjunctions, pronouns, prepositions, particles, discourse connectives (*however, therefore, moreover*), discourse particles (*OK, well*), expletives (*hell!*), and words of greeting and leave-taking (*hello, goodbye*). Since there are few of each class, it is not so important as it was with the major classes to provide operational definitions. Rather, we can list all, or almost all, the members of each class. We will also, of course, explore some of their grammatical and semantic properties.

Articles and Demonstratives: "Determiners"

Articles (*a, the*) and demonstratives (*this, that, these,* and *those*) are grammatically quite similar: they all occur right before nouns:

35. a book, the tree, this branch, that girl, these toys, those cats

Moreover, they can occur before an adjective + noun combination:

36. the tall tree, that steep hill, those juicy grapefruits

Articles and demonstratives also share a general characteristic of meaning or function: speaking loosely, they "modify" nouns. Because of this, and because of the similarity in these words' place of occurrence (before nouns), some traditional grammarians call these words "adjectives." Of course, grammatically they are not like real adjectives. They don't occur with comparative *-er* or *more,* they don't occur before *-ly,* and they don't occur "predicatively" (that is, in a frame like *The puppy is _____*). Also, they have to occur first in a series—*the little red hen*—whereas genuine adjectives can occur in any order[7] before nouns (*the little red hen, the little red hen*). Rather, their similarity in function and in place of occurrence makes it sensible to group them into a super-category of "determiner."

Articles

A, an, and *the* are the articles of English. Actually, *a* and *an* are allomorphs of a single morpheme, in complementary distribution with each other, with a difference in spelling reflecting the pronunciation difference. The distribution, of course, is that *a* occurs before words that begin with a consonant sound (*a man, a house*), and *an* occurs before words that begin with a vowel sound (*an apple, an honest effort*).

The has two allomorphs too: [ði] and [ðə]. They are in complementary distribution too, [ði] occurring before words beginning with a vowel (*apple, orange*) and [ðə] occurring before words beginning with a consonant (*pear, strawberry*).[8]

The is the **definite** article, *an/an* the **indefinite** article. Briefly, this means that *the* is used with nouns and noun phrases that both speaker and

---

7. This is not to say that a given adjective has no constraints on order relative to other adjectives. To the contrary, such restrictions are prominent; we must say *the little red hen,* not **the red little hen,* etc. The point is just that in a series of adjectives and a noun, in general adjectives can occur first, last, and in the middle, whereas words like *the* or *this* must occur at the beginning.

8. The form [ði] is dying out in some American dialects, e.g., Californian. Many young Californians say [ðə æpɫ, ðə ɔrənǰ] for *the apple, the orange.*

hearer have a specific, unique referent in mind for, and *an/an* with nouns and noun phrases that the hearer, at least, doesn't have a specific referent in mind for:

37. a. George bought *the* car in National City.
    b. George bought *a* car in National City.

The speaker of (a) assumes that the hearer knows about George's new car, but the speaker of (b) assumes that the hearer doesn't. Since the definite-indefinite distinction can be expressed otherwise than by the choice between *the* and *a/an*, we will look at this distinction in more detail in Chapter Five, where we will deal with typical grammatical properties and features of nouns.

Demonstratives

This, that, these, and *those* are the demonstratives of English. They get their name from the Latin word *monstrare*, "to point out," because they are used to point out the thing that a noun refers to. English, obviously, has a distinction among demonstratives between "near" and "far" as well as between singular and plural, *this* signaling "near" and "singular," *that* signaling "far" and "singular," *these* signaling "near" and "plural," and *those* signaling "far" and "plural." This is not the only possible way to categorize the world of demonstratives. Japanese does it differently. Japanese lacks a singular-plural distinction, but has a three-way distinction of distance: "near me," "near you," and "near neither of us": [kono] translates as "this, or these, near me," [sono] translates as "that, or those, near you," and [ano] translates as "that, or those, over there," or "that, or those, near neither of us."

Quantifiers

The basic English quantifier words are *all, both, most, much, each, every, many, some, any, few, several, little,* and *no.* There are also some comparative and superlative quantifiers: *more, most, fewer, less, least.* Numbers are also quantifiers. Besides quantifier words, there are quantifier phrases, such as *a couple, a few, a great deal of, lots of, not any, hardly any,* etc. Obviously the meaning or function of quantifiers is to indicate the relative quantity or amount of "stuff" referred to by the following noun. This may be either large or small, from the perspective of the speaker, positive quantifiers including *all, much, many, most, a great deal,* and *lots of,* negative quantifiers including *few, little,* and *no. Some* and *any* are in a middle ground.

Quantifiers can occur exactly as do determiners, right before nouns or adjective-noun combinations:

38. Quantifiers: **Determiners:**

All students	*The* students
Much paper	*This* paper
Some strange elephants	*These* strange elephants
Few candidates	*Those* candidates
Little soup	*That* soup
Seventeen kittens	*A* kitten

But they can also occur before determiners, and consequently are not exactly parallel with them:

39. a. *All* (of) the students
   b. *Much* of the paper
   c. *Some* of those candidates

Some can even occur after determiners:

40. a. The *many* giraffes
   b. Those *few* oranges

And there can even be quantifiers on both sides of a determiner:

41. *Some* of the *many* candidates

In Chapter Six we will examine in more detail the internal grammar of noun phrases—the rather complicated rules governing order of words which occur before nouns (articles, quantifiers, and adjectives of various sorts).

EXERCISE 8. In the following paragraph, identify all articles, all demonstratives, and all quantifiers.

Fourscore and seven years ago, our forefathers brought forth on this continent a new nation, conceived in liberty and dedicated to the proposition that all men are created equal. Now we are engaged in a great civil war, testing whether that nation, or any nation so conceived and so dedicated, can long endure. We are met on a great battlefield of that war. We have come to dedicate a portion of that field, as a final resting place for those who here gave their lives that that nation might live. It is altogether fitting and proper that we should do this. (Lincoln, *Gettysburg Address*)

Auxiliaries

Auxiliary verbs (abbreviation: **aux**) are the words that move to the front of a sentence to form a question:

42. Mo will leave tomorrow. → Will Mo leave tomorrow?
Greg should fire Judy. → Should Greg fire Judy?
Jane is kissing Tarzan. → Is Jane kissing Tarzan?
Sally has gotten John a job. → Has Sally gotten John a job?

These helping verbs are few: *will, would, can, could, may, might, must, shall, should, have, be* and *do*. The last three are cross-classified as verbs; they occur with tense, and can appear in sentences where verbs normally do— after a subject noun phrase and before an object noun phrase (e.g., *Max did his homework*). The others, called **modals**, don't take tense, and can't appear between a subject noun phrase and an object noun phrase (e.g., **Mo must the building*). Rather, they—and all auxes—occur between a subject noun phrase and a verb. There is a simple rule for the relative order of auxes; we'll go over this in Chapter Six. Historically modals were verbs, and a vestige of tense appears with some of them. There are contexts in which *could* is the past tense of *can—Last year I could fit into these pants, but now I can't*—and contexts in which *should* and *would* are the syntactic past tense versions of *shall* and *will*, respectively:

43. Max: Shall I pick up Martha?
Jo: Max asked if he should pick up Martha.
Smith: I will pick up Martha.
Jones: Smith said he would pick up Martha.

These "past tenses" are not semantically past; they are only syntactically past, required by the previous past tense (Jo's verb *asked* and Jones' verb *said*). In the same way, historically *might* was the past tense of *may*, and archaically can be so used today: *Mother says I may have some → Mother said I might have some*. Other than these cases, modals are tenseless.

The Infinitive Marker *to*

To marks the **infinitive** form of a verb: *to love, to go, to be*. The term 'infinitive' comes from the fact that, since it has no tense, an infinitive verb is unlimited—"nonfinite"—with respect to time. In a way, the infinitive marker is an alternative to tense and any aux, since they can't co-occur:

44. a. *We must to go now.
b. *To went, to baked, to walked

(The *have* in *We have to go* is not an aux; observe that it can't be fronted to form a question: **Have we to go?*.) When a complex sentence containing two identifiable sentences is changed to form another kind of complex sentence, *to* replaces the tense on the embedded verb:

45. a. The press corps believed [the senator was a liar]. →
      b. The press corps believed the senator to be a liar.
      c. [(That) a star lives there] seems (to be the case).[9] →
      d. A star seems to live there.

Complex sentences of these kinds will be discussed in Chapter Eight.

Participles and Gerunds

Participles and gerunds are types of words formed from verbs by suffixing *-ing* or the "past participle" *-en* (with its allomorphs) to verb roots, as in *taking* and *taken*.

Participles

In traditional terms, participles are "verbal adjectives," meaning that they are adjectives based on verb roots. Some participle uses are verbal, though, rather than adjectival, so don't take the traditional definition too seriously. We'll distinguish verbal from adjectival uses below.

Present participles

A **present participle** has a suffix *-ing* attached to a verb root. One use of present participles is in the complex **progressive** verbal construction meaning "be in progress": *Max is reading, The girls were laughing*. This is a verbal, not adjectival, use. Adjectival uses include both predicate and attributive positions:

46. a. Predicate position:

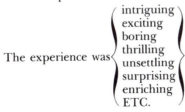

The experience was {
intriguing
exciting
boring
thrilling
unsettling
surprising
enriching
ETC.
}

---

9. Sentences embedded within other sentences sometimes require special markers, like *that* here; and the main verbs of some types of complex sentences require completing phrases, like *to be the case* here. Complex sentences will be taken up in detail in Chapter Eight.

b.   Attributive position:

We had a(n) { intriguing / exciting / boring / thrilling / unsettling / surprising / enriching / ETC. } experience.

These participles are adjectives because they satisfy criteria (9) and (10) (see page 116). Like ordinary adjectives, they can occur with intensifiers and with comparative and superlative *more* and *most:*

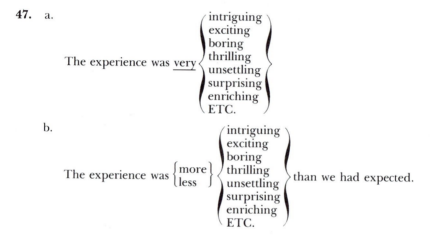

47.   a.

The experience was <u>very</u> { intriguing / exciting / boring / thrilling / unsettling / surprising / enriching / ETC. }

b.

The experience was { more / less } { intriguing / exciting / boring / thrilling / unsettling / surprising / enriching / ETC. } than we had expected.

Not all present participles allow such fully adjectival uses. The ones that do all have a meaning having to do with "emotional impact," and any verb with such a meaning seems to allow formation of an adjectival participle. But try substituting words like *sleeping, running, borrowing, cooking, decaying,* and *developing* into a frame like *This was very* _____ or one like *This was more* _____ *than that.* You'll see that they don't fit. Yet participles like these do have "modifying" uses, and can appear in the attributive position:

48.   a.   the sleeping children
b.   the running players
c.   the borrowing agencies
d.   the simmering onion
e.   the decaying wood
f.   the developing crisis

In (apparent) predicate position, though, they are actually verbs, part of the **progressive** construction, as in *the children are sleeping, the players are running,* etc. Expressions like these are near paraphrases of the examples in

(48); the precise paraphrases involve **relative clauses** (e.g., *the children who are sleeping*). (We will take up relative clauses in Chapter Nine.) Since the expressions in (48), and their paraphrases of the sort just given, are progressive, i.e., have the form *be V-ing* and the meaning "be in progress," which is clearly a verbal meaning, it seems likely that even before nouns, as in (48), such participles are verbal rather than adjectival, despite fitting into the Art _____ N slot given as a test frame for adjectives (see **9** on page 116). This conclusion is supported by the ungrammaticality of intensifiers and *more* with such participles.[10]

Participles can also occur after the noun they "modify," often (though not necessarily) with accompanying material:

49. a.   a man *sleeping* in the hay
  b.   Tickle the man *sleeping*, not the one *reading*.
  c.   a dog *resembling* a horse

Such expressions, which, with certain exceptions, have relative clause paraphrases as well (e.g., *a man who is sleeping in the hay*), are basically verbal as well.[11]

Present participles following nouns can also occur as the main verbs of **complements** ("completers") of noun phrases. In the following example the bracketed expression is a complement of the noun phrase *Lucy.*

50.   The police saw Lucy [<u>driving</u> away from the scene].

Notice that this sentence does not have a relative clause paraphrase; (50) does not mean "The police saw Lucy, who was driving away from the scene." The participle *driving* has a verbal use, of course, since it functions as the main verb of its "sentence" *Lucy driving away from the scene.*

To sum up the uses of present participles, we can list the following:

---

10. But nonoccurrence with intensifiers or *more* is not enough to establish that a word is not an adjective, for there are numerous adjectives which cannot so occur. See Chapter Three, footnote 2.

11. The exceptions are expressions like (49c). Such expressions contain participles of **stative** verbs. As you will see in Chapter Five, stative verbs and adjectives are those which denote states. Stative verbs include *resemble, want,* and *own;* nonstative verbs include *run, study,* and *smile.* Stative adjectives include *tall, beautiful,* and *interesting;* nonstative adjectives include *polite, agreeable,* and *helpful.* Progressive relative clause paraphrases are unavailable for stative participles, as can be seen from the ungrammaticality of **a dog which is resembling a horse.* The reason is that, in simple sentences, at least, statives and the progressive can't co-occur: **Jo is resembling/wanting/owning a Volvo.* However, the clash between stative forms and the progressive is not sharp. Although in simple sentences stative forms cannot occur with the progressive, in some more complex sentence types they can (*Jo seems to be resembling/wanting/owning a Volvo these days*). Consequently, it would not be prudent to conclude from the impossibility of progressive relative clauses paraphrases for expressions like (49c) that they are not verbal in nature.

51.   **USES OF PRESENT PARTICIPLES:**

Adjectival uses:
attributive: an *intriguing* experience
predicate: the experience was *intriguing*

Verbal uses:
in the present progressive construction:
    the children are *sleeping*
prenominally: the *sleeping* children
postnominally: a man *sleeping* in the hay
as main verb of a noun complement:
    I heard Tom *arriving*

Past participles

Morphologically, past participles are formed by suffixing *-en* (or one of its allomorphs, the most common being *-ed*—i.e., [t], [d], and [əd]) to a verb root. Fundamentally, the past participle has two uses, each as part of a complex construction: in the **perfect** construction—*Max has taken the cookies*—and in the **passive** construction—*The cookies were taken by Max.* In each case the suffix *-en* can be regarded as part of a discontinuous morpheme, i.e., as part of *have -en* and as part of *be -en*.

The traditional term "past participle" is misleading, since only the perfect construction (*have..-en*) has past time reference. All the other uses— to be exemplified below—involve what we might more properly call the *passive participle.* That is, all the other uses of this form are related to the passive construction, containing (perhaps in abbreviated form) the morpheme *be..-en.*

Past (or passive) participles have roughly the same range of uses as present participles:

52.   **USES OF "PAST" PARTICIPLES:**

Adjectival uses:
Attributive: very *bored* students; the *packed* boxes
Predicate: the students were *excited*

Verbal uses:
the perfect construction: you have *eaten* my soup
the passive construction: the flight was *announced*
postnominally: the bike *stolen* by the gang
as main verb of a noun complement:
    We saw the victims *stoned* by the angry mob.

One difference between present participles and "past" participles is that present participles have a distinction between prenominal adjectival participles and prenominal verbal participles, whereas all prenominal past participles are adjectival. We used the existence of a progressive paraphrase as a criterion for saying a present participle had a verbal sense. With past participles, the analog would be a passive paraphrase. Cases like *very bored students* are clear; the intensifier makes *bored* a true adjective, and the putative passive paraphrase *the students were very bored by X* is not a passive, as can be seen from the ungrammaticality of the active form related to it: **X very bored the students.* But cases like *the packed boxes,* which don't permit intensifiers (**the very packed boxes*), are harder. One might suppose these are verbal, on the basis of parallelism with similar present participle expressions, and on the (weak) grounds that they don't take intensifiers and consequently can't be adjectival—and therefore must be verbal, by elimination of the alternative. But we know that there are adjectives which don't allow intensifiers (*criminal, agricultural,* etc.). And a sentence like *The packed boxes are on the porch* doesn't seem particularly well paraphrased by something like *The boxes which were packed (by someone) are on the porch.* Notice the past tense. If *the packed boxes* is a verbal construction, it needs a tense in its passive paraphrase. Since the boxes WERE packed (by someone) in the past in order for them to BE "packed" now, the tense needed is the past. But *the packed boxes are on the porch* does not seem to contain even a hint of any past tense meaning. It doesn't mean "the boxes were packed"; it means "the boxes are packed, i.e., in a state of packed-ness." This meaning seems intuitively adjectival. Therefore we may be justified in labeling prenominal past participles "adjectival," even those that don't allow intensifiers.

Gerunds

Traditionally, **gerunds** are verbal nouns, meaning that they are nouns derived from verbs. They have the same form as present participles, being composed of a verb stem and a suffixed *-ing* (*running, swimming, studying,* etc., are all both participles and gerunds). "Gerund" comes, interestingly enough, from the word *gerundum,* itself a gerund of the Latin verb *gerere,* 'to carry on'; that is, the ancestor of the grammatical term was an example of itself.)

Gerunds differ from participles simply in that they are nouns, whereas participles are verbs or adjectives. They occur after determiners: *His driving really impresses me, The sanding of the floor will take place tomorrow.* When used to refer to countable events, they can occur with the plural: *We went to three openings/viewings/poetry readings last weekend.* Like all nouns, they can function as subject and direct object.[12]

---

12. Nouns, including gerunds, can function in other ways too. These functions will be taken up in Chapter Seven.

53. a.   As subject: *Swimming* is good for you.
         As direct object: I love *swimming.*

And they form compound nouns, as in <u>*sleeping*</u> *bag* (= *bag for* <u>*sleeping*</u> [noun]).

EXERCISE 9.

A. Identify every underlined word below as a present participle, a "past" participle, or a gerund. For every participle, say whether you believe it represents a verbal or an adjectival use.
  1.   Everyone <u>charged</u> with a crime deserves a fair trial.
  2.   The <u>building</u> of the temple took 20 years.
  3.   Rome wasn't <u>built</u> in a day.
  4.   Clark heard Barbara <u>working</u> in her studio.
  5.   That explanation was <u>disturbing.</u>
  6.   Charlotte needs a new <u>washing</u> machine.
  7.   <u>Leaving</u> town I had a flat tire.
  8.   <u>Leaving</u> town will be good for both of us.
  9.   The <u>roaring</u> crowd drowned out the candicate.

B. Explain, in terms of our discussion of participles, the ambiguity of *Joe was really entertaining last night.*

Conjunctions

You probably learned in school that conjunctions were "linking" or "joining" words, words which joined together various things—not a very useful definition. If a conjunction "joined" words, then any word that could occur between others would be a conjunction. *Is* would be a conjunction, in *A giraffe is an herbivore,* because it "joins" *giraffe* and *an herbivore.* Of course that is silly; no English teacher would tolerate a statement that *is* was a conjunction. Because there are so few conjunctions, we need not formally define them (especially since it is hard to)—instead, we can simply list them (and we shall, below)—but we can describe some of their more salient characteristics.

Traditionally, there are two kinds of conjunctions, **coordinate** and **subordinate**.

Coordinate conjunctions

What is characteristic of coordinate conjunctions is faintly reminiscent of the "joining" notion: the rule that they can occur only between two words or phrases of the same type—two nouns, two verbs, two sentences, etc. The expressions below, which observe this rule, are all right—

54. a. *Bob* and *Kathleen* left. (two nouns)
    b. Bob *ate* and *drank*. (two verbs)
    c. *Bob ate* and *Kathleen drank*. (two sentences)

—but the following, which violate it, are not—

55. a. *I love *Sadie* and *to sunbathe*. (noun and infinitive verb)
    b. *I believe *Morris meowed* and *Ronnie*. (sentence and noun)

Actually, the rule about conjoining like items is stronger than these examples indicate. This can be seen when we try to conjoin subclasses of different sub-categories, e.g., a "concrete" noun like *desk, cat, tree,* or *cup* with an "abstract" noun like *honesty, truth,* or *beauty.* Sequences like the following are decidedly strange:

56. a. ??I love *cats* and *truth*.
    b. ??I love *my mother* and *skiing*.

So far all our examples have been with *and.* The other "coordinate" conjunctions are *but* and *or* (*nor* is also a coordinate conjunction, but it is really a combination of *and* and *not.*[13]) *Or* generally has the same requirement for having the "same type" of item on either side that *and* has; the following examples are OK—

57. a. Nancy went dancing with *Buzzy* or *Izzy*. (two nouns)
    b. *We must all hang together* or *we shall all hang separately*. (two sentences)

—but this one is strange:

58. ??Bob and Carol tried either *re-plumbing their house themselves* or *to do it with only a little bit of help,* and it didn't work. (two different kinds of verb phrases)

But *or* can conjoin two different types of sentences, an **imperative** and a tensed one:

59. *Open up* or *I'll break down the door.*[14]

---

13. That is, *Saul didn't go, nor did Leo* can be paraphrased *Saul didn't go, and Leo did not go (either).*
14. In fact, *and* can conjoin unlike sentence types, as in *Do that again and I'll knock your block off.* This construction is highly informal, though, and may be an exception rather than a counterexample to the generalization that *and* can conjoin only like constituents.

But has the same-type restriction; it cannot conjoin unlike items:

60. a.   Jo *left town Tuesday* but *got back Friday.* (two verb phrases of the same type)
    b.   *I like *to go to bed early* but *getting up late* (infinitive phrase and gerund phrase)

Meanings of coordinate conjunctions

There is more to the meaning of coordinate conjunctions than meets the eye. The scholars who have studied coordinate conjunctions the most are formal logicians. Let us see, in a rather informal way, what logicians have had to say about coordinate conjunctions, and contrast the logical *and, or,* and *but* with their everyday English counterparts.

And: Logicians describe the meaning of *and* in a "truth table," a chart showing the truth value (True or False) of a complex sentence as a function of the truth values of component sentences:

61.   Truth table for *and:*

Sentence 1	Sentence 2	Sentence 1 *and* Sentence 2
T	T	T
T	F	F
F	T	F
F	F	F

If you've never run across truth tables before, persuade yourself that this truth table makes sense by means of the following examples. Take the first case, the one in which both Sentence 1 and Sentence 2 are true. Suppose Sentence 1 is *Moscow is the capital of the USSR* and Sentence 2 is *London is the capital of England.* The big sentence that results from conjoining Sentence 1 and Sentence 2 with *and* is *Moscow is the capital of the USSR and London is the capital of England,* which is true—just as the "T" in the rightmost column of the truth table predicts it should be.

Case two has Sentence 1 being true and Sentence 2 being false. Suppose Sentence 1 is, again, *Moscow is the capital of the USSR,* but now suppose Sentence 2 is *London is the capital of Albania.* Sentence 2 is, of course, false. The truth table predicts that *Moscow is the capital of the USSR and London is the capital of Albania* should be false, and it is.

For practice, you should make up examples for cases three and four from the truth table above.

For a logician, *and* has only the meaning represented by the truth table. That is, the "message" of *and,* from the logical point of view, is that the speaker of *and* is committed to the truth of both of the sentences that *and* is being used to conjoin. (Things get more complicated for cases where *and* joins things other than sentences.) That is, what *and* conveys to the hearer is that the speaker is claiming that both the sentences on either side of *and* are true. And that's all. That's what *and* "means," from the logical point of view.

One difference between logical *and* and the *and* of everyday English is that only logical *and* can be used between two sentences which have nothing at all to do with each other. The following is perfectly well-formed, from the logical point of view: *Kenya is in East Africa, and I promise never to spill cookie dough on the floor again.* But such a sentence is of course quite bizarre, from the point of view of normal language use. English *and,* but not logical *and,* has to be used between sentences that are somehow mutually relevant.

Another difference between logical *and* and English *and* is that English *and* often conveys (i.e., "means," if "means" is taken rather loosely) more than just that the two sentences it connects are true. For one thing, it often conveys that the events or situations denoted by the two sentences on either side of it are ordered in time the same way the sentences are ordered relative to each other in the larger sentence in which they occur. For example, if you say *I climbed out of bed and I jumped into the shower,* you "mean" that you climbed out of bed FIRST and THEN jumped into the shower. Because we tend to order things in language the way they are ordered in the world, it would be strange to say *I jumped into the shower and I climbed out of bed.* But although it would be strange, it would be logical, and in fact the two sentences *I climbed out of bed and jumped into the shower* and *I jumped into the shower and I climbed out of bed* are logically equivalent. That is, they are identical in their "truth conditions"—what the situations in the world must be like in order for the sentences to be true. But the way these sentences are almost all the time used in English, they "mean" different things—the difference being the order in which the two events are implied as having happened.

In the same way, *and* often conveys a relation of causation between the first sentence and the second. If you say, after ice-skating, *I fell on the ice and I scraped my elbow,* you probably mean that your fall caused your elbow-scraping; you most likely aren't talking about two unrelated events, or about the elbow-scraping causing the falling.

So *and,* as used normally in English, frequently carries with it an implication that the sentence to its left is temporally or causally "prior" to the sentence to its right. It is generally believed that these temporal and causal implications are not part of the "meaning" of *and,* but rather that they follow from general principles governing the presentation of information in conversation, to the effect that it is natural and orderly (and therefore appropriate) to present descriptions of events in the same temporal and causal order in which they occur. If this view is right, then we can say that logical *and* and English *and* do not differ in whether or not they imply priority, the apparent difference between them being due to the application of these general principles governing normal conversation. A similar point can be made about the "mutual relevance" requirement. That is, there may be a general requirement that things mentioned adjacently to each other (within some discourse or discourse segment) have to be somehow mutually relevant. If so, this isn't a feature specifically of English *and*, and therefore English *and* and logical *and* can be considered identical, with the general mutual relevance requirement accounting for the oddity of *Kenya is in East Africa and I promise never to spill cookie dough on the floor again*, rather than a feature of the meaning of English *and*.[15]

But: Logicians treat *but* as a synonym of *and;* that is, it has *and*'s truth table. Indeed, the difference between *and* and *but* in natural language has nothing to do with truth, or with truth-conditions, but with expectation. What *but* conveys is that the material that follows it is contrary in some way to an already-built-up "discourse model," i.e., a set of propositions included in or implied by the discourse previous to *but*.

One other aspect of the meaning and grammar of *but* is that there must be at least two meaning differences between the two clauses it connects. Observe:

62. a. *Maya left but Sarah left. (One difference)
    b. *Maya left but Maya stayed. (One difference)
    c. Maya left but Sarah stayed. (Two differences)
    d. Maya left but Maya stayed, too. (Two differences, with *too* in the second clause counting as a difference.)

Or: The logicians' truth table for *or* is different from the one for *and*. It looks like this:

63.   Truth table for *or:*

Sentence 1	Sentence 2	Sentence 1 *or* Sentence 2
T	T	T
T	F	T
F	T	T
F	F	F

Most *or*'s used in natural language convey an **exclusive** meaning, one with alternatives—that is, that either Sentence 1 or Sentence 2 is true, but not both. For instance, if you stay, *Well either the Yankees will win or they will lose*, you are asserting that only one of two possibilities will occur. Since most occurrences of *or* in everyday talk are part of utterances which convey such

---

15. The work of, and inspired by, H. P. Grice is the source of the ideas here about general principles governing cooperative conversation. Grice's most influential work is the paper "Logic and Conversation," in P. Cole and J. Morgan, *Syntax and Semantics 3: Speech Acts* (New York: Academic Press, 1975).

an assertion, the first line of the truth table above seems counterintuitive to many people. But in fact **inclusive** *or* does occur in English:

64. a. Anyone who fails a test or who turns the term paper in late will automatically get no higher than a D− in the course.
b. If you are a senior, or over 17, you have to meet with the job information counselor in the principal's office.

It is consistent with (a) that a person could, according to the assertion conveyed by the sentence, BOTH fail a test AND turn in a term paper late, and have no hope of getting a higher grade than a D−. It is consistent with (b) that an 18-year-old senior has to meet with the counselor. In both cases, *or* is inclusive.

Inclusive *or* as in these cases must be accounted for, as well as cases of exclusive *or*. But since a sentence like *London is in England or Washington is in the U.S.* does not seem false—rather, it seems true but a funny thing to say—it is possible to treat all *or*'s as having the same meaning (the logical one, represented by the truth table), and assume that the exclusive interpretation of an *or* sentence, when necessary, comes from context rather than a different *or*. That is, the exclusive interpretation comes not from a different *or*, but is added from the situation described by a sentence, if the situation is one which involves an exclusive choice (like winning vs. losing a baseball game).

EXERCISE 10.

A. Identify the following sentences as conveying an exclusive or inclusive interpretation:
1. Which is worse, a strikeout or a groundout?
2. If you buy tires or jewelry you have to pay excise tax.
3. Max had no formal training in illustrating, graphic arts, or paste-up.
4. Who owns that beach house—or rather, who rents it?
5. Ripe tomatoes are red or yellow.
6. Take it or leave it.
7. Should an ambitious college graduate be barred from gainful employment just because he cannot read, write, or cipher very well?

• **B.** Explain what is odd about each of the following sentences (if you find some sentences not odd at all, try to see what might seem odd to some speakers):
1. ?That halfback may be small, but he is slow.
2. ?Bugs jumped into his hole and dashed away from Elmer Fudd.
3. ?The President is the executor of the laws but he is the Commander-in-Chief of the armed forces.
4. ?I wrote a letter to my grandmother yesterday, and six men can fit into the back of a Ford.

Subordinate conjunctions

Subordinate conjunctions include *although, while, when, since, because, after, before, until, unless, as,* and *if.* The word *that* can be considered a subordinate conjunction, too, but it is a different kind from the others. The first set can be called "adverbial" subordinate conjunctions, for reasons that will become clear momentarily. *That* is usually called a "complementizer," and will be discussed separately.

Adverbial subordinate conjunctions

What makes words like *although, while,* and *when* "subordinate"? How are they different from coordinate conjunctions?

Let's examine a few examples. In the sentences below, the italicized sequences are "subordinate clauses" (i.e., subordinate sentences), the underlined words are subordinate conjunctions.

65. a.   Max was complaining, although *he had won the pizza.*
     b.   Sky King re-roofed his garage while *it was raining.*
     c.   David Carkeet's latest novel surprised me when *I read it.*
     d.   Ronnie relied on Nancy, since *she had never let him down.*

What makes the clauses subordinate? Mainly, they are part of larger constituents that cannot stand alone:

66. a.   *Although he had won the prize.
     b.   *While it was raining.
     c.   *When I read it.
     d.   *Since she had never let him down.

Therefore these containing constructions are not "independent"; rather, they are dependent. Since the clauses are inside them, they are dependent too.

We have just suggested that subordinate conjunctions are connected to the subordinate clauses that follow them. This may surprise you; you may feel that the two sentences below are structured similarly:

67. a.   Jo left early and Max stayed late.
     b.   Jo left early since Max stayed late.

But there is good reason to believe they are not. There is a strong reason to believe that *since* and *Max stayed late* are, in fact, very closely connected to each other: the fact that they "move" as a unit. As we shall see in Chapter Six, if a group of words in a sentence "moves" as a unit, it makes sense to assume that the group is a unit of syntactic structure. What does "move as a unit" mean? It means that there is a related sentence with the same meaning as the original, in which a sequence of words appears in a different position:

68. Since Max stayed late, Jo left early.

The relation between example (67b) and example (68) can be thought of as one in which the sequence *since Max stayed late* was "moved" from its position in (67b) to its position in (68).

69.

No such "movement" is possible for the sequence *and Max stayed late:*

70. *And Max stayed late, Jo left early.

Hence it is reasonable to conclude that the conjunction *and* is not syntactically connected to the sentence that follows it, but that the conjunction *since,* and conjunctions like it, are.

All the "subordinate" conjunctions have the property of "movement" which we have just described:

71. a. Rae left although Jon stayed. = Although Jon stayed, Rae left.
  b. Sam smiled when Jane laughed. = When Jane laughed, Sam smiled.
  c. Al smoked while Mo drank. = While Mo drank, Al smoked.
  d. Mannie painted the ceiling since Kim had painted the walls. = Since Kim had painted the walls, Mannie painted the ceiling.
  e. Smith criticized the report because Wesson asked him to. = Because Wesson asked him to, Smith criticized the report.
  f. Martinez doubled after Gwynn singled. = After Gwynn singled, Martinez doubled.
  g. Nixon erased the tapes before anyone could hear them. = Before anyone could hear them, Nixon erased the tapes.
  h. Ike will keep smoking until he gets cancer. = Until he gets cancer, Ike will keep smoking.
  i. Susan will go unless Mary urges her not to. = Unless Mary urges her not to, Susan will go.
  j. I will tickle your feet mercilessly if you do that again. = If you do that again I will tickle your feet mercilessly.

The "subordinate conjunction" that

That as a "subordinate conjunction" occurs as in the following examples:

72.　a.　Smith believes *that* Wesson spilled the beans.
　　　b.　No one doubts *that* the moon is made of green cheese.
　　　c.　*That* Rosencrantz should leave Guildenstern is clear to all.
　　　d.　*That* you left the computer on proves *that* you were present at the scene of the robbery.

In the sentences above, *that* signals that what follows is a sentence within a sentence. *That* is used at the front of embedded clauses when those clauses function rather like noun phrases, that is, as direct objects (as in a and b) or as subjects (as in c). (In d *that* introduces a subject clause to the left of the verb *proves* and an object clause to the right of the verb *proves*.) In Chapter Eight, we will examine more extensively these subordinate clauses introduced by the "complementizer" *that*.

Pronouns

Traditionally, pronouns are words that stand in place of a noun:

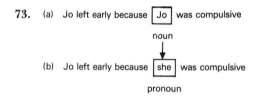

73.　(a)　Jo left early because ⌈ Jo ⌉ was compulsive
　　　　　　　　　　　　　　　noun

　　　(b)　Jo left early because ⌈ she ⌉ was compulsive
　　　　　　　　　　　　　　　pronoun

If we modify the definition so as to include not just nouns, but noun phrases, it will work fine for examples like this:

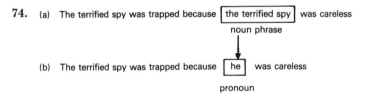

74.　(a)　The terrified spy was trapped because ⌈ the terrified spy ⌉ was careless
　　　　　　　　　　　　　　　　　　　　　　　noun phrase

　　　(b)　The terrified spy was trapped because ⌈ he ⌉ was careless
　　　　　　　　　　　　　　　　　　　　　　　pronoun

So a reasonable revised definition of "pronoun" is: a word used in place of a noun phrase.[16]

One technical term prominent in any examination of pronouns is **antecedent**. The antecedent of a pronoun is the noun phrase that occurs in the same sentence or text as the pronoun and which gives the pronoun its reference. In the examples above, the antecedents of *she* and *he* are the previous occurrences of *Jo* and *the terrified spy*, respectively.

---

16. Even a proper noun can be considered a noun phrase as well as a noun, as we shall see in Chapter Six.

EXERCISE 11. Identify the antecedents of the italicized pronouns in the following sentences.

1. Several of the fans threw beer on the umpire, because *they* were dissatisfied with his decision.
2. Jones decided that the reporters covering the story were being devious, and that *they* should be replaced.
3. The possibility that snow might slow down our trip worried my parents, and *it* did me, too.
4. If anyone comes in late, *they* should go quietly to the back of the room and take a seat.
5. Like any language, at *its* most basic level English is raw sound.
6. As he dodged, Smiley swung the chain into the chest of his pursuer. *Doing so* prevented his pursuer from grabbing his arm as he dashed down the dark alley.

First-person and second-person pronouns

The preceding discussion has applied to "third person" pronouns, that is, *he, she, it, they,* etc.

First and second person pronouns—*I, me, you, we,* and *us*—do not fit the definition we have established for pronouns. That is, they don't replace anything. Nor do they have antecedents, ever. If Rose is speaking, she cannot use the name *Rose* as antecedent for *I:* she cannot say *Rose left early because I was anxious to get home before dark* if she means *I* to refer to *Rose.* So, by the traditional definition of pronouns, first and second person "pronouns" aren't pronouns.

However, because of their morphological similarity to third person pronouns, they are standardly given the name "pronoun." The morphological similarity shows up in the following table:

75. English pronoun morphology:

	Subject	Object	Determiner	Possessive Pronoun
Singular:				
1st person	I	me	my	mine
2nd person	you	you	your	yours
3rd person	he	him	his	his
	she	her	her	hers
	it	it	its	its
Plural:				
1st person	we	us	our	ours
2nd person	you	you	your	yours
3rd person	they	them	their	theirs

From this table, it can be seen that the patterning that shows up with "real" pronouns, that is, third person pronouns, also shows up with first and second person "pseudo-pronouns." The patterning, of course, is that all pronouns have a parallel set of related forms, for subject, object, determiner, and possessive pronoun functions.

There is a grammatical distinction, of course, between possessive forms like *my* (labeled "determiners" in the chart above) and possessive forms like *mine* (labeled "possessive pronouns"). Forms of the first type are blends of a morpheme referring to the possessor and a morpheme meaning "possessive," i.e., "-'s". Consider *my* as an example. *My* contains a morpheme referring to the possessor of something—the speaker, since *my* is related to *I*—and a morpheme that means "possessive." Abstractly, we can regard *my* as being equivalent to an underlying form *I's*. Similarly, *your* is, abstractly, *you's*. *His* doesn't look all that different from its underlying form, *he's*. Forms of this type are determiners; they occur exactly where articles and demonstratives do:

76. a.   my book, your book, his book, her book, our big book
   b.   a book, the book, this book, that big book

So we'll call them **pronominal determiners**. In some traditional grammars, they are called possessive adjectives. Of course they're not adjectives, by our earlier definition, but they do have a modifying function, so the traditional term is not entirely inappropriate.

Possessive pronouns of the *mine, yours, theirs* type abstractly contain three morphemes: the two that make up pronominal determiners and a third one serving as a pronoun for the thing possessed. So *mine* is, abstractly, *I's "thing"* or *I's "one."* We'll call these forms **possessive pronouns**.

The following diagrams show the grammatical distinction between these types of pronouns in terms of the kinds of antecedents they can have.

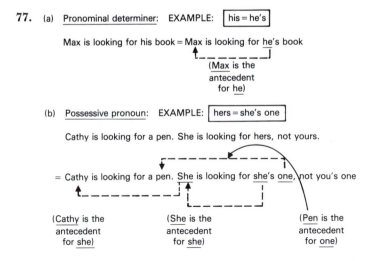

Other kinds of pronouns

Reflexive pronouns

A reflexive pronoun, which always ends with *-self* or *-selves,* refers back to the noun phrase functioning as subject of its own clause. Observe the following examples.

78. a. *Max* loved *himself*
b. **Max* believed that Sheila loved *himself*

In (a), the reflexive pronoun *himself* refers to the subject noun phrase *Max.* But in (b), the reflexive pronoun *himself* cannot refer to subject noun phrase *Max* because *Max* is not the subject of the clause that *himself* is in. The word sequence *Sheila loved himself* is a clause (or would be, if it were grammatical).

Reciprocal pronouns

There are only two reciprocal pronouns in English, the phrases *each other* and *one another.* Like reflexive pronouns, reciprocal pronouns have to have their antecedents in their own clause:

79. a. *Alex* and *Sadie* admired *each other.*
b. **Alex* said that *Sadie* admired *each other.*

Demonstrative pronouns

Demonstrative pronouns include *this, that, these,* and *those,* when they are used without a following noun, as in *This* (pointing) *I like.* When these words have a following noun, they are determiners.

Indefinite pronouns

The only indefinite pronoun which refers to an antecedent (and thus, the only "true" indefinite pronoun by our definition of a pro-word as a word which replaces a phrase) is the word *one. One* actually has as its antecedent only a part of a noun phrase, not a whole noun phrase, as the following example shows:

80.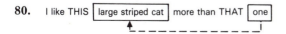

The interpretation is that the speaker likes "this" large striped cat more than "that" large striped cat. There is, of course, another interpretation of this sentence, in which the speaker likes "this" large striped cat more than "that" CAT. (A diagram showing the latter interpretation would have a box around the word *cat*.) In the example above, the boxed phrase *large striped cat* is not a noun phrase. This is clear from the fact that it doesn't occur in normal noun phrase positions: for example, at the beginning of a sentence, functioning as subject—

81. *Large striped cat sat on the window sill.

—or after a verb, functioning as object—

82. *I love large striped cat.

So *one* is a "pro-partial noun phrase"—a cumbersome name indeed, and we will somewhat inaccurately continue to call it a pronoun.

Indefinite "pronouns" which don't have antecedents (like the personal pronouns *I* and *you*) are the *some-* and *any-* words: *someone, somebody, somewhere, something, somehow* and their *any-* counterparts, *anyone, anybody, anywhere,* and *anything.* (*Anyhow,* which at first glance fits into this group, is not a pronoun, but a "discourse connective." Discourse connectives will be discussed below.)

Relative pronouns

Relative pronouns stand for a noun phrase in a **relative clause** (a construction which will be discussed in Chapter Nine). The italicized words below are relative pronouns. Relative pronouns have antecedents, the capitalized words.

83. a. A MAN *whom* I know bought a smoked ham from Vermont.
   b. This is THE WOMAN *whom* I told you about.
   c. Here is THE OAK DESK *which* is missing a drawer.
   d. This guy I know bought A CAR *that* didn't have any doors.
   e. A word processor is A USEFUL TOOL with *which* you can write all your term papers.
   f. Mother, this is THE BOY with *whom* I climbed Mt. Washington last summer.
   g. I know A PLACE *where* you can get banana-orange milkshakes for fifty cents.
   h. There will be A TIME *when* all this will seem funny to you.

The examples (a)–(f) contain relative pronouns which replace noun phrases. Thus, example (a) can be awkwardly paraphrased "A man (I know the man) bought. . . . ," with *who* replacing *the man.* The relative pronouns in examples (f), (g), and (h) replace noun phrases which contain prepositional phrases. That is, *where* in (g) stands for "a place at which," and *when* in (h) stands for "a time at which." Note that *when* can be a relative pronoun, as here, as well as a subordinate conjunction, as in *They left when she came.* The difference is that the relative pronoun *when* has an antecedent (always a word with some time meaning, like *time*), but the subordinate conjunction has no antecedent.

Interrogative pronouns

Interrogative pronouns are *wh-* words used as question words in *wh-* questions—questions like *Who is there?* and *Which did you buy?* All the relative pronouns except *that* can be used as interrogative pronouns. Interrogative pronouns also include some words which are not relative pronouns: *what* and *how.*

Pro-words for other phrase types

English has a small set of pronoun-like words which refer to words and phrases other than nouns and noun phrases. For instance, the word *so* can be a pro-word for a sentence:

84. Jo asked if | Max would quit | , and I responded that I didn't really think | so |
          sentence

It can function the same way: *Max says it will rain today, but I don't believe it.* *So* can also be a pro-adjective:[17] *Willie isn't really lazy; he just seems so.* The phrase *do so* is a "pro-verb phrase":

85. Roxie | wrote the great American novel | before her major rival could | do so |
          — VP —

Thus can function as a pro-manner adverb:

86. Manny cut the paper | painstakingly | ; doing it | thus |
        — Man. Adv.

he was able to avoid the mistakes he had made the first time.

The word *there* can function as a pro-Prepositional Phrase:

---

17. Actually a pro-Adjective Phrase.

87. Mo was ⎡in his room⎤ , and he stayed ⎡there⎤ until allowed to leave

PP — diagram with dashed connector line

EXERCISE 12. In the following paragraph, identify all pronouns or other pro-forms, and identify the antecedent for each one.

> Whenever Max went to a ball game, he sat in the distant left-field stands, alone, with an empty seat to either side, so he could store at first his evening refreshments and later their refuse: a succession of empty beer cups, a dusting of broken peanut shells, mustard-smeared wrap from his hotdogs. Sitting thus arranged, during lulls in the game Max would shout "we want Sims!," in a voice made small and tinny by its isolation. Sims was the bullpen catcher, a team employee not on the playing roster. Whenever Max did this, other fans looked at him curiously, but without malice. The home team was no good—they lost regularly, with an average run differential of 2.5, Max had computed—so fans, including Max, didn't attend games to cheer victories. Rather, for most, the game was a social occasion. For Max it was something else. He amused himself remembering, in the shiny new stadium, the cigar smells of Connie Mack Stadium from his boyhood in Philadelphia.

Prepositions, Particles, and Two-word Verbs

Prepositions

It's not easy to define prepositions. They are typically little words, and often have meanings which have something to do with location or direction: *in, on, above, under, behind, across, inside, below, at, from, to, with.* But not all do: *of* has nothing to do with location, and neither does the *by* of passive sentences (*The press was not deceived BY Nixon*).

Prepositions occur right before noun phrases:

88. (a) in ⎡the cavern⎤
NP

(b) from ⎡Washington⎤
NP

(c) beside ⎡the newly painted lamppost⎤
NP

(d) at ⎡the center of the ring⎤
NP

although sometimes the noun phrase gets moved away from the preposition:

89. 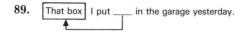 I put ___ in the garage yesterday.

But "possibility of occurrence right before noun phrases" isn't sufficient to identify prepositions, since other word classes can occur there, for example verbs. It is possible to "define" prepositions by means of a list, since prepositions are a small closed[18] class. Here is a list of the more common English prepositions:

90. about, above, across, after, along, among, around, at, before, behind, below, beneath, beside, between, beyond, by, despite, down, during, for, from, in, inside, into, like, near, of, off, on, out, outside, over, since, through, throughout, till, to, toward, under, underneath, until, up, upon, with, within, without

When noun phrases sometimes get moved away from prepositions (as in Example 89 above), sometimes a preposition is left ending a sentence. There is a prescriptive rule against this, as most students have been told. This rule is honored more in the breach than in the observance; anyone who says, in casual conversation, "There goes the girl with whom I went to the movies last night," would probably be subject to severe criticism, for using an inappropriate level of formality. No less a figure than Winston Churchill supposedly made fun of this prescriptive rule, with his famous retort, "That, Madam, is something up with which I will not put."

Particles and two-word verbs

Particles look just like prepositions, and, in fact, form a proper subset of the words in the class of prepositions. Some differ from prepositions in that they are "movable":

91. a. I want you to look *over* this report   =
   b. I want you to look this report *over*
   c. Ruth quickly drank *down* her beer   =
   d. Ruth quickly drank her beer *down*
   e. Izzy ate *up* all his spinach   =
   f. Izzy ate all his spinach *up*

In fact, such particles HAVE TO move, if the noun phrase they occur with is a pronoun:

18. Prepositions depart the language rarely, and are added to it even more rarely. One that is alive only vestigially (possibly known only to crossword puzzle fans and readers of older literature) is *anent,* meaning "in line with, in front of," as in *A cricket ball on a line with the wicket is anent it* (Oxford English Dictionary, compact edition, p. 81).

92. a. Liz fired up *the team* with her fighting spirit.
   b. *Liz fired up *them* with her fighting spirit.
   c. Liz fired *them* up with her fighting spirit.

But some particles are immovable:

93. a. I came *across* a promising review.
   b. *I came a promising review *across*.

94. a. The Smiths call *on* their relatives without warning.
   b. *The Smiths call their relatives *on* without warning.

How are immovable particles to be distinguished from prepositions? First, by meaning: an immovable particle forms a semantic unit with the verb immediately preceding it, whereas prepositions are semantically independent of preceding verbs. In (93) and (94), it makes sense to take *came across* and *call on* as "two-word verbs" (sometimes called "phrasal verbs"): *came across* being paraphrasable by *find* or *encounter, call on* by *visit.* When *across* or *on* are prepositions, as in *walk across the street* or *sit on the table,* they don't form meaning chunks together with preceding verbs.

Second, two-word verbs can be distinguished from a sequence of verb + preposition grammatically: a preposition and its following noun phrase is movable, whereas a particle and a following noun phrase is not:

95. a. Preposition + noun phrase:
      i.   sit on the chair
      ii. sit on what?
      iii. on what should I sit?
   b. Particle + noun phrase:
      i.   come across a review
      ii. come across what?
      iii. *across what did you come?

In (a), the preposition + noun phrase sequence *on what* can be moved to sentence-initial position, but in (b) the particle + noun phrase sequence *across what* cannot.

EXERCISE 13. Explain, both semantically and grammatically, the differences between the following two sentences:

a. I turned him on.
b. I turned on him.

The Negator: *Not*

In traditional grammar often the class of "adverbs" is used as a kind of trash-heap to put hard-to-classify words in. *Not* is often thus dumped into the adverb class, but it is probably better described as the only member of the class "negator." It has a unique place of occurrence: directly after the first auxiliary verb.

96.

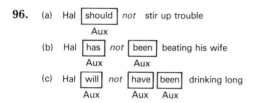

If there is no (overt) auxiliary verb, *not* goes into the auxiliary slot in the sentence, preceded by an occurrence of *do* with the same tense and number as the original verb (details will be given in Chapter Six):

97. a. Ann studied hard.
 b. Ann did not study hard.

In (b), *did* is past tense, as is *studied* in (a).

The Existential Marker: *There*

There are two *there*'s in English. One expresses location, often as a pro-word for a locative prepositional phrase, as in *Don't go <u>near the woods</u>; I told you never to go <u>there</u>!*

Another *there*, the **existential** one, expresses the existence of something: *There is a god in heaven; there ought to be a traffic light on corner of Chestnut and Main; In 1492 there was a widespread belief that the earth was flat.* In traditional grammar, this *there* is sometimes called an (or the) "expletive." English is not alone in using what is otherwise a locative word for the existential marker; French uses *y*, meaning *there-locative*, for the same purpose:

98. Il *y*   a   trois chiens dans la rue
 It *there* has three dogs in the street
 "There are three dogs in the street"

French also uses—in the same construction—the word for 'have'—*a*—for the existential construction. Many other languages do this as well, for instance Spanish, which uses an archaic form of the verb meaning 'have':

99. *Hay* tres perros en el camino
It-has three dogs in the street
"There are three dogs in the street"

Discourse Connectives

Words like *however, nevertheless, moreover, therefore,* and *thus,* traditionally labeled "conjunctive adverbs," function to establish some sort of connection or relevance between a sentence and the preceding discourse context. In the following discourse, notice how *nevertheless* and *however* tie a sentence to preceding context:

100. It is true that purely quantitative reductions do not remove the factors of instability and the incentives for preventive attack that the developments of the past fifteen years . . . have created. Nevertheless, reductions in weapons that cannot be used without disastrous consequence . . . are obviously desirable; and an agreement on reducing their numbers would also improve the political relations between the great powers.
However, even this road remains strewn with obstacles . . .

(Stanley Hoffman, "An Icelandic Saga," *New York Review of Books,* Nov. 20, 1986, p. 15)

Nongrammatical Word Classes

There are various words and word-types which play no grammatical role in sentences; that is, they have no grammatical connection to other words in the utterances in which they occur. These include politeness markers like *please, thank you, excuse me, pardon,* etc.; attention-getters like *hey!* or *yo!;* words of greeting and leavetaking like *hello* and *goodbye;* and expletives or interjections[19] like *hell!, shit!, damn!, Christ!, wow, man, psst!,* and *shh.*

SUMMARY AND CONCLUSION

This wraps up our examination of the defining or typical characteristics of all the English "parts of speech." We have replaced traditional semantic definitions with grammatical ones, and examined in some detail the basic grammatical properties of the major and minor word classes.

Our next task is to look a little deeper into the mysteries of nouns and verbs. Each class requires some division into subclasses, and there are important grammatical and semantic characteristics exhibited by members of each class.

19. In traditional grammar these words have sometimes been referred to as "ejaculations."

ADDITIONAL EXERCISE

Identify the word class of every word in the following text, except the italicized *it*.

When in the course of human events, *it* becomes necessary for one people to dissolve the political bands which have connected them with another, and to assume among the powers of the earth the separate and equal station to which the laws of nature and of nature's God entitle them, a decent respect to the opinions of mankind requires that they should declare the causes which impel them to the separation.

We hold these truths to be self-evident, that all men are created equal, that they are endowed by their creator with certain inalienable rights, that among these are life, liberty, and the pursuit of happiness.

REFERENCES

GRICE, H. P. 1975. "Logic and Conversation," in P. Cole and J. Morgan, eds., *Syntax and Semantics 3: Speech Acts.* New York: Academic Press.

HOFFMAN, STANLEY. 1986. "An Icelandic Saga," *New York Review of Books,* Nov. 20, p. 15.

MITCHELL, RICHARD. 1979. *Less Than Words Can Say.* Boston: Little, Brown and Company.

Chapter Five

NOUNS AND VERBS: SUBCLASSES AND FEATURES

To say that a certain word is a particular "part of speech" does not always tell enough about it. There are grammatical properties which have to be described partly in terms of "subclasses," divisions within word classes. In this chapter we will discuss some important subclasses of nouns and verbs. Besides examining subclasses, we will look at certain grammatical features that are typical of almost all nouns and almost all verbs—e.g., number on nouns and tense on verbs.

NOUNS: SUBCLASSES AND FEATURES

Subclasses

Calling a word a noun accounts for its ability to take a possessive suffix, to function as subject, direct object, and indirect object, and to occur after an article or an adjective. But there are other grammatical properties which only some types of noun have. For instance, in Chapter Four, we saw that the ability to occur with a plural suffix seemed a reasonable criterion for calling a word a noun. But this was not quite as reasonable as it seemed. Although only nouns can take plurals, not all nouns can. *Honesty* and *rice* can't, for example. One important distinction in the class of nouns, then, is between those that can, and those that cannot, take plurals. These two subclasses of nouns are **count** nouns and **mass** nouns.

Count and mass nouns

Count nouns are those which take plurals, and which have the further properties of being able to occur with numbers, the quantifiers *many* and *few*, and the article *a(an)*:

1.   **COUNT NOUNS:**
   a. Five *sticks* lay upon the table.
   b. Did they sell many *pots* at the crafts fair?
   c. I only saw a few *sailboats* on the bay.
   d. I want to buy a *car*.

Mass nouns cannot occur with any of these:

2.   **MASS NOUNS:**
   a. *Five *butter* lay upon the table
   b. *Did they sell many *rice* at the market?
   c. *I only saw a few *sand* at the beach.
   d. *I want to buy a *salt*.

Mass nouns can occur with the quantifiers *much* and *little*, but count nouns cannot:

3. a. Did you buy much *butter*? (Mass noun)
   b. *Did you buy much *sticks*? (Count noun)
   c. I didn't get much *satisfaction* from that movie. (Mass noun)
   d. *I didn't get much *laughs* from that movie. (Count noun)
   e. We sold very little *rice* at the bazaar. (Mass noun)
   f. *We sold very little *houses* working as real estate agents last summer. (Count noun)

(Of course, (f) is acceptable if *little* is taken as an adjective modifying *houses* rather than as a quantifier.)

The count/noncount distinction has a semantic basis; typical count nouns can be used to refer to things which are by their nature countable—things which occur in the world in discrete, individual pieces: cars, sticks, trees, people, windows, beliefs, games, events, etc. Typical noncount nouns are used to refer to things which are by their nature uncountable—things which occur in the world in liquid or mass form, or in nondiscrete quantities: masses like fog, oil, water, butter, air, electricity, and glass, and abstract "things" like honesty, beauty, truth, satisfaction, and significance. But don't take this apparently sensible semantic basis too seriously. Many mass nouns denote things that do occur in little countable pieces: rice, salt, sand, sugar; and there are count nouns like *oats*[1] which denote things just

---

1. *Oats* is a count noun by virtue of being plural and occurring with count determiners: *these*,

as mass-like and uncountable as most things denoted by mass nouns. Moreover, while many mass nouns denote things which actually occur in nondiscrete masses (*water, air*) in most people's experience, many other mass nouns denote things which IN MOST PEOPLE'S EXPERIENCE actually occur in packaged quantities—*butter* (in sticks or in pats), *oil* (in cans), *milk* (in cartons), *ice* (in cubes). It would be almost as logical for these words to be count nouns. Some, of course, are count nouns in the language of young children acquiring English as a first language ("Mommy, can I have some of those ices?"), and others are count nouns in jargons or in special situations: in restaurants, *milk* is regularly a count noun. (Because of this, arriving home after a cross-country car trip which required many restaurant meals, my four-year-old requested "a milk" for his dinner beverage.) In addition, there is a regular process of turning mass nouns into count nouns when a speaker wishes to focus on the type or class of something. In this way oenologists can talk of *wines,* cheese fanciers can compare *cheeses,* and agricultural scientists can contrast *grains,* although in everyday speech *wine, cheese,* and *grain* are mass nouns.

EXERCISE 1. Identify the following nouns as count or mass:

paper, steel, glue, pen, truth, hydrogen, uranium, brick, lamp, love, muscle, stomach, typography, spelling, footnote, democracy.

The proper/common distinction

Proper nouns are names. A name is a word which has a unique **referent** and no other meaning beside this referent. (The "referent" of a noun or noun phrase is the thing in the world that the noun or noun phrase is used to refer to.) The meaning of *Jack* is the guy we all know as Jack; the word has no other meaning.

Common nouns have much more complicated meanings than just their referents. The meaning of *table* is a complicated set of information which enables a speaker of English to pick out possible referents for *table.* (Some linguists believe that the "meaning" of a word is a kind of function— in the mathematical sense—from this complicated set of information to a set of possible referents.)

So much for the semantic differences between proper and common nouns. What about the grammatical differences?

---

those rather than *this, that.* However, it doesn't occur in the singular, nor can it take specific quantifiers (e.g., numbers: **five oats*).

Proper nouns occur without determiners. Common nouns require them, except when they are plural.

4. a. Proper nouns:
    i.   *Max* left on time.
    ii. I visited *Jane* in the hospital.
    iii. *The *Max* left on time.
    iv. *I visited *that Jane* in the hospital.
  b. Common nouns:
    i.   The *yo-yo* got broken.
    ii. I persuaded a *farmer* not to sell his corn.
    iii. *Yo-yo* got broken.
    iv. *I persuaded *farmer* not to sell his corn.
  c. Plural common nouns:
    i.   *Yo-yos* can get tangled up easily.
    ii. I love to visit *farmers*.

Besides semantic and grammatical differences, proper and common nouns have the obvious orthographic difference that proper nouns are most often written with a capital first letter, and common nouns are not.

EXERCISE 2. The claim was made above that proper nouns had no meaning other than their reference. Is this true? Do *George, Alice, Fido,* and *Fluffy* mean no more than the individual they refer to? Are nicknames like *Fatso* and *Red* relevant here? What about *Antarctica?* If proper nouns do mean more than just their reference, how are these meanings like and unlike the meanings common nouns have?

A note on semantic subclasses of nouns

Nouns like *man, Joe, girl, student,* and *analyst* are semantically distinguished from nouns like *cup, tree, stag,* and *molecule;* the first group denotes humans, the second non-human entities. This has repercussions for co-occurrence: human nouns can serve as subjects for verbs like *graduate, chuckle, marry, tease,* and *seduce,* while non-human nouns can't: e.g., *The cup will graduate next spring.* This is not a grammatical fact, though, as can be seen from the fact that if someone told you *The cup will graduate next spring* or *My toothbrush seduced my razor,* you would be inclined to suggest psychiatric help for your interlocutor, not a remedial English class.

A host of restrictions of this sort can be found. But since they're not grammatical restrictions, but have to do with our beliefs and expectations about the world, we will have no more to say about them in this book. (Since they are not grammatical restrictions, go ahead and mentally delete the asterisks in the previous paragraph.)[2]

Features

Grammatical features that are associated with nouns include **person, number, gender case,** and **definiteness.**

Person

Person[3] is the choice among different points of view: the speaker's ("first" person), the hearer's ("second" person), and another's ("third" person). First person is represented in English by the singular pronoun *I* (and its associated forms *me, my, mine,* and *myself*) and the plural pronoun *we* (and its associated forms *us, our, ours,* and *ourselves*). Second person is represented by *you* and its associated forms. Third person is represented by the the pronouns *he, she, it,* and *they,* and their associated forms, and by most nouns. Person is also represented by verb agreement. But English verbs have minimal agreement requirements in terms of person: with most verbs, only present tense forms are marked for person, and then only third person singular (e.g., *he sees*). *Be* is the only verb that has special forms to agree with subject noun phrases in other persons, and then only in the singular:

5. a. 1st person singular: I now <u>am</u>
   b. 2nd person singular: you now <u>are</u>
   c. 3rd person singular: she now <u>is</u>
   d. 1st, 2nd, and 3rd person plural: we/you/they now <u>are</u>

Number

Number is the choice among one, two, or more than two referents for a noun. English distinguishes only between one and more than one referent, but there are languages (ancient Greek, for example), which have three numbers: singular; dual, for exactly two referents; and plural, for

---

2. Actually, semantic subclasses of this sort do have a minimal grammatical effect. As we saw in Chapter Four, conjunction is possible only between a pair of nouns of the same "type," as shown by impossible constructions like **I love my mother and skiing.* Just as impossible is something like **I hate Bob and dishonesty.*

3. Person is usually thought of as being more associated with verbs and pronouns than nouns, but it is basically a pattern in which a verb agrees with its subject noun phrase. Since the noun phrase determines the person agreement, it is convenient to discuss person as a feature of nouns and pronouns.

three or more. English number is marked on nouns by the plural suffix *-s* (realized as [s], [z], and [əz]) and by the absence of a suffix on singular nouns. Third person present tense verbs agree, singular ones taking the suffix *-s* (i.e., [s], [z], and [əz]), plural ones taking Ø.

One problem with numbers has to do with whether **collective** nouns like *committee, team, Congress,* and *aristocracy* take singular or plural verb agreement. In British usage they generally take plural agreement: *the committee have decided . . . , the aristocracy are up in arms.* In American usage, they almost always take singular agreement (*the committee has decided,* etc.). In both dialects (as pointed out in Celce 1970) plural agreement involving pro-forms is possible, depending on the speaker's view of the referred-to group as a unit or as a set of individuals:

6. a. The committee criticized itself.
   b. The committee criticized themselves.
   c. The committee criticized its chair.
   d. The committee criticized their chair.

A similar problem is whether nouns with Latin plural endings—e.g., *data, criteria*—are plural in English. Most Americans treat *data* as a mass noun, both saying and accepting *this data shows . . . ,* and simply do not have as part of their system a singular *datum.* Fewer Americans use *criteria* as a singular; more have a singular *criterion* and a plural *criteria.*

More serious are agreement conflicts of the following types, discussed in Celce-Murcia and Larsen-Freeman 1983:

1. With **correlative** expressions (*either . . . or* and *neither . . . nor*): which is right, the (a) or the (b) sentences below?

7. a. Either the department heads or the dean decide.
   b. Either the department heads or the dean decides.
8. a. Neither the department heads nor the dean decide.
   b. Neither the department heads nor the dean decides.

Prescriptive grammar requires the noun phrase nearest the agreeing verb to determine the verb's number, so prescriptively both (b) sentences above are right. This reflects most actual usage, but by no means all, with more doubt being manifested in contexts with *neither . . . nor* than with *either . . . or.* Such doubt about the correct grammar is rather uncommon in language, but far from unknown; as the great anthropological linguist Edward Sapir said, "All grammars leak."[4]

2. With *none:* which is better, (a) or (b) below?

---

4. A nice example of a leak, or hole, in English grammar is tag questions, as mentioned in Chapter One. On the model of *she is late, isn't she?,* what is the proper tag question for *I'm late. . . ?* For more such problems with tags, see Langendoen 1970.

9. a.   None of the ties really fits him.
    b.   None of the ties really fit him.

Prescriptively, *none,* as the head word of a noun phrase (which contains a prepositional phrase, *of . . .),* governs the agreement, and prescriptively *none* is singular. So prescriptively (a) above is right, and (b) wrong. But actual usage, according to Celce-Murcia and Larsen-Freeman, seems to divide fairly evenly between singular and plural agreement. Number agreement with *none,* then, is another "leak" in English grammar.

Another problem with English number agreement—a fairly minor one, but the target of much prescriptive attention—is the choice of number (singular or plural) for pronouns which refer to **singular indefinite noun phrases,** often quantified phrases like *each person* or *every student.* According to prescriptive grammar, these are not only singular, but masculine, so that the "correct" pronoun for such a phrase is *he.* So semantic mismatches between language and the world occur as when a gender-mixed group is referred to in the following way: *Every student who turns in his paper late will lose half of his grade.* Often speakers attempt to get around the problem by using a plural pronoun like *they* or *their: Every student who turns in their paper late will lose half of their grade.* This makes semantic sense,[5] at least, but is prescriptively ungrammatical. What English needs, of course, is a new gender-free third-person singular pronoun. It is unlikely that one will be developed, however, since pronouns are so commonly used that they are resistant to change. More likely is a continued "incorrect" use of the gender-free third person plural pronouns to refer to singular antecedents, and other avoidance tactics—like the use of plural antecedents, as in *All students who turn in their papers late will lose half of their grade.*

Gender

Gender is a pattern in which nouns of various classes ("genders") require agreement in other words that interact grammatically with them, such as pronouns and adjectives. For example, in Spanish, a "feminine" noun like *casa* ('house') requires that an adjective modifying it have a "feminine" suffix, but a "masculine" noun like *arbol* ('tree') has to have adjective agreement with a "masculine" suffix: 'white house' in Spanish is *casa blanca,* but 'white tree' is *arbol blanco.* A pronoun that has a feminine antecedent has to be feminine: *La quiero* means 'I want it' when 'it'—*la*—looks back to a feminine antecedent like *casa. Lo quiero* means 'I want it' when 'it'—*lo*— looks back to a masculine antecedent like *arbol.*

---

5. It makes semantic sense in that *every X,* loosely speaking, has a plural set of referents, and can be appropriately used in a sentence about a situation in which more than one individual is referred to by the noun or noun phrase modified by *every.*

Some languages have sex-based **natural** genders, according to which the gender of a noun depends on the sex of the things it denotes. In such systems, nouns like *man, boy,* and *father* are masculine in gender, nouns like *woman, girl,* and *mother* are feminine in gender, and nouns like *house, tree,* and *stick* are neuter. Others, like French, Spanish, and German, have **arbitrary** gender systems in which the so-called masculine or feminine or (e.g., in German) neuter gender of a noun may have nothing to do with the sex of the things it denotes. In these languages, it turns out, most nouns denoting humans are "natural" in their gender, but nouns for non-humans are arbitrarily masculine, feminine, or (in German) neuter. The French word for 'pen,' *plume,* is feminine, but the word for 'pencil,' *crayon,* is masculine. Obviously the Spanish *casa* and *arbol* are equally arbitrary in their gender. Some words in these languages that refer to humans even are arbitrary in their gender: the German word for 'maiden' is *mädchen,* which is neuter in gender!

Is gender in English arbitrary or natural? Clearly natural, because nouns denoting things (*tree, table, sky*) are neuter, as we can see from their pronoun, *it,* while nouns denoting female beings are feminine (their pronoun is *she* or its variants), and nouns denoting male beings are masculine (taking the pronoun *he* or its variants). English does, however, have small relics of a former arbitrary gender system: the practice of referring to boats (and sometimes cars and planes and other things) by means of feminine pronouns.

What word-class agrees in gender with nouns? In English, just pronouns. English thus has a relatively impoverished gender system, in contrast with other European languages. And in contrast with some other languages of the world, the English gender system is rudimentary indeed. Swahili, for example, has about eleven (depending on how they're counted) "genders." They are not sex-based genders, but are regular patterns of agreement between noun and adjective, pronoun, verb, and demonstrative. Here is an example showing noun-adjective agreement for just four "genders":

10. a. i. m-tu   m-kubwa.
             gen-man gen-big = 'big man'
         ii. m-toto   m-zuri.
             gen-child gen-good = 'good child'
     b. i. ki-su   ki-kubwa.
             gen-knife gen-big = 'big knife'
         ii. ki-ti   ki-zuri.
             gen-chair gen-good = 'good chair'
     c. i. n-dege   n-zuri.
             gen-bird gen-good = 'good bird'
         ii. n-yumba   n-dogo.
             gen-house gen-small = 'small house'

d.   i.   ma-yai   ma-kubwa
          gen-eggs gen-big = 'big eggs'
    ii.   ma-cho   ma-dogo.
          gen-eyes gen-small = 'small eyes'[6]

There are large numbers of other nouns that pattern like the nouns in each of these examples.

Case

What is the difference in function between *I*, *my*, and *me* in the following sentence?

11.   I saw my kitten playing near me.

You might answer "*I* is for subject, *my* for possession, and *me* for object." The differences in pronoun form according to function (e.g., 'subject') are **case** differences. Case in other languages can involve nouns, determiners, and adjectives (agreeing with modified nouns), as well as pronouns.

English used to have a much more elaborate case system than it has now. Now case in English is restricted to pronouns and to the -'s possessive ending on nouns. English pronouns have four case forms:

12.   a.   Subject case:
              I/you/he/she/it/we/they bought a record.
         b.   Object case:
              The cops arrested *me/you/him/her/it/us/them*.
         c.   Possessive case for pronominal determiners:
              my/your/his/hers/its/our/their book
         d.   Possessive case for pronouns used as full noun phrases (NPs):
              This book is *mine/yours/his/hers/ours/theirs*.[7]

In most languages, English included, the subject-marking case is felt to be the most basic. It is typically the case form in which the word is listed in the dictionary. For example, the *Concise Oxford Dictionary* (Oxford, 1964) gives the subject case form *he* a normal entry:

13.   pron. (obj. *him*, poss. *his*, pl. *they*, obj. *them*, poss. *their*), & n. (pl. *hes*). 1. pron. The male person in question . . . (p. 563)

---

6. You may have noticed some semantic content to the Swahili "genders": the "m-" class, exemplified in (a), contains nouns denoting people, the "ki-" class, exemplified in (b), contains nouns for everyday objects, and the "ma-" class, exemplified in (d), contains plural nouns. Actually, it contains plural nouns of a certain "gender," the gender mainly nouns for liquids and masses, but including other nouns as well. The "n-" class, exemplified in (c), has no clear semantic content.

7. There is no possessive case for the pronoun *it* used as a full NP: *This is its*. It is unclear why not.

But the entry for *him* relates it to the base form *he:*

14. pron. Objective case of HE . . . (p. 576)

Because of this perceived basicness of the subject-marking case, a terminological distinction exists between subject-marking case and other cases, the nonsubject-marking cases being termed **oblique**.

Traditionally, cases have Latinate names: **nominative** for the subject-marking case, **genitive** for the possessive, **dative** for the case which marks indirect objects (English has no separate case for this function), and **accusative** for direct objects.

Although many languages have no morphological case system at all (Chinese is one), some languages have much more elaborate case systems than English. Ancient Greek had five cases, all showing up on nouns. The basic noun [anθro:pos] 'man, human being' could appear, for example, as follows:

15. a. as subject ("nominative" case):
 [ho anθro:pos epʰe: . . .] 'the man spoke . . .'
 b. as possessive ("genitive" case):
 [to biblion tou anθro:pou] 'the book of the man'
 c. as indirect object ("dative" case):
 [ho⁸ so:krate:s to:i anthro:po:i dido:si . . .] 'Socrates gives to the man . . .'
 d. as direct object ("accusative" case):
 [ho so:krate:s ton anθro:pon etimato] 'Socrates honored the man'
 e. as direct addressee ("**vocative**" case):
 [o: anθro:pe!] 'O man!'

In Ancient Greek, as you see, both the definite article and the noun are marked for case. In German, the bulk of the case-marking is on the article. Modern German has four cases:

16. a. nominative: *der* mensch 'the man' (as subject)
 b. genitive: *des* menschs 'of the man'
 c. dative: *dem* mensch 'to the man'
 d. accusative: *den* mensch 'the man' (as direct object)

Russian (which has no articles) has six:

17. a. nominative: *dom* 'the house' (as subject)
 b. genitive: *doma* 'of the house'
 c. dative: *domu* 'toward the house'
 d. accusative: *dom* 'the house' (as direct object)
 e. instrumental: *domom* 'the house' (as agent by which something was done, or with certain verbs or adjectives)
 f. prepositional: *dome* 'at the house'

---

8. Ancient Greek required proper nouns to be preceded by articles.

EXERCISE 3. Identify the case of the underlined pronouns, choosing from "subject case," "object case," "possessive determiner case," and "possessive pronoun case":

1. <u>Her</u> I really like, now.
2. <u>She</u> saw <u>her</u> kite escaping <u>her</u>.
3. <u>He</u> who laughs last laughs best.
4. <u>They</u> gave <u>them</u> to <u>them</u>.
5. Chapter Four needs <u>its</u> heading revised.

Definiteness and specificity

What is the meaning difference between a noun phrase like *a Canadian* and one like *the Canadian?* Obviously the meaning difference is expressed by *a* vs. *the*, that is, by the indefinite vs. the definite article, so we can label the difference indefiniteness vs. definiteness. (In other words, initially let's define definite noun phrases as those with definite articles, and indefinite noun phrases as those with indefinite articles.) But what is the meaning difference? To understand, we need to begin with a discussion of a related concept, **specificity**.

Specificity

Contrast (a) and (b) below:

18. a.   Nancy wants to marry a Canadian. She has flown to Winnipeg to try and meet a nice one.
    b.   Nancy wants to marry a Canadian. Her family has met him and they're dead set against it.

The noun phrases in question in both these sentences, with the form *a Canadian,* are indefinite, since they contain the indefinite article. Sentence (a) contains a **nonspecific** noun phrase, *a Canadian.* In the situation described in (a), Nancy wants to marry any (nice, etc.) Canadian, not some specific Canadian. In contrast, (b) contains a **specific** noun phrase, *a Canadian.* Nancy wants to marry a particular Canadian. What makes a noun phrase specific? Based on (18), what makes an noun phrase specific is for the speaker to have a particular referent in mind for it. Here are a few more examples of indefinite noun phrases, specific and non-specific.

19. a.   Specific:
    i.   <u>A woman</u> in my class came up to me yesterday and invited me to a party.

      ii. Dominique was looking for a book, the one she had been reading.
      iii. If you look in the top drawer, you'll find a red marking pen. Please
          bring it to me.
   b. Non-specific:
      i. Lonely old Will has been yearning for a woman to keep him company for years.
      ii. A computer would be a really good addition to this office.
      iii. I went to the bookstore to get a red marking pen.

So indefinite noun phrases may be specific or nonspecific, with "specific" defined as "referring to a particular referent which the speaker has in mind."

Definite noun phrases, now, like *the Canadian*, are used when BOTH the speaker and the hearer have a particular referent in mind. A further characteristic of definite noun phrases is that they refer to unique referents. There are millions of Canadians, but in a particular discourse *the Canadian* picks out just one,[9] the one that either has been previously introduced into the discourse or is otherwise present in the minds of both speaker and hearer.

Definite noun phrases may be introduced by a definite determiner, like *the, this,*[10] *that,* or a possessive; may be proper names; or may be pronouns.

Definite noun phrases may be definite by virtue of denoting unique things—e.g., *the moon, the sun;* by being unique to a particular setting—*the blackboard, the dog;* by being entailed, in that the definite noun phrase denotes something unique which exists as part of some larger whole—*the door, the kitchen, the back yard* (in talking about a house); or by previous mention: As soon as an entity "X," represented by an indefinite noun phrase, even a non-specific one, is mentioned in a conversation, it takes on definiteness. The reason it does is that it is now identifiable to both speaker and hearer, even if only as 'that X which has been mentioned.' The definiteness shows up in subsequent mentions. In the following example, *a Canadian* is non-specific (and, of course, indefinite), but *he* is definite:

20. Nancy wants to marry a Canadian. He must love hockey and be a good fisherman, that's all she cares about.

EXERCISE 4. Identify the italicized noun phrases below as indefinite specific, indefinite non-specific, or definite.

1. *Max* took *his jacket* off when he got to *Cathy's house.*

2. *A man* is coming up to *the door.* I can see *him* from *the window.*

---

9. Except for the **generic** use, in which a phrase like *the Canadian* means 'the typical Canadian' or 'Canadians generally': e.g., *The Canadian tends to be an outdoorsman.*

10. *This* can also be indefinite (but specific), as in *There's this guy in my linguistics class that I'm really dying to meet.*

3. Usually when *you* go whale-watching in *February* you'll see *a whale* or two.
4. Think of *a number between five and ten.*
5. You know what? Yesterday when I was at the mall I saw *this cute puppy* in the pet store and I'm dying to get him.

VERBS: SUBCLASSES AND FEATURES

Transitivity

One simple basis for verb subclassification is the traditional "**transitive-intransitive**" distinction. Transitive verbs "take" direct objects, i.e., must occur with following nouns or noun phrases functioning as direct object; intransitive verbs can't. *Build, use,* and *scare* are transitive:

21. a. *Frank built.
    b. Frank built the cabinet.
22. a. *Grandma used.
    b. Grandma used brown sugar.
23. a. *Martha scared.
    b. Martha scared the children.

Sleep, chuckle, and *disappear* are intransitive:

24. a. The tired counselors slept.
    b. *The tired counselors slept the young campers.
25. a. Everybody chuckled.
    b. *Everybody chuckled the joke.
26. a. The bug spray disappeared.
    b. *The bug spray disappeared the mosquitoes.

As you might guess, matters aren't so simple as this two-way distinction suggests. First, some verbs can apparently be both transitive and intransitive:

27. a. Paul ate.
    b. Paul ate dinner.
28. a. Jean read.
    b. Jean read the newspaper.
29. a. Isaac paints well.
    b. Isaac paints wonderful portraits.

Paying attention to the meaning of such verbs can resolve this apparent paradox. The situations corresponding to each of these verbs always contain two participants, denoted by the pre-verb noun or noun phrase (the "subject") and, if present, the post-verb noun or noun phrase (the "direct object"). Presumably it is impossible to eat, read, or paint, without eating, reading, or painting SOMETHING. Consequently, it makes sense to say these verbs are basically transitive, but allow a speaker optionally to omit their direct object noun or noun phrase when its meaning is unspecified. One way to think of this is that you can omit an "empty" word like *something* as in *Isaac was painting something* to produce *Isaac was painting,* but not a meaningful word or phrase, like *a nude* in *Isaac was painting a nude.* The principle governing omission is thus that information may not be lost. Observe that the transitive verbs we looked at first—*build, use,* and *scare*—do not allow this optional omission (from *I used something* we cannot create **I used*).

The second problem connected with the notion of transitivity is that it is too limited. "Transitivity" is restricted to the property of taking a direct object, i.e., of requiring two nouns or noun phrases, one functioning as subject and one functioning as direct object. Some transitive verbs, though, require not only subject and direct object noun phrases but one or two additional nouns or noun phrases. An example is *put:* you can *put the eggs in the fridge,* but you can't just **put the eggs.* It would be nice to have a way to label, in the same general way as the transitive-intransitive distinction, verbs that require three, or even four, nouns or noun phrases, instead of simply labeling them transitive. Unfortunately, there are no generally accepted labels for such verbs. The best we can do is the following. Using the abbreviation "NP" for noun or noun phrase, we replace the transitive-intransitive distinction by a distinction among "one-NP verbs" (intransitive verbs), "two-NP verbs," "three-NP verbs," etc. Verbs requiring three NPs, besides verbs like *put,* include those that require NPs functioning as indirect objects, like *give* and *donate:*

30. a. Abel gave a rose to Emily.
    b. We donated $50 to the building fund.

There aren't many verbs that require four NPs. One is *trade,* which fairly freely permits (*something*-type) NP omission:

31. a. Ellie traded Mo an issue of *Mad* for a *Scrooge* comic.
    b. Ellie traded Mo an issue of *Mad.*
    c. Ellie traded with Mo.
    d. Ellie traded for a *Scrooge* comic.
    e. Ellie traded an issue of *Mad* for a *Scrooge* comic.

EXERCISE 5. How many NPs do the following verbs require, in terms of their logical meaning?

1. see   **2.** hear   **3.** buy   **4.** send
5. exchange   **6.** careen   **7.** imagine   **8.** listen

A third problem with transitivity has to do with verbs like *melt* and *freeze,* which can apparently be both one-NP verbs and two-NP verbs:

32. a. The popsicle melted.
  b. The hot sun melted the popsicle.
  c. The iced tea froze.
  d. The cold snap froze the iced tea.

We could simply say the transitive and intransitive versions of each of these verbs are two separate verbs, homonyms, but this solution would miss their obvious meaning connection. A better solution involves noting that the two-NP versions have interpretations of the following sort:

33. a. The hot sun melted the popsicle =
  b. The hot sun caused the popsicle to melt.

Sentence (b), in turn, can be analyzed as follows:

34.   The hot sun caused this: the popsicle melted.

In (34), and by extension, (33b) and ultimately (33a), *melt* is a one-NP verb, the only NP interacting with it being *the popsicle*. The solution, in other words, is to treat **causative** verbs (e.g., *melt, freeze*) as being basically one-NP verbs, their two-NP uses being explained by their causative meaning.

EXERCISE 6. Which of the following verbs are, or can be, causative, in the above sense? Give your evidence.

1. break   **2.** shatter   **3.** build   **4.** ruin   **5.** dent
6. itch   **7.** hurt   **8.** tickle

Voice: Active, Passive, Middle

Unlike transitivity, **voice** doesn't divide verbs into subclasses. Rather, any verb use is, to use traditional terminology, "in" one voice or another. The most interesting features of voice in English are marked by sentence structure, and will be discussed in the next two chapters. The most familiar voices are active and passive:

35. Active: Dean kicked the ball.
  Passive: The ball was kicked by Dean.

Almost all verbs requiring two or more NPs can occur in both the active and passive voices.

36. Active:

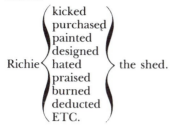

Richie { kicked, purchased, painted, designed, hated, praised, burned, deducted, ETC. } the shed.

Passive:

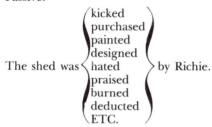

The shed was { kicked, purchased, painted, designed, hated, praised, burned, deducted, ETC. } by Richie.

There are a few "measure" verbs that have only an active, e.g.,

37. a.   *cost:*
    Active: This coat costs a great deal of money.
    Impossible passive:
            *A great deal of money is cost by this coat.
b.   *weigh:*
    Active: This package weighs twenty-seven ounces.
    Impossible passive:
            *Twenty-seven ounces is weighed by this package.

And there are even fewer verbs which occur only in the passive. One is *be rumored:*

38. a.   passive:
    It is rumored that the dean is resigning.
b.   Impossible active:
    *Someone rumors it that the dean is resigning.

In Chapter Six, we will discuss the forms of active and passive sentences.
    Besides active and passive, there is also a **middle** voice available to some verbs, e.g., *sell* and *show:*

39. a.   *sell:* These cards sell well.
b.   *show:* That print will show to good advantage with that kind of lighting.

The NP functioning as logical direct object (i.e., the NP denoting the thing that the action of the sentence happens to) of a middle voice sentence functions as its actual subject: *these cards* and *that print,* in the examples above. In addition, the logical subject NP is missing. (Who sells the cards? Who shows the print?)

EXERCISE 7. Identify the following sentences as active voice, passive voice, or middle voice.

1. The leaders were criticized by the press.
2. We left the room early.
3. This new fabric folds nicely.
4. Madonna photographs incredibly well.
5. Sean photographed Madonna yesterday afternoon.
6. Madonna was photographed yesterday afternoon.
7. Mike surfs like a world-classer.
8. The lake lay flat and glassy before the campers.
9. The water was disturbed occasionally by wild leaping game fish.
10. Everyone passed the course.

Mood, Tense, and Aspect

The grammar of the verbal categories **mood**, **tense**, and **aspect** is complex in English, mainly because of a rather inexact match of meaning to form, with one form often expressing several meanings, and one meaning being expressed by means of different forms. In our discussion, we will first examine these categories from the perspective of meaning, and then with form as the starting point.

Mood

Mood can be defined as the grammatical expression of the speaker's attitude toward what he or she is saying. If you say *Julius Caesar ruled Rome* your attitude toward what you are saying is presumably that it is true; you are making an assertion. If you say *Please pass the salt* your attitude toward what you are saying is that you want the event denoted by your sentence to occur. And if you say *Long live the Queen* or *God bless America* your attitude is hopeful about the situation denoted by the sentence.[11]

---

11. The conditions on the speaker's beliefs or attitudes for uses of moods are actually more complex that this brief discussion indicates. This topic is part of the inquiry into the conditions (of various sorts) governing appropriate carrying out of **speech acts**, which include asserting, warning, threatening, promising, christening, denying, apologizing, and many more—acts that are carried out specifically by means of talk.

Indicative mood is the mood of assertions: *Julius Caesar rules Rome, Max left, Tomorrow is Tuesday, The pen is in the drawer.* Requests and wishes are often expressed by **subjunctive** mood: *Long live the Queen, I demand that he be arrested.* **Imperative** mood is associated with direct commands, suggestions, invitations, and requests: *Please pass the salt, Shut up, Stand at attention, Come for dinner Friday, Try this!.*

Indicative mood is expressed by the presence of tense and person endings on verbs.

Subjunctive mood can be expressed by the absence of tense and person endings: *Long live the Queen, I demand that he leave, it is crucial that the fugitive be captured.*[12] What is sometimes called subjunctive mood is also expressed by "past tense" form: *If beggars were kings, If John left I would just fall apart.* The first of these forms is used to express desires, the second to describe contrary-to-fact or hypothetical situations.

Imperative mood is expressed by the absence not only of tense and person endings, but also of subject: *Please pass the salt, Shut up.*

However, in the whole area of tense, mood, and aspect, there is seldom a simple relation between form and meaning. Commonly, a given form can express several meanings, and a given meaning can be expressed by a variety of forms. The indicative form can express more than assertions; it can express both requests and commands:

40. a. Indicative expressing a request:
I want you to bring that report to my office.
   b. Indicative expressing a command:
You will depart for Botany Bay at 0700 hours.

Moreover, the semantic notions of commanding and requesting can be carried by certain lexical items, especially modals:

41. I would like you to invite Marca.

Thus, mood as embodied in form is relatively impoverished in English.

Tense

Too often, the term "tense" is used for any verbal morphology whatsoever: "passive tense, subjunctive tense, progressive tense." Since subjunctive is a mood, passive a voice, and progressive an aspect (see below), these uses of "tense" don't make much sense. We'll reserve our use of the term to verbal time reference.

12. The ending-less subjunctive used for wishes or desires seems to be dying out. In an official notice (not a news story) in a west coast college newspaper I found the following: *It is crucial that each student brings his or her registration permit to the registration site.*

Let's define tense as follows:

42. Definition: Tense is the grammatical expression of the time relation between two events or situations.

Recall the "grammatical" - "lexical" distinction made in Chapter Three. "Grammatical" means general as opposed to idiosyncratic, and by "grammatical" we exclude from the purview of tense lexical items (words) like *yesterday* and lexically complex expressions like *six days from now*. By "time relation" we mean 'is before,' 'is after,' and 'is simultaneous with.'[13]

One of the two events or situations our definition refers to is the event or situation the speaker talks about, the "narrated event." Often the other is the "event of speaking." In this case, past tense means "the narrated event is before the event of speaking"; present tense means "the narrated event is simultaneous with the event of speaking"; and future tense means "the narrated event is after the event of speaking." (Recall that at this point we are considering tense from the perspective of meaning.) In this case, then, the following diagrams apply:

Past tense

43. Past tense:

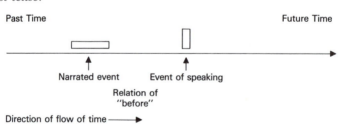

That is, if you say *Bobby defeated Boris,* the narrated event is Bobby's defeating Boris, the event of speaking is your saying "Bobby defeated Boris," and the meaning of the past tense *-ed* in your utterance is that the time of Bobby's defeating Boris is before your saying so.

---

13. Some languages include in what is called tense the expression of relative time order. For example, in Swahili, *a-li-andika* translates as 'he wrote,' and *a-ka-andika* as 'he next wrote' or 'and then he wrote.' Some languages use tense forms to express concepts of different degrees of remoteness from some temporal reference point. According to Sandra Chung and Alan Timberlake (1985), reporting work by Michael Silverstein (1974), a dialect of Chinook, an American Indian language of the Northwest, has a four-way tense distinction among forms meaning 'long ago,' 'some time ago,' 'recently,' and 'just now.'

Future tense

44. Future tense:

In *Bobby will defeat Boris,* the narrated event and the event of speaking are the same as in our past tense example. The main difference, of course, is that the future tense expresses the relation "after"; that is, the meaning of the future tense is that the time of Bobby's defeating Boris is after the time of your saying so. A second difference is that at the moment you speak, the defeat of Boris by Bobby has not yet occurred, so the narrated event has less reality than a past narrated event. As a result, statements about the future are necessarily less certain than statements about the past. This is responsible for future tense assertions often having a connotation of contingency. We will have more to say about this later.

Present tense

45. Present tense:

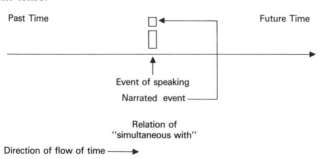

According to this diagram, the narrated event coincides in time with the time for the event of speaking. If you say *I live at 315 Chestnut Street,* you mean, literally, only that you live there just as you speak. Because of the nature of "living at" in our culture, we understand that your living there very likely has much greater duration than that, extending backwards into the past for an unspecified period and into the future for an unspecified period. Our understanding this is an inference we make from what you say together with what we know about the world—in particular, the nature of 'living at.' Strictly, however, the sentence means only that your living there is simultaneous with the time of speaking. If you wish, you can cancel our inference, e.g., by saying . . . *but I am in the process of moving out* or . . . *I just moved there.* A case where no such inference is needed is the following. Imagine being a radio basketball sportscaster. During a broadcast of a game you say, *Kaplan shoots, and it is good!*. The meaning of your present tense on *shoots* and *is* is that first Kaplan's shooting, and then the shot falling through the hoop, is simultaneous with your saying that these things happen. This is so even though the actual moment of Kaplan's shooting or the ball going into the basket may be different from the precise time of your utterance. You're just being a tiny bit inaccurate in your tense usage.

Another case where no such inference is needed is with **performative** expressions like *I promise that the report will be finished by Thursday* and *I hereby resign the office of President of the United States.* Performative expressions accomplish acts by virtue of being spoken: when you say *I promise,* you have made a promise, and when you say *I resign* . . . , in the proper context you have resigned. The significance of the present tense is that at the exact moment that the sentence is uttered, the act denoted by the verb is accomplished. Performative sentences are important in certain legal contexts: *I now pronounce you husband and wife; I sentence you to six years of Linguistics 101.* In the first case, the happy couple may be said to have entered the state of matrimony at the exact moment that the sentence is uttered by the marrying official. Similarly, in the second case, the individual may be considered sentenced at the moment of utterance. Verbs which can have performative uses include, among others, *warn, demand, christen, bless, admit, apologize, authorize,* and *condemn.*

Tense without reference to time of speaking

Sometimes the two events or situations related by tense do not include the time of speaking. This is the case in the so-called "future perfect" and "past perfect" tenses:

46. a. "Future perfect":
 When I get there, Laurie will <u>have</u> arrived already.
 b. "Past perfect":
 When I got there, Laurie <u>had</u> arrived already.

In the situations denoted by both (a) and (b), the two events related by the underlined tense markers[14] are my getting there and Laurie's arriving. In both, the latter is before the former. That is, both are a kind of past tense.

---

14. In complex tenses, *have -en* marks past tense; i.e., it is, in effect, an allomorph of the past tense morpheme.

The "future perfect" is a "past in the future," and the "past perfect" is a "past in the past."

The grammar and meaning of English time expressions, including tense, are complex, partly because of the issues we have just discussed, but partly because a tense morpheme typically expresses **aspect** as well as tense. Let's turn our attention to aspect now.

Aspect

Traditional grammars of English usually make no mention of the term **aspect**, but it is well attested in traditional grammars of other languages, for example Slavic languages (Russian, Polish, etc.), where aspect is a prominent part of the grammar of verbs.

Let's define aspect as follows:

47. <u>Definition</u>: Aspect is the grammatical expression of the internal time structure of an event or situation.

Aspect thus encodes such features of events and situations as progressiveness, habituality, boundedness, duration, and instantaneousness. Aspect differs from tense in that tense deals with the external time relations between two events, while aspect deals with the way the internal time structure of a single event is represented. *Zellig is leaving* and *Zellig was leaving* are distinguished by tense; *Zellig left* and *Zellig was leaving* are distinguished by aspect.

Duration and boundedness

Two important parameters to aspect are **duration** and **boundedness**. Duration involves a distinction among verb subclasses: **instantaneous** verbs like *shatter, arrive,* and *find,* **durative** verbs like *work, read,* and *stay,* and **stative** verbs like *love, resemble,* and *have.* The boundedness parameter involves a distinction between **bounded** and **unbounded** expressions, sometimes associated with individual verbs, sometimes with phrases: *reach (the top)* and *take a walk* are bounded; *draw, sleep,* and *drive* are unbounded. We will examine these distinctions and meanings below.

Duration: instantaneous, durative, stative

Verbs in the **instantaneous** subclass can be identified by their possibility of occurrence with expressions like *at ten sharp.* Non-instantaneous verbs often sound slightly strange with such expressions:

48. a. Instantaneous verbs:
    i.   Mr. Staples arrived at ten sharp.
    ii. At six minutes after three, Ellen broke the piece of chalk.
    iii. The window shattered at noon.
  b. Non-instantaneous verbs:
    i.   ?At six p.m. sharp Ellen lived on Pine Street.
    ii. ?At 12:15, Jim worked hard.
    iii. ?Cathy loved Max at 9:17.
    iv. ?Sharon knew French at six p.m. last evening.

Moreover, instantaneous verbs can't co-occur with expressions like *for two hours* or *for two years*, while non-instantaneous verbs can:

49. a. Instantaneous verbs:
    i.   *Greg arrived for two hours.
    ii. *Ellen broke the piece of chalk for a half hour.
    iii. *The window shattered for the whole afternoon.
  b. Non-instantaneous verbs:
    i.   Max lived on Chestnut Street for twelve years.
    ii. Jane worked hard for a solid hour.
    iii. Romeo loved Juliet for six weeks.
    iv. We owned a Saab for four years.

Non-instantaneous verbs divide between stative and durative verbs. **Stative** verbs denote non-volitional states, with no change over time; durative verbs can (but need not be) volitional, and often indicate or assume some change through time. Stative verbs include *resemble, have,* and *know;* durative verbs include *work, stay,* and *play.* The two sub-types of verbs can be distinguished by certain co-occurrence requirements. Durative verbs can occur with the progressive *be -ing* aspect marker (which we will discuss below), but stative verbs can't, at least in simple sentences:

50. a. Duratives:
    i.   Max was working.
    ii. Uncle Martin was staying here.
  b. Statives:
    i.   *Max was resembling Uncle Martin.
    ii. *Next year I'll be having a Volvo.

Statives also do not easily serve as antecedents for *do so,* while duratives can:

51. a. Statives:
    i.   *Lou had a Volvo before anyone else did so.
    ii. *Whenever Beth knows the answer, she does so before anyone else.
  b. Duratives:
    i.   Lou worked at Fred's Market before anyone else did so.
    ii. If Beth plays like her sister, she does so because she practices an hour a day.

Actually, the stative subclass is not so well-defined as this data suggests; in certain contexts, the constraints we have identified simply don't hold. In complex sentences, for instance, some statives CAN occur with the progressive: *More and more, Max is resembling his uncle; Little Wendy seems to be wanting some candy.* Nevertheless, there is enough validity to the subclass for you to be aware of it; just take the claim that a stative subclass exists with a couple of grains of salt.

The instantaneous vs. non-instantaneous distinction is fairly well-founded. However, even it can be overruled by sentence structure. For example, inherently instantaneous verbs like *arrive* can be made to occur with durative expressions by being given plural subject NPs:

52. The guests <u>arrived</u> all evening long.

EXERCISE 8. Identify the following verbs as inherently <u>instantaneous</u>, <u>durative</u>, or <u>stative</u>, giving evidence in each case:

1. hear	**2.** listen	**3.** amuse
4. know	**5.** think	**6.** appoint
7. realize	**8.** receive	**9.** explode

Bounded and unbounded

Another inherent aspect distinction is between boundedness and unboundedness. The durative verbs *walk, read, draw,* and *smoke* are inherently unbounded, because they require no end point of action. (Unlikely though the event is, you can say *she will walk forever.*) A test for unboundedness is possibility of occurrence with *until . . .* constructions, since an *until* expression establishes an end point of action. You can say *She will walk (read, draw, smoke) until she is exhausted.* In contrast, instantaneous verbs like *arrive* are inherently bounded, as shown by the ungrammaticality of **She will arrive forever* and **She will arrive until she is exhausted.* But instantaneous verbs are not the only bounded verbal expressions. Unbounded verbs like *walk* can be made bounded by certain limiting expressions, like destinations: *She will walk to school* is bounded, since **She will walk to school forever* (note: ignore, for the time being, the "repeated" interpretation) not only describes an unlikely event, but is ungrammatical, as is **She will walk to school until she gets there.* In fact, the addition of a destination to *walk* makes the resulting expression something we can't even call durative, since it can't occur with a *for [a period]* expression: **She will walk to school for an hour.* With *draw,* something even stranger happens. It can be made bounded by a certain kind of direct object NP, but with another, it remains unbounded:

53. a. With no object, and unbounded:
          She will draw forever/until she is exhausted.
      b. With an object, and bounded:
          *She will draw a circle forever/until she is exhausted.
          (Ignore, again, the "repeated" interpretation.)
      c. With an object, and unbounded:
          She will draw a line forever/until she is exhausted.

Expressions like *draw a circle,* labeled "accomplishment terms" by the philosopher and linguist Zeno Vendler (1967), are necessarily bounded. *Draw a line* isn't bounded, because of the nature of lines: as soon as you start drawing one, you have drawn one, and as you continue, you are still drawing it. *Draw a circle* is, though, because you have not drawn a circle until the circle is complete, and, once complete, drawing it can't continue.

You may have noticed that some examples to which we have prefixed an asterisk are in fact all right, in an **iterative** (repeated) interpretation. For instance, with such an interpretation, *She will walk to school forever, because she will never buy a car or ride a bus* is, of course, perfectly grammatical. So is *She will draw a circle until she gets exhausted,* again, with an iterative interpretation. We'll discuss iterativity below.

EXERCISE 9. Identify as bounded or unbounded, giving evidence in each case:

1.	run	**7.**	run a mile
2.	drive	**8.**	drive the car
3.	cross the street	**9.**	read
4.	win the game	**10.**	win
5.	have a drink	**11.**	drink
6.	nap	**12.**	dream

Progressive

The discontinuous morpheme *be -ing* signals **progressive** aspect, meaning 'be in process' (or 'be in progress'): *Max is sleeping, Sue is cooking soup, Selma is not telling the truth.* Unchanging states can't be in progress, since they are static. This is why stative verbs don't easily occur with the progressive. Instantaneous verbs don't usually occur with the progressive either, because the events they denote don't take long enough for us to be able to talk about them as being in progress (?*The window was shattering as I* *watched*).[15] The domain of the progressive, then, is a middle range of verbs on a scale ranging from instantaneous to stative, i.e., durative verbs:

54. Domain of the progressive aspect in English:

Briefest duration of event		Longest duration of situation
Instantaneous	....	Stative
verbs	Durative verbs	verbs
	↑	
	progressive	

Iterative

The progressive is one way to express a different aspect meaning, the **iterative.** When an instantaneous verb is acceptable with the progressive, it indicates repetition:

55. a. A light flashed. (*instantaneous*)
    b. A light was flashing. (*progressive and iterative*)

Only iterable events can be described with the progressive-iterative; instantaneous verbs which don't denote iterable events, like *shatter*, can't take the progressive (**The window was shattering*), unless they have plural subjects or objects. With plural subjects or objects, though, the plurality creates a kind of iteration: *The windows were shattering throughout the evening, The enemy was exploding mines all night long.*

As we saw in our discussion of boundedness, iterativity can occur in other ways than with the progressive. For instance, a durative expression like *for an hour* can make an instantaneous verb denoting an iterable event iterative—and therefore durative, in a derived sense: *Ann jumped for an hour/hopped for twenty minutes/kicked the ball for three hours.*

Not only instantaneous events, but any bounded event, can be iterated; thus we can use durative bounded expressions like *Jane was fixing chairs all last summer.*

Habitual

Habitual aspect conveys the idea of an event or situation being characteristic of some period of time. In English one way to mark habituality is by means of *used to: Joe used to live here, Sal used to ride to school.* Sentences like the latter one have iterative interpretations, but iterativity alone doesn't imply habituality: *The professor sneezed ten times before going on* is iterative but not habitual. Nor does habituality require iterativity, as shown by *Joe used to live here.*

---

15. But in viewing time-lapse motion pictures, it might be possible to say *The window was shattering*, and the like.

Habituality can be conveyed by other forms than *used to*. For example, it can be conveyed by past iteratives—*Diane wrote a poem every Tuesday, Sam dated Ellie for six months*—and by progressive constructions: *Sam is dating Ellie.*

Our discussion so far of tense and aspect (and mood as well) has focussed on meaning. We have identified a number of distinct meanings that the grammar has to recognize, and mentioned some ways English encodes them. Our next effort at making sense of the tense-aspect area will be to use form as our starting-point. We will now look at the range of English verb forms and the variety of tense and aspect interpretations each can have. (We'll ignore mood in the following discussion.)

Form and meaning in English tense and aspect

As we have seen, a difficulty in analyzing tense and aspect in English is the rather chaotic match of form to meaning. Rather than having one form equalling one meaning, the tense-aspect area contains several different forms which express one meaning, and several different meanings expressed by a single form. To muddy the picture further, some of the meanings expressed by "basically" tense or aspect forms have nothing to do with tense or aspect. In order to make sense of this, we will list and exemplify briefly the forms of the English tense-aspect system, together with the meanings each form can have.

SIMPLE PRESENT TENSE FORM (expressed by third person singular *-s*, and by Ø in other persons and numbers: *I swim, he swims, they swim*) can have the following meanings:

1. Present time reference:

56. The quarterback fade<u>s</u> back. Now he look<u>s</u> left and throw<u>s</u>.

57. I promise <u>Ø</u> you that.

In these examples the present tense form refers to the actual present moment. Example (56) is "sportscaster talk," used to represent to the listener what occurs in a game in real time. Example (57) is a **performative** sentence, one which carries out the effect identified by the verb by virtue of being said. That is, when you say (57), you have made a promise, and the promise is made by the saying.

With a stative verb, the present tense form can refer to the present moment, but because of the nature of the situation denoted by the verb—because it is a state—we understand the present tense as, in effect, referring to a longer stretch of time. This is exemplified in (58):

58.   Max loves Cathy.

Somewhat different are duratives:

59.   Max works hard.

The interpretation of the present tense form on durative verbs like *work* is less tightly connected to the actual present moment. Durative verbs can occur with the progressive, as in *Max is working hard,* which ties the ongoing activity to the present moment. The present tense without the progressive has an interpretation of iteration or habituality. The present tense form still has present time reference: "At this moment, it is true that 'hard' applies to Max's working." But at the present moment Max may not be working hard. Rather, his working hard is one of Max's characteristics throughout a period which includes the present moment, without it being required that Max work at every moment throughout this period.

Another kind of present tense use is "timeless truths":

60.   Two plus two equals four.

The present tense with (in effect) timeless truths also has present time reference, but with an even greater implied stretch of time during which a sentence is considered true: in general, forever in both directions, unless it is specifically said to be otherwise (e.g., in fantasy, *In the past, two plus two equaled five*). "Timeless truths" don't have to be logically true like example (60): they can be contingently true, like *Horses have manes and tails.*

2.   Future time reference:

61.   My plane leaves tomorrow at seven-thirty.

In this example, the "present tense" form has future time reference, not present. This construction has been called "futurate" (Prince 1973). It differs from future tense in being restricted to planned or scheduled events; while you can say *I take a test tomorrow,* you can't say **I get an A on a test tomorrow.*

Another kind of future time reference shows up in the following:

62.   When Max leaves, I'll be glad.

The present tense form has future time reference in subordinate clauses, when the main clause has future tense.

3. Past time reference:

63. Yesterday this amazing thing happened to me. I was walking down Market Street, on my way to the subway, when this guy comes up to me and says, "Hey, wanna buy a watch?"

The present tense form can be used in a past time context to refer to events in that frame, i.e., past events. Presumably this "conversational historical present" creates a sense of vividness and immediacy for the hearer, possibly because present time events are generally higher in relevance and interest than other events, and hence a hearer will empathize with a speaker who describes a past event in the present tense.

SIMPLE PAST TENSE FORM (*-ed* and its allomorphs) can have the following meanings:

1. Past time reference:

64. Laurie decided on a motorcycle.

65. The Kaplans lived in South Jersey for 12 years.

66. Spenser biked the Charles River route every day last year.

Example (64) refers to a single past event, (65) to a past situation that endured for a period, and (66) to repeated past events. These differences have to do with aspect, of course, not tense; the interpretation of the past tense morpheme is the same in each case. That is, one would not say that the past tense morpheme is ambiguous among three meanings (single past event, enduring past situation, and repeated past events). Rather, it is unspecified for aspect, and the aspect interpretation derives from what verb is used and other features of sentence structure.

2. Contrary to fact, and hypothetical, conditionals:

67. If cabbages were kings, . .

68. If Magic passed less, he would score more.

Such a use does not express a time reference, of course; this is a use of the "past tense" form to express a **mood**, called, in the traditional literature, both "conditional" and "subjunctive."

3. Present time reference for politeness or deference in requests:

69. Professor Webb, I wanted to ask you about getting an "incomplete."

Presumably present-referring past tense form in examples like this distances the request, thereby achieving politeness or deference.

PROGRESSIVE *BE -ING* can have the following interpretations:

1. Reference to events or situations in progress at time referred to by the tense:

70. Present: Mom is mowing the lawn.

71. Past: Dad was washing the car.

72. Future: Ida will be arguing with Oscar.

2. Iteration:

73. Saul is shooting baskets.

74. Coach Monska was always yelling at Hook Jackson.

75. I'll be running laps.

3. Reference to scheduled or planned future events ("futurate" use):

76. Present tense form: I am leaving tomorrow.

77. Past tense form: I was leaving tomorrow, but my plans changed.

Note that the *be -ing* futurate can occur with the past tense, as in (77), but the simple futurate cannot (**I left tomorrow, but my plans changed.*)

<u>FUTURE WITH *WILL*</u> can have the following interpretations:

1. Future time reference:

78. At 5:17 p.m., the train from Frankfurt will arrive.

Since the future doesn't exist yet, we can't be as certain about it as we can be about the present and the past. Hence there is often an implication of prediction rather than certainty about future-referring expressions. This fact is underscored by the existence of the "futurate" expressions, which are restricted to denoting scheduled or planned events, i.e., those we can be more certain about. This leaves to the *will* future the expression of predictions:

79. a. The Red Sox will lose the playoffs.
   b. Max will ask Cathy out.
   c. Diane will fire Bob.
   d. The sun will rise tomorrow.

2. Probability in the present:

80. Speaker A: Where are the canned peaches?
   Speaker B: Oh, they'll be over in aisle seven next to the nuts.

An additional comment about expressions with *will* is in order. Future expressions with *will* often have an implication of contingency, which can be seen most clearly in contrast with *be going to*. Contrast the following:

81. a. Ted will loan Sam the money.
   b. Ted is going to loan Sam the money.

If the loan is assured, both sentences are possible, but if it depends on Sam's making a request, only (a) is possible. That is, (b) is more certain. The loan depends on nothing. Similarly, contrast these:

82. a.   I've got something that'll fix you right up.
b.   I've got something that's going to fix you right up.[16]

The first of these depends on some conditioning factor, such as drinking the potion, while the second is more certain and is not contingent at all.

EXERCISE 10. Identify the meaning or function of the underlined verbs and verb constructions in the following sentences, using the tense and aspect meaning categories just identified. EXAMPLE: *Jones picks it up on one hop and fires it to first.* Tense form: present. Tense form meaning: present time event. Aspect form: inherently instantaneous. Aspect form meaning: instantaneous.

1.   Tomorrow afternoon the Mets play the Reds.
2.   Smith is painting his garage right now.
3.   If you mowed your lawn more, your neighbors wouldn't complain so much.
4.   The earth revolves around the sun.
5.   I warn you: don't hand your paper in late!
6.   If you are asking me where Jones is, I think probably he'll be in his workshop.
7.   Smith owns a VCR, a PC, and an IRA.

Perfect expressions

The English **perfect** construction is expressed by *have -en,* as in *has taken, have stolen, had bought,* etc. We have said nothing about this form yet. As a particularly vexing construction, it deserves separate treatment. With the discussion below, we will conclude our consideration of tense and aspect in English.

This construction can occur with present, past, or future tense:

83. a.   Tom has stolen the donuts.
b.   Tom had stolen the donuts.
c.   Tom will have stolen the donuts.

It can also occur with the progressive, in all three tenses:

84. a.   Sandy has been reading *Catch-22.*
b.   Sandy had been reading *Catch-22.*
c.   Sandy will have been reading *Catch-22.*

16. These examples, and their interpretation, come from Robert Binnick 1971.

A general, but not very satisfactory, formulation of the interpretation of this construction is that it refers to an event or situation that has some "relevance" to another, later, time, e.g., the present. As such, it seems to have characteristics of a tense and an aspect at the same time. Tense-like, it refers to two times, that of the narrated event, and that of another one, often the speech event. Aspect-like, it looks at the span of time between those two events.

One enlightening analysis of the perfect construction was suggested by James McCawley in 1971. McCawley identified four uses of the present perfect:[17]

85. McCawley's uses of the perfect[18]
   a. "Universal" use, indicating that a situation has endured from a time in the past up to the present:
       We have lived here since 1979.
   b. "Existential" use, indicating the existence of past events:
       I have read *Moby Dick* twice.
   c. "Stative" use, indicating that the effects of a past event continue to the present moment:
       I need a ride; my car has broken down.
   d. "Hot news" use, for reporting brand new information:
       A bunch of students have occupied the President's office!

There is, of course, an aspect difference between the first of these and the rest, in that only the latter three can be used with instantaneous verbs or accomplishment terms, the first requiring verbs like *live, know, work,* and *love*—i.e., statives and duratives. It might be thought that uses (b), (c), and (d) are really the same, but McCawley argues that they are distinct, offering an example like the following—

86. Bud has been fired.

—which is ambiguous between three interpretations:

   There are occasions on which Bud has been fired (*Existential*)
   Bud is currently out of work, having been fired (*Stative*)
   Bud has been fired, which I presume is news to you (*Hot news*)

That these interpretations are truly distinct, rather than special cases of a more general interpretation of the perfect, is supported by the following

17. McCawley does not say this, but each of the four uses can be thought of as representing a different sense of "present relevance."
18. McCawley's analysis refers to the present perfect, but it applies just as well to past perfect and future perfect.

sentence, in which the two parts must receive the same interpretation:

87. But has been fired and Ollie has too.

Both halves of this sentence get the same interpretation—"existential," "stative," or "hot news." If these were merely instances of a more general perfect interpretation, you would expect that the first half of (87) could mean, for example, that Bud has, in the past, had the experience of being fired, and Ollie has just now got fired; or that the first half could mean that Bud is in the state of being unemployed, having gotten fired, and Ollie has, in the past, had the experience of being fired. But it can't. The reason is that conjunctions of ambiguous sentences which are ambiguous in the same way always require the same interpretation in each conjunct. This can be seen in *The chickens are ready to eat and the children are too,* in which the humor derives from this requirement. Since sentence (87) requires identical interpretations of each conjunct, ambiguity rather than vagueness seems to be the proper analysis of perfect constructions. This means that the interpretations listed above are significantly distinct from each other.

EXERCISE 11. Which use of the perfect construction—Universal, Existential, Stative, or Hot News—is manifested by each sentence below?

1. On election night, the newscaster announces, "America has elected a new president tonight."
2. After someone accuses you of being poorly educated, you rather defensively argue, "I've read a lot of books in my time."
3. Your excuse for not attending a party is "I've been handed a tough linguistics assignment and I need to go to the library."
4. You tell a sailboat rental agent who is reluctant to rent you a boat, "I've been sailing for fourteen years."
5. You don't want to go to a movie, because it is one that *you have seen.*
6. After twenty years on a desert island, you are rescued and returned to your home. Your friends and family fill you in on what *has happened* during your absence.
7. The last, summing-up, sentence of a chapter reads, in part, "We have considered the nature and structure of morphophonemic rules . . ."
8. You say to the man or woman of your desires: "I have loved you shamelessly for ten years."

SUMMARY AND CONCLUSION

In this chapter we have examined subclasses and characteristic grammatical features of nouns and verbs. Nouns divide into mass vs. count, and proper vs. common, subclasses, and exhibit features of person (actually and definiteness. A given verb requires a set number of noun phrases to interact with grammatically; such a formulation is an improvement over the transitive-intransitive distinction. Verbal features include mood, tense, voice, and aspect. English expression of these features is extremely complex, with a given form capable of encoding a wide range of meanings.

We have laid a foundation now of understanding English word classes and their characteristic grammar. Our next step is to launch our investigation of syntax, the study of sentence structure.

ADDITIONAL EXERCISE

For each underlined word or phrase in the following passages, say everything you can about it: its word class and subclass, and whatever features of grammar it exhibits that you can identify from among those discussed in this chapter.

> The rabbit-hole went straight on like a tunnel for some way, and then dipped suddenly down, so suddenly that Alice had not a moment to think about stopping herself before she found herself falling down what seemed to be a very deep well.
>
> Either the well was very deep, or she fell very slowly, for she had plenty of time as she went down to look about her, and to wonder what was going to happen next. First, she tried to look down and make out what she was coming to, but it was too dark to see anything; then she looked at the sides of the well and noticed that they were filled with cupboards and book-shelves: here and there she saw maps and pictures hung upon pegs.
> (Lewis Carroll, *Alice's Adventures in Wonderland,* Chapter One)

> We hold these truths to be self-evident: that all men are created equal; that they are endowed by their Creator with certain unalienable rights; that among these are life, liberty, and the pursuit of happiness. That, to secure these rights, governments are instituted among men, deriving their just powers from the consent of the governed.
> (Declaration of Independence)

REFERENCES

BINNICK, R. 1971. *"Will* and *be going to."* In *Papers from the Seventh Regional Meeting,* Chicago Linguistic Society, Chicago: Chicago Linguistic Society, pp. 40–52.

CELCE, MARIANNE. 1970. "The Duality of Collective Nouns." *English Language Teaching* 24.2.

CELCE-MURCIA, M., and D. LARSEN-FREEMAN. 1983. *The Grammar Book: An ESL/EFL Teacher's Course.* Rowley, MA: Newbury House.

CHUNG, SANDRA, AND ALAN TIMBERLAKE. 1985. "Tense, Aspect, and Mood." In *Language Typology and Syntactic Description, Vol. III: Grammatical Categories and the Lexicon,* ed. by Timothy Shopen, Cambridge: Cambridge University Press, pp. 202–258.

McCAWLEY, JAMES D. 1971. "Tense and Time Reference in English." In *Studies in Linguistic Semantics,* ed. by Charles J. Fillmore & D. Terence Langendoen, New York: Holt, Rinehart, & Winston, pp. 97–113.

PRINCE, ELLEN F. 1973. "The Futurate in English." Unpublished paper.

SILVERSTEIN, MICHAEL. 1974. "Dialectal Developments in Chinookan Tense Aspect Systems: An Areal-Historical Analysis," *International Journal of American Linguistics, Memoir 29.*

VENDLER, ZENO. 1967. *Linguistics in Philosophy.* Ithaca: Cornell University Press.

Chapter Six

PHRASE STRUCTURE

From words we move to phrases, significant groupings of words. Here, our goal will be to discover the phrase structure of simple English sentences (complex ones we'll deal with in later chapters), justify specific analyses of phrase structure, and explain a notation for phrase structure. The notation is one we have already used (briefly, in our discussion of morphology in Chapter Three), "tree" diagrams like this one:

1.

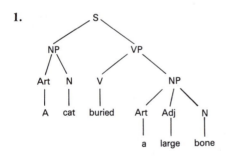

WHAT IS PHRASE STRUCTURE?

Phrase structure is the division of a sentence into parts, and the division of those parts into subparts. For instance, the sentence *A white horse cantered eagerly around the corral* can be first divided into two parts as follows:

2.

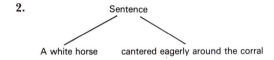

Sentence

A white horse   cantered eagerly around the corral

It's usually easy to split a sentence into two parts. The left part normally functions as subject, the right part as predicate. Within the subject and the predicate, though, the division isn't always so straightforward. In (2), there are three possibilities for dividing up the subject phrase *a white horse:*

3.   (a) | a white | horse |

(b) | a | white horse |

(c) | a | white | horse |

Let's look now at how we might choose among these possibilities.

HOW TO DETERMINE PHRASE STRUCTURE

One approach to determining phrase structure is a **substitution** test: whatever you can substitute a single word for, preserving grammaticality, is a "chunk," a phrase. In our *white horse* sentence, if we can find a single word to substitute for *a white*, then we are justified in calling *a white* a phrase, and boxing it as in (3a). If we can find a single word to substitute for *white horse*, then *white horse* is a phrase, as in (3b). If we can't find a suitable substitution for either one, then presumably neither is a chunk, and (3c) represents the phrase structure.

For *a white* we can substitute *the, my, this, one,* in each case preserving grammaticality: *the horse, my horse, this horse, one horse,*

4.

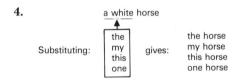

a white horse

Substituting: | the
my
this
one | gives: the horse
my horse
this horse
one horse

On the basis of this, we can divide the phrase like this: *a white - horse.* However, for *white horse*, we can also find grammatical substitutes: *piano, horse, tree, man, soul: a piano, a horse, a tree, a man, a soul.*

5.

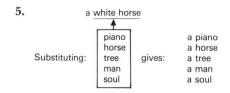

Substituting:

piano		a piano
horse		a horse
tree	gives:	a tree
man		a man
soul		a soul

On the basis of this, we can divide the phrase like this: *a - white horse*.

So which of the two groupings is right? At this point we simply cannot tell.

Fortunately, substitution usually works better than it seems to here. It supports the intuitive division of a whole sentence into subject and predicate:

6.

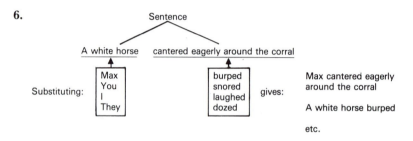

Substitution produces sentences like *A white horse burped* and *Max cantered eagerly around the corral*. Since these are grammatical, the division of the sentence into the two parts *a white horse* and *cantered eagerly around the corral* is supported. If we tried other sorts of substitutions, they would not work. Suppose we believed that the sequence *horse cantered eagerly* was a phrase, a "chunk" of the sentence. We would search in vain for a substitution for it that would preserve grammaticality:

7.

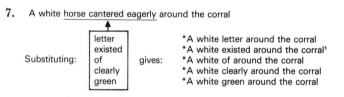

Because the results of substituting are not grammatical sentences, *horse cantered eagerly* is not a phrase.

---

[1] If *white* is taken as a noun, this sentence approaches acceptability.

EXERCISE 1.

A. Apply the substitution criterion to justify the following groupings:

1. [very very large] [tree]
2. [put] [the apple] [in the barrel]
3. [Seventeen freshmen] [got into a Volkswagen]
4. [[You][believe [that I know [that you believe a me]]]]

B. Provide evidence against the following groupings by showing that various substitutions are impossible:

1. [try to] [prove that the] [president can read]
2. [for best] [results use] [Sears staples in] [the right size for each] [job]

In the ways we have just used it, the substitution criterion involves substituting a single word for a word sequence. It is useful to extend the substitution criterion beyond this, in two ways: first, by substituting not just a single word, but a word sequence, and second, by examining mutual substitution possibilities in a range of environments. The idea is that word sequences which are mutually substitutable in a given environment are likely to be phrases; and if they are mutually substitutable in different environments they are even more likely to be phrases. Suppose we suspect that the underlined word sequences in the following sentences are phrases:

8. a. The puppy scratched at the screen door.
   b. I want that little striped kitten.
   c. Max yawned.
   d. I really like swimming in the reservoir.

They are all mutually substitutable. In the context of (8d), *I really like . . . ,* all the other candidate phrases can occur:

9. a. I really like the puppy.
   b. I really like that little striped kitten.
   c. I really like Max.

In the contexts of (8a, b, and c), *the puppy, that little striped kitten,* and *Max* are mutually substitutable:

10. a. That little striped kitten scratched at the screen door.
    b. Max scratched at the screen door.
11. a. I want the puppy.
    b. I want Max.
12. a. The puppy yawned.
    b. That little striped kitten yawned.

In these contexts we cannot place *swimming in the reservoir:* e.g., **Swimming in the reservoir scratched at the screen door* is ungrammatical. But in other contexts it is mutually substitutable with the other candidate phrases:

13.
$$\left\{ \begin{array}{l} \text{The puppy} \\ \text{That little striped kitten} \\ \text{Max} \\ \text{Swimming in the reservoir} \end{array} \right\} \text{ can really be fun}$$

14.
a. I just love
$$\left\{ \begin{array}{l} \text{the puppy} \\ \text{that little striped kitten} \\ \text{Max} \\ \text{swimming in the reservoir} \end{array} \right\}$$

b. What
$$\left\{ \begin{array}{l} \text{the puppy} \\ \text{that little striped kitten} \\ \text{Max} \\ \text{swimming in the reservoir} \end{array} \right\} \text{ means to me is a good time}$$

Consequently, we can tentatively conclude that all four of these candidate phrases are in fact phrases.

With the substitution criterion, negative evidence is not as convincing as positive evidence. Even if we find no grammatical substitutions for some word sequence, we can't be sure that there aren't any; there might be some we haven't thought of yet. Unfortunately, positive evidence does not fully determine phrase structure either; we have not yet found a basis for deciding among *a - white horse, a white - horse,* and *a - white - horse.* Let's see what other criteria for phrase structure might help.

Conjoinability

Phrases can be **conjoined** with *and,* but non-phrases cannot. All the conjoined word sequences below are phrases:

15. a. *Max left* and *Stella stayed.*
     b. *King Arthur* and *Queen Guinevere* both lusted after gold.
     c. Rod *batted .385* and *played errorless ball* last season.
     d. A *very large* and *kind of scary* dog is barking next door.

Do you feel intuitively that the italicized sequences are phrases? If they are, they are different kinds of phrases, in each case. In (a), *Max left* and *Stella stayed* are phrases since they're both sentences. In (b), the italicized sequences are both **Noun Phrases** (NPs). (As an informal exercise, try the substitution criterion with these NP sequences. In particular, observe that they are mutually substitutable with the sequences that we identified as phrases in the preceding section: *the puppy, that little striped kitten, Max,* and *swimming in the reservoir,* which are noun phrases too.) In (c), *batted .385* and *played errorless ball* are **Verb Phrases** (VPs). And in (d) the conjoined items are **Adjective Phrases** (APs). We'll discuss these phrase categories below. But non-phrases cannot be conjoined:

16. *The *boy ran into the* and *girl dashed out of the* schoolyard.

The reason this example is ungrammatical is that *boy ran into the* and *girl dashed out of the* are not phrases.

The way to apply the conjoinability test is to try to conjoin a suspected phrase with one containing different words, but what seems to be the same internal structure. For instance, if you suspect (as you should) that in the sentence *Max devoured the sweet jam* the word sequence *the sweet jam* is a phrase, you should try to conjoin it with something similar, like *The stale toast: On the table is the sweet jam and the stale toast.* This is a grammatical sentence, so you conclude, tentatively, that *the sweet jam* is a phrase.

EXERCISE 2.

A. Use the conjoinability criterion to support the following groupings:
1. [A large python] curled around Sharon's leg.
2. Max believed [that the moon was made of green cheese].
3. John is [taking it with him].
4. A [little child] shall lead them.
5. Mannie and Mo [tried to convince Jack to resign].

B. Use the conjoinability criterion to argue against the following groupings:
1. A large [python curled] around Sharon's leg.
2. Max [believed that the] moon was made of green cheese.
3. John is taking [it with] him.
4. A little [child shall] lead them.
5. Mannie [and Mo tried] to convince Jack to resign.

How helpful is conjoinability in helping us decide on the phrase structure of *a white horse*? Unfortunately, not very. Both *a white* and *white horse* are conjoinable with similar sequences:

17. a. *A white horse* and *gray pony* were delivered yesterday.
 b. *A white* and *a gray* horse were delivered yesterday.

Therefore, as with the substitutability criterion, according to the conjoinability criterion both *a white* and *white horse* are constituents. But they can't both be, since they overlap. Fortunately, there are other criteria for phrase-hood.

Movement

Any sequence of words that **moves** as a unit, linguists have reasoned, is a unit. For instance, in *Max bought some great toys for Alison's four-year-old daughter,* the word-sequences *some great toys* and *Alison's four-year-old daughter* can both be switched:

18.

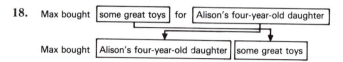

Both movements indicate "phrase-hood."

Don't worry about the fact that the word *for* disappears when these movements occur. Movements often result in the deletion (or, in some cases, the introduction) of grammatical function words or morphemes, like *for.* We will see more examples of this below.

You should corroborate, with substitution and conjoinability, that the boxed word sequences in the example above are indeed phrases. When we can find evidence from more than one criterion, the case for a particular sequence being a phrase is obviously strengthened.

Here are some other examples of how the movement criterion justifies identifying certain word-sequences as phrases:

19.

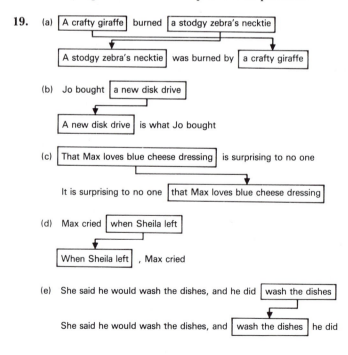

EXERCISE 3. Use the movement criterion, as just demonstrated, to support the phrase groupings below:

1. My neighbor Eddie mowed [the sidewalk] late last night.
2. Hippy the hippo roared with laughter [when her keeper came].
3. It annoyed Cathy [that Max was late so often].
4. He can [catch a lot of trout].
5. [For Smith to fire Wesson] would be really stupid.

What does the movment criterion have to say about the phrase structure of *the white horse?* To see, look at the movement pattern shown below:

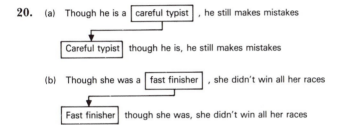

20.　(a)　Though he is a │ careful typist │ , he still makes mistakes

│ Careful typist │ though he is, he still makes mistakes

(b)　Though she was a │ fast finisher │ , she didn't win all her races

│ Fast finisher │ though she was, she didn't win all her races

Significantly, this pattern applies to *white horse,* but not to *a white:*

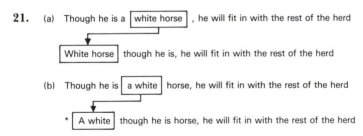

21.　(a)　Though he is a │ white horse │ , he will fit in with the rest of the herd

│ White horse │ though he is, he will fit in with the rest of the herd

(b)　Though he is │ a white │ horse, he will fit in with the rest of the herd

*　│ A white │ though he is horse, he will fit in with the rest of the herd

Since the result of the movement in (a) is grammatical, but that in (b) is ungrammatical, it seems reasonable to conclude that the phrase structure of *a white horse* is:

22.　│ a │ │ white horse │

So while the first two criteria we applied to discover the phrase structure of *a white horse* were inconclusive, the third provides evidence in favor of one possible phrase structure analysis, and against another. This is not unusual in the often difficult task of finding out what the phrase structure of a sentence or word sequence is. The next criterion for phrases we shall discuss will corroborate our finding about *a white horse*.

Antecedent for a Pro-Form

Pronouns, pro-verb phrases, pro-sentences, pro-prepositional phrases, and pro-adjective phrases all take phrases as antecedents, not non-phrase strings of words. In the following examples, the italicized sequences of words (all phrases) are the antecedents for the underscored pro-forms:

23. a. Pronoun: *The old men* stopped because they were tired.
     b. Pro-verb phrase: Jeff *asked Sandy to dance* before Peter could do so.
     c. Pro-sentence: *Smith now plays the horses,* and it doesn't surprise me one bit.
     d. Pro-prepositional phrase: We put the bugs *in the jar* and left them there overnight.
     e. Pro-adjective phrase: Lavern is *really obese* but she didn't become so until after she inherited all that money.

This criterion will corroborate our finding about the phrase structure of *a white horse* in the following way. There is a so-called "pronoun," *one,* that can refer to *white horse* as an antecedent, if not in *a white horse,* at least in the identically structured *the white horse:*

24. I want the *white horse* by the gate, not the one in the stall.

With *white horse* as antecedent for *one,* this sentence means that the speaker doesn't want "the *white horse* in the stall." (This sentence also has another meaning, in which *one* refers just to *horse.*) But *one* cannot possibly refer to *the white:*

25. *I want *the white* horse by the gate, not one horse in the stall.

On the basis of **movement** and **being an antecedent for a pro-form**, then, we can be fairly confident about assigning the phrase structure *a - white horse* to the phrase *a white horse.*

EXERCISE 4. Use the criterion of being a possible antecedent for a pro-form to support the phrase-hood of the italicized sequences below.

1. Greg and Steve *built a mountain house.*
2. I doubt *tomorrow will be sunny.*
3. *Automobile companies* resist attempts by consumer groups to get them to recall vehicles for safety reasons.
4. Put the tinsel *on the trees,* not under it.

To sum up, we have examined four criteria for establishing phrase structure: substitution, conjoinability, movement, and the ability to be an antecedent for a pro-form. Not all will always work; we had to struggle a bit before establishing the correct phrase structure of *a white horse*. In fact, two of our four criteria failed to determine which of two possible phrase structure analyses was right. But two criteria worked, and you can be confident that every word sequence that is justifiably called a phrase will be supported by at least one of these criteria. You can be even more confident about an analysis if two or more criteria support it, and none provides evidence against it—as with *a white horse*.

PHRASAL CATEGORIES

Sequences of words established by these criteria are "phrases." Each phrase belongs to a category, like Noun Phrase (NP), Verb Phrase (VP), Sentence (S), Adjective Phrase (AP), Prepositional Phrase (PP), etc.

Phrasal categories are named according to the most important word of the phrase. **Noun Phrases** (NPs) are so labeled because they typically contain nouns.[2] **Verb Phrases** (VPs) always contain verbs. **Adjective Phrases** (APs) are so-called because an adjective is the only required word; intensifiers are optional:

26.

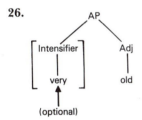

Prepositional phrases (PPs) contain a preposition and an NP:

27.

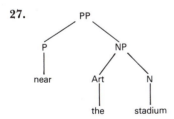

---

[2]When they don't, they function similarly to NPs that do—e.g., as subjects, direct objects, etc. In *To fantasize is delightful*, the infinitive *to fantasize*, even though it lacks a noun, is an NP functioning as subject, parallel to *Max* in *Max is delightful*.

Later in this chapter, we will examine the details of the internal structure of NPs, VPs and APs.

A NOTATION FOR PHRASE STRUCTURE

We will use "tree" diagrams to represent phrase structure. Let's begin by looking at the tree for the sentence *A bear scared the campers.*

28.

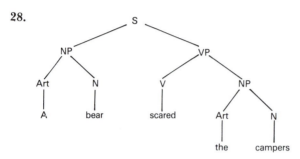

This diagram embodies the following claims: The entire sequence of words *A bear scared the campers* is a sentence (the top "S," which "dominates" the whole string of words, makes this claim); the sentence comprises a noun phrase (NP) *a bear* and a verb phrase (VP) *scared the campers;* the initial NP itself comprises an article (Art) *a* and a noun (N) *bear;* and the VP comprises a verb (V) *scared* and an NP *the campers,* which is itself made up of an Art *the* and an N *campers.*

You can see that a tree provides the following information: the **word class** of each word, the **phrase structure** of the whole sentence (what the word-groupings are, and their hierarchical structure—how they are nested or not nested inside each other), and the **phrasal category** of each phrase (what kind of phrase each phrase is).

Every branch in a tree must ultimately end in a word or morpheme, and every word or morpheme must be at the bottom of just one path of branches starting from the "S" at the top ("root") of the sentence. The latter requirement means that a tree like this is illegal—

29.

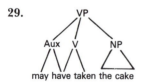

—despite apparently making sense, in a way, because *have* might be termed both an auxiliary and a verb. In addition, branches are not allowed to cross each other. So, for *Cigars, Leonard loved* a tree like this is illegal—

30.

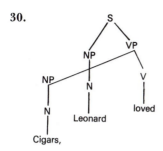

—even though it makes a certain amount of sense, because *cigars* functions as the direct object of the verb *loved,* and therefore might be thought to belong inside the VP with that verb. But phrase structure is only one kind of syntactic structure, and there are other levels and kinds of structure to capture that kind of relation. Phrase structure trees represent only "continuous" phrases.

Trees and Functions

A tree does not show, directly, information about the **function** of phrasal categories. A tree does not indicate directly whether a particular NP functions as subject, direct object, or indirect object. (We'll take up these notions in the next chapter.) However, it is possible to define two of these functions "configurationally." In English, an NP functioning as subject of a sentence can be defined as any NP which is in the circled position in a sentence:

31.

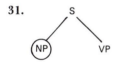

A direct object NP in English can be defined as any NP which is in the circled position in the following tree:

32.

However, indirect object is so semantic a notion that it cannot usefully be defined in configurational terms. For an NP to be an indirect object its verb must have a meaning that has to do with giving in some way. We'll discuss this in the next chapter.

Trees and Ambiguity

Certain kinds of ambiguous sentences can be "disambiguated" with trees. For instance, *Josie bought the car in Miami* means either that Josie bought the Miami-located car, or that the buying occurred in Miami.[3] In other words, *in Miami* either identifies which car Josie bought or tells where the purchase was made. A useful way to think about this is in terms of such a sentence being actually two sentences, both made of the very same words in the very same order, but with different phrase structures:

33. (a)

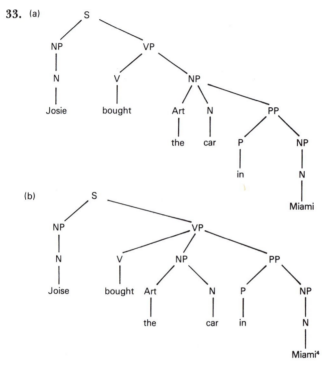

(b)

---

[3]There is a third meaning, due to the ambiguity of the tense. The first meaning divides between a meaning in which the car is in Miami now, and one in which it was in Miami when Josie bought it.

[4]Another possibility is the following tree:

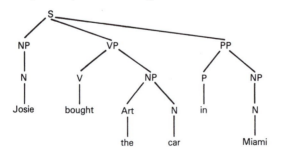

The sentence represented by tree (a) answers the question "which car did Josie buy?"; the sentence represented by tree (b) answers the question "Where did Josie buy the car?" The key to the meaning is the location of the PP *in Miami,* inside or outside the NP containing *the car.* When it is inside, as in tree (a), it may be thought of as modifying the noun *car.* When it is outside, as in tree (b), its "scope" is the whole VP, and may be thought of as modifying the rest of the material in the VP—*bought the car.*

EXERCISE 5.

A. Draw trees for the following sentences, paying special attention to the location of PPs:
1. The koala consumed the leaves with boredom.
2. Greg put the toothbrush inside the piano.
3. The professor with the sunglasses paid for the bubblegum.
4. Bugs fled from the wrath of Elmer.

B. In the trees you have just drawn, draw a circle around every NP that functions as direct object, and a rectangle around every NP that functions as subject.

C. Here are some ambiguous sentences. For each one, paraphrase it in two different ways to bring out the two meanings. Some of these sentences can be disambiguated by means of different phrase structure trees, but some can't. For every one that can be disambiguated by different phrase structure trees, draw the trees (one for each meaning).
1. I don't like hot chili and curry.
2. I love visiting in-laws.
3. Popeye loved Olive more than Pluto.
4. I decided on the truck.
5. They found the treasure under the stairs.
6. The young ones are ready to eat.

CANONICAL AND NON-CANONICAL SENTENCE FORM

Most of the sentences we have discussed so far have had the global structure "NP + VP." As the most common, and in a sense the most basic, sentence form in English, this is **canonical** sentence form for English. (Other languages have other canonical sentence forms. Arabic, for example, has the basic order "Verb + Subject NP + Direct Object NP." That is, the canonical sentence form for Arabic is "V + NP + NP.") But English allows for other sentence structures too, like the structures of these sentences:

34. 1. Shut up!
2. Did Mickey leave Minnie?
3. Asparagus I hate.
4. Up jumped a little rabbit.
5. "Please go," begged Mary.

We'll discuss the structures of "non-canonical" sentences like these later in this chapter.

Both canonical and non-canonical sentence forms can contain optional elements in addition to NPs and VPs. For instance, in English, *not* can be present in any kind of sentence. A sentence like *Max will not paint the garage* is canonical just as *Max will paint the garage* is. Sentence Adverbs are also optional elements. Sentences like *Obviously Martha loves George; Jack liked Jacquie, fortunately;* and *James clearly favored Dolly* are canonical sentences containing Sentence Adverbs:

35.

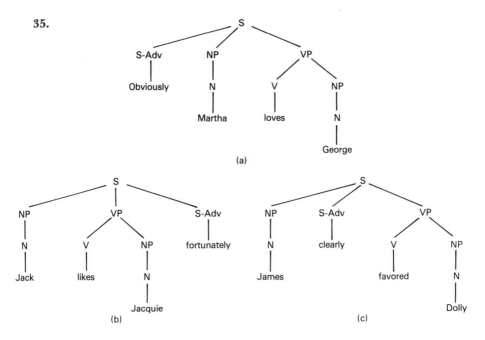

With this as a foundation, let's turn our attention now to some special characteristics of NPs and VPs.

INTERNAL STRUCTURE OF MAJOR PHRASE TYPES

Some Details of NPs

Head nouns

Most NPs contain a **head** noun which determines the number (singular or plural) of the entire NP. In the following example, the noun *tree*, which is singular, determines the number of the whole NP of which it is a part.

36.

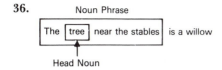

Agreeing with this singular NP is the singular verb, *is*. *Tree* therefore is the head noun of the NP *the tree near the stables*. Contrast this with the following example:

37.

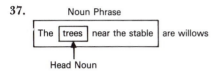

Here, the plural head noun *trees* determines the number of its NP. Agreeing with this plural NP is the plural verb *are*.

A head noun imposes its gender, as well, on its NP, so that any pronoun for which that NP is the antecedent must bear that gender:

38.

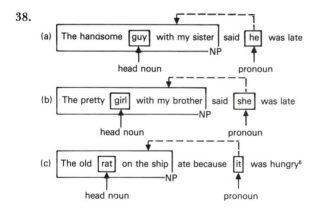

In (a), the masculine noun *guy* imposes its gender on the NP of which it is the head, so the pronoun which takes that NP as antecedent is masculine (*he*). In (b), the feminine noun *girl* imposes its gender on its NP, so the pronoun which takes that NP as antecedent is feminine (*she*). In (c), the neuter noun *rat* imposes its gender on its NP, so the pronoun which takes that NP as antecedent is neuter (*it*).

---

[5] Pronouns can, of course, refer to NPs within NPs, and consequently not bear the gender of the head noun of the containing NP. In place of *he* in (a), *she* could occur, referring back to the embedded NP *my sister*, and similarly *he* could occur in place of *she* in (b), referring back to the embedded NP *my brother*.

NP-internal structures

So far we have seen three kinds of NPs:

39.

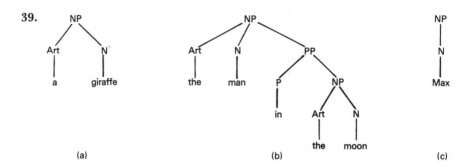

(a)   (b)   (c)

You may wonder about the structure of single-word NPs like tree (c) above. Why does it makes sense to say a single noun is also an NP? You might think the structure of a sentence like *Max left Shelley* would be

40.

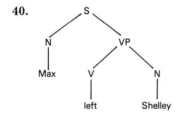

But evidence from substitution—especially mutual substitutability with other, longer phrases which we have called NPs—supports the idea that single nouns in subject or direct object positions (among other positions) are also NPs. In the example above we could substitute, for either *Max* or *Shelley*, longer NPs like *the girl who sits next to my brother*. Other evidence supports labeling single Ns as NPs as well. For practice, you should apply the other criteria for phrase-hood to this question.

The same point holds for pronouns like *he, him, she, it, they* and *them;* they are single-word NPs too.

N̄s

In our discussion earlier about the phrase structure of *a white horse*, we examined data which we can now interpret as evidence for phrase structures intermediate in size between a single word (a noun or pronoun), and a full phrasal category (NP). There are major implications of this for the internal structure of NPs.

Adjective phrases inside NPs

NPs can contain adjectives, e.g., in the example we have been beating to death, the NP *a white horse*. In our earlier discussion we found evidence from the pro-form *one* and from the movement criterion to support a phrase structure like *a - white horse*, or, in tree form.

41.

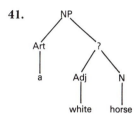

What shall we call the phrase *white horse?* There is no commonly accepted name for this type of phrase, midway in size between a noun and an NP, but a widely-used abbreviation is N̄ (pronounced "N-bar"). The tree for *a white horse*, then, might be the following:

42.

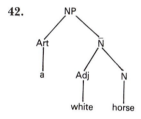

This is a significant step in the right direction, but for two reasons the tree for *a white horse* is actually slightly more complicated than this. First, the Adjective must be labeled "Adjective Phrase" as well as "Adjective." The reason for this will be discussed below. Second, the noun *horse* must be an N̄ as well as an N. That is, we need a tree like this—

43.

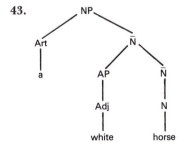

The reason for this comes from the fact that *horse* can be an antecedent for a pro-form, the "pronoun" *one*, just as *white horse* can in *the white horse,* indicating that in this construction *white horse* and *horse* are the same kind of phrase. To see this, observe that in one meaning of the following sentence, the antecedent of *one* is *horse.*

44.   I like this white horse, not that one.

(The meaning this sentence has when *horse* is the antecedent for *one* is "I like this white horse, not that horse." To pronounce this sentence with this meaning, stress *white.*) Consequently the noun *horse* must be an N̄ as well as a noun.

What is an N̄? At this point, we can define it as follows: a possible antecedent for *one,* or an AP-N sequence. We will see below that there is another structure an N̄ can have as well.

Are all nouns also N̄s? No. Proper nouns aren't, since they don't occur in NPs that contain other words; they don't co-occur with articles, quantifiers, or demonstratives (**The Max, *Some good Linda, *This Jane*[6]), and consequently can't be referred to by *one.* Some occurrences of common nouns aren't N̄s either, for the same reason. Consider the two meanings of *the Russian teacher.* One meaning is 'the teacher of Russian'; the other is 'the teacher who is Russian.' In the first meaning, the teacher may or may not be of Russian nationality; in the second, the teacher may or may not teach Russian. Only one of these meanings allows *one* to refer to *teacher,* the one in which *Russian* identifies national origin, not subject taught. That is, *That guy with the booming voice is the Russian teacher, not the French one* means only '. . . is the teacher who is Russian, not French,' never '. . . is the teacher of Russian, not French.' In light of this, it has been proposed (by the syntacticians Norbert Hornstein and David Lightfoot [1981]) that there are two trees for NPs like *the Russian teacher:*

45.

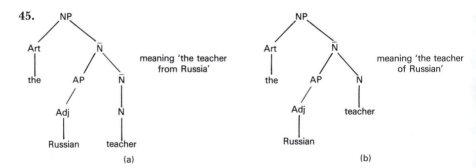

[6]When they do, as in *this is the Max I was telling you about* or *This good Linda, not the bad one, can be in our play,* the "proper" noun is actually being used as a common noun.

EXERCISE 6. Draw trees for the following sentences, paying special attention to the internal structure of the initial NPs:

1. The gray rabbit greeted Elmer Fudd.
2. This little house is near the town.
3. This poetry essay bores me.
4. This steel mill closed in March.
5. Those Russian farmers need this tractor.

Adjective phrases inside N̄s

What is the phrase structure of *very large green tree?* Substitution would seem to support *very large green - tree,* because we can substitute *beautiful* for *very large green,* giving *beautiful tree:*

46. very large green tree
       ↑   = beautiful tree
     beautiful

We would thus have an Adjective Phrase made up of an intensifier *very* and two adjectives, perhaps in a tree like this:

47.

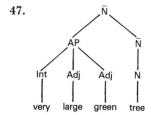

But another substitution is possible: *beautiful* for *very large,* giving *beautiful green tree*:

48. very large green tree
       ↑   = beautiful green tree
     beautiful

Movement provides evidence for calling *very large* a phrase: *Very large though this green tree is, . . . ,* whereas no movement is possible of the hypothetical phrase *very large green*. Consequently, the N̄ *very large green tree* should be divided *very large - green tree:*

49.

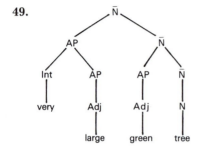

The single words *large* and *green* must be APs as well as Adjectives, since intensifiers can precede them: *very very large intensely green tree.*

An interesting result of this is that N̄s can have any number of APs inside them, nested in the following way:

50.

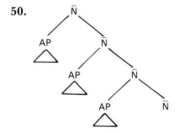

For example:

51.

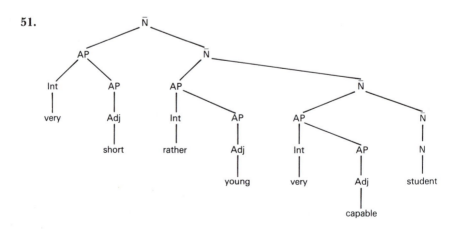

EXERCISE 7.

A. Draw trees for the underlined Ñs:
1. A rather interesting envelope is waiting for you on the table.
2. Give me some of those juicy red apples.
3. A very very tall gentleman wants to see you.

B. What does the criterion of conjoinability suggest about the phrase structure of *very large green tree?*

PPs inside NPs

What does *one* refer to in the following sentence?

52. This writer of suspense novels has sold more books than the one you were telling me about.

In one meaning, it refers to the N + PP sequence *writer of suspense novels,* thus arguing for an Ñ phrase.[7] That this sequence is a phrase is also supported by conjoinability:

53. This *writer of suspense novels* and *designer of motorcycle engines* is a real renaissance man.

Substitution supports this:

54. This writer of suspense novels
    $\uparrow$ = this guy
    guy

Consequently, we can conclude that the NP *this writer of suspense novels* has the following phrase structure:

55.

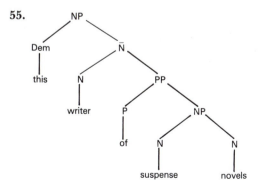

[7] Intuitions differ on whether another meaning is possible, one in which *one* refers just to *writer.*

In this tree, we see an N̄ composed of an N and a PP.

Now we encounter the problem of figuring out whether a noun right before a PP (*writer*, in the tree above) is an N̄ or just an N. The *one*-pronoun test suggests the latter, because of the ungrammaticality of *I like this writer of suspense novels better than that one of romances*, which is ungrammatical because *one* can't refer back to *writer*. As a result, calling *writer* just an N, as we did in tree (55), seems to have been right.

In contrast, *one* can refer to *writer* in the following sentence:

56.   I admire the <u>writer</u> in my novel class more than the *one* in my poetry class.

The tree for the NP *the writer in my novel class*, then, must be this:

57.

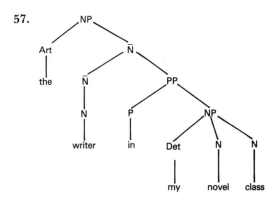

As you can see, determining whether a single noun is an N̄ (as well as an N) can be tricky. The tests we have established as useful for deciding are: (1) whether an adjective can precede the noun: if so, the noun is probably an N̄, and if not it probably isn't; (2) whether the "pronoun" *one* can take the noun as antecedent: if so, the noun is probably an N̄, and if not it probably isn't. (A third test, implicit in our discussion of PPs following Ns, is whether a PP could follow the N, but doesn't in the example under consideration: if so, the noun is probably an N̄, and if not it probably isn't.)

To summarize, N̄s are phrases inside NPs. An N̄ can be made up of a single noun, an AP and a noun (or N̄), or a noun (or N̄) and a following PP.

EXERCISE 8. Draw trees for the underlined NPs in the following sentences, paying special attention to the issue of N vs N̄.

1.   The librarian questioned <u>the borrower of mysteries</u>.
2.   The librarian questioned <u>the borrower with a backpack</u>.
3.   Max is <u>a student of literature</u>.

4. Max is <u>a student with a crewcut.</u>
5. Max is <u>a student of literature with a crewcut.</u>

Pre - N̄ elements

Determiners

Articles and demonstratives. The articles (*a/an* and *the*) and demonstratives (*this, that, these,* and *those*) occur before an N̄:

58.

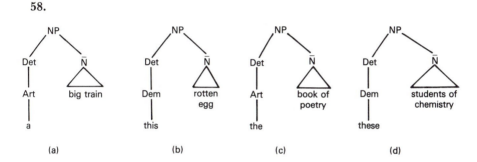

| (a) | (b) | (c) | (d) |

These trees make explicit the fact that articles and demonstratives are determiners. However, our trees in this book will generally identify articles just as articles, and demonstratives as demonstratives, without further identifying them as Determiners.

Possessives. Simple possessive pronominal determiners, e.g., *my, his, its,* etc., can occur before an N̄, just as do Articles and Demonstratives:

59.

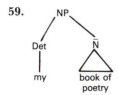

Full NPs can also be possessive determiners, for example possessive versions of proper nouns—*John's book of poetry*—and full NPs with common nouns—*The fat football coach's playbook.* These possessive determiners are NPs with the possessive morpheme following:

60.

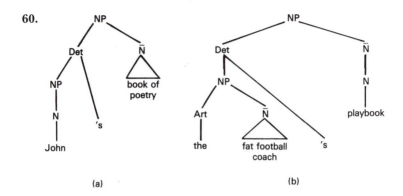

(a)   (b)

Since any NP can be plugged in in front of *-'s*, substitution argues strongly for hanging the possessive morpheme *-'s* from the Determiner node instead of attaching it directly to the NP.

EXERCISE 9. Draw trees for the underlined NPs:

1. Your brother is a crybaby.
2. I want your brother's cupcake.
3. Max's lawyer's sister's house is rather impressive.

Quantifiers

Quantifiers (*all, some, any,* etc.), introduced in Chapter Four, are semantically and grammatically complex. One easy thing about them is their number. Some go only with singular count nouns, some only with plural ones, some only with mass nouns, and some with either plurals or masses. The two singular quantifiers are *each* and *every.* Quantifiers which take only plural nouns are *several, many,* and *few.* Those which take only mass nouns are *much* and *little.* Those which can go with either plurals or masses are *some, any, no, all, more* and *most.*

More complicated is the distribution of quantifiers—where they can occur. Here we'll examine their distribution inside NPs. Sometimes quantifiers occur immediately before an N̄ (*every cat, some delicious bagels, many cars*). Sometimes they precede Prepositional Phrases (*all of the cats, some of the bagels*). Sometimes they precede NPs (*all these adult cats, all the good movies*). Sometimes they occur inside N̄'s (*the few good students*). Examples:

61.

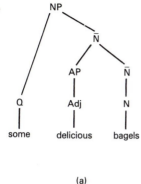

(a)

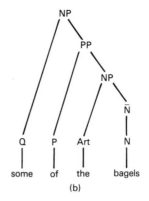

(b)

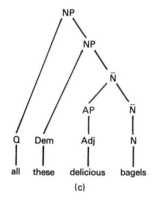

(c)

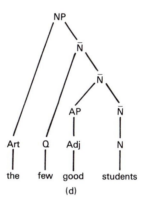

(d)

(As an informal exercise, justify these trees for yourself by seeing that everywhere there is an N̄, there could be an Adjective-Noun or N-PP sequence, and everywhere there is an NP, a Determiner-Noun sequence is possible.)

Among the quantifiers, only *all* can fit into the pattern of tree (c) above. Trying other quantifiers produces results like **many the houses* and **some the trees*.

A final way quantifiers can occur within NPs is as pronouns, as in *All were here*.

EXERCISE 10. Draw trees for the following NPs:

1. each apple
2. many good poets
3. some of the many good responses

Summary of NP Possibilities

From this discussion we can extract the following obligatory and optional components of NPs:

An NP may be made up of a Q followed by an N̄, a PP, or an NP; a Det followed by an N̄; an AP followed by an N or N̄; an N alone; or a Pronoun (which may be a Quantifier).

62.

$$NP = \begin{Bmatrix} Q & \begin{Bmatrix} \bar{N} \\ PP \\ NP \end{Bmatrix} \\ Det & \bar{N} \\ AP \begin{Bmatrix} \bar{N} \\ N \end{Bmatrix} \\ N \\ Pro \end{Bmatrix}$$

In this notation the curly brackets mean "pick one and only one of the listed elements." The sequence beginning with AP is needed to account for plural Adjective - Noun (or N̄) sequences, like *old trees*, which are complete NPs, while their singular counterparts—*old tree*, for example—are only N̄s.

An N̄ may be made up of a single noun, an AP or Q and a noun (or N̄), or a noun (or N̄) and a following PP:

63.

$$\bar{N} = \begin{Bmatrix} N \\ \begin{Bmatrix} Q \\ AP \end{Bmatrix} \begin{Bmatrix} N \\ \bar{N} \end{Bmatrix} \\ \begin{Bmatrix} N \\ \bar{N} \end{Bmatrix} PP \end{Bmatrix}$$

An AP may be made up of an intensifier and an AP, or of an Adjective alone, in either case optionally followed by a PP:

64. $$AP = \begin{Bmatrix} Int\ AP \\ Adj \end{Bmatrix} (PP)$$

The optional PP is to account for phrases like *was tall for a child*, in which *tall for a child* can be seen to be a constituent by virtue of the movement criterion (e.g., *Tall for a child though Max was, . . .*).

EXERCISE 11.

A. Draw trees for the underlined NPs in the sentences below, making sure that our trees conform to the possibilities allowed by formulas (62), (63), and (64):

1. The excited seagulls dove for the fish scraps.

2. Some of the students' papers are publishable.

3. <u>Any reader of old novels</u> will know who Silas Marner was.

4. <u>Those big green trees</u> near the red barn are a good hiding place.

B. Formula (63) above doesn't allow for N N sequences like *poetry essay* or *stone wall.* (Sequences like *White House,* of course, are compound nouns, and, as such, can be considered single Ns. Recall the characteristic stress patterns of compound nouns, discussed in Chapter Three). In fact, longer sequences are possible: *poetry essay index, desk top finish control,* etc. Try to revise the formula so it will allow for such "noun strings."

C. Our description of NPs has omitted any mention of conjoined elements. Figure out what trees for the following underlined phrases ought to look like, and draw them.

1. <u>The short and stocky catcher</u> threw the ball into center field.

2. <u>Those fat watermelons and bananas</u> look incredibly delicious. (two trees, one for each meaning)

3. Squirrels can live <u>in trees and holes in the ground.</u> (one tree only; ignore the 'trees in the ground' meaning)

4. <u>Max and Jane and Dottie</u> were fishing for compliments. (three trees)

Verb Phrases

Verb Phrases are not as internally complex as NPs are, but they do come in a variety of shapes. Here is a list of possible VP contents:[8]

65.
a. V alone: Mike <u>snored</u>
b. V + NP: Mike <u>built a cabin</u>
c. V + PP: Mile <u>lived in the forest</u>
d. V + NP + PP: Mike <u>put the box on the table</u>
e. V + AP: Mike <u>is cheerful</u>
f. V + AP + PP: Mike <u>seems cheerful to us</u>
g. V + NP + NP: Mike <u>sent her the cookies</u>
h. V + Q: Mike's complaints <u>were many</u>

Additionally, Manner Adverbs and "Manner Prepositional Phrases" can co-occur with all these possibilities—*Mike snored <u>quietly</u>, Mike smiled <u>with effort</u>,* etc. The following formula summarizes the possibilities for VPs in simple sentences:

66.

$$\text{VP} = \text{V} \left\{ \begin{array}{l} (\{{\text{NP} \atop \text{AP}}\}) \ (\text{PP}) \ (\{{\text{Man.Adv.} \atop \text{PP}}\}) \\ \text{Q} \end{array} \right\}$$

---

[8]Not an exhaustive list; additional structures will be discussed below.

In this and similar formulas, parentheses indicate optional elements, and (as before) curly brackets indicate obligatory selection of just one listed element.

EXERCISE 12. Draw trees for the following VPs. Don't worry about the internal structure of NPs. (Use triangles to abbreviate.)

1. put the cat on the porch
2. cheered for the team lustily
3. looks short for a basketball player
4. built a house of logs for the twins

Auxiliary verbs

What the VP formula (66) doesn't include is the option of auxiliary verbs (**auxes**), which were briefly introduced in Chapter Four. Auxes are the "helping verbs"—*have, be,* and modals (*can, will, shall,* etc.), as well as "dummy *do*" (the *do* used in negation, questions, and emphasis (*Max DID buy a car*) when other aux elements are absent). These elements occur in a fixed order: a modal first, *have* second, and *be* third. Of course, they are all optional, but if any occur, the modal-*have-be* order is obligatory:

67. a. Max may have been studying.
    b. *Max has may been studying.
    c. *Max may be have studied.
    d. *Max is may have studied.

The aux elements *have* and *be* are peculiar in that they demand that the next element after them have a particular ending. *Have* requires that the next element carry the past participle suffix (*taken*, etc.), and *be* requires that the next element carry the *-ing* suffix:

66. a. Max has taken the cake.
    b. *Max has take the cake.
    c. Max is sleeping.
    d. *Max is sleep.

(*Be* can also be followed by a past (really passive) participle, as in *John will be taken to jail.* Ignore this fact for the time being; we will deal with the passive construction separately.) As mentioned in Chapter Three, the relation between the aux and the required suffix is so close—if one is present the other must be present too—that some linguists have referred to them as "discontinuous" morphemes.

The place of "Aux" in sentence structure

In the theoretical syntactic literature, the most common analysis of auxiliary elements places all the aux elements together in an **Aux** constituent separate from the VP:

69.

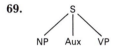

However, the substitution criterion supports joining auxes with VPs, since substitutions like the following are possible:

70.

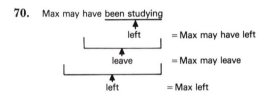

This evidence supports a tree like the following, in which each word sequence that can be substituted for is represented as a phrase:

71.

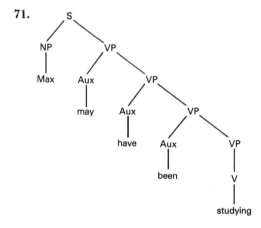

Let us see what the other critera for phrase-hood suggest about the structure of sequences of aux elements.

Movement. The movement criterion provides evidence against the idea that aux elements form constituents with other parts of the VP, since *been studying, have been studying,* and *may have been studying* cannot move. To see this, observe that if we begin with *Though Max may have been sleeping all* *afternoon, he still passed the test,* and try to move various parts of the first clause, only a sequence beginning with the verb can move:

72. a. *Been sleeping all afternoon though Max may have, he still passed the test.
     b. *Have been sleeping all afternoon though Max may, he still passed the test.
     c. *May have been sleeping all afternoon though Max, he still passed the test.
     d. Sleeping all afternoon though Max may have been, he still passed the text.

Pro-form. The pro-form-antecedent criterion likewise argues against a phrase made up of aux elements and VP elements, since *do so,* a pro-form for VPs, can refer only to verbs and following elements:

73.

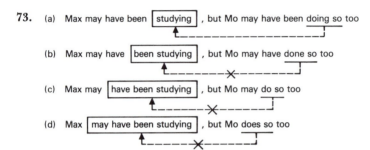

Although all the sentences in this example are grammatical, in only the first one does the underlined pro-form take as antecedent the boxed element earlier in the sentence. Example (b) does not mean '. . . but Mo may have been studying too'; rather, it means '. . . but Mo may have studied too.' A similar point can be made for examples (c) and (d).

Conjoinability. The conjoinability criterion, however, supports inclusion of the first aux element inside the VP—and hence, necessarily, other aux elements as well. However, second and third auxes, according to the evidence from conjoinability, do not form a constituent with further VP elements:

74.

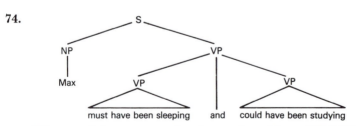

(This grammatical sentence supports a phrase made up of Aux and VP elements.)

(a)

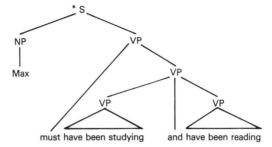

(This ungrammatical sentence argues against a phrase made up of a second Aux element and later VP elements.)

(b)

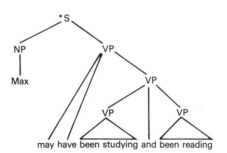

(This ungrammatical sentence argues against a phrase made up of a third Aux element and later VP elements.)

(c)

(Of course, main verbs can be conjoined—*Max may have been studying and reading.*)

Consistent, then, with the evidence from conjoinability is a structure like the following, in which all the aux elements are grouped with the VP, but *have* and *be* do not form a constituent with the main verb VP:

75.

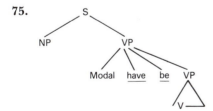

Such a structure is, in fact, compatible with the evidence from the movement criterion, the antecedent-for-pro-form criterion, and the conjoinability criterion. The only data a structure like this is not fully compatible with is that from substitution. But, as we saw earlier, substitution evidence is not completely reliable (it's too free). So, with some caution, we will adopt the structure above as our model for the placement of auxes in sentences.

To be consistent with our notation, now, we should distinguish between the phrasal category of the "old" VP—the one that contains a true verb, i.e., the VP whose contents are summarized in (66)—and the "new" VP, the one that contains aux elements. Following the "bar" approach introduced for NPs, let's label as "VP" the new, inclusive, VP, and let's label as "V̄" ("V-bar") the old, contained, main-verb VP. So we'll have trees like these:

76.

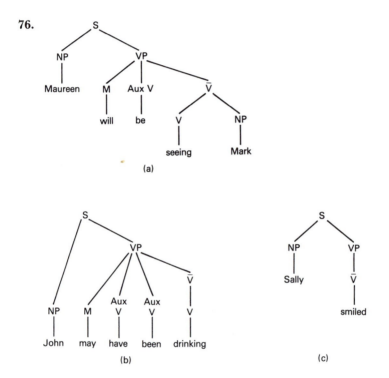

Notice that these trees apply the word-class designation "Aux V" (for "Auxiliary Verb") to the aux elements *have* and *be*. These words are verbs, of course, since they take tense (as can be seen in *was, had,* etc.). They need to be distinguished from their main verb homonyms: *be* as in *Max will be at practice* and *Don't be silly,* and *have* as in *Max has a truck.* Main verb *have* is clearly different in meaning from the aux *have,* since it means "possess" (as well as having other meanings, e.g., "causative," as in *Max had Belle arrested*); and it is not unreasonable to assume that main verb *be* similarly is semantically different from the aux *be.* The latter, always co-occurring with the suffix *-ing* attached to the following verb, is part of the progressive construction, as discussed in the previous chapter. (Again, we are ignoring passive *be* for the time being.) For this reason it makes sense to label aux *have* and *be* differently from main verb *have* and *be*.

EXERCISE 13. Draw trees for the following sentences. Don't worry about the internal structure of NPs.

1. Linda is making Paul a cake.
2. Ringo argued with Brian.
3. George will be writing a novel.
4. John might have been telling a joke.

At this point you should have a fairly clear picture of how simple, canonical sentences are structured in English, as well as a basic understanding of the empirical motivation for these structures. In the rest of this chapter we will look at some special varieties of canonical sentences and some non-canonical sentences.

SOME SPECIAL VARIETIES OF CANONICAL SENTENCES

Four types of structure deserve special comment at this point: the **passive**, **indirect object**, **cleft** (e.g., *it was Max who left*), and **verb-particle** constructions (e.g., *look up the number*). These structures fit the NP-VP template for canonical sentences, but they are slightly unusual internally. Some of these structure types create paraphrases or near paraphrases of basic sentences. Their existence alongside their basic counterparts allows speakers additional options for expressing emphasis, focus, and other nuances of meaning.

Some of the discussion below will treat non-canonical sentence structures as being "derived" from the basic canonical forms. This metaphor will be used not only because it is easier to grasp something new in terms of something already understood, but also because there are intuitively felt relations between basic sentences and non-basic ones. More importantly, certain significant grammatical generalizations can be expressed through positing such a connection.

Passives

Passive sentences—those "in the passive voice," in traditional terminology—include sentences like these:

77. a. Max was struck by lightning.
    b. The pudding was served by the waitress.

    c. Deep Throat may have been seen by Woodward.
    d. The flight was announced.

Intuitively, they are related to, and may be thought of as being derived from, "active" sentences—

78. a. Lightning struck Max.
     b. The waitress served the pudding.
     c. Woodward may have seen Deep Throat.
     d. Someone announced the flight.

What makes a sentence passive is for its "logical" direct object NP to be its actual subject, and its "logical" subject NP to be "no longer" the subject. Altogether, English passives have the following specific characteristics:

1. The presence of logical direct object in subject position, and presence of logical subject in post-verb position;
2. The presence of *be* as the last Aux element;
3. The presence of the past participle suffix on the verb; and
4. The presence of *by* in front of the "moved" logical subject.

The first and fourth characteristics need a small amendment. The *by*-phrase may be optionally omitted, if the NP in it (the logical subject) means only 'some unknown agent,' e.g., *someone,* as in the (d) sentences in (77) and (78) above.

    There is nothing unexpected about the phrase structure of passives:

79.

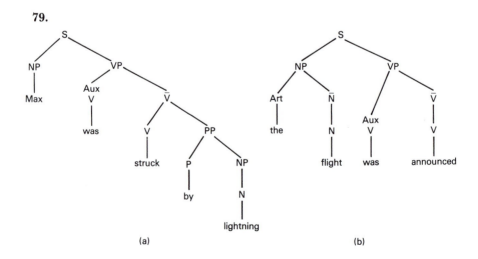

(a)   (b)

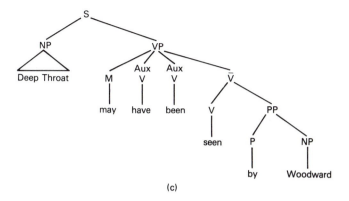

(c)

EXERCISE 14. Speculate about why a passive construction is likely to be chosen over an active one in each of the circumstances described below. What is it about the passive construction that makes it a better candidate than the active for each of these situations?

1. Waiting at the airport, you remind your friend that "the flight was just announced."
2. In a scientific paper, you read "the solution was then heated."
3. In a conversation about Max, someone asks where he is. You answer, "Oh, he's in the hospital. <u>He was struck by lightning.</u>"

EXERCISE 15.

A. The "*get*-passive" construction uses *get* in place of *be: Max got struck by lightning, Irene got promoted.* From conversations you hear around you, collect a few dozen examples of *get*-passive sentences and analyze them with respect to how they differ in use from *be*-passives. What, if any, differences in meaning or nuance can be found between these two similar constructions? (Don't focus on structure; focus on how the situations differ in which the two constructions would be likely to be used by speakers.)

B. Are the sentences below passive or not? What is your evidence?
1. Bill and Bonnie got married.
2. Doug got drunk.
3. The Dripping Palms resort is located next to a toxic waste dump.
4. My front window is broken.

In Chapter Five, we saw that besides active and passive, there is also a **middle** voice available to some verbs. Repeating the Chapter Five examples:

80. a.   sell: These cards sell well.
      b.   show: That print will show to good advantage in that corner.

Middle voice sentences have canonical structure. In terms of form, they are marked by use of logical direct object as actual subject, as with passives, absence of logical subject, as with some passives, and absence of passive morphology (*be*, past participle ending, and *by*).

Indirect Object Constructions

The grammatical function "indirect object" will be discussed in Chapter Seven, but trees showing the phrase structure of indirect object sentences are in order here. (Indirect object NPs refer to the individual who receives something, or who benefits from something, in the situation represented by a sentence.) Indirect object NPs occur in two ways, in PPs—

81.

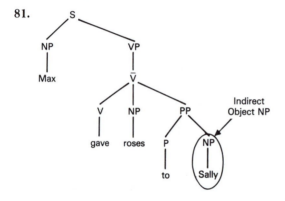

—or right after a verb, with the direct object NP appearing to the right of the indirect object NP—

82.

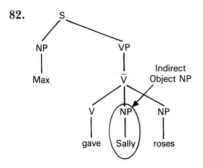

EXERCISE 16. Assume that we can treat as a process both the relation between a sentence like *Max gave roses to Sally* and one like *Max gave Sally
roses,* and the relation between active and passive sentences. In the following
sentence, both processes have applied. Which process must have applied
first? Why?

Diane was given a ring by Mark.

Assume that the starting point for the analysis is the basic sentence *Mark gave
a ring to Diane.*

Cleft Constructions

Cleft sentences come in two varieties, "*it*-clefts" and "*wh*-clefts":

83. *It*-clefts:
   a.   It was Mrs. Swalm whom Jane saw.
   b.   It may have been Sally who called you.
84. *Wh*-clefts:
   a.   What Max loves is garlic ice cream.
   b.   What convinced Spenser was the broken lock.

Structurally, cleft sentences look like the following:

85.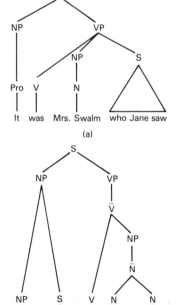

A couple of things in these trees deserve comment. First, in (a), don't worry about the internal structure of the "embedded" S; there are theoretical issues concealed in the triangle which go beyond the scope of this book. Second, in (b), it might seem strange to you to call *Max loves* an "S." But it is an S, albeit one that has "lost" a phrase. The entire subject NP, *What Max loves,* is an altered form of a relative clause structure. We will take up relative clauses in Chapter Nine. Think of *What Max loves* as being, "basically," "That [which Max loves]," in which the bracketed sequence is a sentence, whose underlying form is "Max loves which," i.e., "Max loves something." In the actual form *What Max loves,* the underlying relative pronoun *which* has merged with the preceding word *that* to create *what.*

Semantically, cleft sentences have two characteristics: they place a certain phrase "in focus," and they assume a certain proposition as background knowledge. In (83a) *Mrs. Swalm* is in focus, and the assumed background proposition is *Jane saw someone.* That is, (83a) does not make sense unless both speaker and hearer assume, already, that Jane saw someone. Similarly, in (84a) the focussed phrase is *garlic ice cream* and the assumed background proposition is *Max loves something.* Obviously there is a relation between the focussed phrase and the assumed background proposition. This relation can be understood in terms of a process: if we turn the cleft sentence into the basic sentence related to it, and then replace the focussed phrase by an indefinite word like *something* or *someone,* we get the assumed background proposition. For example, we can turn (84a) into the following related basic sentence: *Jane saw Mrs. Swalm.* We then replace the focussed phrase *Mrs. Swalm* with *someone,* resulting in the assumed background proposition *Jane saw someone.*

EXERCISE 17. For each cleft sentence below, identify the focussed phrase and the assumed background proposition.

1. What ruined the stew was the onions.
2. It may have been Sally who called you.
3. It was Bill's cat that bit the mail carrier.
4. What Mary does is smoke pot in class.
5. It's washing last night's dishes in the morning that I really hate.

Phrasal Verbs

Phrasal verbs show up in sentences like *Max looked up the number, Rose drank down her milkshake, The plane took off late,* and *She put up with his foolishness much too long.* They're "phrasal" verbs because they function semantically and grammatically as single verbs, but are composed of two or more words. Try to apply our criteria for phrase-hood to persuade yourself that the proper tree for a sentence of this sort is as follows:

86.

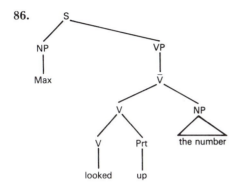

rather than this:

87.

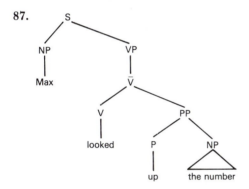

(You should be able to use the criteria of movement and conjoinability to find evidence favoring the first of these over the second.)

As we saw in Chapter Four, the "particles" in these sentences look just like prepositions, but are not. Some are movable: *Max looked up the number* → *Max looked the number up*. This movement is obligatory if the direct object NP is a pronoun: **Max looked up it.*[9] Others are not movable: *She came by her wealth honestly* ↛ **She came her wealth by honestly*. Though not movable, words like *by* here are still not prepositions, because they do not form a prepositional phrase with a following NP. This can be seen in the immovability of the supposed prepositional phrase: **By her wealth she came honestly*. Rather, just like movable particles, immovable words like *by* here form

---

[9]Of course, if *up* here is a preposition, the sentence is fine.

phrases with their preceding verbs, as can be seen by their synonymy (and mutual substitutability) with one-word verbs; e.g., *came by* = *acquired*.

EXERCISE 18. Draw trees for the underlined VPs in the sentences below.

1. The IRS examiner <u>looked over my calculations</u> and smiled.
2. Mikey <u>peered over his cereal</u> and said, "I like it."
3. The cat <u>threw up a hairball on the carpet</u>.
4. Stein <u>will drink down his beer with gusto</u>.

NON-CANONICAL SENTENCES

A small number of simple sentence types don't fit the canonical mold. Especially common among these are three kinds of **questions**, "yes-no" questions, so-called *wh*-questions, and tag questions; **imperatives**; **preposings**; and "**inversion**" constructions. A unique, but very common, non-canonical sentence form is the **existential** *there* construction (*There was a frog in my soup*). Because of important similarities with the way questions are formed, **negations** will also be discussed here, although they are canonical. Here are examples:

88.

> Negation: You should not untie this widget.
> Questions:
> > Yes-No question: Can you untie this widget?
> > *Wh*-question: Who can untie this widget?
> > Tag question: You can untie this widget, can't you?
> Imperative: Untie this widget.
> Inversion construction: Never had Babar untied so many widgets.
> Existential *there* construction: There was a widget in my soup.
> Preposing: Widgets I hate; gizmos I love.

Negation

The formation of negative sentences is simple: the negator, *not*, is placed after the first aux:

89.   (a)   Max must have been flirting

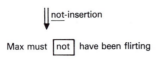

(b) Max has been flirting

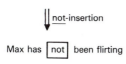

not-insertion

Max has [not] been flirting

(c) Max is flirting

not-insertion

Max is [not] flirting

In this simplest case, there is only one added wrinkle: *not* can optionally form a contraction with the preceding word (*couldn't, hasn't, isn't*).

If there is no aux, things are a little more complicated. What happens is that *not* is placed where the first aux would have been, and right in front of it the "dummy" morpheme *do* is inserted, carrying the same tense, person, and number ending as the main verb of the sentence. At the same time, the main verb loses its tense, person, and number suffix. Metaphorically, if you want, think of the verb suffix as moving from verb-final position to a position right in front of the inserted *not*, where *do* suddenly enters the sentence to carry it.

90. (a) Max flirted with Jean

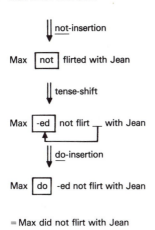

not-insertion

Max [not] flirted with Jean

tense-shift

Max [-ed] not flirt ⎯ with Jean

do-insertion

Max [do] -ed not flirt with Jean

= Max did not flirt with Jean

(b) Max flirts with Jean

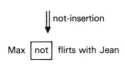

not-insertion

Max [not] flirts with Jean

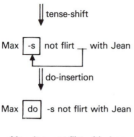

Max $\boxed{\text{-s}}$ not flirt $\rule{0.5cm}{0pt}$ with Jean

do-insertion

Max $\boxed{\text{do}}$ -s not flirt with Jean

= Max does not flirt with Jean

Just as with the simpler case, here *not* can optionally contract with *do: didn't, doesn't, don't.*

Questions

Yes-No Questions

Very simply, yes-no questions are those which call for a 'yes' or 'no' answer. Equally simply, they are formed by placing the first aux—the same word so important in negation—at the front of the sentence:

91.

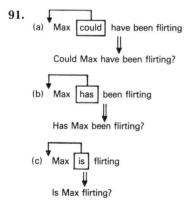

(a) Max $\boxed{\text{could}}$ have been flirting

Could Max have been flirting?

(b) Max $\boxed{\text{has}}$ been flirting

Has Max been flirting?

(c) Max $\boxed{\text{is}}$ flirting

Is Max flirting?

We will refer to this movement as the rule of "Subject-Aux Inversion."

If there is no aux, things happen similarly to the way they happen with negation. *Do* is inserted where the first aux would have been moved to, carrying the same tense that the main verb has in the original affirmative sentence. The main verb, at the same time, loses its tense morpheme. In a sense, the tense suffix of the verb is taken from the verb and moved to the front of the sentence, where *do* is brought in to carry it.

92.

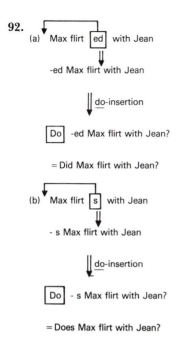

(a) Max flirt ed with Jean

-ed Max flirt with Jean

do-insertion

Do -ed Max flirt with Jean?

= Did Max flirt with Jean?

(b) Max flirt s with Jean

- s Max flirt with Jean

do-insertion

Do - s Max flirt with Jean?

= Does Max flirt with Jean?

Negative questions

There are two kinds of negative questions, those like *Hasn't Max been flirting?* and those like *Has Max not been flirting?*. The difference between them, of course, results from whether or not the *not* has been contracted. If so, the whole contraction, including the contracted *not* (*hasn't,* etc) is shifted to the front by Subject-Aux Inversion. If not, only the aux, without *not,* shifts to the front. In each case, our earlier generalization, that the first aux shifts, holds true.

Wh-*questions*

Wh-questions focus the query on *wh*-words like *what, who, which, whose, when, where, why*—and *how,* which lacks an initial *w* but grammatically is a *wh*-word all the same.

Wh-questions conveniently divide into those focussing on the subject *wh*-phrase and those focussing on a *wh*-phrase which has another grammatical relation (direct object, indirect object, object of preposition, etc.). We'll examine the latter type first.

Wh-questions focussing on non-subject phrases

Here are some examples of *wh*-questions focussing on non-subject phrases:

93. a. What could you have done?
b. Who will you give that cantaloupe to?
c. Where has Miriam been hiking?
d. How would Max have been able to say that?
e. What did the president know and when did he know it?

Two features of these sentences stand out. First, as with Yes-No questions, they show the effect of Subject-Aux Inversion: in (a), for example, the subject NP, *you*, follows the aux *could*. Second, the *wh*-word appears at the front of the sentence. Logically, this *wh*-word originates in another position in the sentence, the canonical position for a phrase that bears a given grammatical relation: direct object right after the verb, indirect object in a PP, location, reason, and time phrases in VP-final adverbial position. That is, the examples above can be thought of as being derived from these:

94. a. You could have done what?
b. You will give that cantaloupe to who(m)?
c. Miriam has been hiking where?
d. Max would have been able to say that how?
e. The president knew what and the president knew it when?

It will be convenient to think of the two movements (of the aux, and of the *wh*-word) as occurring separately, and in a fixed order—first the aux-fronting by Subject-Aux Inversion, then the *wh*-fronting. (Why this order makes sense will become clear momentarily.) So our model for *wh*-questions focussing on non-subject phrases will be a derivation like this, in which the blank spaces mark where elements "were moved from":

95. You could see what

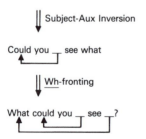

Wh-*questions focussing on subject phrases*

Here are examples of *wh*-questions focussing on a subject:

96. a. Who can read these Sanskrit texts?
  b. What broke?
  c. Who will be bringing the chocolate chip cookies?

Like the *wh*-questions we discussed above, these sentences have a *wh*-word at the beginning of the sentence. But unlike the *wh*-questions focussing on non-subject phrases, these sentences do not show the effect of Subject-Aux Inversion. The subject NP of (a) above is the *wh*-word *who,* that of (b) is *what,* and that of (c) is *who.* These are in normal subject position. In fact, these sentences have canonical structure:

97.

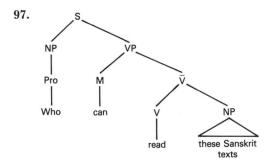

A simple description of this kind of sentence—but not a very insightful one—would let it go at that; we would just say that *wh*-questions focussing on subjects, unlike other questions, were structured exactly like affirmative sentences. An alternative description would relate *wh*-questions focussing on subjects to other questions, in the following way:

Suppose that in *wh*-questions focussing on subjects, Subject-Aux Inversion takes place exactly the way it does in Yes-No questions and *wh*-questions focussing on non-subjects. The partial derivation, then, would be:

98. (a) Who can read these Sanskrit texts

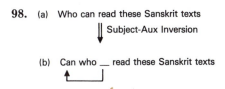

Next would be the movement of the *wh*-word, *who,* to the front of the sentence, resulting in just what we want:

(c)   Who can __ __ read these Sanskrit texts

Is this perverse, this movement which is, in effect, undone immediately? Not if it is taken to be important to preserve the generalization that questions—Yes/No questions, and both kinds of *wh*-questions—are formed via Subject-Aux inversion. According to this approach, the superficial structure of these sentences masks a deeper similarity to the other question types.

Now you can see why we chose to apply Subject-Aux inversion before *wh*-movement. If, in the derivation of *wh*-questions focussing on subjects, we used the other order, this is what would happen:

99.   a. Who can read these Sanskrit texts
   ↓ *wh*-movement applies vacuously
   b. Who can read these Sanskrit texts
         Subj.-Aux.Inv.
   c. *Can who read these Sanskrit texts[10]

EXERCISE 19. Propose "logical" forms for the following *wh*-questions, putting the *wh*-words in their "logical" positions. (Example: the logical form for *who(m) did Max visit* is *Max visited who(m)*, since the *wh*-word functions as direct object of *visited*.)

1.   What did you give to Sam?
2.   Where did you see Sam?
3.   Where did you stay with Sam?
4.   What did you exchange for the socks?
5.   What happened?
6.   Who will come to Sam's party now?
7.   When did Sam come to my party?

Tag Questions

Here are some sentences containing tag questions (which are underlined):

100.   a.   We're late, aren't we?
   b.   Max has left, hasn't he?
   c.   Tanya and Bonnie can't stay up late, can they?

---

[10]This sentence is OK as an "echo" question, asked as a request for clarification, e.g., if one didn't hear what had been said.

As an informal exercise, try to state as clearly as you can how tag questions are formed from simple declarative sentences.

A simple recipe for tag questions might look like this:

1. Copy a pronoun version of the subject NP at the end of the sentence.
2. Copy the first aux of the main sentence to the left of the copied pronoun. Do not copy a negative element.
3. If the main sentence is positive, make the tag question negative by attaching a contracted *not* to the right of the copied aux.

This set of rules is more or less "descriptively adequate"; it suffices to account for most tag questions, and those it fails to account for are equally problematic for other descriptions.[11] But it is not very insightful. It fails to reflect the fact that tag questions are, in fact, questions. They function like questions; if you say to me, *"We're late, aren't we?,"* I am under some obligation to respond just as if you had asked, *"Aren't we late?."* And tag questions are structured like other questions, too: they have subject NPs and auxes in inverted order. That is, tag questions show the effect of Subject-Aux Inversion.

In light of this, let's describe tag questions as follows:

1. Copy a pronoun version of the subject NP at the end of the sentence.
2. Copy the first aux to the right of the copied pronoun, at sentence-end. Do not copy any negative morpheme.
3. If the main sentence is positive, insert *not* to the right of the copied aux, at sentence end. (Note: Observe that this is no different from Negative-Placement in main sentences.)
4. Optionally contract *not* with the preceding aux.
5. Apply Subject-Aux Inversion to the tag question.

So the derivation of sentences containing tag questions will proceed like this:

101. a. Basic structure:
   Max has finished
   ⇓ Pronoun copying

---

[11] These include cases like the following:
   1. Sentences with the subject NP *I*: ?*I'm late, aren't I?*
   2. Sentences with certain indefinite pronoun subject NPs:
      a. ?Everyone was late, wasn't he?
      b. ?No one was late, was he?
   3. Sentences with *ought:*
      ?Max ought to leave early, oughtn't he?
   4. Sentences with negative sentence adverbs:
      a. ?Max rarely stayed late, didn't he?
      b. ?Cathy phoned Max infrequently, didn't she?
   There are others, as well. A nice source for such cases is D. Terence Langendoen's *Essentials of English Grammar* (New York: Holt, Rinehart, and Winston, 1970).

   b.   Max has finished he
           ⇊ Aux copying
   c.   Max has finished he has
           ⇊ Negative-insertion
   d.   Max has finished he has not
           ⇊ Contraction
   e.   Max has finished he hasn't
           ⇊ Subject-Aux inversion
   f.   Max has finished hasn't he

According to this approach, tag questions are not special, uniquely structured phrases unrelated to any others; they are just questions that are found at the end of sentences. They have the structure of questions in all respects. The only things unique about them are their location at sentence-end and the fact that their subjects are pronoun copies of the subjects of the main sentences to which they are attached.

   The negative contraction seen in step (d) → (e) is, of course, optional; tag questions are possible without the contraction, such as *Max has finished, has he not?* Just as with questions formed on main sentences, if the *not* does not contract, the word that gets fronted by Subject-Aux Inversion is the aux alone, not including the *not*.

   A negative basic sentence, of course, won't have rule (3) apply; the aux alone gets copied word-finally: *Max hasn't finished, he has*, after which Subject-Aux Inversion applies, producing *Max hasn't finished, has he?*.

Imperatives

   Imperatives, like *shut up!*, *close the door!*, and *come for dinner*, are simply structured. They are sentences made up of only a VP, a V̄, in fact:

102.

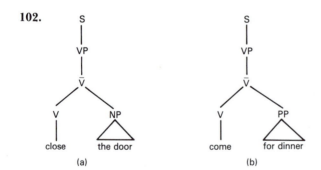

(a)   (b)

In school you probably learned that, because of their meaning, imperative sentences had an "understood *you*" as subject. But in addition to this semantic evidence for an "understood" subject *you*, grammatical evidence is available. Tag questions formed at the end of imperatives provide syntactic evidence about the structure of imperatives. Recall how tag questions are formed. Imperative tags show that imperative basic structures must contain not only *you,* but also the aux *will,* since the tag questions all do:

103. a.   Shut up, *won't you?*
      b.   *Shut up, *won't I?*
      c.   Close the door, *will you?*[12]
      d.   *Close the door, *must you?*

If we assume, as is reasonable, that tag questions attached to imperatives are formed just as other tag questions are, both the subject NP *you* and the aux *will* must be present in the basic structure of imperatives. From these observations we can conclude that imperatives are derived from basic structures like the following:

104. a.   You will shut up
      b.   You will close the door

Preposing

Preposing constructions contain "fronted" phrases:

105. a.   He said it would be hot, and hot it was.
      b.   He said he would wash the dishes, and wash the dishes he did.
      c.   Jon claimed God lived on Neptune. For that unusual assertion there was no immediate evidence.
      d.   Bean soup I can't stand.

In (a), an AP is fronted; in (b), a VP; in (c), a PP; in (d), an NP. The phrase structure of preposing constructions offers no problems; the fronted phrase simply occurs at the beginning of the sentence, and the rest of the sentence is canonical:

106.

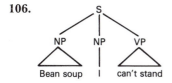

Inversion Constructions

Inversion constructions have their subject NP shifted to the right of the aux or the verb. They are syntactically more complex than preposings, which have subject NP and aux (and often verb) in canonical positions.

---

[12]Tags with imperatives can optionally have the same polarity (positive or negative) value as the main sentence to which they are attached. An interesting question is how such tags differ semantically or in discourse function from opposite-polarity tags on imperatives.

By far the most common inversion constructions in English are the question constructions we have already discussed: Yes-No Questions, *wh*-questions, and tag questions. But inversion occurs also in other cases, for instance:

107. a. In a little hole in the ground lived a white rabbit.
  b. Up jumped Mr. McGillicuddy.
  c. "Gracious!" exclaimed Miss Glatzert.
  d. Now circling under the ball is the center fielder.
  e. Max loves bean soup, and so does Doug.

You can see that inversion constructions often—as in the examples above—contain a preposed phrase. In (a) the preposed phrase is the PP *in a little hole in the ground*. Since it has been moved, it is a phrase, as with preposings. The only question, then, for the phrase structure of the whole sentence is where the verb is placed—with the preposed phrase, with the postposed subject, or by itself.

'By itself' is the best answer. In (a), the verb *lived* cannot be shown by any of our criteria for phrase-hood to be connected with either the preceding PP or the following subject NP. (Try each of the criteria for yourself to see this.) Consequently inversion constructions like those above are best represented in a tree like the following:

108.

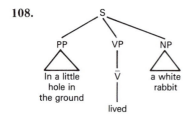

Existential *There* Sentences

Sentences announcing the existence of something, like *There may be a frog in my soup, There is a god, There were 13 colonies which rebelled against England,* have a peculiar structure. The subject NP occurs immediately to the right of an occurrence of *be:*

109.

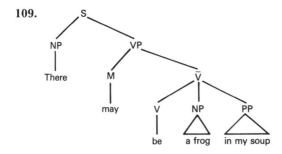

EXERCISE 20. Some occurrences of *be* are auxes, and some are main verbs. Which kind of *be* does the logical subject of an existential *there* sentence go after, or does it matter? Here are some data sentences you can use to answer this question.

1. There were twenty men on the deck.
2. There may have been twenty men parading in front of us.
3. There will be seven players released by the Packers today.
4. There might be some problems with that analysis.
5. There should have been somebody to meet me at the train.
6. There should have been somebody appointed to meet me at the train.
7. There are some flies swimming happily in my chowder.

SUMMARY AND CONCLUSION

We have looked at the whole range of simple English sentences from the perspective of their structure. We have focussed on the tree notation for representing phrase structure, and have investigated how we can determine the phrase structure of a phrase or sentence, by means of various criteria that can be applied empirically.

Next on the agenda is grammatical relations—subject, direct object, and the like—which we have already used and referred to non-systematically. It is time to examine closely what these notions mean.

ADDITIONAL EXERCISE

Write a short paper explaining to a friend who has not had linguistics one of the following ideas that have been discussed in this chapter:

1. What phrase structure is and how to determine the phrase structure of a sentence.
2. What underlying structure in syntax is and how it can explain some grammatical facts about English sentences—i.e., how it can be revealing to posit basic sentence forms from which certain sentences may be said to be derived.

REFERENCES

HORNSTEIN, N., AND DAVID LIGHTFOOT. 1981. *Explanations in Linguistics.* London: Longman.
LANGENDOEN, D. TERENCE. 1970. *Essentials of English Grammar.* New York: Holt, Rinehart, and Winston.

Chapter Seven

GRAMMATICAL RELATIONS

We now move from structure to function, to the roles phrases play in a sentence. The function of VPs is to make predications, i.e., to say something about subjects; that of APs is to modify an N, N̄, or NP, i.e., to affect its interpretation; and that of the varieties of adverbs and adverbial phrases is similarly to modify the interpretations of words or other phrases. In this chapter we will regard a sentence as being composed of a verb and a small number of NPs, each of which stands in a certain relation to the verb. So the major NP roles—**subject**, **direct object**, and **indirect object**—will be discussed in detail. Minor NP roles—including **predicate nominative** and **object complement**—will also be discussed, in somewhat less detail. Our basic question will be "What does it mean for an NP to function as a certain role?"

A technical term for the notion of function or role is **grammatical relation**. The idea is that the main roles NPs play in sentences—subject, direct object, indirect object—involve different relations to the verb.

SUBJECTS

Most people are taught in school that the subject of a sentence represents either what the sentence is about (the **topic**) or the doer of the action (the **agent**). According to these definitions, the subject of *The President of the United States is a very important man* would be *the President of the United States*, because that is what the sentence is about, and the subject of *Max sniffed the roses* would be *Max,* because Max did the sniffing (as well as, perhaps, because Max is what this sentence is about). Since these definitions are different, it is obviously possible for them to conflict, and they sometimes do, by picking out different NPs in a sentence: e.g., *The President of the United States is elected by the people.* This sentence is about the President of the United States, but the doers of the action are the people. So by one definition of subject the subject is *the President of the U.S.,* and by another it is *the people.*

There are other reasons that these definitions are inadequate. Some of them we will discuss below. However, as with many claims found in traditional grammar, these traditional definitions shouldn't be discounted completely. Many subject NPs do in fact denote either agents or topics, often both. Since we are going to define 'subject' differently, an interesting question is why so many subject NPs do denote agents or topics—i.e., why do agent or topic NPs "get attracted" to the subject slot?

The phrase 'the subject slot' presupposes that there is such a slot, and for most English sentence types, that is certainly the case.[1] A fairly useful definition of 'subject' in English is "the NP immediately before the aux or verb":

1.

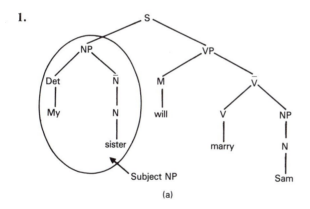

(a)

---

[1]For many languages there is no subject slot. In Latin, for example, a "free word order language," the subject NP can appear essentially anywhere in a sentence, always marked by a "nominative" case ending, as discussed in Chapter Four.

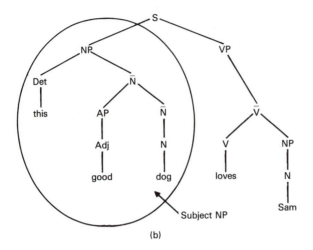

(b)

The subject NP need not be sentence-initial:

2.

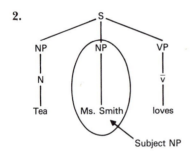

Let us now examine what difficulties arise in defining subject in terms of topic and agent.

Subjects As Topics

Let's begin with the following trial definition:

3. Trial definition:
   The subject of a sentence is the NP which denotes the sentence's topic.

In the following little discourse, all the subject NPs, which are underlined, represent topics, what each sentence is about:

4. Unbeaten Roger Clemens, the hottest pitcher in baseball, relived the past for Ron Guidry on Monday night. Clemens won his 12th straight game with a four-hitter as the Boston Red Sox ripped Guidry and the New York Yankees, 10-1. Clemens' start is the best in the major leagues since Guidry opened the

1978 season with 13 straight victories. The major league record for con-secutive wins at the start of a season is 19 by Rube Marquard in 1912.
(*Yankees Are No Match for Clemens—He's 12-0, LA Times,* Sec. III., p. 1, June 17, 1986.)

So this example supports our trial definition. But it is easy to find examples in which the topic of a sentence is not represented by the sentence's subject. Here is one (again, subject NPs are underlined):

5. You know that guy in my anthropology class? I saw him last night at the movies.

The subject NPs are *you* and *I,* but the topic of both sentences is presumably the guy in the speaker's anthropology class. Note that a 'topic' is a thing—in the world or in speakers' mental worlds—whereas "being a subject" is a property of a linguistic item, a phrase. Hence, in our discussion of subjects and topics, subject NPs are italicized, whereas topics are not (since they are not linguistic items). Example like (5) make it clear that our trial definition won't work.

Sentence topic or discourse topic?

If we could define subject somehow in terms of topic, we would need to distinguish **sentence topic** from **discourse topic**. If a discourse, or part of a discourse (e.g., a paragraph), is well-composed, one should be able to determine what it is about. But a sentence which holds to the discourse topic may at the same time have a different topic of its own. Look at these initial sentences from Samuel Clemens' *The Prince and the Pauper.* The sentences are numbered for ease of reference.

6. (1) In the ancient city of London, on a certain autumn day in the second quarter of the sixteenth century, a boy was born to a poor family of the name of Canty, who did not want him. (2) On the same day another English child was born to a rich family of the name of Tudor, who did want him. (3) All England wanted him too. (4) England had so longed for him, and hoped for him, and prayed God for him that now that he was really come, the people went nearly mad for joy. (5) Mere acquaintances hugged and kissed each other and cried. (6) Everybody took a holiday, and high and low, rich and poor, feasted and danced and sang, and got very mellow; and (7) they kept this up for days and nights together.
(Samuel Clemens, *The Prince and the Pauper*)

The discourse topic is the birth of the prince and the pauper, inferrable not only from the text itself, but also from the fact that "The Birth of the

Prince and the Pauper" is the title of the two-page chapter in which this passage appears. Probably the topic of the first sentence is the pauper, expressed by the subject NP *a boy*, and that of the next three sentences is the prince, expressed by the NPs *another English child, him*, and *he*. But what are the topics of sentences (5), (6), and (7)? Most likely the public joy, a generalization over some specifics in each of these sentences. That is what these sentences seem to be about. The public joy is a discourse sub-topic, a topic of a part of the discourse. But this topic would not be determinable from any one of these sentences in isolation, out of the context of this discourse. Consequently, at least for some sentences, what the topic is depends partly on the surrounding discourse. But subject is a concept having to do purely with a sentence. And the public joy does not find expression in any particular words or phrases in any of these sentences as distinct from the whole sentence; all of sentence (5), for example, is about the proposition that the joy is public. So this topic does nothing to identify some particular word or phrase in sentence (5) as the one that bears the grammatical relation 'subject.'

It seems reasonable to conclude that we can't define subject in terms of topic. However, it remains true that many subject NPs do in fact refer to topics. There must be something about subjects that is useful for topics. Since subjects usually occur early in English sentences, and topics tend to be familiar rather than brand new (since it is hard for something to be a topic unless both speaker and hearer know about it), possibly a tendency to place "old," or given, information earlier in sentences accounts for why so many subjects are topics.

EXERCISE 1. In the following text, identify the topic of each sentence. The sentences are numbered for ease of reference.

(1) When it rains on the Pittsburgh Pirates, it pours—even at home. (2) Jack Clark backed Danny Cox's four-hit pitching with a home run Monday night as the St. Louis Cardinals defeated the Pirates, 4-1, in a rain-shortened, protested game at Pittsburgh. (3) The game was called after two rain delays totaling 39 minutes with the Cardinals batting with one out in the top of the sixth. (4) "That's the quickest I've ever seen a game called in this league. (5) This has to go down in the Guinness Book of World Records," said Pirate General Manager Syd Thrift. (6) Pirate Manager Jim Leyland said he would file an official protest. (7) "I've never heard of any game being called in less than 45 minutes," he said. (8) "We didn't get something we had coming."

(*LA Times*, "Pirates Lose to Cardinals, 4-1; Plan to Protest the Rain Call," Tuesday, June 17, 1986, p. 111-7)

Subject As Agent

Let's consider another trial definition of subject:

7. Trial definition: The subject of a sentence is the NP denoting the agent, the doer of the action described in the sentence.

Very commonly, this definition works. Here are some sentences with subject NPs denoting agents:

8. a. Paul blew out the candles.
   b. A large dog tore up the petunia beds.
   c. Germany defeated France in the Franco-Prussian War.

Agents are assumed to be sentient, consciously and purposefully acting beings who are responsible for bringing about the action described in a given sentence. 'Agent' is a semantic rather than grammatical role. Let's examine a few other semantic roles. One role is **Instrument**. The Instrument in the situation represented by a sentence is the inanimate, nonsentient thing by whose action or use the action described in the sentence comes about. Instrumental NPs can accompany Agentive ones functioning as subject, as in *John opened the door with a key*, in which *John* is Agentive and *a key* is Instrumental, but—crucially for the putative association between subject function and the semantic notion of Agent—Instrumental NPs can also function as subjects:

9. a. The key opened the door.
   b. The runaway car knocked over the lamp post.
   c. The lawn mower damaged the flower bed.

On this basis then, it is obviously impossible to define subject as Agent.[2]

Another semantic role is **Patient**, sometimes called **Object**. (This semantic notion is obviously related to, but should not be confused with, the grammatical notion 'direct object,' which will be discussed below.) The Patient or Object in a situation described by a sentence is the affected entity, the one that the action happens to, for example *the ball* in *John kicked*

[2]Sometimes it is hard to decide whether a NP is Agentive or Instrumental:
   i. The sun heats the earth.
   ii. The avalanche buried the skiers.
   iii. The wind opened the door.
The NPs in cases like these can be labeled Agents, under a broader definition of Agent as "self-energy source," which encompasses both volitional Agents as well as non-volitional sources for events, like weather phenomena. With this broader definition of Agent, the term 'instrument' can be reserved for entities used or controlled by Agents. This of course won't save our trial definition, because of sentences like *The key opened the door*, in which *the key* cannot be considered a "self-energy source."

the ball. However, also damning for our trial definition of subject as Agent, sometimes Patient NPs can function as subjects:

10. a.　The door opened.
　　b.　The ice melted slowly.
　　c.　The window shattered when the ball hit it.

NPs referring to human beings can designate Patients:

11.　(Knocked out,) James Bond fell hard to the floor.

But a distinction is often drawn between Patients and **Experiencers**. Experiencers are sentient beings, e.g., people, to whom events happen or who are the locus of the situation or event of a sentence, for example *Brian* in *The news hit Brian hard.* Sometimes Experiencer NPs can function as subjects—

12. a.　Colleen fell in love with Brian.
　　b.　The reporters heard the announcement.

—which also constitutes evidence against our working definition of subject as Agent. Experiencers, unlike Agents, do not act; they experience passively. In *The reporters listened to the announcement,* the NP *the reporters* refers to an Agent, but in (12b) above, it refers to an Experiencer. Unlike Patients, Experiencers are psychologically affected through the situation represented by the sentence.[3]

Other semantic roles include **Locative**, **Source**, and **Goal**. NPs expressing each usually occur in positions other than subject, as, for example, in the following:

13.　Locative:　Greg lives in Chicago.
　　Source:　i.　The letter came from San Clemente.
　　　　　　ii.　She carved a bird out of wood.
　　　　　　i.　Rose gave a gold watch to Manolo.
　　Goal:　　ii.　We sent it to headquarters.

Here are examples of sentences in which NPs expressing these roles func-

---

[3] The distinction among Agent, Patient, and Experiencer can account for certain ambiguities. Consider *Max hit the wall.* This sentence has three **readings** (interpretations):
1.　Max (willfully) struck the wall (e.g., with his fist) (the Agentive reading).
2.　Max accidentally or through the act of some other person or force struck the wall (e.g., he bumped it) (the Experiencer reading).
3.　Max's unconscious body struck the wall (e.g., his body was thrown against it) (the Patient reading).

tion as subjects, thus further invalidating our working definition of subject as Agent:

14. a. Locative: Chicago is windy.
  b. Source: Harvard has sent many leaders to the Senate.
  c. Goal: Headquarters received the package.

All the semantic roles we have considered in this section can be encoded in NPs which function as subject. Obviously we have come a long way from being able to identify subject with Agent! To put it more strongly, a definition of subject in terms of semantic role is out of the question, since subject NPs can express such a wide range of semantic roles—Agent, Instrument, Patient, Location, Source, and Goal.

All our examples so far have involved canonical sentences. But in non-basic or non-canonical sentences, a correlation between Agent and subject is no more possible than in canonical sentences. First, an Agentive NP may function other than as subject:

15. (a) The candles were blown out by all the birthday kids
           Subject   *Agent*

  (b) It was Max who spoke up
       Subj. *Agent*

  (c) What Max wrote was a really subtle poison pen letter
             Agent
             Subject

Second, an Agent may not be overtly expressed in a sentence:

16. a. Max's flight was announced.
  b. Please don't smoke.

In (a), while *Max's flight* is the subject NP, the Agent is the person who announced the flight, whose identity is unimportant. In (b), there is not even an expressed subject (although if there were, it would be *you*, which would be Agentive).

However, it remains true that there is something typically subject-like about the Agent role. (There may even be something prototypically Agent-like about the subject slot.) Agentive NPs are much more commonly found as subjects than as any other grammatical relation. In basic canonical sentences, there is a hierarchy among the semantic roles of Agent, Instrument, and Patient:

17. Likelihood to function as subject: Agent > Instrument > Patient

If a canonical sentence contains an Agentive NP, it is likely to function as subject; if a sentence contains no Agent, but does contain an Instrument, the Instrument NP will probably function as subject; if it contains no Agent or Instrument, but has a Patient, the Patient will probably fill the subject slot. Consider the canonical sentence *Max dented the fender with a rock.* The subject NP is *Max,* and is Agentive. The NP *the fender* is Patient, and the NP *a rock* is Instrumental. There is no other way to express the meaning of this sentence so simply. Other ways to express the same meaning are non-basic (e.g., a passive sentence: *The fender was dented by Max with a rock,* in which the subject NP *the fender* is Patient), or, if canonical, are more complex (e.g., *A rock is the instrument which Max used to dent the fender*). If there is no Agent, but both a Patient and an Instrument, the Instrument must take the subject role: *The rock dented the fender,* but **The fender dented with a rock.* (With some verbs, however, Instrument and Patient are of equal rank: *The key opened the door, The door opened with a key.*)

To sum up, it is impossible to define subjects as NPs which denote Agents. However, it remains true that while subject cannot be defined in terms of Agent, it is nonetheless true that many subject NPs do denote Agents (just as many denote topics).

EXERCISE 2. Identify the semantic role of every underlined NP below. Choose from Agent, Patient, Experiencer, Instrument, Source, Locative, and Goal.

1. The boys broke the glass with a stone.
2. The ice melted.
3. Steve lives in Newton Corner.
4. Mary Ellen has a new Chevy.
5. Peter bought a new Chevy for Mary Ellen.
6. The kids burst from the door.
7. Charlie liked Hallie.
8. Greg was becoming accustomed to the weather in Chicago.

Grammatical Properties of Subject NPs

Since subjects cannot be defined either by denoting topics, or by manifesting some particular semantic role, like Agent, it makes sense to look for a grammar-based definition.

Generally, a subject NP in English occurs immediately before an aux or verb. In the following examples, subject NPs, in each preceding an aux or verb, are underlined:

18. a. The boys have stolen the potato chips.
    b. Max likes Mozart.
    c. This coffee even Ms. O'Reilly wouldn't drink.

In sentences with inversion, however, like the following, again with subject NPs underlined—

19. a. Standing in the rear of the hall was Ira Smith.
 b. (The Prez has left already,) . . . and so has the Senator.

—the subject NP is not before an aux or verb. Of course, in the "pre-inversion" versions of these sentences—

20. a. Ira Smith was standing in the rear of the hall.
 b. . . . and the Senator has [left already] too.[4]

—the subject NPs do immediately precede the verbs or auxes. So it is possible to define subject NPs structurally as follows:

21. Definition:
 In a sentence without inversion, the subject NP of a sentence is the first NP to the left of the main Aux or Verb; in a sentence with inversion, the subject NP is the first NP to the left of the main Aux or Verb in the corresponding pre-inversion sentence.[5]

This definition is so simple that it is perhaps a bit surprising that the faulty definitions of subject as topic and agent still persist in traditional grammar.

Other common characteristics of English subjects include **governing verb agreement** and being the **antecedent for a tag question**. As we will see below, neither of these characteristics can serve as a definition, but they are nonetheless significant typical properties of English subject NPs.

Subject as governor of verb agreement

In present tense sentences, subject NPs govern verb agreement. Below, in (a), the singular subject NP *the kitten* requires singular verb agreement, and in (b), the plural subject NP *the puppies* requires plural verb agreement.

22. a. The kitten *is* chasing the string.
 b. The puppies *are* chasing the ball.

---

[4] In Chapter Ten we shall see how it makes sense to say that a sentence like this is the "pre-inversion" version of sentence (19b).
[5] We say "first NP to the left of . . ." instead of "NP immediately preceding . . ." to allow parenthetical expressions or adverbs to occur between subject NP and Aux or verb:
 Max, unfortunately, has already departed.

Past and future tense auxes and verbs do not change form depending on the subject NP:

23. a. Tom had already stolen the donuts.
   b. Tom and Huck had already stolen the donuts.
   c. I had already stolen the donuts.
   d. Tom stole the donuts.
   e. Tom and Huck stole the donuts.
   f. I stole the donuts.
   g. Tom will steal the donuts.
   h. Tom and Huck will steal the donuts.
   i. I will steal the donuts.

Subject as antecedent for tag pronoun

Another grammatical characteristic of subject NPs is how they work in the formation of tag-questions. Recall from Chapter Six how tags are formed: the subject NP is copied at the end of the sentence, in pronoun form:

24. a. Frank poured Ms. Hernandez some tea, didn't he?
   b. This tea even Ms. Hernandez wouldn't drink, would she?
   c. Tea is what Ms. Hernandez loves, isn't it?

In (a), the subject NP *Frank* is copied in the tag question in the pronoun form *he*. In (b), the subject *Ms. Hernandez* is copied in the tag question in the pronoun form *she*. In (c), the subject NP *tea* is copied in the pronoun form *it*.[6]

In sentences with existential *there*, the characteristics of verb agreement and tag-question formation conflict. Notice what governs verb agreement in these sentences:

25. a. There is a fly in your soup.
   b. There are flies in your soup.

[6]To see that *Tea* is indeed the subject of this sentence, by our definition (21), a tree will be helpful:

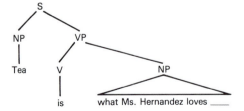

In this tree, *tea* is the first NP to the left of the main verb *is*. Within the post-verbal NP, of course, is an embedded sentence, whose subject is Ms. Hernandez

In both cases, the NP AFTER the verb (in (a), *a fly*, in (b), *flies*) governs verb agreement. But look at the corresponding tag-questions:

26. a. There is a fly in your soup, isn't there?
　　 b. There are flies in your soup, aren't there?

The copied NP is *there*, so by the tag-question criterion *there* functions as subject.

　　It is not important which of these two properties is better for identifying subjects. What is important is the fact that a subject NP, DEFINED as the first NP to the left of the aux or verb, TYPICALLY has the property of being copied in tags, and of governing verb agreement.

EXERCISE 3. Identify the subject NPs of the following sentences, showing in each case how the NP you pick as subject is identified as such by the tag rule and the verb-agreement rule. Comment on any difficulties.

1. Glen and Molly love cheesecake.
2. The auditor believes the claims of the lawyers.
3. The jury has not yet arrived at a verdict.
4. It is raining cats and dogs.
5. Yesterday was a day we'll never forget.
6. The lawyer in charge was Mary Ann.

Logical and Superficial Subjects

　　It is sometimes convenient to distinguish between the "actual," or "superficial," subject NP of a sentence and the "underlying" or "logical" subject. For our purposes, the actual or superficial subject NP will be as defined in (21) above—the first one to the left of the verb or aux—and typically the one that governs verb agreement or that would be copied to form a tag question. The underlying or logical subject NP will be the one that has these characteristics at a deeper level of structure. For instance, in passive sentences the actual subject is the initial NP, but the logical subject is the NP in the *by*-phrase: the actual subject of *Max was bitten by Rover* is *Max*, but on the assumption that active sentences are more basic, the underlying or "logical" subject is *Rover*, the subject of *Rover bit Max*.

EXERCISE 4. Identify the (a) actual (superficial) and (b) logical subjects of each sentence. In some cases they may be the same.

1. Marie is accused by the people of high crimes.
2. The ball was knocked into the stands by the lunging fielder.

3. There were a lot of people being arrested by the police.
4. The announcement was made that the chairman was resigning.
5. A hundred dollars was given to Peri Lou by her aunt.
6. Book authors are often stymied by the indexing problem.
7. Notice what happens with imperative sentences.
8. Also indicted for perjury was Senator Crookshark.

EXERCISE 5. Select three or four paragraphs from written discourses of different genres (e.g., a sports news story, a physics textbook, and an autobiography). For each representative of a genre, find out what percentage of subject NPs are topics, what percentage are Agents, what percentage are both, and what percentage are neither.

DIRECT OBJECTS

Let's express the traditional definition of a direct object NP in the following trial definition:

27. Trial Definition:
    The direct object NP of a sentence is the NP which represents an entity which, in the situation described by the sentence, receives the action signified by the verb.

The direct object thus, according to this definition, represents the "target" for the "transfer of action." So the underlined NPs below function as direct objects:

28. a. Max dented the new Corvette.
    b. The principal scolded the misbehaving 7th graders.
    c. We ate lobster stew with the other Down Easters.
    d. When better automobiles are built, Buick will build them.

Prototypical direct object NPs have this semantic property, but it won't work as a definition. Consider the range of "action" the back pasture "receives" in the various situations described by the following:

29.

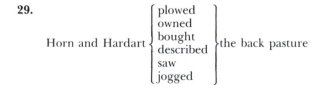

Are all these occurrences of *the back pasture* to be considered direct objects? Traditionally, all but the last would be. But it is hard to see what action is transferred to the back pasture by the action symbolized by *described* or *saw*. And while something may happen to the back pasture when it is <u>bought</u> or even <u>owned</u>, presumably much less than when it is <u>plowed</u>. These facts call our <u>trial definition</u> into question.

Consider next cases like these:

30. a. We loaded the truck with hay.
     b. We loaded hay onto the truck.

Objectively, these sentences are nearly identical in meaning. In the situation these sentences describe, which is more affected, the truck or the hay? Probably they are in fact equally affected, and equally receivers of the action symbolized by the verb. Which NP—*the truck* or *hay*—functions as direct object? Traditionally, in (a) *the truck* does, and in (b) *hay* does. Indeed, there is a small but significant semantic difference; most native English speakers will probably feel that in (a) the truck is the more affected and in (b) hay is the more affected. Why? Presumably because of the position of the NPs. It seems that the position immediately after the verb is especially conducive to the interpretation of being the most affected. But if this is so, we might as well define object structurally, as being the grammatical relation of the NP immediately following the verb! Let's try out another working definition:

31. Trial definition:
The direct object NP of a sentence is that NP which immediately follows the main verb of the sentence.

If this definition works, we can dispense with the semantic definition entirely in favor of the more easily applicable structural one, while remembering that prototypical direct object NPs have the semantic property of denoting the entities which are the most affected.

Taking this structural perspective will help with another, more serious problem. Sometimes the NPs which the traditional semantic definition identifies as direct objects function as subjects, by our earlier definition:

32. a. <u>The new Corvette</u> was dented by Max
     b. When <u>better automobiles</u> are built . . .

(They function as subjects because they precede auxes or verbs, they govern verb agreement, and they would serve as sources for pronoun copies in tag questions.) But if direct object NPs have to be right after verbs, as our current proposal has it, the underlined NPs above can't function as direct objects. However, we can distinguish, as we did earlier with subjects, between logical or underlying direct objects and actual or superficial ones. In (32), the underlined NPs function as actual subjects, but logical or underlying direct objects. If the sentences in (32) are "de-passivized," this becomes clear: *Max dented the new Corvette; When [someone] builds better automobiles.*

Defining direct objects as those NPs which immediately follow verbs is an improvement over the traditional semantic definition. However, as we shall see below, it is not sufficient. Our aim will be to come up with a definition which is both satisfactory—in that it identifies the "right" range of NPs as direct objects—and explicit.

Grammatical Characteristics of Direct Object NPs

The most obvious grammatical characteristic of direct object NPs is their position. They occur immediately after the verb:

33. a. Tabitha drew a picture of a cow for Bonnie.
     b. The council fired the city manager for corruption.
     c. Everyone knows that story really too well.
     d. Grandma's apple pie tickles my taste buds.

But while generally accurate, this isn't enough. For one thing, it won't do to say that every NP immediately following a verb functions as direct object, since the NPs following certain measurement verbs are not labeled direct object in traditional grammars:

34. a. Leon weighs 212 pounds.
     b. Those avocados cost 59 cents.

For another, certain intransitive verbs like *be* and *seem* can be followed by NPs which don't function as direct objects, traditionally:

35. a. The press secretary was a liar.
     b. Ivan seems a good leader.[7]

---

[7]Some speakers find this ungrammatical. If you do, simply accept on faith that many find it perfectly acceptable.

The main grammatical characteristic of direct object NPs is that they can be shifted to the front of sentences to become ("derived") subjects, in passive sentences. Let's define direct objects this way:

36. Definition: A direct object NP is one which immediately follows a verb and can be passivized.[8]

Observe:

37. a. Frances will build <u>a dream house in the Sierras</u>. ⇒
  b. <u>A dream house in the Sierras</u> will be built by Frances.
  c. Greg must send <u>those travel forms</u> to New Jersey. ⇒
  d. <u>Those travel forms</u> must be sent to New Jersey by Greg.
  e. Al exchanged <u>those socks</u> for a tie at Bloomies. ⇒
  f. <u>Those socks</u> were exchanged by Al for a tie at Bloomies.
  g. Peri put <u>the pencil</u> in the drawer with my socks. ⇒
  h. <u>The pencil</u> was put in the drawer with my socks by Peri.

An implication of defining direct objects in terms of passivization is that NPs following measure verbs do not function as direct objects, even though they occur in canonical direct object position:

38. a. Tom weighed <u>290 pounds</u> last week.
  b. Those grapefruit cost <u>39¢</u> today.

---

[8]This definition of direct object fails in the case of certain sentence-types. The underlined NPs below function as direct object, despite not following the verb:

i. <u>Tea like this</u> Ms. Hernandez would never drink.
ii. <u>What</u> can you see from up there?

However, recognizing the presence of a "gap" from which the direct object NP "was moved"—as we did in our discussion of *wh*-questions in Chapter Six—offers a solution. Let's assume that sentences (i) and (ii) above are structured as follows (the arrows, of course, are not part of the structure, but simply indicate the movement):

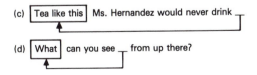

In these structures, the gaps are in the proper position to bear the relation of direct object; and if the gaps were filled with the phrases that have been moved, these phrases would be passivizable:

e. Tea like this would never be drunk by Ms. Hernandez.
f. What can be seen (by you) from up there?

They are not direct objects, because they cannot be passivized:

39. a. *290 pounds was weighed by Tom last week.
b. *39¢ is cost by those grapefruit today.[9]

This is also true for an NP following a verb like *jog:*

40. a. Horn and Hardart jogged the back pasture.
b. *The back pasture was jogged by Horn and Hardart.

The same holds for NPs following *be, seem,* and other intransitive verbs; since they cannot be passivized, we are justified in saying they don't function as direct objects:

41. a. The press secretary was a liar. ⇒
*A liar was been by the press secretary.
b. Leon seems a good leader. ⇒
*A good leader is seemed by Leon.

EXERCISE 6. Identify all direct object NPs. Discuss any questionable cases.

1. I put the pencil into the drawer with the socks.
2. Many is the time Max has punched John in the mouth.
3. There are seven dwarves in this story.
4. I built this table out of redwood pieces.
5. You need oregano, sage, curry, butter, garlic, and onions.
6. I gave at the office.
7. The chairman called me at home yesterday.
8. The caravan reached the oasis yesterday.
9. Max entered the courtoom cautiously.
10. Jane left the room hurriedly.
11. Smoke filled the hall.
12. This can contains turnips.
13. Steve's brother resembles a basset hound.
14. George Washington slept in this bed.

---

[9] Verbs like *weigh* and *cost* can occur with direct object NPs, but only when they are interpreted as meaning that the denotation of the subject NP actively causes the action of the verb to occur, as, for example, if Max is a "weigher" in a warehouse—a worker whose job it is to weigh things. Then we can say both *Max weighed 290 pounds last week* and *290 pounds were weighed by Max last week.*

INDIRECT OBJECTS

Indirect object NPs are "second objects," showing up canonically in PPs:

42.

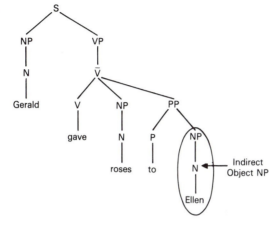

But they can also show up where direct object NPs normally do, right after the verb (we'll resolve the conflict with our direct object definition shortly):

43.

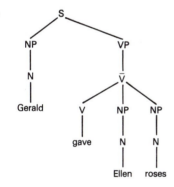

But not all NPs in PPs, or after Vs, function as indirect objects. The underlined NPs in these examples, in PPs, do not:

44. a. Max threw the ball in the river.
   b. Maureen mailed a package to <u>England</u>.

And, of course most NPs right after Vs don't:

45. a. Max threw <u>the ball</u> in the river.
   b. Maureen mailed <u>a package</u> to England.

What makes a second object NP function as indirect object is the semantic property of denoting the entity that, in the situation denoted by the sentence, receives something. Let's define indirect objects in this way:

46. Definition: An indirect object NP is one which appears in post-verbal position or in a PP headed by *to* or *for* within the VP, and refers to an entity which receives something, in the situation denoted by the sentence.

Examples:

47. a. Gerald gave roses to Ellen.
   b. Smith sent Wesson a nasty telegram.
   c. I gave that old porch bench a new coat of paint.
   d. If John doesn't watch out, I'm going to give him a punch in the mouth.
   e. The girls made mustard pancakes for Mrs. McGillicuddy.

Mere directional result—i.e., the thing referred to by the direct object NP ending up somewhere else—is not enough; in *we sailed our dinghy to Hawaii, Hawaii* is not an indirect object NP. In *We sent the results to Chicago,* however, *Chicago* may be an indirect object NP, if *Chicago* is personified—for example, if it denotes not the city, but a corporate head office.

Typically, a given indirect object NP can occur in two positions: in a PP, as in tree (42), and directly after the verb, as in tree (43). This double pattern of occurrence is typical enough to make it a useful test, but it is not strong enough to define the notion 'indirect object.' It is useful in that any NP that can occur in both positions may be said to function as indirect object. Thus, the underlined NPs in the examples below may be said to function as indirect objects:

48. a. Gerald gave roses to Ellen.
   b. Gerald gave Ellen roses.
   c. Sarah baked a cake for Sally.
   d. Sarah baked Sally a cake.
   e. Barbara sent a note to Clark.
   f. Barbara sent Clark a note.

But this pattern isn't a defining one, because there are NPs which we would want to call indirect objects which occur in only one or the other of the two patterns. Indirect object NPs with *cost* occur only post-verbally:

49. a. The trip cost Greg a lot of money.
   b. *The trip cost a lot of money to Greg.

This example is interesting, because it shows that the "thing" received by the entity referred to by the indirect object NP need not be the referent of the direct object NP, though it usually is. In (49) what is received is the cost of the trip—the loss of the money.

Indirect object NPs with a number of verbs—e.g., *open, explain,* and *describe*—occur only in canonical indirect object position, in the PP:

50. a. Max opened the door for <u>Cathy</u>.
    b. *Max opened <u>Cathy</u> the door.
    d. Bill described the situation to <u>John</u>.
    e. *Bill described <u>John</u> the situation.
    f. Mr. Staples explained the theorem to <u>the class</u>.
    g. *Mr. Staples explained <u>the class</u> the theorem.

Consequently we need to rely on the partly semantic definition provided in (46).

Post-Verbal NPs: Direct Object or Indirect Object?

Earlier, direct object NPs were defined as those NPs which immediately follow a verb and which are passivizable. Above, indirect object NPs were said to be able to occur immediately after verbs, in examples like *Gerald gave <u>Ellen</u> roses*. But notice that such "indirect object" NPs are passivizable: *<u>Ellen</u> was given roses by Gerald*. But by the direct object definition, then, these NPs must function as direct objects. Can an NP function as both a direct and an indirect object?

Yes, if we invoke the metaphors of "underlying structure" and "derivation." In "underlying structure," indirect objects occur in canonical PP position, that is, as in *Gerald gave roses to <u>Ellen</u>*. A sentence in which the original indirect object NP occurs right after a verb is "derived" by a movement process which moves the NP from its PP position to its post-verbal position, and as a consequence changes its grammatical relation from indirect object into direct object. The process also shifts the original direct object NP to the position of the original indirect object (the two NPs trade places), and "demotes" it from direct object to a state of having NO relation to the verb:

51. a.

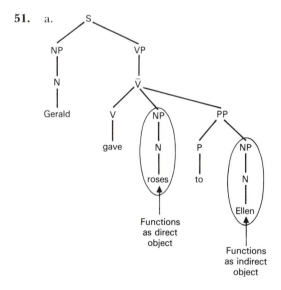

Functions as direct object

Functions as indirect object

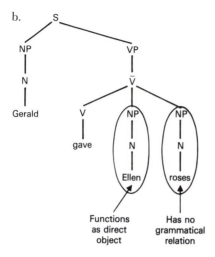

The reason the NP *roses* is said to bear no grammatical relation is that it seems generally to be true that in a simple sentence there can be no more than one NP bearing a given grammatical relation.[10]

The clash between the grammatical definition of direct object (passivizable NP immediately following a verb) and the semantic and grammatical definition of indirect object (NP denoting recipient, in immediate post-verbal position or following *to* or *for*) is resolved, then, in the following way: A given NP can bear only one grammatical relation at a given level of structure, that is, at either of the two levels of structure we have considered: actual—surface—structure, and underlying structure. Post-verbal NPs denoting recipients will be considered surface direct objects derived from underlying indirect objects. So (to pick new examples) the post-verbal NP *Don* in *Sue gave Don a cookie* functions as direct object (not indirect object) at the surface (i.e., actual) level, indirect object only underlyingly. But the post-verbal NP *Dad* in *The meal cost Dad a fortune* functions at the surface level as indirect object, since there is no passive **Dad was cost a fortune by that meal,* and hence *Dad* doesn't function as direct object.

---

[10]This generalization runs into trouble in connection with the following example, which is acceptable to some speakers:

> *Roses were given Ellen by Gerald.*

In this example, the "original" direct object NP has been passivized, but presumably from a non-direct object position, the one it occupies in tree (51b). If such an NP is passivizable, it might make sense to call it a second direct object. A possible way to avoid this is to say that in *Gerald gave Ellen roses* the sequence *gave Ellen* might be "reanalyzed" as a verb, whose direct object is *roses.*

EXERCISE 7. Identify all NPs below which function as surface (actual) indirect objects, and all that function as underlying indirect objects.

1. Max made brownies for the cub scouts.
2. The aged history teacher was pleased by the gifts from the students.
3. I wrote my invalid aunt a long letter yesterday.
4. We paid Celia the money for the meeting expenses.
5. Pass the salt, please.
6. She mentioned the new proposal to me yesterday.
7. We exchanged the socks for gloves with the neighbors at the Swap Meet on Sunday.
8. That mechanic charged me a lot to tune up my lawnmower.

With this discussion of indirect objects, we have concluded our examination of the so called "major" grammatical relations in English: subject, direct object, and indirect object. Next we will look briefly at three minor grammatical relations.

MINOR GRAMMATICAL RELATIONS

Predicate Nominative

In traditional grammar, the NP after the verb in *Leon is a leader* is said to function as **predicate nominative**, so called because it is in the VP, which functions as the predicate, and in languages with Latin-like case systems has a nominative case ending. Hence the name. Another label for this function is **subject complement**, because the NP is a complement for, i.e., completes, the meaning of the subject NP. Predicate adjectives (as in *Manute is tall*) are also subject complements.

Object Complements

Object complement NPs and APs parallel predicate nominatives and predicate adjectives semantically; they "complete" the meaning of direct object NPs:

52. a. We considered the senator a fool.
    b. The committee elected Jane chair.
    c. The storm made the air fresh and clean.
    d. Paul named one of his kittens Athena.

Semantically, there are two kinds of object complement sentences, those in which the verb denotes a belief—e.g., (a) above, and those in which the verb denotes a change of state for the direct object NP—e.g., (b), (c), and (d) above. The latter type has implications the former type lacks: for instance, the implication that because of the event denoted by the sentence, the entity denoted by the direct object takes on the state denoted by the object complement. Thus, it would be reasonable to infer from sentence (b) that Jane became chair.[11] But it would not be reasonable to infer from sentence (a) that the senator was, or became, a fool.

A Note on Objects of Prepositions

An NP preceded by a preposition, in a PP, functions as object of the preposition:

53.

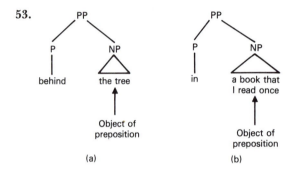

(a)   (b)

A sentence can have indefinitely many objects of prepositions—as many as there are prepositions:

54.

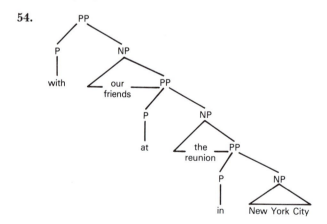

---

[11] This implication is not as strong as a logical consequence, or entailment, since someone elected to a position may decline.

In this tree, each NP functions as an object of a preposition: *our friends at the reunion in New York City, the reunion in New York City,* and *New York City.* Unlike the major grammatical relations (subject, direct object, indirect object), object of a preposition does not involve a relation between an NP and a verb; the NP in question bears a relation to a preposition. The relation is purely structural: any NP following a preposition, and within a PP, functions as object of the proposition. (So do NPs which have been moved from the post-preposition slot, leaving a gap: *Whom did you give the radio to _____?.*) Still, the NP is affected by the preposition in much the same way that a subject or direct object NP is affected by the verb, in that it gets its case from it: *who* as subject form, but *to whom; he* as subject form, but *beside him,* etc.

An NP which functions as an object of a preposition may, of course, bear another relation: indirect object. The two relations are to different elements of the sentence, the verb and the preposition. There are no other cases of an NP bearing two grammatical relations, at least at a given level of structure. It is possible, of course, for an NP to function as direct object at the level of logical structure, and as subject at the level of superficial or actual structure. Similarly, an NP can function as indirect object at one level of structure and direct object at another level.

SUMMARY AND CONCLUSION

In this chapter we have examined the major grammatical relations **subject**, **direct object**, and **indirect object**, with a view to characterizing them semantically and grammatically. In the first two cases, semantic properties were found unworkable for definitions (while being useful to understanding prototypical cases of the grammatical relation in question), but in the third case, a semantic characterization proved necessary, along with some grammatical properties.

We have also looked briefly at the grammatical nature of the minor grammatical relations **predicate nominative** (and predicate adjective), **object complement**, and **object of a preposition**.

Next on the agenda is the application of the ideas discussed in this and the previous chapters to complex sentences—sentences which contain sentences inside them.

ADDITIONAL EXERCISE

Identify the grammatical relation(s) of every underlined NP in the following sentences. Deal with superficial (actual) structure only. If an NP has no grammatical relation, say so.

1. The trailer was more expensive than the boat.
2. Those students sent cookies to the dean.
3. Smith found Wesson a bore.
4. Willie bought Sandra a new beach house.
5. Early poets studied the effect of sports on humans.
6. Linguistics is the scientific study of language.
7. Seven old ladies got stuck in the lavatory.
8. The bone was severely chewed by Rover.
9. Alice was beginning to get very tired of sitting by her sister on the bank, and of having nothing to do: once or twice she had peeped into the book her sister was reading, but it had no pictures of conversation in it, "and what is the use of a book," thought Alice, without pictures or conversation?
   (Lewis Carroll, *Alice's Adventures in Wonderland*)

Chapter Eight

COMPLEX SENTENCES

Complex sentences contain sentences inside them. For the most part, complex sentences have the same sort of structure simple sentences have, which by now should be familiar to you. Embedded sentences typically play roles in the complex sentences which are familiar, too: as we will see, they function as subjects and direct objects and as sentence-adverbial phrases.

One technical term which will be useful from here on is **clause**. A clause is a sentence, embedded or not. The term is used mostly with reference to complex sentences, however. In complex sentences it is sometimes useful to distinguish between the **main** or **matrix** clause—the embedding one—and the embedded clause(s).

Embedded clauses often have the same form as ordinary non-embedded sentences:

1. a. Roses are red but violets are blue.
    b. That <u>Lou stole six bases</u> doesn't surprise me at all.

Embedded clauses can also be found in altered form, as **infinitive** constructions—

2.

Max strongly desires (for) the Packers to win

—or as **gerund** constructions:

3.

Everybody greatly enjoyed Lulu's defeating Max

In this chapter we shall first discuss embedded clauses which have the same form as ordinary non-embedded sentences.

EMBEDDED SENTENCES WITH ORDINARY SENTENCE FORM

Coordination

Coordinate structures have embedded clauses on either side of a co-ordinate conjunction (*and, or,* and *but*). Sentences of this type are called **compound** in traditional grammar:

4.

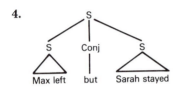

In this example, *but* does not form a constituent with either of the clauses it conjoins. We will see below that this makes sense.

Coordinate structures are not limited to two conjuncts:

5. Roses are red and violets are blue and sugar is sweet and so are you.

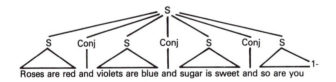

[1]There may be semantic reasons for grouping some embedded sentences in compounds together, for example *Max is five-eight and Pete is six feet even, and we therefore had two short forwards last year and that's why we lost the championship game,* which has a phrase structure tree like the following:

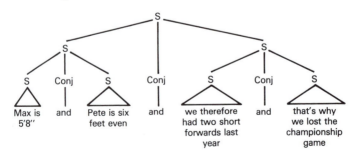

"Extraposition" of sentential subjects

Sentences with sentential subjects occur infrequently in discourse, especially in speech. Much more common are sentences in which the sentential subject appears to the right, being replaced in its original subject position by the pronoun *it:*

19.   <u>*It grossed everyone out*</u> <u>that Mary swallowed a goldfish</u>

Embedded clauses "moved" in this way are said to be **extraposed**,[3] and the movement process is called **extraposition**. Although firm evidence is lacking, let's assume that the extraposed, S-containing, NP is inside the VP:[4]

20.

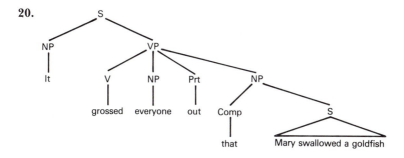

EXERCISE 2. Draw trees for the following sentences. Don't worry about N̄ and V̄.

1.   That the Dodgers won infuriated the Yankees.
2.   It infuriated the Yankees that the Dodgers won.
3.   That the proposal will pass seems very likely.

---

[3]One interesting issue is why extraposed structures are so much more commonly used than sentential subject structures. One reason presumably has to do with the relative length of the sentential subject and the predicate, the former almost always being much longer (e.g., *That Max swallowed a frog* [sentential subject] - *surprised me* [predicate]). All else being equal, longer constituents tend to be placed at the end of a sentence (e.g., in an **extraposed** structure like *It surprised me that Max swallowed a frog*). However, a separate tendency exists to place old, given information earlier in sentences than new information. Sentential subjects always represent old information, either overtly present in a preceding part of the discourse, or easily inferrable from the preceding discourse. So we would expect them to occur in the sentential subject slot, rather than at the end. Possibly part of the answer to the question of why sentential subjects are so uncommon in discourse is simply that the tendency to place longer elements toward the end of a sentence outweighs the tendency to place elements representing old information early. But more research is needed on this, and on the question of what motivates choice of a sentential subject structure, when it does occur, over one with the embedded sentence moved to the end.

[4]The other possibility, which we will not discuss here, is that it is attached to the S.

4. It seems very likely that the proposal will pass.

5. That the soup contains garlic proves that Max made it.

The actual subject of a sentence containing an extraposed element is the "dummy" pronoun *it.* The logical subject, of course, is the extraposed sentence.

Any sentential subject can have an extraposed paraphrase, with one notable exception: complex sentences with sentential constituents after the verb:[5]

21. a. That the moon is full is good.

⇓ Extraposition

It is good that the moon is full.

b. That the moon is full means that we can have the snipe hunt.

⫶ Extraposition

*It means that we can have the snipe hunt that the moon is full.

The material after the verb in (a) is just the adjective *good;* the material after the verb in (b) is the sentential direct object NP *that we can have the snipe hunt.*

Noun-Complement Clauses

Embedded sentences can appear inside NPs functioning as subject or direct object in constructions slightly different from those we have been discussing:

22. a. The idea that frogs eat spaghetti is preposterous.
b. Jill denied the accusation that she had sideswiped me.

---

[5]Below, we will discuss infinitives (e.g., *to know*) which can be considered truncated embedded sentences. Infinitives in subject position can be extraposed:

a. To know him is wonderful.
b. It is wonderful to know him.

But when an infinitive follows a verb, no extraposition is possible:

c. To know him is to love him.
d. *It is to love him to know him.

These **noun-complement** clause constructions are, of course, NPs containing Ss:

23.

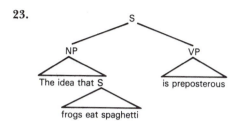

But what is the internal structure of the NP? One possibility is the following:

24.

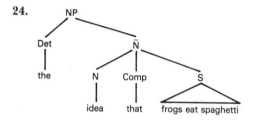

But the movement criterion supports uniting *that* and the S into a single phrase:

25.

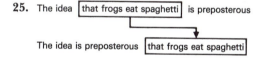

Because of this movement (extraposition), the phrase structure must be

26.

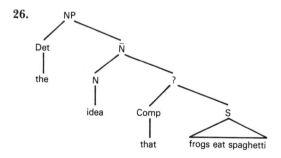

That is, complex NPs (those containing Ss) contain an N̄ made up of an N from a restricted set (*idea, fact, hypothesis, proof*, etc.), and a constituent made up of the complementizer *that* and an S.

What kind of constituent is *that* + S, labeled "?" in tree (26)? In previous examples, such a phrase was labeled NP on the basis of evidence from movability and substitution. But here substitution argues against its being an NP: **the fact Max, *the claim the garden*, etc. (Movement, as we saw in Ex. 25, indeed argues for *that* and the S to be a constituent together, but provides no answer as to what kind.)

A widely accepted answer is that *that* + S is a new kind of constituent, called S̄ (pronounced "S-bar"), made up of an S and a complementizer. With S̄ in our system, we can replace tree (26)'s "?," resulting in tree (27):

27.

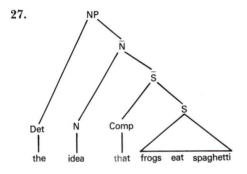

Accepting S̄ into our system will require a simple revision of previous analyses: we can no longer represent NPs like *that Max left* like this

28.

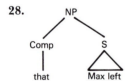

but must represent them like this instead:

29.

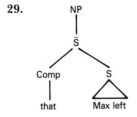

Adjective-Complement Clauses

Embedded sentences can show up inside APs, too:

30. a. Leon is <u>very happy that Sarah won the race.</u>
   b. We were <u>delighted that you were able to come.</u>

Trees for such sentences are straightforward:

31.

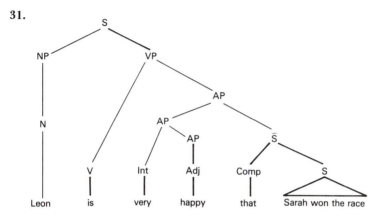

Notice that the S̄ in such a sentence is not dominated by an NP node.

EXERCISE 3.

A. Draw trees for the following sentences. Use triangles for embedded sentences.
  1. I love the idea that grasshoppers can sing.
  2. Max was very sad that Cathy left early.
  3. The proof that Tom stole the donuts is before your eyes.
B. Only a few adjectives can be followed by adjective-complement clauses (*happy, sad, pleased, excited,* etc., but not *red, tall, shiny,* etc.). What semantic property is shared by the adjectives which take adjective complement clauses? To investigate this question, think up ten or so adjectives which do, and a like number of adjectives which do not.

REDUCED SENTENCES: INFINITIVES AND GERUNDS

The embedded sentences discussed so far have all had the form of ordinary non-embedded sentences. Some phrases, however, that don't look like sentences are best analyzed as embedded sentences which have been changed in certain respects because of the way they are embedded. Some of these embedded sentences have **infinitive** verbal morphology instead of a tensed verb:

32.   For the Packers *to win* this game would be a miracle.

In this example, the underlined sequence is the embedded sentence, and the italicized sequence is the infinitive verb. (As mentioned in Chapter Four, the term 'infinitive' derives from the fact that inifinitive verbs have no tense, and are therefore, with respect to time, unlimited—"non-finite," that is.)

Another alternative to tense is **gerund** morphology:

33.   Max's *defeating* Lulu surprised everyone.

Again, the underlined sequence is the embedded sentence, and the italicized form is the gerund. Lacking tense, gerunds are "non-finite" like inifinitives, and were once called "cases" of infinitives. Nowadays this connection between gerunds and infinitives is not made, and gerunds are simply considered morphologically distinct versions of verbs.

One reason the underlined stretches in the examples above deserve to be called "sentences" is that they have internal *NP + VP* structure, in which the NP functions as subject and the VP as predicate, like the regular sentences they are obviously related to *The Packers win this game* and *Max defeated Lulu*.

Are embedded sentences of this sort NPs as well? Let's try applying some familiar constituency tests: function, substitution, and movement. If the concept of subject is to have any meaning, only NPs can function as subjects, and in (32) and (33), infinitive and gerund clauses function as subjects of their matrix sentences. So they must be NPs. As far as substitution is concerned, for each of the underlined phrases in (32) and (33), we can substitute a garden-variety NP like *the visit:*

34.   (a) <u>For the Packers to win this game</u> would be a miracle

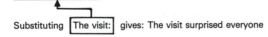

Substituting | The visit | gives: The visit would be a miracle

(b) <u>Max's defeating Lulu</u> surprised everyone

Substituting | The visit: | gives: The visit surprised everyone

Infinitive clauses with *for* move like NPs, too. Look at the movements indicated below:

35. (a) <u>This red model</u> really moves.

⇓

(b) What really moves is <u>this red model</u>.

⇓

(c) <u>For the Packers to win this game</u> would be a miracle.

⇓

(d) What would be a miracle is <u>for the Packers to win this game</u>.

The underlined phrase in (a) and (b) is an ordinary NP. The infinitive construction in (c) and (d) can undergo the same movement, indicating that it is an NP as well.

Gerund phrases move like ordinary NPs too. NPs can generally move by "passivization," and gerund phrases are no exception:

36. a. <u>Max's defeating Lulu</u> surprised everyone. (*active*)

⇓ Passivization

b. Everyone was surprised by <u>Max's defeating Lulu</u>. (*passive*)

It seems reasonable to conclude, therefore, that gerund and infinitive phrases of the sorts we have examined are NPs.

What about the internal structure of these embedded sentences? In place of tense, the gerund type has its subject NP in possessive form and *-ing* attached to the verb, and the infinitive type has an occurrence of *for* initially and an occurrence of *to* where aux would appear in a non-embedded sentence. These markers of embedding can be thought of as discontinuous complementizers overlain on the sentence:

37.

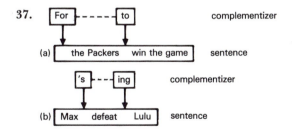

(A tree diagram cannot do justice to such structures, since tree diagrams cannot represent discontinuous constituents.)

Infinitive and gerund constructions can function as direct object as well as subject:

38. a. Infinitive:
      i. Leon wants for the Packers to win the game.
      ii. Leon wants the Packers to win the game.
   b. Gerund: Everybody enjoyed Max's defeating Lulu.

You can see in (aii) that in direct object position, an infinitive construction can omit its *for*. However, whether or not *for* is omissible is dependent on what the main verb is:

39. a. Leon hoped *for* the restrictions to be removed.
   b. *Leon hoped the restrictions to be removed.
   c. The President strongly desires *for* the Secretary to resign.
   d. The President strongly desires the Secretary to resign.

Hope requires a direct object infinitive construction to keep its *for; desire* allows it to be omitted.

EXERCISE 4. Identify all subject and direct object NPs, including sentential ones and the subject and direct object NPs within embedded clauses, including infinitive and gerund constructions:

1. That Sheila left early proves that she loves you.
2. Sheila's leaving early proves her love for you.
3. For Sheila to leave early would prove her love.
4. I admire your leaving early.

Infinitive Constructions with Subject Deletion

The infinitive constructions we have discussed so far in this section have overt subject NPs, e.g., *the Packers* in *Vince desires (for) the Packers to win the game.* Trickier are constructions in which the subject NP of an embedded clause is not overt in the superficial structure of the sentence, but "understood":

40. The Packers want to win.

In (40), *to win* can be viewed as an embedded sentence that is missing its subject NP:

41.

The Packers want _____ to win

The "understood" subject NP of this sentence is, of course, *the Packers*. This makes semantic sense: in the situation the sentence denotes, the ones who the Packers desire to win are, of course, the Packers (not, for example, the Giants). Therefore, a more explicit version of this sentence might be the following:

42. ?The Packers want the Packers to win.

(The sentence has a question mark because the omission of the repeated subject NP is nearly obligatory.)

Besides this common-sense semantic reasoning for the nature of "understood" subjects, strictly grammatical justification can be found:

Thinking of the active - passive relation as a derivational process— "passivization"—note that infinitive constructions can be passive as well as tensed constructions:

43. a. O'Donnell wanted <u>a doctor to examine Linda</u>.
⇓ "Passivization"
b. O'Donnell wanted <u>Linda to be examined by a doctor</u>.

This example contains an infinitive construction with an overt subject NP. But an infinitive with a covert (i.e., understood) subject NP can also be passive:

44. O'Donnell wants *to be examined* by a doctor.

What non-passive form is this related to? Presumably this:

45. O'Donnell wants a doctor to examine him.

Crucially, this example contains an embedded sentence, one with an infinitive construction instead of tense: *a doctor to examine him*. Passivization, applied to this example, would produce the following "abstract" structure:

46. O'Donnell wants <u>he/him/himself to be examined by a doctor</u>.

What is the relation between the above sentence (46) and *O'Donnell wants to be examined by a doctor* (44)? Suppose there is a correspondence between a sentence like (46) containing two NPs with the same reference and meaning, (*O'Donnell* and *he/him/himself*[6]), and a sentence like (44) with the second NP omitted. Diagrammatically:

---

[6]Which particular form is not clear, nor does it matter.

47.

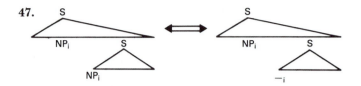

In this diagram, the small *i*'s indicate sameness of meaning and reference. If this makes sense, the following relation holds:

48.   O'Donnell$_i$ desires [himself$_i$ to be examined by a doctor]
⇓
O'Donnell$_i$ desires [——$_i$ to be examined by a doctor]

In this relation, the absence of the subject NP in the embedded sentence can be thought of as resulting from a "process" of deletion, under the condition of sameness of reference and meaning between main sentence subject NP and embedded sentence subject NP.

If such a relation holds for passive sentences, there is no reason why it shouldn't hold for active sentence as well:

49.   The Packers$_i$ want [the Packers$_i$ to win]
⇓
The Packers want [—— to win]

This means that sentences with missing subjects of infinitives have structures like the one below, in which the second *i* indicates that the blank space—the "gap"—is understood as if it contained a copy of the NP bearing the other *i*.

50.

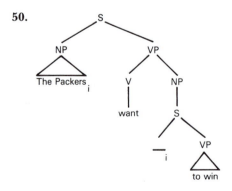

Let's review this argument. Assumptions: Passive sentences can be thought of as being derived from active ones. The process of passivization applies to a full sentence, one with subject and direct object NPs. Given these assumptions, the only way to explain the form of a sentence with a subjectless passive infinitive (e.g., *O'Donnell wants <u>to be examined</u> by a doctor*) is to conclude that it is related to a sentence containing an embedded full active sentence—"full" meaning complete with subject and direct object NP. This embedded active sentence can be passivized, resulting in a sentence in which the embedded subject is identical (in reference and meaning) to the main subject (e.g., in effect, *O'Donnell wants O'Donnell to be examined by a doctor*). Such a sentence is the one that the subjectless infinitive sentence is directly related to. Once forced to make such an analysis for subjectless passives, the way is open to make it for subjectless actives as well, ones like *The Packers$_i$ want ____$_i$ to win.*

Infinitives after adjectives and verb-like NPs

Essentially the same as the sentences we have just discussed are sentences like the following:

51. a. Zack is eager for Cate to arrive.
    b. Zack is eager to arrive.

52. a. Mannie has a plan for Kim to run for office.
    b. Mannie has a plan to run for office.

All four of these sentences—the first pair, with the adjective *eager*, and the second pair, with the NP *a plan*—pattern just like sentences with a verb like *desire:*

53.

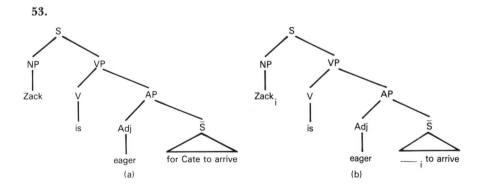

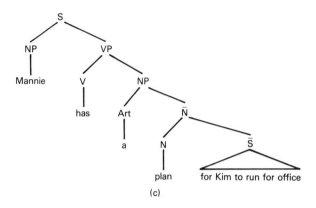

(c)

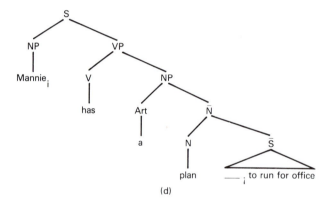

(d)

In these sentences, the *V* + *AP* or *V* + *NP* combinations are semantically—though not grammatically—equivalent to a simple verb.

You will undoubtedly have noticed that the trees above contain S̄s, not Ss. Of course the S̄s actually have Ss inside them. The reason for the presence of the S̄s is that *for* is a complementizer, and therefore, strictly speaking, outside the boundary of the S that it precedes. Complete versions of the trees in (53a and b) above are the following:

54.   Complete version of 52(a):

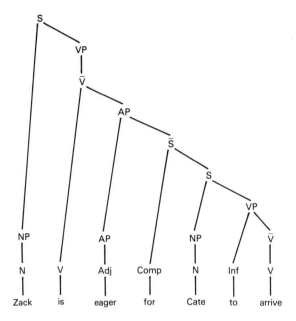

Complete version of 52(b):

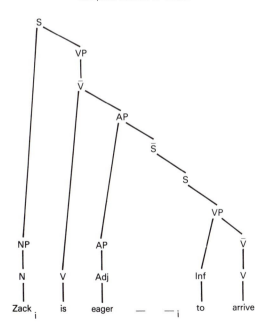

Another detail in (54) is that the embedded S̄s are not NPs. Substitution supports not calling them NPs, since no garden-variety NP can be substituted for them in these environments: *Zack is eager <u>the tree</u>; *Mannie has a plan <u>the truck</u>.*

EXERCISE 5. Draw trees, with gaps where NPs have been deleted, for the following sentences. Don't worry about V̄. Use triangles for S̄s.

1. That guy wanted to buy my truck.
2. Jane declined to be interviewed.
3. Senator Fogbottom always endeavours to be seen at parties.
4. Max had a scheme to win Cathy's heart.
5. Cathy was not anxious to get close to Max.

Subjectless infinitives governed by main-sentence objects

All the examples of subjectless infinitives above have linked the understood subject—the "gap"—with the main sentence's subject NP:

55. a. The Packers$_i$ want _____$_i$ to win.
    b. Leon$_i$ wants _____$_i$ to be examined by a doctor.

But some sentences govern the gap with the main sentence direct object NP:

56.   Max persuaded Bill$_i$ _____$_i$ to go.

One argument for this analysis comes from the semantic interpretation of this sentence, which is that it is Bill, not Max, who will go. We will see below there is grammatical evidence for it as well.

Let us see how there is a significant grammatical difference between a pair of sentences which seem, on the surface, to have identical structures:

57. a. Max wanted Bill to go.
    b. Max persuaded Bill to go.

Both (a) and (b) are made up of the sequence *NP V NP to V*. But in (a), the direct object NP is the whole "infinitive clause" *Bill to go*, whereas in (b) the direct object NP is the simple noun *Bill*. How do we know? By what happens with *wh-* clefting, for one thing:

58. a. Non-clefted sentence with *want* and an ordinary direct object NP:
   Max wanted *a party.*

   b. *Wh*-clefting with *want* and an ordinary direct object NP:
   What Max wanted was *a party.*

   c. Non-clefted sentence with *want* and a direct object infinitive clause:
   Max wanted *Bill to go.*

   d. *Wh*-clefting with *want* and a direct infinitive clause:
   What Max wanted was *for Bill to go.*

   e. Non-clefted sentence with *persuade:*
   Max persuaded *Bill to go.*

   f. Attempt at *wh*-clefting with *persuade:*
   *What Max persuaded was *for Bill to go.*

The ungrammatical example sentence in (f) results from trying to create a *wh*-clefted sentence with *persuade* on the model of the example sentence in (d), with *want*. Since the example sentence in (f) is ungrammatical while the one in (d) is fine, the two basic sentences underlying them must be structured differently, despite their superficial similarity. (These two basic sentences are those in c and e, i.e., those in 57.)

Another reason for saying that sentences like (57a and b) are structured differently comes from their respective passive versions. (We will here substitute *desire* for *want* in (57a), since *want* doesn't permit a passive, for reasons that have nothing to do with our current topic.) The passive of *Max desired Bill to go* is *For Bill to go was desired by Max,*[7] while the passive of *Max persuaded Bill to go* is *Bill was persuaded by Max to go.* Trying to passivize the *Bill to go* sequence after *persuaded* produces the ungrammatical **For Bill to go was persuaded by Max,* and trying to passivize just the simple NP *Bill* after *desired* produces the ungrammatical **Bill was desired by Max to go.* Summarizing the allowable movements diagrammatically:

59. (a)

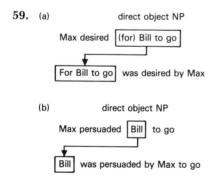

(b)

---

[7]The *for* is optionally present in direct object position (*Max desired [for] Bill to go*) obligatory in subject position.

Consequently, *Max desired Bill to go* and *Max persuaded Bill to go* have different structures:

60.

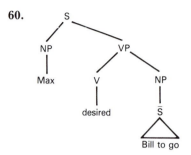

61.

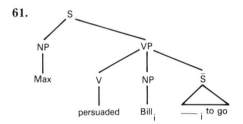

So far, we have seen three different kinds of infinitive structures:

62. (a) With no gap:

Max $\begin{Bmatrix} \text{wanted} \\ \text{desired} \end{Bmatrix}$ Bill to leave.

(b) With a gap referring back to main sentence subject NP:

Max$_i$ $\begin{Bmatrix} \text{wanted} \\ \text{desired} \end{Bmatrix}$ —$_i$ to leave.

(c) With a gap referring back to main sentence object NP:

Max persuaded Bill$_i$ —$_i$ to leave.

If a gap is present, usually it refers to the nearest preceding NP; if there is an object NP the gap refers to it (as with *persuade*) and if not the gap refers to the subject NP (as with *want* and *desire*).

We have seen, then, a structural ambiguity in the sequence *NP V NP to VP:* the structure is either *NP V [NP to VP]* or *NP V NP [_____ to VP]*. Which structure a sentence has depends on what its main verb is. If it is a verb like *want* or *desire* the structure is the former, and if it is a verb like *persuade* the structure is the latter.

EXERCISE 6.

A. Are the following sentences like the *want/desire* examples or like the *persuade* examples? In each case give your reasoning for your decision. Then draw the tree for each sentence, including gaps and little *i*'s for sameness of meaning and reference. Use triangles to abbreviate S̄s.

   1. The cop forced Sheila to pull over.
   2. Al needed Jo to bring the pies. (Note: Take this sentence to mean that Al needed a particular event to occur, that of Jo bringing the pies.)
   3. Ernie begged Bert to give back his hat.
   4. Terry likes Marry Ellen to read to him.

B. Consider the verb *promise*. Is it like *want/desire*, like *persuade*, or like neither? In the sentence *Max promised Bill to leave*, is there a gap? If so, why? Where is it, and to what NP does it refer? If there is no gap, why not?

Another kind of infinitive structure

A different kind of infinitive structure shows up in the following:

63. Everybody expected Bill to leave

Surprisingly, sentences like this have characteristics of both *want/desire*-type and *persuade*-type structures. There is a *wh*-cleft version of (63): *What everybody expected was for Bill to leave,* which makes (63) look like a *desire*-type structure, but both kinds of passives are possible for it, a passive like *desire* and one like *persuade:*

64. a. For Bill to leave was expected by everybody. (like *desire*)
   b. Bill was expected by everybody to leave. (like *persuade*)

Sentence (64a) makes (63) look like a *desire*-type sentence, but (64b) makes it look like a *persuade*-type sentence. Paradoxically, then, *expect* sentences appear to have two types of structure.

   One resolution of this paradox is to assume that—for sentences containing *expect* and similar verbs—the two structures *NP V [NP to VP] and NP V NP [_____ to VP]* are related. That is, a sentence like *Everybody expected Bill to leave* may indeed have two structures, but not at the same time—rather, one may be, metaphorically speaking, turned into the other. Which one do you think is more basic? Using meaning as a guide, we can observe that in *Everybody expected Bill to leave,* everybody didn't expect Bill; they expected "that Bill would leave," that is, a proposition, i.e., basically, a sentence meaning. Now, *NP to VP* is a sentence structure. Consequently, let us take *NP V [NP to VP]* as basic, and assume a derivational process *NP V [NP to VP]* → *NP V NP [_____ to VP]*, which doesn't alter phrase order, but significantly changes internal structure, by removing the subject NP from an embedded sentence functioning as direct object and making it the main sentence's new direct object:

65.

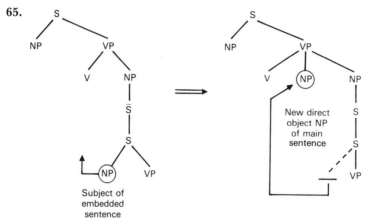

Raising a subject NP to direct object position

Because this process "raises" a subject NP out of an embedded sentence into a "higher" sentence, making it a derived direct object, it has been called "Raising to Object" in the syntactic literature.

In the choice between (64a) and (64b), the passive which is found depends on whether passivization occurs before or after Raising to Object. If it occurs before Raising to Object, the passive would be (64a), *For Bill to leave was expected by everybody* and if it occurred after Raising to Object, it would be (64b), *Bill was expected by everybody to leave.*

Some verbs permit Raising to Object even though they lack a passive of the form *[For NP to VP] be V-en by NP*. One such a verb is *believe*. The sentence *Everybody believes Bill to be a crook* is made up of our current favorite sequence, *NP V NP to VP*. The only passive we can make from it is *Bill is believed by everybody to be a crook;* the other passive—**For Bill to be a crook is believed by everybody*—is ungrammatical. This suggests the *persuade*-type structure, *NP V NP [_____ to VP]*, in which the gap is simply construed with the main sentence direct object NP, not a structure involving the Raising to Object process. That is, the passive evidence suggests simply that in sentences containing *believe* there is no "pre-Raising to Object" structure.

However *believe* sentences may involve a pre-Raising to Object structure, and Raising to Object may apply. Here is why.

The logical direct object of *believe* is a sentence; one believes that something is the case, i.e., one believes something that can be either true or false. Of all the phrase categories (S, NP, VP, etc.), only sentences can be true or false. It is thus semantically sensible to assume that *Everybody believes Bill to be a crook* has a pre-Raising to Object structure *Everybody believes [Bill to be a crook]*, in which the bracketed sequence is a sentence, rather than

Everybody believes Bill [_____ to be a crook]. Raising to Object must apply to such a structure, to enable passivization to produce *Bill is believed by everybody to be a crook,* since the NPs that are affected by passivization must be inside the same simple sentence (i.e., Ss are what the process of passivization applies to). Raising to Object moves the NP *Bill* into the same simple sentence as the subject NP *everybody.*

To understand this argument further, consider the following sentence:

66. Bill is believed by everybody to be suspected by the police.

In this sentence, as before, logically Bill isn't what (or whom) everybody believes; rather, everybody believes that something is the case. So the (logical) direct object of *believe* must be a sentence. Moreover, *Bill* is logically the direct object of *suspect,* so it must—at some level of structure—be in proper direct object position with respect to that verb. The word sequence *to be suspected by the police* is a truncated passive sentence; it "originated" as the active form *the police to suspect Bill,* and "got passivized" into the form *Bill to be suspected by the police.* In the whole sentence *Everybody believes [Bill to be suspected by the police],* then, the subject NP *Bill* must have been raised to main sentence direct object position, from which it can be passivized. The derivation looks like this:

67. Logical structure:

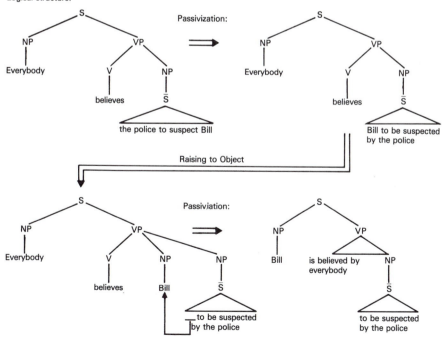

EXERCISE 7. Using the above derivation as a model, propose a "logical structure" and a derivation for *MacArthur was thought to be greatly admired by the
President.*

Tough *infinitives*

Earlier, we discussed infinitives in sentences like these—

68. a.   Zack is eager to arrive.
     b.   Mannie has a plan to run for office.

—in which a V + AP (*is eager*) or V + NP (*has a plan*) acts like the verb in a
sentence like *Max desires to win.*

Superficially similar to (a) and (b), but actually quite different, are
sentences like the following:

69. a.   With an adjective:
        Zack is easy to love.
     b.   With an NP:
        Mannie is a joy to visit.

The superficial similarity, and underlying difference, can be brought out
with the following pair of sentences:

70. a.   Marty is eager to please.
     b.   Marty is easy to please.

Sentence (a) is of the type discussed earlier: the verb - adjective sequence *is
eager* functions like a verb, e.g., *desires.* Sentence (b), however, represents a
new structure.

The two sentences of (70) are at first glance identical in structure,
each being made up of the sequence *NP is Adj to V.* The difference between
the two types is a difference in grammatical relations, and, correspondingly, a difference in the location of a gap. In (a), the main sentence
subject NP (*Marty*) functions also as the subject of the infinitive:

71.   Marty$_i$ is eager [_____$_i$ to please]

This sentence means that Marty is the one who will do the pleasing. But in
(b), the main sentence subject NP also functions as the direct object of the
infinitive:

72.   Marty$_i$ is easy [to please _____$_i$]

This sentence means that Marty can be pleased, rather than is the pleaser.

Another difference between the *eager*-type and the *easy*-type is that *easy*-type sentences have extraposition paraphrases:

73. a. It is easy to please Marty.
   b. It is a joy to visit Mannie.
   c. It is easy to love Zack.

Eager-type sentences, on the other hand, do not have such paraphrases:

74. a. Max is eager to please. ≠ It is eager to please Max.
   b. Zack is eager to arrive. ≠ *It is eager to arrive Zack.

Semantically, in *easy*-type sentences, the adjectives and NPs before the infinitives function as part of predicates about sentences. That is, logically:

75.

S

(For one) to please Marty   is easy

(a)

S

(For one) to visit Mannie   is a joy

(b)

S

(For one) to love Zack   is easy

(c)

The subject NPs of the embedded sentences in these logical forms are indefinite, with a meaning of "one," "someone," or the like. That is why they can be omitted: omission results in no information loss. Seeing this kind of sentence in "logical" form, with sentential subjects, as in (75), allows us to see why extraposition is a possible paraphrase: as we saw earlier, sentences with sentential subjects have extraposed variants. The reason that *eager* sentences do not have extraposition paraphrases is that *eager* is not part of a predicate about a sentential subject; rather, it is a predicate about a simple NP subject (in 74, *Max* and *Zack*).

EXERCISE 8. What are the logical forms of the following sentences? Write them out linearly, with brackets around any embedded sentences and <u>one</u> to indicate indefinite subjects.

1. This jar is tough to open.
2. Jane is anxious to leave.
3. Jasper is just a delight to babysit for.
4. Tony is struggling to succeed.
5. Lou is hard to catch.

Gerunds

As we saw in Chapter Four, gerunds are "verbal nouns," derived from verb roots by suffixing *-ing*.

76.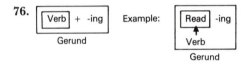

Not every verb with *-ing* attached to it is a gerund, however, since a different *-ing* forms the "present" participle. Gerunds are a fourth type of embedded sentence (in addition to *that*-clauses, noun- and adjective-clauses (e.g., (22) and (30), and infinitives). Basically, the gerund ending *-ing* is accompanied by a **genitive** NP (one with the "possessive" *-'s* suffix, or a variant):

77. a. [Shelley's winning the championship] surprised me.
b. I hate [Oscar's driving].
c. [My leaving early] shocked everybody.

The genitive NP functions, of course, as subject of the embedded sentence. That is, in (77), *Shelley, Oscar,* and *I* are the subject NPs of the embedded sentences. The subject NP can be omitted, as you might expect, when it is indefinite:

78.   One's reading *Ulysses* is a deep and difficult experience.
=   Reading *Ulysses* is a deep and difficult experience.

Sometimes discourse context can lead a listener to infer that an omitted subject NP refers to a specific individual:

79. Winning the championship would be a real surprise.

Sentence-Adverbial Phrases

Sentences inside sentence-adverbial phrases are subordinate to the main sentence. In traditional grammar, this type of clause-containing sentence, and all others we shall discuss in this chapter, are called **complex**. In the sentence below, *when Max snored* is a sentence-adverbial phrase containing a subordinate clause:

6. Julia laughed when Max snored.
                           ↑
              subordinate clause

What is the structure of such a complex sentence? You may feel that the two sentences below have the same structure:

7. a. Julia laughed and Max snored.
    b. Julia laughed when Max snored.

Based on our discussion of sentence conjunction above, a reasonable tree for (a) would be:

8.
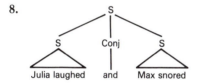

Applying the same analysis to (7b), we would get the following tree:

9.
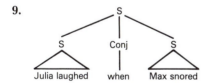

But, as we saw in Chapter Four, the movement criterion for constituenthood provides evidence for grouping the subordinate conjunction and the S together:

10.

No such "movement" is possible for the sequence *and Max Snored:*

11.

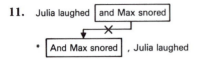

So the correct structure for (7b) might well be the following:

12.

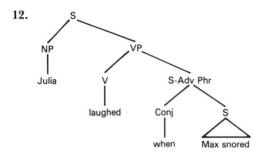

Because of the impossibility of movement, (7a) could not have such a structure.

The constituent made up of a subordinate conjunction (*when,* in 12) and an embedded S is an "Adverbial Phrase," so called because it functions like a sentence-adverb, "modifying" the rest of the complex sentence. (Observe that the kind of paraphrase that sentence-adverb-containing sentences were said to have in Chapter Four is possible with these subordinate clause sentences, albeit awkwardly: *Julia's laughing was when Max snored.*)

When moved to the front, a sentence-adverbial phrase of this sort is attached to the top S:

13.

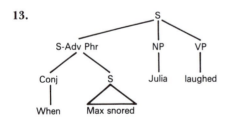

EXERCISE 1. Draw trees for the following sentences:

1. Tacos are good but enchiladas are better.
2. We scored the runs when we needed them.
3. Before she fired George, Nancy apologized to him.
4. While the nation slept, the volcano erupted and the tidal wave threatened the coast.

Embedded Clauses Functioning as Subject and Direct Object

We know that in *Max suspects Rudy* and *Max suspects the truth*, the phrases *Rudy* and *the truth* are NPs. By substitution, the underlined word sequence in *Max suspects that Sheila stole the donuts* is an NP as well, since *Rudy* and *the truth* can substitute for it. By movement, too, it is an NP, since it moves exactly as do the NPs *Rudy* and *the truth:*

14.

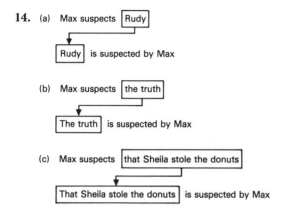

(a) Max suspects [Rudy]

[Rudy] is suspected by Max

(b) Max suspects [the truth]

[The truth] is suspected by Max

(c) Max suspects [that Sheila stole the donuts]

[That Sheila stole the donuts] is suspected by Max

The movement in these examples is brought about by passivization; therefore, by our definition of direct object NPs as passivizable NPs (recall our discussion of direct objects in Chapter Seven), these NPs bear the grammatical relation "direct object." The one in (c) we might call a "sentential direct object," since the sentence *Sheila stole the donuts* is contained within it.

What is the internal structure of such an NP? Besides an S, it contains the **complementizer** *that*. **Complementizers** are words that signal that what follows is an embedded sentence.[2] So *that* + *S* NPs have the following type of structure:

15.

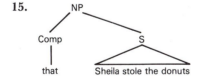

There is nothing to prevent indefinitely long and complex sentences with unbounded nestings of verbs and sentential direct objects:

---

[2]The idea of a complement is that it "completes" another word or phase. Embedded sentences in NPs functioning as direct objects may be thought of as completing the transitive verb. Below we shall see embedded sentences in NPs functioning as subjects; these may be thought of as completing the verbs too—by providing their subjects.

16.   I know that you think that I believe that Max suspects . . .

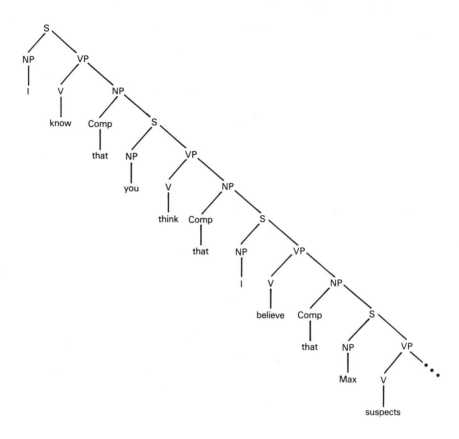

Sentences can have **sentential subjects**, too:

17.   a.   That Mary swallowed a goldfish grossed everyone out.
    b.   That Rocky wants to build a better mousetrap is clear.

The trees for these are straightforward. Here is the tree for (a):

18.

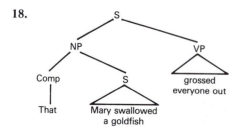

This sentence means that Marty can be pleased, rather than is the pleaser.

Another difference between the *eager*-type and the *easy*-type is that *easy*-type sentences have extraposition paraphrases:

73. a. It is easy to please Marty.
    b. It is a joy to visit Mannie.
    c. It is easy to love Zack.

Eager-type sentences, on the other hand, do not have such paraphrases:

74. a. Max is eager to please. ≠ It is eager to please Max.
    b. Zack is eager to arrive. ≠ *It is eager to arrive Zack.

Semantically, in *easy*-type sentences, the adjectives and NPs before the infinitives function as part of predicates about sentences. That is, logically:

75.

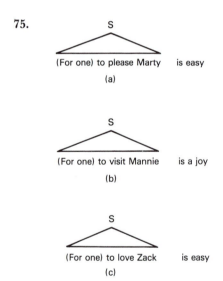

S

(For one) to please Marty   is easy

(a)

S

(For one) to visit Mannie   is a joy

(b)

S

(For one) to love Zack   is easy

(c)

The subject NPs of the embedded sentences in these logical forms are indefinite, with a meaning of "one," "someone," or the like. That is why they can be omitted: omission results in no information loss. Seeing this kind of sentence in "logical" form, with sentential subjects, as in (75), allows us to see why extraposition is a possible paraphrase: as we saw earlier, sentences with sentential subjects have extraposed variants. The reason that *eager* sentences do not have extraposition paraphrases is that *eager* is not part of a predicate about a sentential subject; rather, it is a predicate about a simple NP subject (in 74, *Max* and *Zack*).

EXERCISE 8. What are the logical forms of the following sentences? Write them out linearly, with brackets around any embedded sentences and <u>one</u> to indicate indefinite subjects.

1. This jar is tough to open.
2. Jane is anxious to leave.
3. Jasper is just a delight to babysit for.
4. Tony is struggling to succeed.
5. Lou is hard to catch.

Gerunds

As we saw in Chapter Four, gerunds are "verbal nouns," derived from verb roots by suffixing *-ing*.

76.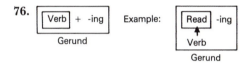

Not every verb with *-ing* attached to it is a gerund, however, since a different *-ing* forms the "present" participle. Gerunds are a fourth type of embedded sentence (in addition to *that*-clauses, noun- and adjective-clauses (e.g., (22) and (30), and infinitives). Basically, the gerund ending *-ing* is accompanied by a **genitive** NP (one with the "possessive" *-'s* suffix, or a variant):

77.   a.   [Shelley's winning the championship] surprised me.
     b.   I hate [Oscar's driving].
     c.   [My leaving early] shocked everybody.

The genitive NP functions, of course, as subject of the embedded sentence. That is, in (77), *Shelley, Oscar,* and *I* are the subject NPs of the embedded sentences. The subject NP can be omitted, as you might expect, when it is indefinite:

78.   One's reading *Ulysses* is a deep and difficult experience.
  =   Reading *Ulysses* is a deep and difficult experience.

Sometimes discourse context can lead a listener to infer that an omitted subject NP refers to a specific individual:

79.   Winning the championship would be a real surprise.

The discourse context around this example would provide a likely subject for *winning: I, you, our team,* or *the team (or individual) we are speaking about.*

When the subject NP is present, it usually has genitive form. The subject NP takes non-genitive form, however, when the subject NP is long:

80. a. I loved Bertha's scratching my back.
    b. ??I loved the new friend I made last night's scratching my back.
    c. I loved the new friend I made last night scratching my back.

Gerund constructions without genitive subjects must be distinguished from the participle complement constructions discussed in Chapter Four, that is, examples like Chapter Four's (50), *The police saw Lucy driving. away from the scene.* Such present participle complement constructions contain simple direct objects—in this example, *Lucy*—with the participle construction modifying the direct object. The structure contains a gap: *The police saw Lucy$_i$ [_____$_i$ driving away from the scene].* In contrast, in examples like (80c) there is no gap, and the direct object is the whole gerund construction, in which the NP following the main sentence's verb functions only as the subject of the gerund construction: *I loved [the new friend I made last night scratching my back].*

EXERCISE 9. Almost any sentence can be made into a gerund construction. Make gerund constructions out of the following sentences, and embed them in complex sentences you invent:

1. Max loved Cathy.
2. The principal was not here.
3. One keeps one's lawn mowed.
4. One jogs.
5. The manager didn't warn Tom not to pitch to Jack.
6. The turkey was basted too often.

ASPECTS OF MEANING IN COMPLEMENT CLAUSES

The Choice between Infinitive and Gerund

After certain verbs, both infinitives and gerunds can occur:

81. a. Max began to smoke.
    b. Max began smoking.
    c. Shelley liked to bake cookies.
    d. Shelley liked baking cookies.

    e. Harry tried to open the window.
    f. Harry tried opening the window.

But after other verbs, only one or the other is possible. *Want* and *decide* need infinitives:

82. a. Jane wanted to cry.
      b. *Jane wanted crying.
      c. Ann decided to resign.
      d. *Ann decided resigning.

Enjoy and *deny* need gerunds:

83. e. Bob enjoys drawing trees.
      f. *Bob enjoys to draw trees.
      g. Tom denied losing the file.
      h. *Tom denied to lose the file.

Proposing a partly semantic basis for the choice, the linguist Dwight Bolinger (1968) suggested that the infinitive often expresses something "hypothetical, future, unfulfilled," while the gerund expresses something "real, vivid, fulfilled." This may be why *want* and *decide* can only take the infinitive; wanting and deciding are inherently future-oriented. And it may be why *enjoy* and *deny* can only take the gerund; enjoying and denying are present- or past-oriented.[8]

    Structures with verbs which can take both infinitive and gerund complements sometimes show an interesting meaning difference which can be attributed to Bolinger's distinction. Contrast the situations in which one would say the following:

84. a. Harry tried to open the window.
      b. Harry tried opening the window.

Version (a) would be used only if Harry did not succeed in opening the window. If Harry managed to open the window but opening it did not bring about desired results (like cooling off the room), (b) would be used. In a similar vein, contrast *Sam remembered to lock the car* and *Sam remembered locking the car:* the former, with an infinitive, has Sam locking the car after remembering, while the latter, with a gerund, has this temporal order

---

[8]Enjoying is necessarily present-oriented; we can only enjoy activities we are presently engaged in. Denying is less present- or past-anchored, since it is possible to make a denial about the past, present, or future. But a negative statement about the future is less appropriately called a denial than one about the present or past. Presumably this is because the present and past are more firmly established in reality; what has happened and what is happening are immutable, but the future is to some extent uncertain.

reversed. Both these examples are just what Bolinger's distinction would predict.[9]

EXERCISE 10. For each verb below, state whether it takes an infinitive complement, a gerund complement, or both, and show—with a brief explanation—whether it fits Bolinger's suggestion or not.

hope, risk, start, continue, admit, refuse, plan

Factives and Implicatives

Factives

Contrast the meanings of the following:

85. a. Jane regrets that Tanya left Henry.
     b. Jane suspects that Tanya left Henry.

The speaker of (a) assumes, as background, the fact that Tanya left Henry, while in (b) it is not necessarily given that Tanya left Henry. Such an assumed background fact, what we called an "assumed background proposition" in Chapter Six, is a **presupposition**. More technically, a presupposition is a sentence (actually, a proposition) that must be true in order for a given sentence to "make sense." One presupposition of *Jane has stopped beating her husband* is that Jane has been beating her husband; another is that she has a husband. One presupposition of *Next time you fly to Hawaii, fly Universal Air* is that you have flown to Hawaii before. Another is that you will fly there in the future.

An interesting semantic property of sentences with presuppositions is that the presuppositions hold under negation:

86. a. Jane doesn't regret that Tanya left Henry.
     b. Jane hasn't been beating her husband.
     c. Next time you fly to Hawaii, don't fly Universal Air.

---

[9]The distinction is not always borne out, however—or if it is, it is very subtle. What meaning difference do you detect between the infinitive and gerund versions below?
a. Max began to smoke
b. Max began smoking
c. Shelley liked to bake cookies
d. Shelley liked baking cookies
Some speakers find that the gerund versions tend to fit actual occurrences of smoking and baking, while the infinitive versions tend to describe habits or recurrent events. These intuitions follow from Bolinger's predictions.

Saying any of these means that you assume the relevant presupposition ("that Tanya left Henry," "that Jane has a husband," "that you have flown to Hawaii before")—just as if you had said the corresponding affirmative sentences.

So—looking back to example (85)—sentence (85a) presupposes that Tanya left Henry, while (b) doesn't. This meaning difference is due, of course, to (a)'s containing *regret* versus (b)'s containing *suspect*. In complex sentences, certain verbs (and predicate adjectives taking complements) require the presupposition that the embedded clause is true:

87. a. Jane *regrets* that Tanya left Henry.
　　 b. It *is odd* that Tanya left Henry.
　　 c. Sam *was amazed* that Tanya left Henry.
　　 d. It *amused* us that Tanya left Henry.

For each of these sentences to make sense, it must be the case that Tanya left Henry.

On the other hand, with many verbs and predicate adjectives the truth of the embedded clause is not presupposed:

88. a. Jane *suspects* that Tanya left Henry.
　　 b. It *is likely* that Tanya left Henry.
　　 c. Sam *was afraid* that Tanya left Henry.

None of these sentences presupposes that Tanya left Henry.

Verbs (or other predicates) which require that a sentence embedded under them be true—i.e., which presupposes them—are called **factive** predicates. *Regret, be odd, amaze,* and *amuse* are factive; *suspect, be likely,* and *be afraid* are non-factive.

As you would expect, given Bolinger's distinction between infinitives and gerunds—that infinitives tend to express "hypothetical, future, unfulfilled" meanings and gerunds tend to express "real, vivid, fulfilled" ones—factive verbs tend to take gerunds rather than infinitives:

89. a. Max regrets Sally's leaving Mark.
　　 b. *Max regrets Sally to have left Mark.

And non-factives tend to take infinitives rather than gerunds:

90. a. Max suspects Sally to have left Mark.
　　 b. *Max suspects Sally's leaving Mark.

EXERCISE 11.

1. For each verb or adjective below, show that it is either factive or non-factive. Use *that*-clauses in your examples.

Assert, believe, note, is astonishing, bother, doubt

2. Try the same verbs and adjectives with gerunds and infinitives in your embedded clauses. Do these verbs and adjectives act as Bolinger's principle would predict?

Implicatives

Similar to factivity is the property shown by *manage* and *fail:*

91. a. Max managed to get a job.
    b. Rose failed to keep the appointment.

The sentences containing these verbs imply either the truth or the falsity of their complement: (a) implies that Max got a job, and (b) that Rose did not keep the appointment. Contrast (91a) with (92):

92. Max hoped to get a job.

(92) does not imply that Max got a job.

The verbs *manage* and *fail* are not factive. *Manage* is not factive, since it is not necessary (in fact, it is impossible) for the speaker to assume, ahead of time, that the hearer believes its complement sentence is true; the same holds for *fail* (the speaker cannot assume ahead of time that the hearer believes its complement sentence is false). Instead, the linguist Lauri Karttunen (1971) calls these verbs **implicative**. *Manage* is a positive implicative verb since it implies the truth of its complement sentence; *fail* is a negative one since it implies the falsity of its complement sentence.

EXERCISE 12. Identify the following verbs as factive, implicative, or neither, and give your evidence in each case. If the verb is implicative, say whether it is positive or negative (giving evidence).

remember, bother, neglect, avoid, seem, appreciate, turn out, suppose, amuse, agree, condescend

---

SUMMARY AND CONCLUSION

In this chapter we have looked at a variety of embedded sentence types, exploring certain of their semantic characteristics as well as their grammar. Looking first at embedded sentences with the same form as non-embedded sentences, we saw that embedded clauses can be conjoined with others to form "compound sentences," and in "complex sentences" embedded clauses can function as subjects, direct objects, and adverbial phrases. We then focussed on sentences with infinitives and gerunds, examining the intricate grammar of the former in some detail. Such embedded clauses, being tenseless, are thereby abstract from ordinary sentencehood. Sometimes their subject NP is missing as well, requiring an even more abstract analysis.

We have not even come close to exhausting the topic of complex sentences and embedded sentences. In the next chapter we shall see how embedded sentences can be modifiers of various phrase types, especially NPs.

ADDITIONAL EXERCISES

1. Think about the following sentences with respect to the question of their logical underlying form:
    1. A computer is likely to be a strong addition to our office.
    2. The meeting seemed to me to be going nowhere.
    3. There is certain to be a parade.
    4. It is apt to be raining.
    The verbs *seems* and *appears,* and the verb-adjective combinations *is certain* and *is apt,* function as predicates. They "say something" about subject NPs. Logically speaking, in the sentences above, what do they make predications about? That is, what are the logical subjects of the above sentences? And what are the abstract "underlying forms"—logical forms—of these sentences? (In the logical forms, predicates should be in canonical position with respect to their subjects—immediately to their right.)

2. In this chapter, we have examined a variety of infinitive structures. In some cases, the structure a sentence has is determined by its main verb (or functionally-equivalent predicate). Review the different infinitive structures which are determined by *want/desire, persuade, expect,* and *be easy.* Then try to figure out what kinds of structures are determined by the following: *try, condescend, be reluctant, imagine, get,* and *proclaim,* in sentences like these:
    1. Max tried to win Cathy's heart.
    2. Cathy condescended to spend some time with him.
    3. Jon was reluctant to go to State College.
    4. Don imagined himself to be intelligent.
    5. Miss Jackson got the class to enjoy *Macbeth.*
    6. Ron proclaimed himself to be above reproach.

REFERENCES

BOLINGER, DWIGHT. 1968. "Entailment and the Meaning of Structures," *Glossa* 2:2, 119–127.
KARTTUNEN, LAURI. 1971. "Implicative Verbs," *Language* 47:2, 340–358.

Chapter Nine

RELATIVE CLAUSES AND PARTICIPLES

In this chapter we will focus on two types of modifying constructions based on sentences: relative clauses and participle constructions. Here are some examples of each:

1. a. Relative clauses:
       i.   These boxes, which Luigi delivered, contain prizes.
      ii.   We came with a driver who talked a bit too much.
     iii.   It's 8° outside, which makes jogging exciting.
    b. Participle constructions:
       i.   The boxes sitting on the table contain prizes.
      ii.   A president elected by popular vote would have a stronger mandate.
     iii.   Mary, standing alone, smiled at the cheers of the crowd.

In many respects the two types of construction are similar. We'll look at relative clauses first. As we will see, much of what we will say about them will apply to participle constructions as well.

RELATIVE CLAUSES

Relative clauses are embedded sentences that modify phrasal categories (NP, S, AP, PP, VP):

2. a. Modifying an NP:
       The boxes which are on the table contain prizes.
    b. Modifying a clause:
       It's 8° outside, which makes jogging exciting.

c.   Modifying an AP:
     I'm *delighted,* which I know you're not.
d.   Modifying a P̄P̄:
     It's *in the bedroom,* where it should be.
e.   Modifying a VP:
     Susan *placed a personal ad,* which I would never do.

The reason they are called "clauses" is that they have the structure of a canonical sentence: subject NP and predicate VP. In (2a), the relative clause *which are on the table* is composed of the subject NP *which* and the tensed[1] predicate VP *are on the table.* In simplified tree form:

3.

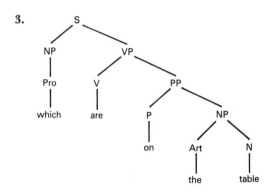

A relative clause usually contains a **relative pronoun**—*who, whom, which,* or *that*:

4.

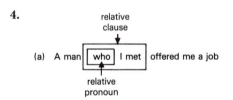

(a)   A man who I met offered me a job

(b)   The friend with *whom* I traveled in Spain is here.

(c)   The pencils *which* I loaned you are due back.

(d)   The comics *that* I bought in 1972 are now worth $95.

One kind of relative clause, called **restrictive**, modifies only NPs. **Nonrestrictive** relative clauses, which are semantically different from restrictive ones, can modify any kind of constituent (including NPs). We will look first at restrictive relative clauses.

As noun modifers, restrictive relative clauses are inside NPs, modifiers of the head noun (cf. Chapter Five):

---

[1] Unlike the infinitive and gerund constructions discussed in Chapter Seven.

5.

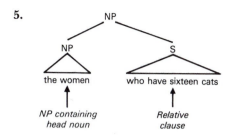

We say a structure of the form *NP + Relative Clause* is an NP on the basis of familiar criteria for constituency—substitution, movement, and function:

6. Substitution:

The women who have 16 cats left early.

↑

Josephine

(Substitution gives *Josephine left early.*)

Movement:

The police arrested the women who have 16 cats. ⇒
The women who have 16 cats were arrested.

Function:

As subject:

The women who have 16 cats left early.

As direct object:

The police arrested the women who have 16 cats.

The antecedent of a relative pronoun is commonly the immediately preceding NP. In the examples above, the subject NP of the relative clause is the relative pronoun *who*, whose antecedent is *the women*. (That is, the ones who have 16 cats are the women mentioned immediately before the relative clause.)

There is one situation in which a relative pronoun doesn't refer to an immediately preceding NP. Relative clauses can be extraposed:

7. a. The man who lives in that funny house is here.
   b. The man is here who lives in that funny house.

In both (a) and (b), the antecedent of *who* is the *man*, which is adjacent to it in (a), but not in (b).

EXERCISE 1. Underline the relative clauses in the following sentences. In each sentence, circle the relative pronoun and box its antecedent.

1. The coach was the one who seemed to be in charge.
2. This is the cat that caught the rat.

3. A car which you buy from a used-car lot can't be relied on.
4. The instructors whom I complained to the dean about are angry.
5. Smith ordered the books about which Jones had boasted to him.
6. The little boy came by who was trying to sell cookies.

The NP in which a restrictive relative clause resides is made up of a determiner and a common noun (or a plural common noun without determiner), and the relative clause. The common noun, by itself, identifies a potential set of things it can refer to (in Examples 5 and 6, the set of all women). The relative clause then **restricts** the possible reference to a subset of that domain (in Examples 5 and 6, the particular women the speaker is talking about who have sixteen cats).

Relative Clauses with Gaps

Because the relative pronoun always occurs at the beginning of a relative clause (or in a PP that is clause-initial, as in *The friend [with whom I traveled] is here*), some relative clauses are harder to recognize as clauses, because they don't have canonical word order. In *A man whom I met offered me a job,* the subject NP of the relative clause *whom I met* is *I,* the direct object NP *whom* having been moved to the front of the relative clause:

8. whom I met

that is:

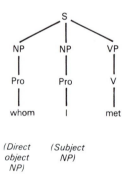

The only relative clauses whose form is canonical are those in which the relative pronoun functions as subject, or in which a determiner relative pronoun (exemplified below) is in a subject NP; in other types the relative pronoun can be thought of as moved from its logical position, just as with the *wh-* questions discussed in Chapter Six.

9.

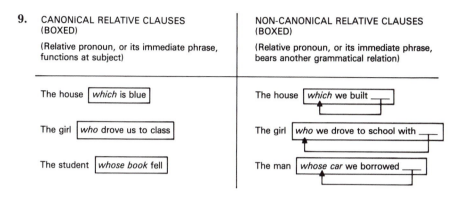

CANONICAL RELATIVE CLAUSES (BOXED)	NON-CANONICAL RELATIVE CLAUSES (BOXED)
(Relative pronoun, or its immediate phrase, functions at subject)	(Relative pronoun, or its immediate phrase, bears another grammatical relation)

EXERCISE 2. Which of the following sentences containing relative clauses have gaps—i.e., have moved relative pronouns? For those that do, write out the sentence linearly, inserting a blank space where the gap appears, and draw an arrow to the moved relative pronoun. In some cases, a phrase containing the relative pronoun may be moved, not just a relative pronoun alone.

Examples: i   This is the store that has the chocolate cookies.
(No gap; relative pronoun *that* functions as subject)
ii   This is the store that Acme Management bought.
= This is the store that Acme Management bought __

1.   This is the cat that caught the rat.
2.   This is the man whom I met yesterday.
3.   This is the cracked pipe which I told you about on the phone.
4.   This is the leaky garage roof about which I was complaining.
5.   This is the class to which I was referring in my report.
6.   This is the park ranger whom I wrote that awful letter to.
7.   The painting that Barbara did of the market needs reframing.
8.   Cats who scratch furniture will be banned from the living room.

Relative pronouns can be moved across an indefinitely long stretch:

10.   The man | *who* Max thought Noel believed Zelig said Ann claimed __ had left |

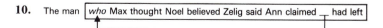

The tree for this example shows its structure more clearly:

11.

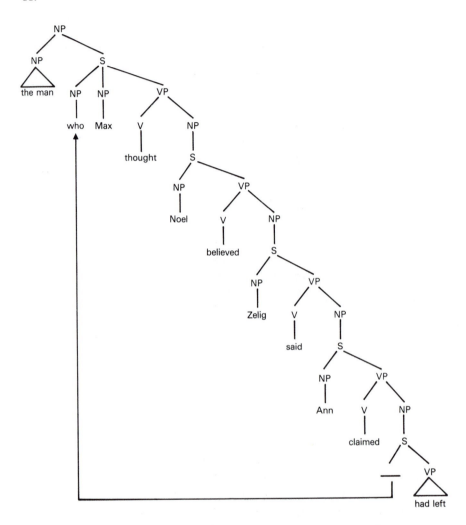

(The arrow showing movement, of course, is not part of the tree.)

EXERCISE 3. Draw trees for the following sentences containing relative clauses. Leave gaps at sites from which any item is moved, and draw arrows to their
derived position. Use triangles to abbreviate where details are irrelevant to the
relative clause.

Example: A crooked car dealer sold me a car which he had stolen.

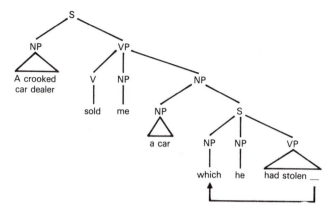

1. The candy bar which Paul bought for Eric has a rich filling.
2. Rose was the one who proposed the moratorium.
3. Bill showed us the court on which we would be playing.
4. The girl whose book I wrote in yelled at me.
5. The man who Rose thought Bill said the chairman had fired has filed suit.

The Grammatical Relations of the NP Containing a Relative Clause

The NP containing a relative clause can occur wherever any NP can, and can bear any grammatical relation:

12. a. As subject:
       The guy whom Ellen flirted with called her up.
    b. As direct object:
       Mr. Gold bought a truck which had an extended cab.
    c. As indirect object:
       We sent the teacher whom we admired most a long-stemmed rose.
    d. As predicate nominative:
       Frank is a guy whom you can always count on.
    e. As object complement:
       We consider Sally an administrator who always listens.

The Grammatical Relations of the Relative Pronoun

The relative pronoun can function as subject of the relative clause—

13. The women *who* have sixteen cats left early.

—or can bear other grammatical relations. In these other cases, you have to use the gap to identify the grammatical relation:

14.   a.   Direct object:
Max restored the car *which* Frank had owned _____ in 1948.
    b.   Indirect object:
       i.   This is the aunt to *whom* I sent those books _____ today.
      ii.   This is the aunt *who(m)* I sent those books to _____ today.
    c.   Object of a preposition (not an indirect object):
I learned the trick by *which* Huey deceived the voters _____ when he ran for editor.
    d.   Object of comparison (in casual speech):
You are the only person *that* I am shorter than _____.
    e.   Sentence adverb:[2]
This is not the place where we will be staying _____ tonight.
Shelly is trying to figure out the reason *why you left* _____.
Bob found out the time *when the silver was taken.*

Relative pronouns can also be determiners:

15.   This is the kitten *whose* ear I tweaked.

Headless relative clauses

The head NPs of relative clauses whose relative pronouns function as sentence adverbs can drop, creating "headless relative clauses":

16.   This is not *where* we will be staying _____ tonight.

Sentence (16) is related to the following structure, which contains the head NP *the place:*

17.

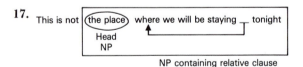

NP containing relative clause

Other examples:

18.   a.   i.   Gary is still trying to understand *why Peri left.*   =
      ii.   Gary is still trying to understand the reason *why Peri left.*
    b.   i.   Bob will never know *when the rugs were taken.*   =
      ii.   Bob will never know the time *when the rugs were taken.*

---

[2]Not, strictly, a grammatical relation.

It was suggested in Chapter Four that the word *when* is cross-classified as both a relative pronoun and a subordinate conjunction. It appears to be a relative pronoun when it has an antecedent, as in (18bii). But is it a subordinate conjunction in (18bi), where it lacks an overt antecedent? No; as suggested above, it is still a relative pronoun. It might be thought that subordinate clause constructions could be distinguished from headless relative clause constructions by the fact that the former can be moved—

19. a. Jo left when Mo came. =
    b. When Mo came Jo left.

—whereas the latter cannot:

20. a. I know when the cookies were taken. ≠
    b. ?When the cookies were taken I know.

But this immovability is only apparent. The movement of the *when* construction is easy when it functions otherwise than as direct object, e.g., as predicate nominative:

21. a. A good time to go would be when Jo arrives. =
    b. When Jo arrives would be a good time to go.

And, in fact, direct object headless relative clauses can move:

22. a. The prosecutor knows when the murder occurred. =
    b. When the murder occurred the prosecutor knows (when the robbery occurred, he doesn't).

All apparent subordinate clause constructions with *when* can in fact be considered headless relatives (contrary to our brief discussion in Chapter Four), with an "understood" occurrence of *(at) the time:*

23. a. Mo left when Jo came. =
    b. Mo left <u>at the time</u> when Jo came.
    c. When the coffee was ready we got up. =
    d. <u>At the time</u> when the coffee was ready we got up.

PPs like *at the time when Jo came* function as sentence adverbial phrases, because they "modify" the rest of the sentence. This is why, when the *at the time* phrase is omitted, the remaining *when . . .* construction functions as a sentence adverbial phrase as well. Within the headless relative clause, the word *when,* of course, functions as sentence adverb, since it expresses the meaning "at a certain time."

EXERCISE 4. Identify the grammatical relation (subject, direct object, etc., and including sentence adverb) of each of the following italicized relative pronouns:

1. I know the teacher *whom* you told me about.
2. This is the man *whom* Sheila is going to marry.
3. This is the cat *that* caught the rat *that* lived in the house *that* Jack built.
4. A saloon stands near the place *where* Abe was born.
5. Lou is the one *whom* we sent the pictures to.
6. The apartment *that* Barbara lives in is cavernous.
7. Clark is the guy *who* works in the book binding factory.
8. I can't understand *how* you identified my car.
9. The press corps knew *when* the President would resign.

Relative Pronoun Choice

What determines which relative pronoun—*who, which,* or *that*—is used? The choice between *who* and *which* is easy; *who* is used with a human antecedent, *which* with a non-human one:

24. a. The man whom I recommended
    b. *The man which I recommended
    c. The apartment which we rented
    d. *The apartment whom we rented

That is an alternative for both *who* and *which:*

25. a. The man that I recommended
    b. The apartment that we rented

With higher animals that we often interact closely with, like household pets, speakers differ in preferring *who* or *which*. Depending on whether you attribute human-like qualities to your cat, dog, or horse, you accept or reject the following:[3]

26. a. I have a kitten who is always crawling onto my lap.
    b. Fido is one dog who can always be counted on to wag his tail at intruders.
    c. Flicka is a horse who can't really be trusted with kids.

---

[3]Interestingly, race track parlance usually refers to horses as *it* and *which*. This may say something about how race track personnel feel about their horses!

Relative Pronoun Deletion

Sometimes a relative pronoun can be omitted:

27. a. a teacher (whom) she once had
     b. the guy (whom) you told me about
     c. the apartment (which) we rented
     d. the girl (whom) I sent a long-stemmed rose to
     e. the place (where) I'm staying

But not always:

28. a. a teacher who really got my attention
       ≠ a teacher really got my attention
     b. the guy who lives next door
       ≠ the guy lives next door

The difference between (27) and (28) is that in (27) the relative pronouns function as direct object, indirect object, object of preposition, sentence adverb—anything but subject; while in (28) the relative pronouns function as subject. Conclusion: relative pronouns functioning as subject cannot be dropped. (However, in some non-standard dialects—e.g., Black English and some varieties of British English—deletion of subject relative pronouns is permitted: *The guy lives next door told me about the 10K race.*)
Another kind of relative pronoun deletion is illustrated below:

29. a. The horse which is standing there won the last race.

     b. The horse __ standing there won the last race.

This is deletion not only of the relative pronoun, but of *be* as well. Such a deletion sometimes results in a participle phrase—in (29b), *standing there*—which modifies the head NP. Participle constructions will be discussed later in this chapter.

Distinguishing Relative Clauses from *That S* Constructions

In Chapter Eight we discussed *that S* constructions, tensed sentences embedded inside larger sentences, introduced by the complementizer *that:*

30. a. That frogs eat spaghetti pleases everyone.
     b. It pleases everyone that frogs eat spaghetti.
     c. Everyone knows that frogs eat spaghetti.

Sometimes these *that*-clauses superficially resemble relative clauses. This is the case when *that S* follows a noun like *idea, fact, proof,* or *claim:*

31. a. the idea that frogs eat spaghetti
b. the fact that Jill had sideswiped me
c. the proof that the earth revolves around the sun
d. the claim that Cheryl might ditch Mike

Superficially, these noun-complement clauses look like relative clauses, having head nouns followed by clauses introduced by *that:*

32. a. Noun-complement construction:

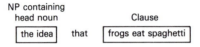

b. Construction containing relative clause:

One difference between these constructions is that any common noun at all can be the head noun of a relative clause, but only a restricted group of common nouns can be head nouns of noun-complement clauses: *idea, proof, fact, idea, hypothesis,* etc. (Nouns not in this set don't work: **the chair that frogs eat spaghetti* is ungrammatical.) But a more significant difference between the two constructions is that the *that* of the noun-complement construction is not part of the clause it is attached to—it just precedes it—while the *that* of a relative clause is an integral part of the relative clause. In the relative clause example above, (32b), *that* functions as subject of the relative clause, whereas in the noun complement example, (32a), *that* has no grammatical relation at all in the clause. Of course, the relative pronoun *that* in a relative clause may function otherwise than as subject, as we have seen (as direct object, object of a preposition, etc.). In such cases, the relative clause will contain a gap related to *that:*

33. a. the man *that I knew* _____
b. the girl *that* Max went to the prom with _____

In contrast, *that-S* constructions never contain gaps related to *that.*

Another way to think of the difference is to notice that *that* in a relative clause is an NP, whereas the *that* in a *that-S* construction is a complementizer.

EXERCISE 5. For each of the nouns listed below, construct two sentences, one containing a relative clause and one containing a *that-S* construction, using the listed nouns as head nouns.

1. proof   2. claim   3. notion
4. possiblity   5. hypothesis   6. dream

Nonrestrictive Relative Clauses

Contrast the following:

34. a. Margaret Louise, who is an artist, is coming to visit.
     b. A woman who is an artist is coming to visit.

The pauses or intonation breaks indicated by the commas in (a), and their absence in (b), are significant. They distinguish two types of relative clauses which have different sorts of meanings. Example (a) contains a nonrestrictive relative clause, (b) a restrictive relative clause. How are these constructions different?

In form, nonrestrictive relative clauses are bracketed by pauses or intonation shifts. Restrictive relative clauses aren't. In meaning, restrictive relative clauses provide information essential to the identification of the referent of the head noun, while nonrestrictive relative clauses provide less important, even parenthetical, information. More precisely, restrictive relative clauses narrow down the set of potential referents for the modified NP (the antecedent for the relative pronoun), restricting it, as it were, while nonrestrictive relative clauses modify NPs with a unique referent, so no narrowing-down is possible.

Besides the phonological difference and the meaning difference, grammatical differences exist between restrictive and nonrestrictive relative clauses. Restrictive relative clauses permit the relative pronoun to be *who, whom, which,* or *that,* but nonrestrictive relative clauses do not allow the relative pronoun *that:*

35. a. Restrictive relative clause:
       The woman that is an artist . . .
     b. Nonrestrictive relative clause:
       i. Margaret Louise, who is an artist, . .
       ii. *Margaret Louise, that is an artist, . .

Restrictive relative clauses cannot modify proper nouns,[4] but nonrestrictive relative clauses can:

---

[4]Except when the proper noun is used as a common noun: *The Margaret Louise who lived in Galveston, not the one from Houston.*

36. a.   Restrictive relative clause:
           *Margaret Louise who is an artist . . .
      b.   Nonrestrictive relative clause:
           Margaret Louise, who is an artist, . . .

Finally, only nonrestrictive relative clauses can modify sentences, VPs, or APs:

37. a.   Modifying a sentence:
           i.   Restrictive:
                *Today is Saturday which means we go swimming.
           ii. Nonrestrictive:
                Today is Saturday, which means we go swimming.
      b.   Modifying a VP:
           i.   Restrictive:
                *Margaret reads mysteries which many artists do.
           ii. Nonrestrictive:
                Margaret reads mysteries, which many artists do.
      c.   Modifying an AP:
           i.   Restrictive:
                *I'm exhausted which I know you're not.
           ii. I'm exhausted, which I know you're not.

EXERCISE 6. Using the following NPs as "heads" for relative clauses, construct, if possible, a restrictive and a nonrestrictive relative clause for each. If it proves impossible to create a relative clause of one type or the other, try to explain why.

1. Seven old ladies   **5.** My disk drive
2. Cathy and Max   **6.** An alligator
3. Anyone   **7.** Administration sources
4. A box of crayons   **8.** The fact that Cathy took typing

Appositives

An **appositive** is a construction immediately following an NP which provides another way to refer to the referent of the NP:

38. a.   Kennedy and Johnson, <u>our new neighbors</u>, recommended this weed whacker very highly.
      b.   Margaret Louise, <u>my boss's cousin</u>, is coming to visit.
      c.   *Catch-22*, <u>Max's favorite novel</u>, was written by Joseph Heller.

Appositives are related to relative clauses. The sentences above are identical in meaning to the following:

39. a. Kennedy and Johnson, <u>who are our new neighbors</u>, recommended this weed whacker very highly.
 b. Margaret Louise, <u>who is my boss's cousin</u>, is coming to visit.
 c. *Catch-22*, <u>which is Max's favorite novel</u>, was written by Joseph Heller.

This meaning relation enables us to regard appositives as reduced relative clauses; the sentences of (39) can be viewed as derived from those of (38) via the deletion of a *wh*-word and an immediately following form of *be*.

Most appositives are derived from nonrestrictive relative clauses, as in the examples discussed above. But restrictive appositives do exist:

40. a. Joseph Kennedy's son <u>John</u> became president.
 b. I was referring to my brother <u>the psychologist</u>.

In these sentences, the NPs *Joseph Kennedy's son* and *my brother* have more than one possible referent. Hence a restrictive interpretation is possible for the appositive NPs which follow. An NP which is necessarily unique, like *my mother*, can be modified only by a nonrestrictive appositive: **My mother the artist is having an opening soon* is ungrammatical, but *My mother, the artist, is having an opening soon* is fine.[5]

PARTICIPLES

As we saw in Chapter Four, a participle is a tenseless verb form used to modify NPs—

41. a. The woman <u>swilling</u> beer over there is my supervisor.
 b. The painting <u>stolen</u> by the burglars was a Picasso.

—or used in certain morphologically complex aspect and voice constructions, namely, the progressive, perfect, and passive:

42. a. Progressive: Elaine is <u>reading</u> the cereal box.
 b. Perfect: Elaine has <u>stolen</u> the muffins.
 c. Passive: Elaine was <u>chosen</u> by the awards committee.

---

[5]What then should we make of constructions like *My husband Jack bought himself a new car*—with restrictive intonation, but a nonrestrictive interpretation? It may be—though further research is needed—that NPs with necessarily unique referents—e.g., *my mother, the sun, the current president of the United States,* and proper names of people known to speaker and hearer, etc.—do not tolerate appositives that appear restrictive by their intonation, because they absolutely do not tolerate semantically restrictive ones, whereas NPs that can, under some situations, have non-unique referents, like *my husband,* do allow appositives that are restrictive by their intonation, even if a nonrestrictive interpretation is intended. The interpretation of such expressions, then, may be something like "My husband—and his name is Jack—bought himself a new car."

As discussed earlier, the progressive, perfect, and passive constructions can be viewed as containing the discontinuous morphemes *be..-ing, have..-en,* and *be..-en.*

As NP modifiers, some participles are in reduced relative clauses:

43.   a.   With full relative clause:
      i.   The man *who was chosen by the chair* was Ernie.
      ii.   The guy *who is standing here* is my roommate.
   b.   With reduced relative clause:
      i.   The man *chosen by the chair* was Ernie.
      ii.   The guy *standing here* is my roommate.

An NP-modifying participle always functions as a predicate about the NP that the reduced relative clauses modifies, i.e., the antecedent of the deleted *wh*-word:

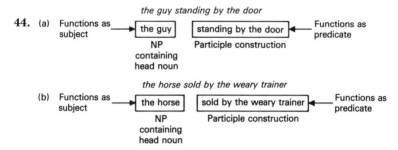

This can be accounted for by the idea that NP-modifying participle constructions like those we have just seen (e.g., those in 41, 43b, and 44) are derived from relative clause constructions, via deletion of both a *wh*-word and a form of *be;* any NP, including a *wh*-word, immediately preceding a verb, in this case *be,* necessarily functions as subject. The deleted *wh*-word, of course, has as its antecedent the NP containing the head noun of the relative clause. This NP must therefore function as subject, the modifying participle construction as predicate.

EXERCISE 7. For each sentence below, expand it with the missing *wh*-word plus *be.* Example: *The woman eating a sandwich laughed: The woman who was eating a sandwich laughed.*

1.   Travelers staying at the conference center will be taken to the banquet by limousine.
2.   Why don't you help those shoppers bagging their own groceries?
3.   I want to own every record made by a Motown group.
4.   Sue pointed out the man hidden in the crowd.

5. Most computers sold by discount stores can't be relied on.

6. Tim remembers every strikeout thrown by Steve Carlton.

Since NP-modifying participle constructions of this sort can be viewed as arising via the deletion of *be* and a *wh*-word, the presence of a past participle in such a construction can only result from a passive expression, never a perfect expression. For while both types contain past participles, passive constructions contain *be,* whereas perfect constructions contain *have:*

45. a. Passive:
Mr. Green was fired by the boss.
   b. Perfect:
Mr. Green has fired the secretary.

While both of these could take the form of relative clauses, if *Mr. Green* were replaced by a relative pronoun—e.g., *who was fired by the boss, who has fired the secretary*—only the first contains *be* and can therefore undergo deletion of the *wh*-word and *be* to produce a participle phrase:

46. a. The guy who was fired by the boss is here to see you. ⇒
The guy <u>fired by the boss</u> is here to see you.
   b. The guy who has fired the secretary is here to see you. ↛
*The guy <u>fired the secretary</u> is here to see you.

Nonrestrictive Participle Constructions

All the examples we have just discussed involve restrictive participle constructions, and are derivable from restrictive relative clauses. You might want to look back over the participle constructions we have just discussed to convince yourself that these are semantically restrictive just the way their relative clauses sources are.

Nonrestrictive participle constructions exist too:

47. a. Margaret Louise, cheered by the crowd, waved.
   b. Mary Ellen, standing alone, smiled quietly.

These are semantically nonrestrictive: they are parenthetical, and do not narrow down the set of possible referents to just the intended one(s). These appear at first glance to be derivable in the same way as restrictive participles, from relative clauses; the apparent sources are *Margaret Louise, who was cheered by the crowd, waved* and *Mary Ellen, who was standing alone, smiled quietly.* Nonrestrictive participle expressions share the grammatical characteristics of nonrestrictive relative clauses, as compared with restrictive ones.

They can modify proper nouns, whereas restrictive relative clauses and participle expressions can't:

48. a. Nonrestrictive:
Mary Ellen, looking grim, peeled the onion.
b. Restrictive:
*Mary Ellen looking grim peeled the onion.

And they can modify sentences, while restrictive participles cannot:

49. a It was Tuesday, indicating that the delivery would probably be made about noon.
b. *It was Tuesday indicating that . . .

For many nonrestrictive participle constructions, however there is a regular meaning difference between the relative clause sentence and the participle sentence: the relative clause seems to modify the head NP, while the participle construction has an adverbial flavor, modifying the VP or the entire sentence. That is, (47a) above is probably better paraphrased "As Margaret Louise was cheered by the crowd, she waved," or "Margaret Louise waved as she was cheered by the crowd," and (47b) perhaps by "As she stood alone, Mary Ellen smiled quietly." Further examples, in each of which the (b) sentence seems the better paraphrase of the (a) sentence than does the (c) sentence, include the following:

50. a. The dancer, losing her balance, slipped off the wire.
= b. As she lost her balance, the dancer slipped off the wire.
not c. The dancer, who was losing her balance, slipped off the wire.
51. a. Max, finally spurned by Cathy, concluded there must be other fish in the sea.
= b. After finally being spurned by Cathy, Max concluded there must be other fish in the sea.
not c. Max, who was finally spurned by Cathy, concluded there must be other fish in the sea.
52. a. The campers, shivering all over, listened to the counselor's instructions.
= b. While they shivered all over, the campers listened to the counselors' instructions.
not c. The campers, who were shivering all over, listened to the counselors' instructions.

The difference is subtle, and may not exist for some nonrestrictive participle expressions; and where it does exist it does not involve a difference in "truth conditions." That is, the conditions in the world under which a sentence containing a nonrestrictive participle expression is true are identical to those under which a nonrestrictive relative clause version of the same sentence are true. But a relative clause paraphrase frequently isn't the best paraphrase. Consequently the connection between nonrestrictive relative clauses and nonrestrictive participles must be regarded as much weaker than that between restrictive relative clauses and restrictive participle constructions, and it probably makes sense to regard nonrestrictive participle expressions not as derived via deletion of *be* and a relative pronoun, but as tokens of an independent type of construction.

The adverbial interpretation some participle constructions get can be seen in cases which lack the characteristic intonation pattern of nonrestrictive participle constructions, but which are nonrestrictive nonetheless.

53. a. Jean spends a lot of time *watching soaps on TV.* ≠
    b. *Jean spends a lot of time who is watching soaps . . .
    d. After the speech the audience stood *cheering.* ≠
    e. *After the speech the audience stood who was cheering.

You can see that these constructions function adverbially to modify the rest of their sentences.

Participle Movement

Nonrestrictive participle constructions are not limited to post-nominal position:

54. a. <u>Shivering all over</u>, fourteen campers climbed onto the truck.
    b. <u>Fourteen campers</u> climbed onto the truck, <u>shivering all over</u>.

"Moved" participle constructions occur mainly in writing or formal speech. The movability of participle constructions underlies a common problem of inexperienced writers: so-called "dangling" participles. There is a simple constraint on moved participle phrases: the moved participle phrase has to modify the sentence subject. In both cases in (54), the participle phrase modifies the subject NP *fourteen campers*. See how nonsensical the sentence becomes if the participle can't modify the main subject: *Shivering all over, the truck now held fourteen campers.* Novice writers who notice that good writing often contains moved participle phrases often try to imitate the moved-participle pattern, but they are not always aware that the participle phrase must modify the subject. Here are some additional examples containing "dangling" participles:

55. a. *Playing his trumpet, we watched Paul lead the band across the field. (*We didn't play Paul's trumpet; Paul did.*)
    b. *Having slaved over those pies, the Thanksgiving dessert was as impressive as I had hoped it would be. (*The Thanksgiving dessert didn't slave over those pies.*)
    c. *Thrilled by the come-from-behind victory, there was nothing to do but

savor the memory of the last two seconds. (*"There" wasn't thrilled by the come-from-behind victory.*)

EXERCISE 8. Some sentences below are grammatical, but some have dangling participle phrases. Underline all dangling participle phrases. Repair them by changing the sentences so that the participle phrase modifies the main subject NP. (Radical surgery may be necessary.)

1. Feeling powerful, Max asked Cathy for a date.
2. Having worked hard all morning, the garage was now completely organized.
3. Studying intensely, there were now over a hundred students in the cafeteria.
4. Having suffered through the ice storm, we were now ready for anything.
5. Pleased by Dana's progress, a B+ seemed to us like the appropriate grade.
6. Ellen's dissertation was finished in six weeks, working round the clock seven days a week.
7. The victory party was scheduled for Friday night, assuming that we would win.

Restrictive participle expressions not related to relative clauses

We saw above that nonrestrictive participle expressions can't with certainty be related to relative clauses. Certain restrictive participle constructions cannot be connected to relative clauses either. One type of such a construction contains a stative verb, like *know, resemble, have,* or *be:*

56. a. The first student knowing the answer will get a nickel. ≠
   b. *The first student who is knowing the answer will get a nickel.

57. a. A man resembling my father . . . ≠
   b. *A man who was/is resembling my father . . .

58. a. Anybody having a book report to hand in, come up here now. ≠
   b. *Anybody who is having a book report to hand in . . .

59. a. Anyone being taller than six feet tall will be excluded from the short man's team. ≠
   b. *Anyone who is being taller than six feet tall . . .

Because the (b) sentences above are ungrammatical, they cannot be the sources of the (a) sentences. The reason the (b) sentences are ungrammatical is that they contain stative verbs in the progressive; as we saw in Chapter Five, stative verbs do not, generally, occur in the progressive construction. Observe, too, that even if they were grammatical, progressive sources would be impossible for the (a) sentences since the (a) sentences are not progressive in meaning. Consequently, participle expressions like those in the (a) sentences in (56)–(59) have to be described on their own terms, not as derivative from some other construction.[6]

EXERCISE 9. Explain why the (b) sentence below cannot be the source for the (a) sentence.

a. Any window shattering near children is dangerous. ≠
b. ?Any window which is shattering near children is dangerous.

Noun Complement Participle Constructions

In Chapter Four, and briefly in Chapter Eight, we encountered expressions like *The police saw Lucy driving away from the scene,* in which *driving away from the scene* is what we called a "noun complement participle construction." In such expressions the main verb always seems to be a psychological verb, like *hear, see,* or *remember.* Other examples:

60. a. John heard Mary fixing her garage door.
  b. We imagined the dog being terrorized by a kitten.
  c. I remember Cathy walking between the rosebushes.
  d. The girls saw the bears driven off by the rangers.

Noun complement participle expressions are not reduced relative clauses; (60a) does not mean "John heard Mary, who was fixing her garage door." Nor are they adverbial. Unlike the adverbial participle constructions we saw in (50) to (52), (60a) does not, in the interpretation in question, have an adverbial sense; it does not, in this interpretation, mean "John heard Mary as she was fixing her garage door." Rather, it means "John heard Mary in the act of fixing her garage door," or, in an awkward paraphrase, "John heard the fixing of her garage door being done by Mary."[7]

---

[6]When *be* is used non-statively, a progressive relative clause and a progressive participle construction are both possible:

  i. Katherine, who was being helpful, carried everything back into the house.
  ii. Katherine, being helpful, carried everything back into the house.

[7]Actually, the sentence is ambiguous, with a second reading, "As John was fixing her garage door, John heard Mary." This reading contains an adverbial participle construction like those in (50) to (52).

  Another adverbial reading may be possible for some expressions which have noun complement readings. Some speakers may be able to interpret (60a) as meaning, in addition to the noun complement reading, something like "John heard Mary as she was fixing her garage door," i.e., John heard Mary (e.g., talking, singing, or whatever), while she was fixing her garage door. Such an adverbial reading is not available to all noun complement expressions; it seems impossible for (60b), for instance.

In these expressions the simple NP following the verb (e.g., in [60a], *Mary*) functions as actual direct object, as can be seen by the fact that it can be moved by passivization (*Mary was heard fixing her garage door*). But because of the meaning of the sentence it is not the logical direct object. Logically, the direct object must be sentential, as in *John heard [Mary fixing her garage door]*, because what John heard was not Mary, but Mary's doing something. Under this analysis, the actual direct object NP *Mary* is underlyingly (logically) the subject of the complement, and is "raised" to direct object position by the process called "Raising to Object" discussed in Chapter Eight in connection with the verbs *expect* and *believe*. The derived structure then would be *John saw Mary_i [______i fixing her garage door]*.

Noun complement constructions are not restricted to participle constructions:

61. a.   John heard Mary <u>close her garage door</u>.
   b.   The police saw Lucy <u>drive away from the scene</u>.
   c.   It was incredible; we smelled his clothes <u>just burn right up</u>.

The superficial structure of these contain gaps—*John heard Mary_i [______i close her garage door]*—whereas underlyingly they have gapless sentential direct objects—*John heard [Mary close her garage door]*. Note that the verbs of these non-participle noun complement expressions lack the usual person + number + tense ending. The absence of this ending suggests infinitives, and this connection is supported by some related passives: *Mary was heard to close her garage door*. But since such a passive is marginal to most speakers, and other noun complement expressions do not permit passives with infinitives (**His clothes were smelled to burn right up*), this connection should not be granted too much credence.

Absolutes

Another kind of present participle phrase not derived from a relative clause is the **absolute** construction:

62. a.   Max stayed home, <u>his white sport coat being dirty</u>.
   b.   A heavy snowfall <u>having blanketed the city</u>, school was canceled and all baseball games were called off.
   c.   <u>The guests arriving</u>, Mary Ellen hurriedly stirred the vegetables into the wok.

Unlike the participle constructions examined in the previous sections, absolutes do not modify an NP. Rather, they modify the entire main clause:

63.

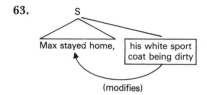

Moreover, absolute constructions have subjects and predicates in actual, superficial structure—i.e., they are clauses—unlike other participle constructions, which, lacking subjects, are clauses only in logical structure. With other participle phrases, there exists identity between the logical subject NP of the participle phrase and some NP in the main clause. In absolutes, such identity is absent:

64. a. Ordinary participle construction:
   i. Max, driving at top speed, chased the escaping felons.
   Logically, this sentence has the form:
   ii. Max (Max was driving at top speed) chased the escaping felons.
   (*The two occurrences of Max have the same referent.*)
   b. Absolute construction:
   The felons escaping, Max drove off after them.
   (*The felons and Max have different referents.*)

In (a), because of this semantic identity between the NPs in the logical form of the ordinary participle construction, omission of the subordinate one is possible. In the absolute construction in (b), on the other hand, there is no pair of semantically identical NPs in the modifying phrase and the main clause.

Because of participle phrase movement, some ordinary participle phrase constructions can resemble absolutes; (64ai) can be paraphrased *Driving at top speed, Max chased the escaping felons.* In this sentence, the preposed participle phrase lacks a subject NP. This distinguishes it from an absolute construction:

65. a. Preposed participle phrase (grammatical):
   __ Sweating and grunting, Bruno lifted the cinder blocks.
   b. "Dangling" participle phrase (ungrammatical):
   *__ Sweating and grunting, the cinder blocks were finally lifted onto the platform.
   c. Absolute construction (grammatical):
   The cinder blocks weighing 70 pounds apiece, it was hard to lift them onto the platform.

In (a) and (b) the sentence-initial gap indicates the site of subject NP deletion, i.e., where a copy of the main sentence subject is understood. In (a), the blank space is co-referential with *Bruno*, in (b) it is co-referential with *the cinder blocks*—that's why (b) is nonsensical. (Cinder blocks can't sweat and grunt.) In (c), with an absolute, there is no gap.

Semantically, there are two kinds of absolutes. One has a paraphrase with a causal adverbial phrase:

66. a. Max stayed home, <u>his white sport coat being dirty</u>. =
Max stayed home, <u>since his white sport coat was dirty</u>.
  b. <u>A heavy snowfall having blanketed the city</u>, school was canceled and all <u>baseball games were called off</u>. =
<u>Because a heavy snowfall had blanketed the city</u>, school was canceled and <u>all baseball games were called off</u>.
  c. <u>The guests arriving</u>, Mary Ellen hurriedly stirred the vegetables into the <u>wok</u>. =
<u>Because the guests were arriving</u>, Mary Ellen hurriedly stirred the vege-<u>tables into the wok</u>.

Rather than being causative, the other kind of absolute adds a detail:

67. a. Cathy stood before Max, <u>her eyes shining</u>.
  b. <u>Trumpets announcing their arrival</u>, the knights' party crossed the <u>drawbridge</u>.
  c. Prof. Fuzzlehead droned on, <u>his voice cracking now and then</u>.

One paraphrase for this kind of absolute is a *with* prepositional phrase: *Cathy stood before Max* <u>*with her eyes shining*</u>, etc.

Since the function of both types of absolutes is to modify the whole main sentence, it makes sense to treat them as subordinate, like their para-phrases; that is, they can be diagrammed in a tree as a sentence adverbial phrase:

68.

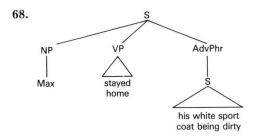

The internal structure of an absolute is that of a clause—it has a subject NP and a predicate VP—although the verb is always a participle and there is no syntactic tense or modal possible. (The only aux elements permissible are *be* and *have*, both in participle form.) Semantically, though, two time references are possible. In the unmarked case, the time reference of the absolute construction is the same as that of the main clause: in *Juliette arrived, her tires squealing* the time of the tires' squealing equals that of

Juliette's arriving. In the marked case, past time is expressed by the participle *having*. In *The sky having turned threatening, the fleet set sail for home,* the time reference of the absolute phrase *the sky having turned threatening* is prior to that of the main clause. To express future time reference, since English, unlike some languages, has no future participle, a complex circumlocution must be used, e.g., *about to: Night being about to fall, the picnickers packed up.*

In all three cases, syntactically we have present participles. For past time reference, the form of the participle is *having,* a present participle, and for future time reference, the present participle *being* is used.

Even cases like the following involve present participles, underlyingly:

69. a. Her fingers stuck in her belt, Jean shyly looked up.
  b. The brown kitten finally ended her destruction, the dissertation torn to pieces.
  c. All the under-performing salespeople fired, Scrooge could finally relax and plan for the upcoming campaign.

The reason they involve present participles is that the past participles—*stuck, torn,* and *fired* above—are remnants of ordinary present participle constructions or passive constructions:

70. a. Her fingers *being* stuck in her belt . . .
  b. . . . the dissertation *having been* torn to pieces
  c. All the under-performing salespeople *having been* fired . . .

Adjectives can appear in absolutes where past participles (i.e., passive participles) can, with optional deletion of *being:*

71. a. Her fingers being numb, she couldn't work the buttons. =
    Her fingers numb, she couldn't work the buttons.
  b. His dissertation being unpublishable, Tom sought employment at Burger King. =
    His dissertation unpublishable, Tom sought employment at Burger King.

In addition, other kinds of complements of *be* can occur, e.g., predicate nominative NPs and PPs, again with optional deletion of *being:*

72. a. i. His shirt being a thoroughly soaked rag, Max shivered in the chill. =
    ii. His shirt a thoroughly soaked rag, Max shivered in the chill.
  b. i. His socks being still on the floor, Jon smiled weakly at Mary. =
    ii. His socks still on the floor, Jon smiled weakly at Mary.

Only *being* and *having been* can be deleted. Other present participles remain:

73. a.   Lucien walked home in bliss, autumn leaves <u>swirling</u> around him.

　　　≠

　　 b.   Lucien walked home in bliss, autumn leaves around him.

The formal tone of the absolute examples we have looked at might suggest to you that absolutes are largely restricted to writing. This is in fact the case. Presumably this is because absolutes are such tight compactions of complex meanings that they require a fair amount of planning, which the real-time nature of speech inhibits.

EXERCISE 10. In the sentences below, identify all absolute constructions and all non-absolute participle constructions.

1. The day dawning clear, Joelle decided to sail to Catalina.
2. Barking madly, the puppy raced around the yard.
3. Cathy and Max strolled along the riverbank, their fingers intertwined.
4. Born to a family of large landowners, Cate nonetheless was a lifelong socialist.
5. The arena roof leaking, officials finally stopped the game.
6. Max sat fidgeting in his seat as the proctors passed out the test.
7. Having failed twice, Jim was unwilling to tackle Linguistics 1 again.
8. Unwilling to tackle Linguistics 1, Jim signed up for Physics for Poets.
9. Linguistics 1 being regarded as one of the most challenging courses in the catalog, Ellie signed up for it bright and early on registration day.
10. The coffee hot and the bagels ready, Dave and Ellie sat down to breakfast.

SUMMARY AND CONCLUSION

We have explored relative clauses, participle constructions, and absolutes in some detail. As with complex constructions generally (cf. Chapters Six and Eight), some abstract syntactic analysis, including the positing of gaps from which something "was moved," proved useful to understanding relative clauses. This is one more case in which it has proved useful to think of sentences "vertically" rather than horizontally, i.e., as having more than one level of grammatical structure instead of being simply a left-to-right sequence of words and phrases.

The relationship between relative clauses and participle constructions proved problematic: restrictive relative clauses, except for those involving stative verbs, can usefully be grammatically related to restrictive participle constructions, but other participle constructions are better treated as independent construction types.

ADDITIONAL EXERCISES

1. Make up fresh examples, or find cases in written texts, to illustrate the following concepts:
   1. nonrestrictive relative clause
   2. restrictive relative clause
   3. appositive
   4. participle construction modifying an NP
   5. participle not modifying an NP
   6. absolute construction
   7. relative clause modifying a VP
   8. moved participle phrase
   9. dangling participle phrase
   10. noun complement participle expression
2. Some of the underlined participle expressions below can be usefully related to relative clauses, some should not be. Identify those that should not be, and in each case explain why not.
   1. Bobbie spent the night walking in the park.
   2. The coach was carried off the field yelling and waving his fist.
   3. Dan made $15,000 selling real estate last summer.
   4. Crying all the while, Maria told me about the loss of her wallet.
   5. Congressmen voting to override the veto will regret it come election time.
   6. Numbers having no factors other than one and themselves are prime.

Chapter Ten

ANAPHORA

In this chapter we are going to ask what it means for a word to be a pronoun. We shall also examine words that act as pronouns do, but aren't pro-NOUNS (they're "pro" forms for other grammatical categories), and words that aren't "pro" anything at all, but still function as pronouns do. We shall also examine some interesting grammatical rules and patterns governing pronouns and related forms. Finally, we will look at how "zero"—a significant "piece of nothing"—can behave like a pronoun.

Traditionally, of course, pronouns are words which are used in place of nouns (more accurately, NPs). In Chapter Four this notion was shown to be inadequate because some personal pronouns (*I, you, we* and their related case-forms like *me*) are simply not used in place of NPs. To repeat the point made in Chapter Four, third person pronouns can usually be thought of as referring (usually back) to other words or phrases:

1.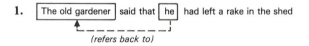

But first and second person pronouns don't. There just isn't any **antecedent** (the technical name for the word or phrase that a pronoun refers back to) for *I, you,* or *we.* Suppose the speaker is named Max, and the hearer is named Willie. Consider the following examples:

2. (a)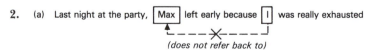

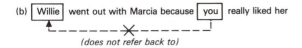

(b) [Willie] went out with Marcia because [you] really liked her

(does not refer back to)

In (a), *I* does not refer back to *Max,* and in (b) *you* does not refer back to *Willie.* Even though speakers know their own names and (usually) those of their hearers, *I* and *you* are not pronouns for those names. The point made in Chapter Four was that *I, you,* and *we* are—by the traditional definition—not pronouns at all, but just alternative names for the speaker and the hearer. Morphologically, however—as was pointed out in Chapter Four—they fit into the same class as real pronouns like *he,* and consequently are labeled with the same term, "pronoun."

Let's make this notion of "referring back" more precise. Used in the way that gave rise to the traditional definition, pronouns are words which get their reference from other words or phrases in a discourse or sentence. These other words or phrases which provide the reference for a pronoun are called **antecedents**. In the following examples, the underlined pronouns get their reference from the italicized antecedents:

3. a. *Max* left because <u>he</u> was eager to get home on time.
   b. *The gray kitten* saw <u>itself</u> in the mirror.
   c. When <u>she</u> arrived, *Diane* saw that the chicken was cold.

In (a), because the word *Max* is the antecedent for *he,* the referent of *he* is Max (the person, not the word). In (b), because *the gray kitten* is the antecedent for *itself,* the referent of *itself* is the gray kitten. In (c), because *Diane* is the antecedent for *she,* the referent for *she* is Diane.

An antecedent does not have to be in the same sentence as the pronoun that it provides reference for; it can be in a previous sentence in the discourse, as in the following examples.

4. a. You know *the guy in my physics class with the silver skateboard?* Well, <u>he</u> asked me out!
   b. Lucy was searching high and low for *a book.* Finally she found <u>it</u> under a pillow on the sofa.
   c. Lucy was searching high and low for *a book.* Finally she took Tim's advice and looked in the living room. She found <u>it</u> under a pillow on the sofa.

Pronouns are not devoid of meaning on their own, but they do get most of their meaning from their antecedents. Take *he.* In isolation, *he* means "third person, masculine, singular." You also know from its form that in context it will function grammatically as a subject, since it is in the subjective ("nominative") case. In context, *he* nearly always has much more meaning than that. What does *he* mean in each of the following examples?

5. a. Max overate because <u>he</u> was binging.

  b. Before <u>he</u> could stop him, Bob saw the robber dash out.

  c. Isaac's black lab gets very excited whenever <u>he</u> gets to go for a walk.

Obviously, in (a), *he* means "Max," in (b) "Bob," and in (c) "Isaac's black lab." (True, each of these sentences has another meaning in which *he* means "somebody else that we are talking about," but let's ignore this meaning for now.)

AN OVERVIEW OF PRONOUN-LIKE WORDS (ANAPHORS)

Let's introduce a technical term: **anaphor.** An anaphor is a word or phrase which has an antecedent. More precisely, an anaphor gets its reference from an antecedent. In Chapter Four we surveyed the different kinds of pronoun-like words—i.e., anaphors—that are found in English. Let's review, by means of the following examples of anaphors:

6. Pronouns (actually, pro-NPs):
  he, she, it, they
  one (actually a pro-N̄)

The pronouns *he, she, it,* and *they* have different forms for different cases: *him, her, their, them,* etc. (see Chapter Four).

7. Pro-VPs:
  do so, do it
  Joe [painted the box]$_{vp}$ before Sam could <u>do so/do it</u>.

8. Pro-APs:
  so, it
  Joe isn't really [<u>lazy</u>]$_{AP}$; he just seems <u>so/it</u>.
  that
  Joe isn't really [lazy]$_{AP}$; for him to be <u>that</u>, he would have to never get any work done at all.

9. Pro-Sentences:
  so, it
  They say [Fidel fired Ernesto]$_s$, but I don't believe it.
  I will believe that [Fidel fired Ernesto]$_s$ if you say <u>so</u>.

10. Pro-Adverbial Phrase:
  thusly (a pro-Manner Adverb)
  Research your presentation [painstakingly]$_{Man\ Adv}$. If you do it <u>thusly</u>, you'll be ready for any kind of question.

11. Pro-PP:
  then
  <u>In the fifties</u> gas prices were low. Also, back <u>then</u>, American cars were reliable.

These are "regular" anaphors. They have very little meaning of their own, deriving most of their meaning from their antecedent. There also exist words and phrases that sometimes get their reference from antecedents, and which we can therefore call anaphors, but which have substantial amounts of meaning on their own. Here are some examples, with antecedent italicized and anaphor underlined:

   12. a. Bob rode his bike *no-handed*. I want to do it <u>the same way</u>.
        b. I tried to reach *Pete* yesterday, but <u>the jerk</u> wasn't home.
        c. Barb is *sixteen*, and Sue is <u>old enough to have a driver's licence</u>, too.

These "ad hoc" anaphors have substantial meaning of their own, as well as—in context—deriving meaning from their antecedents. For example, obviously the meaning of *old enough to have a driver's license* is complex, but on its own the phrase doesn't entail "being sixteen" (since minimum driving ages vary by state). That element of meaning is added to *old enough to have a driver's license* in the context of sentence (12c). Similarly, the phrase *the jerk* obviously has meaning, but, on its own, it doesn't mean Pete; in (12b), however, *the jerk* does refer to Pete.

    One other kind of anaphor should be mentioned before we proceed: "Ø," or the omission of something repeated. Zero anaphora will be discussed in a section of its own below, but let's look briefly at a small set of examples here:

   13. a. Cate ordered fish, Laurie Ø soup.
        b. Charlotte writes travel books and Jennie does Ø too.
        c. Sam walked to the store and Ø bought the paper.
        d. Speaker A: What did Sam get?
            Speaker B: Ø Ø the paper.

In (a), the "Ø" is anaphoric to the verb *ordered* of the first clause; in (b) the Ø is anaphoric to *write travel books* in the first clause;[1] in (c) the antecedent of Ø is *Sam;* and in (d) the pair of zeroes are anaphoric to the subject and the verb of the first (Speaker A's) clause, i.e., to *Sam got.*

    An obvious question—but one that will not be answered in this book—is what determines the choice between pro-form anaphora and zero anaphora, in cases where both are grammatically possible (e.g., *Sam walked to the store and Ø/he bought the paper.*)

---

[1] The antecedent is *write travel books*, not *writes . . . ;* the third person singular present tense, in the second clause, is on the auxiliary *does.*

ANAPHORIC AND NON-ANAPHORIC PRO-FORMS

Pro-forms aren't always used anaphorically. Sometimes they are used to refer to something speaker and hearer can directly perceive, or otherwise jointly know about:

14. a. (Police officer to individual being arrested:)
       Ok, up against the car. Now, drop *it*.
    b. (One baseball fan to another, seeing base-steal attempt:)
       There *he* goes!

The referent of the pro-form in these cases is the most relevant possibility in the environment. In the situation in which (a) is uttered, there might be several things the hearer might be able to drop (his key, his wallet, his jacket, his hat), but probably only a weapon or booty is relevant to a police officer's command to drop something. In the situation in which (b) is uttered, if both speech-event participants are at a baseball game, there are probably thousands of candidates for referent for *he*, but probably the one most relevant to the situation, and therefore the referent—is the player attempting to steal a base.

ORDINARY VS. REFLEXIVE PRONOUNS

Two of the anaphors mentioned above deserve special attention: pronouns and pro-VPs. We will examine pronouns first. There are two basic kinds: ordinary pronouns and reflexive pronouns. Ordinary pronouns are *he, she, it,* etc., and their related oblique case forms (*him,* etc.). Reflexive pronouns always end in *-self* (or the plural *-selves*): *myself, himself, ourselves,* etc. The antecedent of an ordinary pronoun must be in a different minimal clause from the pronoun, while the antecedent of a reflexive pronoun must be in the same clause as the pronoun. What it means to be in the same or a different minimal clause is exemplified in the diagrams below:

15.

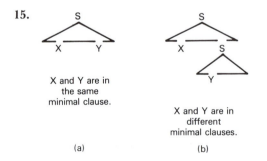

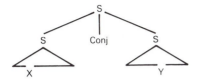

X and Y are in different
minimal clauses.

(c)

When two items are in the same minimal clause, the first S-node up from
one is also the first S-node up from the other. To see how this structural
pattern distinguishes ordinary and reflexive pronouns, consider the examples below. In these examples, the subscripts indicate sameness or difference of reference; if two NPs have the same subscript, they refer to the
same individual in the world; if they have different subscripts they refer to
different individuals.

16.   a.   The coach$_i$ loves himself$_i$.
      b.   The coach$_i$ loves him$_j$.

In (a), *himself* necessarily refers to the coach; in (b), *him* cannot refer to the
coach. It must refer to some other individual. To complete the argument,
compare the sentences below:

17.   a.   The coach$_i$ knows that the quarterback$_j$ respects him$_{ik}$.
      b.   The coach$_i$ knows that the quarterback$_j$ respects himself$_j$.

In (a), *him* cannot refer to the quarterback; it can refer to either the coach
or someone else (thus the subscript "$_{ik}$"); in (b) *himself* necessarily refers to
the quarterback. Look at the trees (below) for these sentences to see that
the pronoun *him* is in a different minimal clause from its antecedent, and
that *himself* is in the same minimal clause as its antecedent:

18.

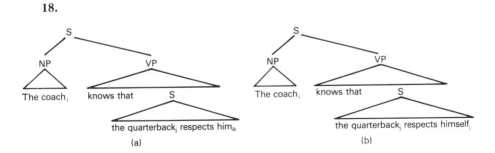

EXERCISE 1.

A. Explain why the following sentence is ungrammatical:
*My brother believes that our mother loves himself.

B. In the following sentence, identify all the possible antecedents for *him:*
Saul said that Bill claimed that Max wanted Neil to send him the records.
Which NP cannot be an antecedent for *him?* Why?

ANAPHORA TO A FOLLOWING ANTECEDENT

What should we make of the following pattern?

19. a. Max_i claimed that he_{ij} was the actual winner.
    b. He_j claimed that Max_i was the actual winner.
20. a. Leo_i stayed late because he_{ij} was having a great time.
    b. He_j stayed late because Leo_i was having a great time.
21. a. We will award the $grant_i$ to the person who has earned it_{ij}.
    b. We will award it_j to the person who has earned the $grant_i$.

Remember, subscripts indicate the same or different reference (sometimes the terms **joint** and **disjoint reference** are used). In (19a), for example, the pronoun *he* can, along with the proper noun *Max,* refer to Max, or it can refer to someone else. In (19b), though, *he* and *Max* must refer to different individuals. In (20a) *Leo* and *he* can refer to the same individual, but in (20b) *Leo* and *he* must refer to different individuals. And in (21a) *the grant* and *it* can refer to the same thing, but in (21b), they cannot.

From this data, you might hypothesize that for a full NP and a pronoun to have joint reference (or **co-refer**), the full NP must precede the pronoun. Your hypothesis would be reasonable, but it would be wrong. Look at the following sentences:

22. a. That he_{ij} was not the actual winner didn't bother Max_i.
    b. Whoever said he_{ij} was a loser doesn't know Max_i at all.
    c. Near him_{ij}, Max_i saw a snake.

In (22a) *he* and *Max* can co-refer, as can *he* and *Max* in (22b), and *him* and *Max* in (22c). Clearly, anaphors can precede their antecedents. They can in (22), but not in (19)–(21). What's the difference?

The difference is structural, and can be seen in trees, once you know what to look for. Let's look at the trees for (19b) and (22a).

23. (19b)

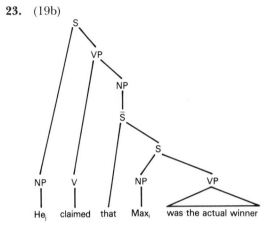

24. (22a)

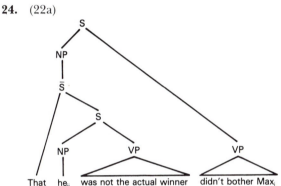

In (23), which has obligatorily disjoint reference (i.e., the subscripted NPs cannot co-refer), the pronoun *he* is in a particular structural relationship to the NP *Max;* that relationship does not obtain in (24). This relation, called **c-command**,[2] is as follows:

25. Definition:
Node A c-commands node B if and only if the first branching node which dominates A also dominates B.

In (23), the first branching node that dominates *he* is the main S-node, which also dominates *Max*. In (24), however, the first branching node that dominates *he* is the embedded S-node (the one over the clause *he was not the actual winner*). This node does not dominate *Max*.

---

[2]The term for the structural relationship that was originally proposed (Langacker, 1969) to handle these phenomena is **command**, which was defined somewhat differently. The "c" in "c-command" stands for "constituent."

Here are some examples of c-command. The circled nodes in the trees below c-command the nodes with boxes around them.

26.

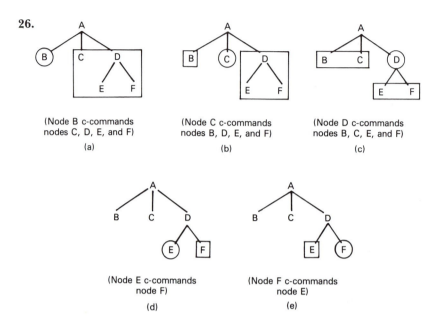

(Node B c-commands
nodes C, D, E, and F)

(a)

(Node C c-commands
nodes B, D, E, and F)

(b)

(Node D c-commands
nodes B, C, E, and F)

(c)

(Node E c-commands
node F)

(d)

(Node F c-commands
node E)

(e)

On the basis of this, you might very reasonably hypothesize that the rule governing when anaphors can precede their antecedents is the following:

27. Rule:
An anaphor can precede its antecedent unless the anaphor c-commands its antecedent.

Your hypothesis would be almost right. A slight addendum is needed to account for the co-reference possibilities in conjoined structures. We will consider this case below.

Anaphors Preceding Antecedents in Conjoined Structures

In conjoined structures, can an anaphor precede its antecedent? No. To see this, consider the following:

28. a.   She$_i$ left but Martha$_j$ didn't go home.
  b.   I love it$_i$ and I'm going to keep this car$_j$ for a long time.

In (a), *she* and *Martha* cannot co-refer, nor can *it* and *this car* in (b). We cannot account for this in terms of c-command, since a node in one conjoined sentence could not possibly c-command a node in another. If branching structures are conjoined—i.e., have structure like the following—

29.

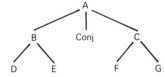

—there is no way an element in one conjunct could c-command an element in the other; for instance, in (29), there is no way node D could c-command nodes F or G. One way to deal with this problem is to define as **primacy relations** both "precedes" and "c-commands," and to reformulate Rule (27) in terms of primary relations:[3]

30. Rule (revision of 27):
An anaphor is not allowed to bear all possible primacy relations to its antecedent.

In non-conjoined structures, the possible primacy relations are "precedes" and "c-commands," and an anaphor can take an antecedent unless the anaphor both precedes and c-commands the antecedent. But in conjoined structures, c-command is irrelevant, since it is not possible for a node in one conjoined clause to c-command a node in another. In conjoined structures the only possible primacy relation is "precedes," so the constraint on anaphors and antecedents in conjoined structures must be simply that anaphors cannot precede their antecedents.

EXERCISE 2.

A. For each sentence, state whether the underlined anaphor can have the italicized NP as its antecedent. Then use Rule 30 to explain why the anaphors can or cannot have the underlined NPs as their antecedents. To do this, you will have to draw trees.
1. The house that she is building will suit *Marian* very well.
2. Ellen asked them whether *Irving and Lynette* could come for dinner.
3. The fact that he studied preposing constructions made *Greg* a big success.
4. We will award it to the one who wins *the prize*.
5. It upset them that *Rose and Leon* had arrived before the others.
6. *John* left early, but he returned quite late.
7. He left early, but *John* returned quite late.

---

[3]This is essentially what was proposed by Langacker, one of the first to describe the conditions governing when an anaphor can precede its antecedent.

B. Explain what problem the following sentences pose for the analysis presented in the last two sections. (Don't try to provide a solution.)
1. Near Max$_i$, he$_j$ saw a rattler.
2. For Joe$_i$'s country, he$_j$ would do anything.

ANAPHORA TO VPS

Do so and *do it* are anaphors that refer to Verb Phrases:

31.

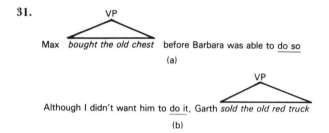

Max *bought the old chest* before Barbara was able to do so

(a)

Although I didn't want him to do it, Garth *sold the old red truck*

(b)

VP-anaphors obey the same primacy constraint as pronouns:

32.

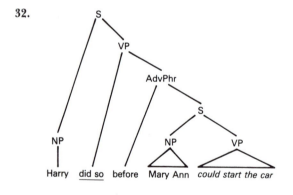

Harry did so before Mary Ann *could start the car*

In (32), *did so* cannot have *started the car* as antecedent, because *did so* bears both the primacy relations "precedes" and "c-commands" to the candidate antecedent. Contrast the following:

33. a. Mary Ann *started the car* before Harry could do so.
b. Before Harry could do so, Mary Ann *started the car*.

In (a), the anaphor *do so* can have *start the car* as its antecedent because it bears neither primacy relation to the antecedent. In (b), *do so* can have *started the car* as its antecedent because it bears only one of the two possible primacy relations to the antecedent: it precedes it, but does not c-command it. (To see this, as an informal exercise, draw the trees.)

Do so is like NP pro-forms in its ability to precede its antecedent in a conjoined structure. In (34), *did so* and *washed some dishes* cannot have joint reference:

34.   Max <u>did so</u> too and Sam *washed some dishes.*[4]

Inverted So

Seemingly similar to *do so,* but with a very different structure, is the **inverted** *so* construction:

35.   a.   Max loves Vermont cheddar cheese and *so do I.*
     b.   Carter was from the South but *so was Strom Thurmond.*
     c.   Nell has painted in Balboa Park for five years and *so has Mo.*

At first glance this construction looks like a variant of the *do so* construction, since it seems synonymous with it (e.g., equivalent to c above is *Nell has painted in Balboa Park for five years and Mo has done so too*). But it isn't. Structurally it is quite different. For one thing, *do so* always contains *do,* but inverted *so* needn't:

36.   a.   *Do so* needs *do:*
        i.   *Harry left before Sam could so. (cf. ok : could do so)
        ii.   *Although Harry left, he shouldn't have so. (cf. ok : shouldn't have done so)
     b.   Inverted *so* doesn't:
        i.   Harry left and so should Sam.
        ii.   Harry will leave and so will I.

For another, the *do* that sometimes occurs with inverted *so* is the "dummy" aux tense-carrier that we met in questions and negation (see Chapter Six), whereas the *do* of *do so* is a real verb, not an aux. (If this seems unfamiliar to you, re-read the sections of Chapter Six that deal with questions and negation.) This can be seen by the fact that in *do so,* other auxes can occur, but with inverted *so,* if *do* is present, no other aux can be, just as with *do* in negation or questions.

37.   a.   *Do so* with other auxes:
        i.   Mae left before Harry <u>could</u> do so.
        ii.   Although Harry left, he <u>shouldn't have</u> done so.
     b.   Ungrammatical inverted *so* with *do* and other auxes:
        i.   *Mae left and so could do Harry.
        ii.   *Mae left and so <u>should have</u> done Harry.

---

[4]This example is a little unfair, since *do so* seems not to occur in conjoined structures of this sort anyway. Although grammatical, sentences like *Sam washed some dishes and Max did so too* seem not to occur.

Of course inverted *so* can occur with other auxes but without *do,* as in (36b).

Another difference between *do so* and inverted *so,* and one significant to the topic of anaphora, has to do with the fact that antecedents cannot be repeated after anaphors. This can be seen with pronouns; in the (b) sentences below the capitalized words are ungrammatically repeated:

38. a. Ellen$_i$ left because she$_i$ was bored.
  b. *Ellen$_i$ left because she$_i$ ELLEN was bored.
  c. Max *started the car* before Jane could do so.
  d. *Max *started the car* before Jane could <u>do so</u> START THE CAR.[5]

But with the inverted *so* construction, such repetition of the apparent antecedent is much more acceptable:

39. Shane is a junior and so is his cousin a junior.

This kind of repetition of the apparent antecedent occurs most frequently after some intervening parenthetical material, and seems to function to indicate emphasis: *Shane is a junior, and—now I really want you to believe me on this, because it's true—so is his cousin a junior.* The inverted *so* construction can even be followed by a phrase synonymous with the "antecedent"—

40. Jane is a sophomore, but, you know, so is Beth in her second year.

—or by a phrase whose meaning is implied by the meaning of the apparent antecedent:

41. Jack is a junior, but, you know, so is Fred an upperclassman.

A reasonable inference from this repeatability is that *so* in the inverted *so* construction is not an anaphor. What is the anaphoric element in the inverted *so* construction? In cases in which there is one—e.g., (35) and (36b), but not (39), (40), and (41)—it seems to be Ø. That is:

42. a. Nell has *painted in the park for years* and so has Mo Ø.
  b. Wilbur will *try many flights* but so will Orville Ø.
  c. Sheila will *fire her butler* and so should you Ø.[6]

The antecedent of the Ø in each case is the main VP of the initial clause, not including the aux.

---

[5]This sentence, and (38b) above, are OK if the capitalized expressions are given non-restrictive appositive intonation, i.e., are set off by comma pauses. You should ignore the appositive reading, of course, for the point being made.
[6]This sentence has the interesting property of "sloppy identity," in which the *her* in the antecedent of Ø may stand for either "Sheila's" or "your."

EXERCISE 3.

1. Draw the tree for the first clause of sentence (42c). You may want to review VP structure from Chapter Six.

2. In the tree you have drawn, what is the antecedent for the Ø in (42c)? Is it a constituent?

3. Now consider *Sheila will be buying a house and so should you.* Draw the tree to figure out what is the antecedent for the Ø. Is it a constituent?

If the anaphor in the inverted *so* construction is Ø, what is *so*? There is evidence that it is related to *too*. As argued in Kaplan (1985), *too* and inverted *so* share a number of properties, including the fact that they cannot occur in clauses following a subordinate conjunction:

43. a. *Max left because so did Sheila.
    b. *Max left because Sheila did too.

The connection between *so* and *too* is supported by the intuition that the same thing—whatever it is—is wrong with both (a) and (b) above. Another trait that inverted *so* and *too* share is that they both must have a main VP, never an embedded one, as their antecedent. Consider the following:

44. a. Max tried to imitate Molly. Sam did Ø too.
    b. Max tried to imitate Molly. So did Sam Ø.

In both (a) and (b), the second sentence can mean only that Sam tried to imitate Molly, not that he imitated her; that is, the antecedent of the Ø is the whole main VP *tried to imitate Molly*, not the embedded VP *imitate Molly*. The VP-anaphor *do so*, on the other hand, can refer to an embedded VP in a context like (44): in *Max tried to imitate Molly. Sam did so* clearly the meaning is that Sam imitated Molly.

A third characteristic inverted *so* and *too* share is that the Ø that accompanies them cannot refer to an antecedent VP that is inside a subordinate clause introduced by *unless, before,* or *until* (whereas other subordinate conjunctions are OK):

45. Antecedent VP inside a clause containing *unless, before,* or *until:*
    a. *Unless Sam left, Joe did Ø too.
    b. *Unless Sam left, so did Joe Ø.
    c. *Before Sam left, Joe did Ø too.
    d. *Before Sam left, so did Joe Ø.
    e. *Until Sam went jogging, Joe did Ø too.
    f. *Until Sam went jogging, so did Joe Ø.

46. Antecedent VP inside a clause introduced by other subordinate conjunctions:

$$
\left\{
\begin{array}{l}
\text{Although} \\
\text{Because} \\
\text{When} \\
\text{Since} \\
\text{If} \\
\text{After}
\end{array}
\right\}
\quad
\begin{array}{l}
\text{a. Sam left, Joe did } \emptyset \text{ too} \\
\\
\text{b. Sam left, so did Joe } \emptyset
\end{array}
$$

Consequently let's treat inverted *so* and *too* as alternative versions—allomorphs, if you will—of the same element, *so* occurring in inversion, *too* otherwise,[7] and let's further assume that the actual anaphoric element in this construction is an occurrence of Ø.

EXERCISE 4. In each sentence below, if there is an anaphor, state what the anaphor is and what its antecedent is. Note if there is no anaphor.

1. Max wrote up the results before anyone else could do it.
2. The Finns have invaded Bulgaria, or so it seems.
3. Max said that Sheila thought that Sam had moved out, and so did Joel.
4. Grace divorced Fred, and Ginger got rid of her old man too.
5. Laffit attempted to catch Willie in the stretch. Marco did so.
6. Laffit attempted to catch Willie in the stretch. So did Marco.
7. Laffit attempted to catch Willie in the stretch. Marco did too.

ZERO ANAPHORA (ELLIPSIS)

The <u>*too*</u>/inverted <u>*so*</u> structure we have just discussed is an example of anaphora by Ø, or **ellipsis**. In this case an occurrence of Ø is anaphoric to a preceding VP. Indeed, often anaphora by Ø is to a single constituent:

47.

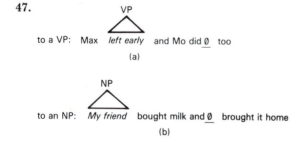

to a VP: Max *left early*   and Mo did Ø̲ too

(a)

to an NP: *My friend* bought milk and Ø̲ brought it home

(b)

[7]A strange coincidence is the interchangeability of *so* and *too* in emphatic constructions:

  i. I can *so* lift fifty pounds!
  ii. I can *too* lift fifty pounds!

V
|
to a V: Fred *ordered* fish, Harry 0̸ a salad
(c)

Sometimes an occurrence of 0̸ stands for a sequence of constituents:

48. a. a subject NP and its following verb:
Speaker A: What did Max get?
Speaker B: 0̸ 0̸ a carton of milk.
(i.e., B means: *Max got a carton of milk*)
b. a subject NP and a following Aux:
0̸ 0̸ see you later.
(Meaning: *I will see you later*)
c. a sequence of aux elements and a main verb:
Max *could have been dating* Marie, and Sam 0̸ Dinah.

EXERCISE 5. Where are the anaphoric 0̸s in the following sentences? Do they have antecedents in the discourse? If so, what are they? If they have antecedents which are recognizable constituents, say what kind of constituents they are.

1. A: I thought that was the football.
B: I did too.
2. A: Who took my red and blue striped tie?
B: I did.
3. A: Has Fred left?
B: Not yet.
4. Max bet on Precious Maiden and so did Lee.
5. Saul wanted to marry Zelda but so did Fred.
6. Saul wanted to marry Zelda but Fred did so.
7. Saul wanted to marry Zelda but Fred DID. (emphatic stress on *did*)
8. A: Who is going to be at the party?
B: Max and Zelda.

Two final, important points about ellipsis: One, it is not true that whatever at all a speaker repeats can optionally be deleted (i.e., be replaced by 0̸). Languages differ in what they allow to be deleted. Although it freely allows deletion of subject NPs, English does not allow an NP functioning as direct object or as object of preposition to be deleted:

49. *Bill bought *a carton of milk*, and he bought 0̸ because we were out of 0̸.

Some languages, however, do allow such a deletion. One that does is
Japanese:

50.   Hiroshi wa sakana o tabemashita ga Taroo wa Ø tabemasen deshita

Hiroshi-topic fish-object   ate   but Taro-topic Ø   not-eat   past

"Hiroshi ate fish, but Taro didn't eat Ø"

(i.e., Hiroshi ate fish but Taro didn't)

Second, whatever is deleted (replaced by Ø) must be **recoverable**; that
is, every Ø must be understandable in a specific way. When the Ø is anaphoric, its interpretation must be available from its antecedent. This formulation allows for the possibility of non-anaphoric zeroes. We have seen
some, e.g., the Ø that occurs in the imperative construction:

51. a.   Shut the door!
     b.   Meaning: <u>You will</u> shut the door
     c.   Structure of (a), with Øs shown:
          Ø Ø shut the door!

While not anaphoric, the meaning of the ellipsis is recoverable from the
sentence form; an imperative sentence has a particular form which signals
that the "emptiness" before the verb is to be interpreted as *you will*.

Comparison

A special kind of ellipsis occurs in comparative constructions:

52. a.   Max is as angry as Tom.
     b.   The rattlesnake is more dangerous than the copperhead.
     c.   Orphan Annie is more cute than beautiful.

We say an occurrence of Ø is present because the alleged Ø can be filled:

53. a.   Max is as angry as Tom <u>is.</u>
     b.   The rattlesnake is more dangerous than the copperhead <u>is.</u>
     c.   Orphan Annie is more cute than <u>she is</u> beautiful.

When the Ø is filled completely, sometimes the result is awkward, but
semantically complete:

54. a.   Max is as angry as Tom <u>is angry</u>.
     b.   The rattlesnake is more dangerous than the copperhead <u>is dangerous</u>.

Another reason for believing Ø is present in comparative sentences is that when there is lack of semantic identity between what is said about the two compared items, a word or phrase is present after the second compared element, instead of nothing:

55. a. Max is as angry as Tom is sad.
    b. The rattlesnake is as dangerous as the garter snake is harmless.

The structure of comparative sentences

Comparative sentences contain two compared words or phrases:

56. a. *Max* is as angry as *Tom*.
    b. *Max* is as angry as *Tom* is sad.

The comparison structure is an Adjective Phrase:

57.

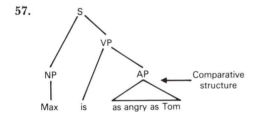

Within the AP is a pair of morphemes which express the "direction" of the comparison (greater than, less than, equal to):

58. a. Max is *more* intelligent *than* Harry.
    b. Sarah is *less* bold *than* Bianca.
    c. Jack is *as* honest *as* the next man.

The suffix *-er* is an allomorph of *more* which occurs with adjectives or manner adverbs of one or two syllables: *bigger, slower, faster, sillier, funnier* exist;[8] **intelligenter, *impressiver* don't. In addition, the familiarity of the base word plays a role in determining which form shows up: among two-syllable adjectives, less common words take *more: more gala* (not **gala-er*), with a fair amount of free variation: *more angry* exists as well as *angrier*. Some relatively uncommon one-syllable adjectives take *more* as well: *more ill,* not **iller*.

---

[8] An irregular comparative form like *better* has structure of the following sort: *good + -er,* with the morphemes *good* and *well* having grammatically conditioned allomorphs *bet-* which occur before *-er*.

The two paired morphemes always go together, even if the second is sometimes "understood"—i.e., present in zero form:

59. a.   Max is tall*er than* Tom.
      b.   A dragon is *as* scary *as* a goblin.
      c.   I want a larg*er* present! [*than* this one]

Consequently we might regard them as two parts of a discontinuous morpheme. But it is more convenient not to, since the two elements occur in different positions: the first one, which we will label a **degree marker** ("Deg" in a tree), in initial position in the AP—where Intensifiers go—and the second one (which we'll call a **comparative conjunction**) in a spot analogous to that occupied by subordinate conjunctions:

60.   Position of first comparison marker:

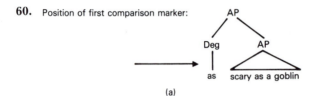

(a)

Position of second comparison marker:

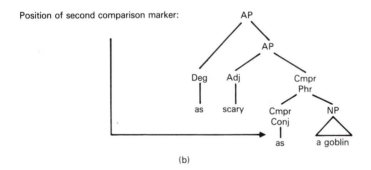

(b)

You can see that we are calling *as a goblin* in this example a **comparative phrase**. Comparative phrases have structures just like complex adverbial phrases made up of a subordinate conjunction and a sentence, e.g., *while Bob was reading*. To see this, observe that an AP like *as scary as a goblin* is a shortened form—containing an occurrence of Ø—of *as scary as a goblin is scary*, in which the clause *a goblin is scary* is found. When a tree spells this out, it is clear that a comparative conjunction is a sort of subordinate conjunction, since it occurs directly before an embedded S in a subordinate construction (here, the comparative phrase):

61.

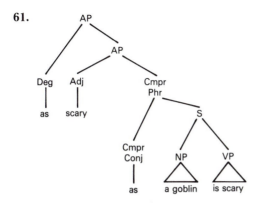

When the allomorph *-er* is found rather than *more*, we simply attach it to the adjective or adverb. We can even represent word-internal structure:

62.

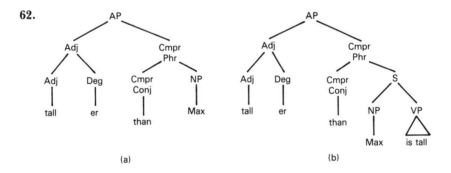

(a)　　　　　　　　　　　　　　(b)

Tree (b) represents the structure of the AP with the implicit Ø filled.

EXERCISE 6. Draw trees for the following APs:

1. more powerful than a locomotive
2. faster than a speeding bullet
3. less significant than a bug
4. more beautiful than you said she would be

Comparative complement sentences

In sentences like *She is so tall that she bumps her head*, the degree marker *so* is paired with the complementizer *that*, not a comparative conjunction (*as, than*). But the structure of such sentences is essentially like that of sentences with paired comparative markers (e.g., as in 61):

63.   She is so tall that she bumps her head.

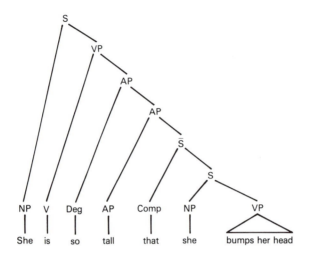

The only differences are (1) that the adjective is an AP, since here, but not in the purely comparative sentences we examined above, it can be preceded by an intensifier (*she is so very tall that she bumps her head;* contrast **she is more very beautiful than* . . .), and (2) that the clause in the comparative phrase is probably best labeled an S̄, since it contains the complementizer *that*. (We might call the Comparative Phrases in examples (60)–(62) S̄'s as well, and call *as* and *than* complementizers. In this book we won't do so, in order to underscore the comparative meaning in comparative sentences.)

DEFINITE NPS AS ANAPHORS

Finally, recall our discussion of definiteness from Chapter Five (mentioned briefly in Chapter Four, as well). We established that definite NPs are used when both speaker and hearer have a particular referent in mind. This can be the case in a number of ways. One way, of interest here, is by virtue of previous mention in the discourse. Consider the following:

64.   While I was working a moth flew into my coffee. The moth struggled a while, but finally I put it out of its misery and consumed it.

In this discourse, the indefinite NP *a moth* introduces the idea of the entity of the moth into the mental model the speaker is leading the hearer to